THE PSYCHOLOGY OF READING

THE PSYCHOLOGY OF READING

Theory and Applications

Paula J. Schwanenflugel
Nancy Flanagan Knapp

THE GUILFORD PRESS
New York   London

© 2016 The Guilford Press
A Division of Guilford Publications, Inc.
370 Seventh Avenue, Suite 1200, New York, NY 10001
www.guilford.com

Printed in the United States of America

This book is printed on acid-free paper.

Last digit is print number: 9   8   7   6   5   4   3   2   1

Library of Congress Cataloging-in-Publication Data

Schwanenflugel, Paula J., author.
   The psychology of reading : theory and applications / by Paula J. Schwanenflugel
and Nancy Flanagan Knapp.
      pages cm
   Includes bibliographical references and index.
   ISBN 978-1-4625-2350-4 (pbk. : acid-free paper)—ISBN 978-1-4625-2351-1
(cloth : acid-free paper)
   1. Reading, Psychology of.   I. Knapp, Nancy F., author.   II. Title.
   BF456.R2S39 2016
   418.′4019—dc23
                                                                    2015024553

About the Authors

Paula J. Schwanenflugel, PhD, is Professor of Educational Psychology at the University of Georgia, where she researches and teaches courses on the psychology of reading, psycholinguistics, and child development. She is also affiliated with the Linguistics and Cognitive Science programs. Dr. Schwanenflugel has carried out both basic and applied research on the topics of reading fluency, lexical processing, semantic development, and vocabulary knowledge, as well as large-scale school-based interventions related to literacy. She has published numerous articles in both psychology and education journals, many book chapters related to reading, and two recent books that describe effective research-based classroom practices related to the development of literacy.

Nancy Flanagan Knapp, PhD, is Associate Professor of Learning, Design, and Technology at the University of Georgia, where she teaches courses in literacy and learning theory. She is also affiliated with the Department of Educational Psychology, for which she taught the Psychology of Reading course for 17 years. Dr. Knapp's current research focuses on helping struggling readers and improving instruction at the K–12 and postsecondary levels. She offers professional development courses and seminars and is the developer of the Reading Apprenticeship Program, a Tier 2 intervention for delayed elementary school readers. She has published numerous articles on literacy and teaching and is a founding editor of the journal *Teaching Educational Psychology*.

Introduction

The study of the psychology of reading exists at the intersection of a multiplicity of fields. This book is intended for two groups of people: those interested in the psychology of thinking, learning, and language, and those interested in reading and reading education. We feel that this book will have much to offer the great variety of professionals whose work intersects with reading: cognitive and educational psychologists, reading teachers and diagnosticians, test developers, school psychologists, speech and language pathologists, professionals engaged in teaching reading in a second language, and applied linguists and psycholinguists.

The processes of reading and learning to read have fascinated psychologists for more than a century, in part because reading (and writing) offers a more permanent, analyzable record of thought and language than does ephemeral speech. Written literacy has become increasingly essential to living well in modern society, and thus it is increasingly the focus of our ever-expanding educational efforts. Educators have sometimes been put off by the hypothetical nature of (and jargon associated with) the theories put forth about reading by psychologists. But they have continued to turn to psychology, searching not only for an understanding of the processes engaged by reading, but for ways to help the many children whose life options are curtailed each year because they do not learn to read adequately.

In this book, we consider the psychology of reading through the dual lenses of the psychologist interested in mental processes and of the educator interested in practical, helpful insights. We draw on the work of scholars who hold widely diverse conceptions of reading and on the ideas about how to assist students in the process of learning to read. Our intention is not to promote a single encompassing theory of the processes of reading and learning to read. Nor do we make unequivocal recommendations for classroom or other educational practices. Rather, we hope our efforts will increase our readers' basic understanding of the developmental processes underlying the psychology of reading. We hope to outfit readers, whether researchers or practitioners, with an understanding that allows them to help the many students who struggle with reading every year. We discuss the implications of how research conducted on the psychology of reading can guide, and has guided, educational practices and standards as well as the assessments developed to measure their effectiveness.

WHY PSYCHOLOGISTS NEED TO KNOW ABOUT READING

For the past century at least, psychologists have regarded reading and the study of reading to be a window into how people think and learn. Edward Thorndike, often described as a founding father of educational psychology (Berliner, 1992), described reading as reasoning (E. L. Thorndike, 1917), noting that "reading is a very elaborate procedure" (p. 323) and suggesting that "reading an explanatory or argumentative paragraph . . . involves the same sort of organization and analytic action of ideas as occur in thinking of supposedly higher sorts" (p. 331). Sixty years later his son, Robert Thorndike, a noted educational psychologist in his own right, asserted that "performance in reading, at least after the basic decoding skills are mastered, is primarily an indicator of the general level of the individual's thinking and reasoning processes rather than a set of distinct and specialized skills" (R. L. Thorndike, 1973, p. 136). Ever since the older Thorndike made his mark on the psychology of reading, psychologists have not only contributed vitally to the study of reading, but have also often used reading-based tasks to develop and test seminal theories about more general human mental processes, including attention (Stroop, 1935), memory (Baddeley, Thomson, & Buchanan, 1975), metacognition (Hart, 1967), incidental learning (Eysenck, 1974), and task persistence (Sandelands, Brockner, & Glynn, 1988).

However, reading is not just a window into thought; there is increasing evidence that reading shapes thought and even the brain architecture that underlies thought. Historians, sociologists, and anthropologists have long observed clear differences between literate and preliterate societies, both historically and currently (Heath, 1989). Today, scientists, using new methods of neuroimaging, are beginning to demonstrate the positive effects of ordinary reading on the brain itself (e.g., Kidd & Castano, 2013; Berns, Blaine, Prietula, & Pye, 2013), offering evidence that confirms the 40-year-old hope of R. L. Thorndike (1973) that "as we improve the understanding with which a child reads, we may concurrently improve the effectiveness with which he processes a wide range of information important in his development" (p. 147). Finally, the ability to read with ease and understanding is increasingly necessary for full participation in modern society. Not only do poor readers find themselves handicapped in school (Stanovich, 1986) and later in the workforce, but they are disadvantaged in many other ways, including poorer health associated with lower levels of health literacy (Andrus & Roth, 2002), higher levels of incarceration (Kutner, Greenberg, Jin, Boyle, Hsu, & Dunleavy, 2007), and even greater susceptibility to depression and suicidal thoughts (Daniel et al., 2006). In the final chapter of this book, we examine in greater detail the potential psychological, social, and cognitive benefits of reading, but the evidence cited here is enough to show that adequate reading skills are a significant contributor to mental and psychological well-being in today's society.

WHY READING EDUCATORS NEED TO KNOW ABOUT PSYCHOLOGY

We can grow impatient with psychological debates regarding the underlying mental processes engaged by reading. Why not just get on with the business of teaching kids to read and simply figure out "*what works*"? We argue that it is not enough to know what works to help people read better. In both scholarship and practice, it is essential to understand *why*, *how*, and *for whom* a particular theory or intervention "works," and psychology is one intellectual path for gaining such understanding. Without this understanding, it is all too easy to misread and misuse the findings of research, and to end up doing more harm than good. For example, the uninformed application of research showing that children learn better in kindergarten if they have been introduced to concepts about reading and writing at home (see Chapters 1 and 2 for more on this issue) has led to the creation of what psychologist Deborah Stipek (2006, p. 741) calls *drill and kill* prekindergarten classes, where 3- and 4-year-olds spend extensive time memorizing flashcards and doing worksheets. A better understanding of child development would have prevented this all-too-common practice, which can be found to have negative impacts on cognitive and motivational outcomes.

In addition, Robert Cole (2008) points out that no strategy or approach works for every student. Both students and teachers are too diverse in their prior knowledge and skills, their talents, their resources, their interests and values, and even their specific ways of thinking for any instructional strategy to work always with everyone. This basic reality does not mean that we know nothing about how people usually read and learn to read; if that were true, you might as well stop reading this book right now. Just as medical science continues to discover more about the human body, so do psychologists continue to gain knowledge about the mental processes that underlie reading and the needs of students who are learning to read. But the field of medicine is increasingly recognizing that medical treatment cannot conform to a one-size-fits-all model; the same medicine or treatment at the same dosage may cure one person, be ineffective for another, and produce intolerable side effects in yet another. Doctors are professionals precisely because they can combine a broad understanding of human physiology with specific knowledge about their patients to better anticipate which medicines may work better for which patients, and make quick adjustments to decide that a patient may need a different treatment altogether. In the same way, education professionals know that they cannot blindly apply educational research in their classrooms; as professionals, they need a broad understanding of how people think and learn as well as specific curricular knowledge that allows them to adapt in ways that will most effectively meet the needs of particular students.

TWO MAIN SCHOOLS OF PSYCHOLOGY THAT PERTAIN TO READING

As you read this book, it will be useful to have some general background knowledge about two of the main schools of thought in psychology that are particularly relevant to reading and learning to read. If you have already had coursework in educational psychology, you will probably recognize much of what follows, but for readers who have not, or who would like to brush up on what they may have learned a while ago, a brief summary of each school of thought may be useful. We hope to illustrate how some main ideas from these schools of thought might apply to reading per se.

Cognitive Information Processing

The theory (or theories) of *cognitive information processing*, at least the classical version of it we discuss, focuses on computers as models of human thought processes. The approach breaks down complex cognitive processes, such as reading, into simpler ones that can be studied somewhat independently from the larger processes in which they are embedded. Sparked by the Cognitive Revolution against behaviorism in the 1950s, which included a devastating critique of Skinner's *Verbal Behaviors* by Noam Chomsky (1959), information processing, with its descendant, cognitive science, remains one of the two dominant paradigms in research on the psychology of reading today.

In early information-processing theory, the human mind was viewed as consisting of different functions, similar to the different parts of a computer. Different scholars use slightly different versions of the information-processing model, but the main parts and how they are thought to work are pretty similar. You may want to refer to Figure I.1 as we discuss the various elements of this theory:

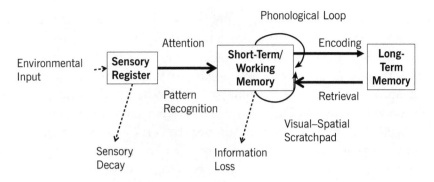

FIGURE I.1. Standard information-processing model.

Sensory register (also called *sensory input* or the *sensory memory*) is the gateway for all information coming into the mind. In a computer, the sensory memory would be connected to such input devices as the keyboard, mouse, modem, and disk drive. In human beings, the sensory memory takes in information from our senses: sight, hearing, touch, taste, and smell. The sensory memory can take in a great deal of information, but the impression made by a stimulus on the sensory memory is very fleeting, a few seconds or mere milliseconds long depending on the sense, unless the sensory impression is passed on to working memory. It is in the sensory register that the graphic input from text is processed.

Because the sensory memory can take in many more pieces of information than the working memory can deal with, *attention* controls which information from the sensory memory transfers into working memory. Directing attention in computers is just a matter of pushing a button to bring up a different program or screen, but attention in humans is much more complex. Some attention patterns originate in the sensory memory itself—loud noises, unexpected movements, and other novel, potentially dangerous stimuli draw our attention automatically; the human nervous system is "hardwired" to pay attention to such stimuli as a matter of survival. Other times, certain stimuli attract attention because they are related to something that is currently engaging working memory (e.g., once you start reading a good novel, it is easy to focus your attention on it and shut out other stimuli), or because they are associated in long-term memory with something either pleasant or upsetting (e.g., consider how quickly you notice a friend's, or an enemy's, face in a crowd). Finally, you can use your executive control to focus attention on certain stimuli deliberately, such as when you search for particular information in a textbook being used in a class.

Working memory is sometimes also called *short-term memory* because information disappears from working memory within 20–30 seconds if attention is not focused on it. Working memory in humans is parallel to the random-access memory (RAM) in a computer, with one important difference. Whereas many computers today have several gigabytes of RAM (which means they can work with several billion bits of information at the same time), we humans can work with only five to nine separate pieces of information simultaneously on the "desktop" of our working memory. This difference is one reason computers can calculate so much faster than humans (although, as you will discover, we have other advantages).

Humans use a number of different processes to deal with these severe limitations to working memory. One of the simplest is *maintenance rehearsal,* which involves repeating information over and over to keep it fresh in memory (much as you might repeat a phone number you have looked up in order to remember it until you can get to a phone). We need our working memories to build and update our current understanding of the text as we read. We notice difficulty with our working memories when there are lots of characters and places to keep track of, causing us to lose track of the identity of a pronoun we have encountered in a text. Children may demonstrate difficulties with their working memories when they try to string together long sequences of sounds as they sound out words in a text.

Perhaps the biggest space-saving function in working memory is that of *automaticity.* Once we have learned to do something very well, we have practiced it to the point that it takes up very little working memory; that is, we have made its retrieval *automatic.* Without automaticity, we could never do all the very complex activities involved in daily life, from driving to reading to even walking or talking—without automaticity, we literally could not walk and chew gum at the same time! In reading, automaticity is a central concept around which many of our activities operate. We can quickly recognize words, quickly interpret the grammatical relationships in a sentence, and quickly retrieve relevant information from our experience to be used in interpreting text.

In addition to the main part of working memory, sometimes called the *central executive,* it seems likely that there are at least two subcomponents: the *phonological loop,* which holds and rehearses sounds and words and is obviously involved in word decoding, and the *visual–spatial scratchpad,* whereupon visual images can be briefly stored and manipulated. Both of these elements are crucial to the act of reading.

Long-term memory is like the hard drive on your computer, but this is where we humans have a huge advantage. First of all, no matter how big your computer's hard drive is, your human long-term memory is larger; in fact, no one has ever found the limits of the storage capacity in human long-term memory. Second, although all information originally enters long-term memory after being processed through working memory, just as information has to be processed through RAM to get to the hard drive on a computer, information in human long-term memory is not stored in hierarchical pathways the way it is on our computers. Instead, it is stored in organized, interconnecting, cross-connecting, and ever-changing networks. The information from your long-term memory is brought to bear when you are reading a text, and it is used in an ongoing way as the meaning of the text unfolds and is updated as comprehension occurs.

Executive control is the part of your mind that chooses goals and decides on strategies for reaching them. An important skill that enhances executive control functioning is *metacognition*, or the ability to reflect upon and control your own thinking. Young children are not very metacognitive; they often are not aware of what they know and don't know or how they learn best. They are not very good at being strategic as they read. As we get older, we can get better at monitoring our understanding *if* we reflect on our own learning and thinking—that is, by knowing when we have understood something we have read, for example, and when we need to go back over it to gain a better understanding. The value of metacognitive reflection is one reason good reading teachers instruct children not only to read the various materials they will encounter, but also to reflect on and discuss them. The more metacognitive children become, the better they can use and add to the information and skills they acquire.

Today few cognitive psychologists would hold to the classical version of information-processing theory that we have presented here. Certainly, one main lesson that emerged from the past few decades of research in cognitive psychology is how interactive and less stage-like cognition is than what we have just described. However, we still see remnants of the "mind as computer" analogy that drove much of the early theorizing from this theoretical standpoint in the current use of computer modeling to test theories found in cognitive-science approaches to reading. Throughout this book you will notice how important the information-processing model of thought is to the study of reading. Concepts generated from this approach—such as *attention, working memory, automatization, long-term memory, semantic networks,* and *metacognition*—will come up repeatedly as we progress from explanations of emergent and early word reading all the way through the study of reading comprehension. We will see that this cognitive-science approach to reading psychology has become very interdisciplinary, seeking theoretical input from the fields of psychology, artificial intelligence, cognitive neuroscience, linguistics, and education.

To a great extent, the cognitive information-processing approach has been useful to classroom teachers by providing guidance in identifying the workings of a particular aspect of reading that they are teaching. It can help provide insight into problems particular children may be having. It can help them answer many questions, such as:

"Do the children in my classroom have the long-term memory concepts required for reading this particular book?"

"Is this child's word reading automatic and accurate enough so as not to gobble up working memory resources and interfere with comprehension?"

"Is the sound identification process and rehearsal process engaged by the phonological loop operating optimally to help this child pair sound to print?"

Constructivism

The theoretical framework of *constructivism* looks at people not as passive recipients of environmental conditioning, nor as just receivers and processors of information, but rather as choosers and builders of knowledge, both their own and their society's. Constructivist psychology, with its emphasis on the learner's active role in learning and the powerful influence of interactions with people in a culture and community, is another major paradigm that dominates the psychology of learning and reading today.

Jean Piaget is often thought of as the father of constructivism because he was one of the first psychologists to elaborate on the idea that we don't just respond to stimuli or soak up information, but often learn intentionally, by trying to construct knowledge to help us adapt to our world (Piaget, 1970). Piaget believed that we learn by forming *schemes* (or *schemas*), which are organized structures of knowledge used to think, talk, and accomplish desired actions. According to Piaget, the motivation to learn arises in response to a feeling of *disequilibrium*, that is, a sense that our current schemes are not adequate to deal with the world around us. For example, while we are reading, we may feel disequilibrium when we try to *assimilate* the information—that is, incorporate the information into our existing ideas—but the assimilation does not work well enough. This may occur when we read something in a book that is surprising, unexpected, or counter to what we already believe or know. We assimilate some ideas well, but others lead to disequilibrium—which forces us to *accommodate*, or change and update, our schemes. It is important to note that, if we as readers experience too much disequilibrium—that is, if a situation we face is too far beyond what any of our schemes can help us make sense of—then we may not be able to assimilate or accommodate, but rather reject or ignore the new knowledge entirely. This last response is what happens all too often when students are required to read texts that are far too removed from their current knowledge base. According to this constructivist theory, we use assimilation and accommodation to build all the rest of our knowledge on previously acquired schemes.

Piaget (1970) also saw children as growing through four distinct stages of development in the way they think and learn, with the corollary that, no matter how well taught, children are not able to learn something that is too far beyond their current developmental stage. According to Piaget's theory, babies up to the age of 2 (approximately) are in what he termed the *sensorimotor stage*. They develop schemes mainly by interacting directly with objects in their environment; they cannot yet develop schemes from other people's knowledge or by imagining new things.

One cognitive accomplishment at the completion of this stage is *object permanence*: the baby's initial realization, at about 8 months old, that objects continue to exist even when they are not directly perceivable by sight or sound. Object permanence is important because it indicates that the baby has developed the ability to form a mental representation of an object. The ability to create and utilize mental representations allows children to represent their concrete experience symbolically through language. The child is now able to attach words to mental representations of objects to capture the symbolic relationship between a pronounced word and the object that it represents. This ability has obvious importance for the development of vocabulary, which expands radically toward the end of this stage.

From ages 2 to 6 or 7, approximately, children are mostly in the *preoperational* stage; children in this stage have many mental representations of people and objects they have experienced, but they cannot yet mentally manipulate, or operate, on those representations (hence the prefix *pre-*). Because of this limitation, they have trouble recognizing that things can be in multiple categories (e.g., Spot is a dog, but he is also an animal and a dalmatian), and they also typically struggle to put more than two things into a series; they can recognize that A happened before B, and B happened before C, but they have difficulty understanding that, in turn, A also happened before C. Finally, children in this stage can be rather egocentric, which means they have trouble taking another person's point of view. They may thus experience difficulty in imagining the psychological goals, emotions, and intentions that guide the actions of characters in stories. All of these limitations affect their abilities in reading comprehension; even if they know all the words in a story, they may struggle to draw appropriate inferences, to understand characters that are much unlike themselves, and even to remember the events of a story in some logical order.

At around age 6 or 7, most children move into the stage of *concrete operations*, which means that they can now mentally manipulate (or operate upon) the huge number of mental representations they have constructed. They can now mentally move, reshape, compare, separate, and recombine representations, but these are still mainly of concrete objects—things children have actually seen, touched, done, or experienced somehow. Children in this stage still do not think well abstractly or hypothetically; that is, they have trouble thinking about things that do not have a concrete referent (e.g., the concept of justice, the value of x) or hypothesizing situations that are contrary to fact (e.g., "What if you had a third eye?"). Children's vocabulary still reflects largely concrete items during this stage. Their reading comprehension will be superior for texts dealing with concrete concepts that resonate well with their experience, perhaps.

Around 12 years of age marks the beginning of the *formal operations* stage, in which children start to form mental representations of things, ideas, events, and possibilities outside their actual experience and, using these new representations, begin to reason hypothetically about previously unknown circumstances. They also become able to reason more abstractly and deductively and to develop ideas and draw conclusions about situations with many more complex factors. Their thinking becomes somewhat less dependent on direct concrete experience; now such experience serves as a means to confirm or dispute *thoughts* regarding those experiences primarily. This is the type of thinking needed to succeed at more advanced levels of schooling and to reason scientifically. Adolescents are able to interact meaningfully with texts that include such abstractions. There is a flurry of new vocabulary that addresses abstract concepts, and reading texts outside their experience does not pose the decided difficulty it once did.

It is important to recognize that these age limits and stages are not absolute; they blend gradually into each other as a child grows, and no one is at the same stage in all areas of knowledge. We tend to be more advanced in areas in which we have more experience, so that a 10-year-old chess expert may have already moved to formal operations in chess, but not in mathematics or reading, whereas an adult who has never played chess will begin learning the game by operating much like a child at the concrete operations level (Chi & Bassock, 1989). In fact, Piaget himself noted that many people might never reach the formal operations stage in a general way. From a constructivist point of view, it is likely that reading is one of the activities that push us to develop intellectually.

Lev Vygotsky is another major thinker who contributed to the theory of constructivism. The theory he originated, often called *social constructivism*, has gained recent prominence in the psychology of reading. Whereas Piaget emphasized learning that occurs through the individual's attempt to figure out his or her world, Vygotsky (1978) placed much more emphasis on the social nature of learning. He was not much interested in the basic types of learning that we share with animals, but rather in what he called the *higher mental functions* that are unique to humans, such as language and culture. He believed that these higher functions are learned naturally by participation in social interaction and activities with a *more knowledgeable other*, such as a parent, older sibling, or teacher. As they work or play together, the learner and the more knowledgeable other talk about what they are doing, and the language patterns and words the knowledgeable other uses are *internalized* by the learner, eventually developing into concepts and thoughts. The interaction between a parent and young child during storybook reading at home, discussed in depth in Chapter 1, is a very common example of this kind of learning experience.

Vygotksy (1978) also emphasized the importance of *cultural tools* to facilitate human learning and thought. Cultural tools are the products of every human culture, both physical (e.g., tractors, computers, shovels, books) and mental (words, symbols, stories, theories). The tools afforded by any culture both facilitate and limit the thinking processes of the people in that culture. Language, a cultural tool of relevance here, can both facilitate and limit thinking. For example, languages differ in terms of the way they capture spatial relations. The Australian

Aboriginal language Guugu Yimithirr uses only absolute directions (i.e., north, south, east, and west) when describing spatial relations, whereas in English we tend to use relative positioning (e.g., in front of, behind, to the left of, to the right of). Using concepts of absolute directions makes it easier for the speakers to carry out activities necessitating such knowledge, such as navigating in open space, compared to speakers of English (Levinson, 2001). A more recently developed cultural tool is the Internet, which allows those of us with adequate computers, broadband connections, and reading ability to access knowledge and think in ways that would have been impossible only 20 years ago.

The *zone of proximal development* (ZPD) is perhaps the element of Vygotskian theory best known to most educators. The ZPD is the psychological "distance" between what a child or learner can do independently and what he or she could do with the maximum amount of assistance from a more knowledgeable other. This psychological ZPD is held to be the ideal level for teaching and learning; it is wasteful to teach children what they can already accomplish without help, and it is useless to try to teach children something they cannot do or even understand, no matter how much help is given. Vygotsky saw this sort of assisted learning within the ZPD as the main source of mental development. Whereas Piagetians would say that a child can learn a new word only after he or she has developed a strong mental representation of the concept to which that word refers, Vygotskian theory suggests that the concept itself is developed through the child's hearing the word from adults or siblings and trying to construct a meaning for it. Some of the effects of reading on vocabulary and even on IQ (discussed later in this volume) could be attributed to this Vygotskian sort of development.

A major outgrowth of Vygotskian learning theory is the idea of *cognitive apprenticeships* (Collins, Brown, & Newman, 1989; Rogoff & Chavajay, 1995). Some cognitive apprenticeships occur very naturally, as when children learn to sing by listening to and singing along with their parents and other adults, but they can also be very effectively arranged within a classroom environment. In a cognitive apprenticeship, a learner works together with a more knowledgeable other (peers and/or the teacher) to accomplish an *authentic task*, a complete task that has some real benefit or purpose beyond the immediate learning situation. The more knowledgeable other *scaffolds* the task by doing the parts of the task that learners (or a single learner) cannot yet do. He or she *models* unfamiliar parts of the task for the learners; this modeling can be physical, such as actually demonstrating an action or procedure, or it can be mental, as when a teacher "thinks aloud" by verbally describing his or her thoughts, questions, and decisions as the teacher performs a task in front of the class. The more knowledgeable other also *coaches* the learners by asking questions or reminding them of important factors at each step of the process, but gradually *fades* this scaffolding, modeling, and coaching as the learners become sufficiently competent to take over more and more of the task. Throughout the process, the more knowledgeable other encourages the learners to *reflect* on what they are doing and *articulate* their ideas, questions, and new learning through conversation or writing. Finally, he or she encourages the now-competent learners to *explore* new ways of doing the task and thereby to create new knowledge of their own. The partner reading common in many elementary school classrooms is one example of a very basic form of this sort of cognitive apprenticeship learning.

Some later followers of Vygotsky have claimed that all human knowledge is merely the result of social construction, so that people living within a culture (which is all of us) have no way to assess the "truth" of their knowledge, since they cannot know reality directly, but must always interpret it through the "lens" of their cultural thought (Gergen, 1985). More moderate social constructivists believe that outer reality constrains but does not determine the knowledge a culture constructs, because such knowledge must "fit" with reality for the culture to survive (e.g., the many Native Alaskan words for *snow*), but they too acknowledge that different cultures can construct very different knowledge that "fits" reality well enough (von Glasersfeld, 1989). For example, cultures over the centuries have developed many different styles of clothing to serve different purposes, and typically each culture believes that its style of dress is the "right" style—that it is more "proper" or "healthier" or "beautiful"—than the "strange" styles of other cultures or other times. (How do you feel about the idea of deliberately scarring the face, as is done by some Maori in New Zealand as a form of decoration, or the long skirts and bustles considered the height of fashion for women in the United States and Europe during the Victorian era?) But clearly, it is also possible for a cultural clothing custom to be "wrong"—that is, harmful to people in the long run—as was the practice of binding young girls' feet that used to be common in China. Moderate social constructivism requires that people recognize that there may be many "right" ways to do something, but there are probably also some really "wrong" ones. These ideas have direct implications for resolving the *reading wars* (Vacca, 1996), the ongoing disputes over the best way to teach reading, that have raged in our schools over the past century, but also for the type of tests that assume, as do almost all standardized tests, that there is a single "correct" meaning for a reading passage or interpretation for a poem.

ORGANIZATION AND ORIENTATION OF THIS BOOK

In this book, we do not take a firm position on most of the debates that have developed on various topics in the psychology of reading, nor do we write solely from the viewpoint of any particular school of psychology. Instead, we try our best to present balanced evidence for and against various hypotheses that have emerged. We provide numerous references so that readers can read for themselves the research that has provided the evidence for any particular theory, debate, or conclusion. We include what we consider to be important additional sources that the readers of this book can pursue to derive their own conclusions. Although we emphasize psychological, developmental, and educational research throughout, we bring in evidence from other fields when it is directly germane to developing an enhanced understanding of the topic. In particular, we have tried to systematically incorporate the exciting new evidence regarding the neuropsychological underpinnings of reading where possible.

This book takes a decidedly developmental focus on reading and learning to read. We think our choice of topics will resonate with both educators and psychologists and other practitioners interested in the psychological foundations of learning to read. For each chapter, we provide a *classroom case study* that describes a child with an issue related to the topic and a teacher considering how to understand the problem and decide on an instructional approach. We also identify questions that readers might want to consider. These case studies do not represent actual, specific children or teachers with whom we are acquainted. Instead, they are composites of various children and teachers we have known over the years, for whom our understanding of the psychology of reading has been particularly helpful.

The psychology of reading has implications for implementing effective instructional practice and for evaluating and creating literacy standards related to instructional practice. Throughout the book, we present information regarding how the research in the psychology of reading has implications for certain areas of instruction, which change in both content and emphasis as children progress in learning to read. We provide examples of instructional practices that seem particularly closely connected to research on the psychology of reading. We examine more recent national standards related to learning to read, especially the Common Core State Standards, in sections that we call *Connecting to the Standards*. We evaluate the consistency of the standards with what we know about developmental processes in learning to read. Issues related to computer-assisted instruction and reading digital texts are addressed in several *Technology Toolboxes*. We also draw implications from the psychology of reading for the development of appropriate assessment practices throughout. The psychology of reading has a lot to offer test developers by identifying the key dimensions of underlying constructs, the psychological processes engaged by reading, and the implications for the remediation of problems.

Contents

CHAPTER 1

Families and Reading

CASE STUDY

Angie woke up Monday morning excited because her fourth birthday was tomorrow; she could hardly wait! As she ate breakfast, she watched one of her favorite *Sesame Street* videos, and then talked with her mother about what she wanted for her birthday as they drove to preschool. Angie wants a *Dora the Explorer* house, and she really wants a puppy, but her mother says they can't have a puppy in the apartment, so maybe she'll just get a book about puppies instead. At preschool, Angie played in the house corner with her friends Bernice and Sandi and really enjoyed the visit of a local storyteller, who told the class two funny Halloween stories. After school, they drove to the grocery store, and Angie told her mother one of the stories. Her mother laughed and laughed; then she let Angie pick her favorite cereal from the shelf for telling the story so well. Angie also spotted a McDonald's sign on the way home, but her mother wouldn't stop. She said dinner would be late enough as it was. After dinner, Angie played with her older sister for a while. Before she went to sleep, her mom read her *Dora's Birthday Surprise* (Reisner, 2010). Angie fell asleep as fast as she could, so her birthday would come sooner.

We begin this book on the psychology of reading by talking about families because learning to read, like all human learning, begins in the home. As Linda Baker and her colleagues have noted, "When children are raised in a literate society, they are in the process of acquiring literacy from infancy onward" (Baker,

Scher, & Mackler, 1997, p. 78). Parents implicitly (and sometimes explicitly) teach their children important lessons about reading through everyday interactions with the written materials that are found in almost all homes in modern society: not only books, magazines, and newspapers, but also bills, letters, labels, ads, and coupons (Purcell-Gates, 1996; Taylor & Dorsey-Gaines, 1988; Teale, 1986), and increasingly, digital text, whether on Facebook or shopping websites or online news (O'Mara & Laidlaw, 2011). Long before they enter kindergarten, children learn not only their first lessons about the meaning and uses of print, but also the oral language and cognitive skills that are the foundations of reading, so to understand how reading skills and attitudes develop, we have to start at home.

ORAL LANGUAGE DEVELOPMENT AND READING

Reading is, above all, a language-based activity, and it has long been known that children's oral language development precedes, accompanies, and greatly influences their learning to read (Snow, 1983). For example, Dickinson and Snow (1987) found that kindergarteners with better listening comprehension and ability to provide formal definitions for common words out of context also had better emergent literacy skills, such as alphabet recognition, reading of simple three-letter words, and even early invented spelling. In a small longitudinal study of a diverse group of pubic school children, Roth, Speece, and Cooper (2002) identified several specific factors in kindergartners' oral development that impacted their reading comprehension skills 2 years later, in second grade, particularly vocabulary and knowledge of narrative structure. General knowledge of syntax (how sentences in English are put together and what sorts of words fit where) seemed to affect both single-word reading and reading comprehension at all three grade levels studied.

In a later and much larger study done with over 1,000 children by the National Institute of Child Health and Human Development (NICHD) Early Childcare Research Network (2005), researchers found that pre-kindergarten comprehensive language skills, including listening comprehension and expressive language ability, were strongly related to both first-grade word recognition and third-grade reading comprehension. Again, in 2007, Durham, Farkas, Hammer, Tomblin, and Catts measured the oral language skills of children entering kindergarten, including vocabulary, listening comprehension, and grammar/syntax, and found that these skills had direct, positive effects on later elementary reading achievement. Clearly, oral language skills matter in preparing children for success in reading.

But where do these oral language skills come from? A full discussion of children's oral language development and the factors that influence it is beyond the scope of this book, since many factors, including health, emotional well being, and general cognitive development, can affect language development. Several specific influences are worth discussing here, however, because they have been shown to impact not only oral development, but also subsequent development in reading.

Quantity and Quality of Conversation

Perhaps the most important home influence on young children's oral and later literate development is the conversations that they hear and, especially, in which they participate. Not surprisingly, children learn language by trying to understand and use it, but the opportunities to do so vary greatly among different home contexts. For example, Heath (1989) carried out a case study of a young single mother living in an urban government housing project, who agreed to tape the interactions she had with her children over 2 years. In over 500 hours of tape and accompanying notes, "she initiated talk to one of her three preschool children (other than to give them a brief directive or query their actions or intentions) only 18 times," and there were only "14 interchanges that contained more than four turns between mother and child" (p. 370). Nor is this an isolated case. Hart and Risley (1995) carried out an intensive in-home study of 42 two-parent families: 13 with professional parent employment, 23 working-class families, and 6 who were on welfare. They found that parents in the six families whose income derived mainly from welfare programs spoke in daily conversation an average of only 616 words per hour, whereas those who had professional jobs averaged 2,153 words per hour, over three times as many; working-class parents averaged 1,251. By age 3 children's own speech in these families followed the same pattern; children whose parents spoke least spoke far fewer words per hour themselves, knew fewer words to use, and eventually, in third grade, scored significantly lower in reading comprehension (Hart & Risley, 2003). Tellingly, by 3 years of age, "86 percent to 98 percent of the words recorded in each child's vocabulary consisted of words also recorded in their parents' vocabulary" (p. 112).

More recent research suggests that differences in the amount of conversation in the home are not always tied to family socioeconomic status (SES). In fact, many low-income families do use considerable levels of complex language with their young children, which can have cumulative effects. Weisleder and Fernald (2013) recorded a typical day's worth of conversation experienced by 19-month-old babies in Spanish-speaking, mainly low-SES homes and followed up with these children when they were 2 years old. They found:

> There was striking variability in the total amount of adult speech accessible to the infant, which ranged from almost 29,000 adult words to fewer than 2,000 words over the course of 10 hours. . . . When only talk addressed directly to the child was considered, these differences were even more extreme: In one family, caregivers spoke more than 12,000 words to the infant, whereas in another family, the infant heard only 670 words of child-directed speech during an entire day. (p. 2146)

Interestingly, the number of words overheard did not seem to affect the child's language development; only children who heard more child-directed talk used more words in talking themselves, thus showing larger expressive vocabularies.

Not only does the sheer quantity of conversation impact children's language development, but the qualities of those conversations matter as well. As implied in the Hart and Risley (1995) study described above, parents' frequent use of new or unusual words contributes to children's vocabulary development, just as their regular use of more complex or unusual sentence structures helps children broaden their knowledge of syntax and grammar (Whitehurst & DeBaryshe, 1989). As the research by Weisleder and Fernald (2013) shows, parents' attentiveness and responsiveness during conversation also matter; conversations in which parents engage positively with children, asking open-ended questions or responding with interest to children's talk, are particularly helpful to children's language development (Debaryshe, 1995; de Jong & Leseman, 2001; Hill, 2001).

Clearly, habits of conversation in the home vary greatly from family to family, and these variations are not always predictable by SES. In turn, the quality and quantity of talk that young children overhear or, especially, in which they are directly engaged powerfully impacts their oral development. One of the best things that parents can do for their children's development is simply to talk with them—early and often and about all kinds of interesting things.

Other Home Factors That Impact Early Oral Language Skills

Although not as well studied, or perhaps as influential, as parent–child conversation, other aspects of the home environment also affect children's cognitive and oral development and thus ultimately their reading. It has long been recognized that experience is crucial to a child's cognitive and language development (Dewey, 1938; Hunt, 1961; Piaget, 1970; Vygotsky, 1934/1986). For preschool children, this means not only lots of talk, but also active play with a variety of objects and toys, opportunities to engage in joint activity with more knowledgeable others, and opportunities for varied experiences outside the home (Rogoff & Lave, 1984; Walberg & Marjoribanks, 1973). The HOME Inventory (Home Observation for Measurement of the Environment; Caldwell & Bradley, 1984) is probably the best-known instrument for measuring this type of support and stimulation for children in their home environments. A deceptively simple observation and interview protocol, with approximately 50 items, its use in multiple studies over decades has clearly shown the impact of these factors on children's early development (Bradley, 1994; Totsika & Sylva, 2004). Two of the qualities it measures—stimulation from toys and learning materials and variety of experiences—have been found to particularly impact children's later reading skills (Bradley, Caldwell, Rock, & Harris,

1986; Roberts, Jurgens, & Burchinal, 2005). For more detailed information about the HOME Inventory, see Box 1.1 below.

The amounts and types of television children watch also seem to affect children's development. Though early studies in the 1950s and 1960s found no effects of television viewing per se on development or reading (Neuman, 1991), more recent studies have found that increased television viewing, especially when it exceeds 4 hours per day or 10 hours per week, is associated with lower reading readiness and achievement scores. Perhaps so much time spent watching television displaces other, more valuable, activities (Clarke & Kurtz-Costes, 1997; Neuman, 1988).

BOX 1.1. The Home Observation for Measurement of the Environment (HOME) Inventory

In the early 1960s, Bettye Caldwell and her colleagues in the University of Syracuse Early Learning Project established one of the first day care facilities in the country dedicated to enhancing the development of underprivileged children. This program became one of the inspirations for the Head Start program (Mabie, 2002). As part of their work, Caldwell and colleagues needed some way to measure the level of support and stimulation available to preschool children in their home environments, so they developed the Inventory of Home Stimulation (Caldwell, Heider, & Kaplan, 1966), which was revised in the 1970s to become the Home Observation for Measurement of the Environment (HOME) Inventory (Caldwell & Bradley, 1984, 2003).

The HOME Inventory is a relatively simple instrument based on a 45- to 90-minute home visit, during which the rater observes natural interactions between the child and the child's primary caregiver and discusses objects and happenings in the child's life with that caregiver. Based on this observation and semistructured interview, the rater answers approximately 50 yes-or-no items, yielding scores with high reliability (alphas and interrater agreement typically > .90) on six to eight subscales, such as Parental Responsivity, Learning Materials, and Variety of Experience. The HOME Inventory is the best-known instrument for measuring the developmental potential of a child's home environment, having been used in literally hundreds of studies and intervention programs in this country and worldwide, because of its relative ease of use and established validity across many different child populations. There are currently four main versions of the inventory, suitable for children from birth through age 15, as well as a version adapted to assess the environments of children with disabilities and another that can be used to assess the quality of nonparental child care in home or homelike settings. For more information on how to purchase or use the HOME Inventory, plus a bibliography of key articles about it, go to the HOME Inventory website at *http://fhdri.clas.asu.edu/home/contact.html*.

In a more nuanced study of 236 children from low- to moderate-income families, John Wright and colleagues (2001) used interviews and parent-kept television diaries to measure the amount and kinds of television children watched. They found that preschool children watched an average of 23.5 hours of television per week, with only 2 of those hours devoted to child-audience informative programs such as *Sesame Street* and *Reading Rainbow*. Two- to three-year-olds who watched more hours of these informative programs scored higher on emergent literacy tests at age 3 than those who watched fewer hours, whereas their peers who watched more hours of cartoons or general-audience programming scored significantly lower. Four- and five-year-olds who watched more cartoons or general-audience programs also scored lower on early reading achievement measures at age 5.

Culture and Language

Finally, children learn not only the elements of language—words, meanings, and syntax—at home; as they get older, they also learn the more complex patterns and purposes of language. They learn how to ask and answer questions, how to tell stories, and how to use language to accomplish various ends. They learn how to talk to people of various relationships and statuses, and which aspects and types of language are valued or not valued culturally. This type of language learning strongly influences children's later reading and school achievement, and indeed, their use of oral and written language throughout life (Gee, 1992). Multiple studies in the ethnographic tradition (e.g., Moll, Amanti, Neff, & Gonzalez, 1992; Taylor & Dorsey-Gaines, 1988; Teale, 1986) have demonstrated that, in all cultural groups, "rich and varied literacy and language practices . . . are embedded in the fabric of children's daily lives" (Paratore, 2002, p. 57), but these patterns of language use can differ greatly among different cultural groups, even those that officially speak the "same" language.

Shirley Brice Heath's (1983; see also Heath, 1982b, 1989) 10-year study of three different communities only a few miles apart who shared a single school system in the Carolina Piedmont area is still one of the best known and most cited studies of this type. Her descriptions of the language practices in Trackton, an African American working-class neighborhood, show especially clearly how children can grow up learning to use language in ways that are useful and competent, but quite different from the mainstream language patterns typically found in schools. In Trackton, much language learning took place in mixed-family and -age groups during outdoor gatherings, on front porches, after church, and in local community spaces. Unlike middle-class European American parents, adults did not adjust or censor their talk around children, and, rather than calling children's attention to important remarks, they typically assumed that children were actively listening and learning from the adult conversation around them. Directions given to children were most often commands, like, "Hush, now," or "Put on your coat," rather than the indirect statements ("It's time to be quiet now") or even pseudo-questions ("Don't you think you should put on your coat now?") through which commands are often "softened" in middle-class environments. Trackton adults also did not tend to ask children the kinds of "school-type" questions that are so common in middle-class homes, questions that are really invitations for children to display their knowledge, such as "Where is your nose?" or "What color is your bear?" Instead, they asked children real questions, questions to which they did not know the answers, such as, "What do you want to drink?," and open-ended questions calling for analogical thinking, such as, "What's that like (*pointing at a neighbor's flat tire*)?" Questions such as, "What was at your Uncle Jake's?" could also be an invitation to "perform" for an appreciative audience, to tell a story or joke, often with dramatic exaggeration or humor. Although such open-ended, divergent questions can be good for language and cognitive development, Trackton children did not know how to interpret teachers' more convergent questions in school. They also did not know how to interpret the "softer" directives ("Wouldn't you like to hang up your coat?") that teachers used in classroom management. As a result, they often appeared to be less cooperative and capable, and frequently failed to do well in school. They were not, in truth, less competent; they just didn't understand the language patterns (typically white middle-class) being used in the classroom. Other researchers have found similar effects for children from many other non-mainstream cultural groups in this country, including Native Americans (Philips, 1972), Hawaiians (Au, 1980), and Hispanic Americans (Moll et al., 1992).

HOME LITERACY FACTORS THAT IMPACT EARLY READING DEVELOPMENT

Beyond the general language and cognitive development discussed so far, children's development of actual reading skills also begins in the home, through a myriad of resources and activities that are directly reading-related and which offer children opportunities to:

1. become familiar with literacy materials,
2. observe the literacy activities of others,
3. independently explore literate behaviors,
4. engage in joint reading and writing activities with other people, and
5. benefit from the teaching strategies that family members use when engaging in joint literacy tasks (DeBaryshe, Binder, & Buell, 2000, pp. 119–120).

Access to Written Materials and Adult Modeling

Scholars and teachers have long known that children whose homes are full of books, especially children's books, usually learn to read more easily and eventually read better than their peers who do not have as easy access to books. In fact, in a recent analysis using data from 42 countries in the Program for International Student Assessment (PISA), Evans, Kelly, and Sikora (2014) found that students whose families owned more books scored significantly higher on the combined reading scale. This effect held true overall and also in every one of the countries measured, both advanced and developing, even after controlling for parents' education and occupation and family wealth. In fact, the size of the home library had a stronger relationship to student reading achievement than did any of these other home factors.

Books, of course, are not all that matters; children encounter a variety of other literate materials at home, including magazines, newspapers, journals, letters, and board games (Taylor & Dorsey-Gaines, 1988; Teale, 1986). Preschool children with greater exposure to print overall tend to better understand the purposes and functions of written text. Simply by living and participating in home contexts that included people reading books and magazines, reading the *TV Guide* for program information, and reading the rules for a board game, young children could begin to construct knowledge about written language and how it works (Purcell-Gates, 1996, p. 423). However, Purcell-Gates and others have also found that children gain much more when, rather than just observing, they are directly involved with their parents in reading-related activities (Burgess, Hecht, & Lonigan, 2002), and by far the best studied of these is shared book reading.

Shared Book Reading

When most of us think about reading in families, the image of a mother or father reading a bedtime story to a child almost invariably comes to mind. So many studies have found that shared book reading has a strong, positive influence on young children's reading development (Sulzby & Teale, 2003) that in their influential report, called *Becoming a Nation of Readers*, Anderson, Hiebert, Scott, and Wilkinson (1985) asserted that "the single most important activity for building the knowledge required for eventual success in reading is reading aloud to children" (p. 23). Despite some who challenged this conclusion (notably, Scarborough, & Dobrich, 1994), a meta-analysis by Bus, van IJzendoorn, and Pellegrini (1995) found significant effects for shared book reading for multiple countries and at different SES levels, providing a "clear and affirmative answer to the question of whether or not parent–child joint storybook reading is one of the most important activities for developing the knowledge required for eventual success in reading" (p. 15).

In describing this common practice, we have deliberately used the term *shared book reading*, rather than the more colloquial *reading aloud*, because there is good evidence that young children don't learn as much when parents simply read a story *to* them as they do when parents interactively read *with* them. That is, it is helpful to children when the adult reader stops to ask open-ended questions, point out pictures, and discuss important or exciting points. To be effective, adults should also adapt their pace and interaction to maximize children's ability to contribute to the activity (Lonigan & Whitehurst, 1998; National Early Literacy Panel, 2008; van Kleeck, 2006). The affective quality of the interaction also matters; children who experience warm and positive interactions around reading benefit more than those whose parents are colder or more corrective of their behavior (Baker et al., 1997; Bus & van IJzendoorn, 1995). In other words, the quality of shared reading in families probably matters just as much as the quantity.

The following is an example of this type of warm, interactive shared reading, taken from Bus and van IJzendoorn's (1995, p. 1010) study of mothers reading *Dudley and the Strawberry Shake* (Taylor, 1986) to their 3-year-olds:

MOTHER: (*Reads that Dudley sees a giant strawberry; the picture shows the dog sleeping behind a leaf.*)

CHILD: But that's a dog. (*Points.*)

MOTHER: Oh, that must be the dog of the notice on the gate "Beware of the dog." (*Here the mother is referring to a previous picture and discussion.*)

MOTHER: (*Reads that Dudley decides to take that strawberry [which is actually the dog's nose] home.*)

CHILD: Oh, what's going to happen now? (*Cuddles up to his mother.*)

MOTHER: (*Puts her arm around the child.*) Well, I haven't a clue, but the dog is still sleeping. Exciting, isn't it?

CHILD: It is.

MOTHER: Yes. Dudley . . . He thinks that that (*points to the dog's nose*) is a strawberry. (*Turns the page and reads on.*)

Such shared reading experiences enhance children's reading development in a variety of ways. Children who regularly experience interactive shared reading tend to have greater receptive (listening) and expressive (talking) vocabularies (Mol, Bus, de Jong, & Smeets, 2008; Sénéchal, LeFevre, Thomas, & Daley, 1998). Examining shared reading in 2,581 low-income mothers and children from birth through 3 years, Raikes and colleagues (2006) found that English-speaking children whose mothers reported reading with them daily in their first year had larger receptive and expressive vocabularies at 14 and 24 months of age, and better cognitive development at 24 months. By 36 months, English-speaking children whose mothers reported reading with them daily over the preceding 3 years, and Spanish-speaking children whose mothers reported daily shared reading during even 1 of those years, all had higher scores on measures of language and cognitive development.

As noted earlier, such language and cognitive advantages can impact children's reading development. Sénéchal and LeFevre (2002) demonstrated this connection directly in a 5-year longitudinal study of 168 children and their families. They found that children whose caregivers had read with them more showed not only greater vocabularies and listening comprehension skills in first grade, but also higher reading comprehension scores in third grade.

Beyond language abilities, children's early reading development depends on their understanding of basic concepts about print. The first and most fundamental concept children need to develop is what Purcell-Gates and Dahl (1991) have called the *big picture*: the idea that print signifies language and is intended to communicate meaning. As discussed previously, most children begin to grasp this idea if they are regularly exposed to various uses of print in their homes. But there are more specific conventions related to books and print that children need to learn before they can really embark upon reading, and which they seem to develop best from shared book reading. Marie Clay (1979) identified some of these print-specific concepts that young children develop from the experience of shared reading, and she developed an easily administered assessment of them that can be given to a child who is holding a book. Examples of these concepts and the related questions can be seen in Table 1.1. Children who have not developed concepts such as these from shared reading prior to formal reading instruction are at increased risk for reading difficulties and failure.

Familiarity with the *written register* is another quality that distinguishes children who learn to read relatively easily from those who may struggle to learn. The language we use in everyday oral communication (the oral register) is quite different from the language we use in print (the written register), even in families that speak a standard or mainstream dialect. There is certainly overlap and blurring between the structures and uses of these two registers; formal speeches use language much more like the written register, whereas narrative fiction comes closer than most writing to the oral register, especially in written dialogue (Chafe & Tannen, 1987), but there are still some common distinctions. Based on Chafe's work (1982; also Chafe & Danielewicz, 1986), Purcell-Gates (1988) identified 15 ways in which written "storybook" language typically differs from oral language narratives. Written language tends to use a broader and more literary vocabulary:

TABLE 1.1. Examples of Concepts of Print Acquired from Shared Reading

Concept	Prompts
Book elements	Show me the right way to hold this book. Where is the front of the book? Where is the back of the book? Where is the title of the book?
Meaningfulness and directionality of print	Show me with your finger where to start reading. (*after first word*) Show me where I should read next? (*at end of first line*) Where do I go now? (*at end of page*) Where do I read after this?
Letters and words	Point to one word. Point to the first letter in the word. Point to the last letter in the word. Point to each word as I read it.
Capital letters	Point to a capital letter. Point to a small letter (or a letter that is not capitalized).
Punctuation (assessor points to a period, then a question mark, then an exclamation point, each time asking . . .)	What is this called? or What is this for?

Note. Based on Clay (1979).

for example, "entered" instead of "went in," "battle" instead of "fight." It is usually less personal in tone, with less use of the pronoun "I," as in "I think," "I felt," "I saw." Because people read written language at different times and in differing contexts, it is necessarily decontextualized, whereas oral language often refers tacitly to objects in the immediate context. For example, someone giving oral directions might say, "Turn there, by that house," whereas someone writing directions will be much more explicit: "Turn left at Oak Street." Finally, written language typically uses more complex sentence structures, with more connected phrases and clauses, so that more meaning is packed into fewer words. For example, a speaker might say, "In the summer we went to the beach a lot. My whole family would go, and we would go swimming. After we went swimming, we'd get ice cream cones. We'd stay and watch the sun set, and then go home." A writer might pack all of that into one sentence: "When my family went to the beach, we usually swam all day, then bought ice cream cones to eat as we watched the sun set before going home." Purcell-Gates found that "well read to" children used many more of these features of the written register when they were urged to "pretend read" a story from a word-less picture book. In their 1995 meta-analysis, Bus et al. confirmed this finding, noting that shared book reading significantly affects children's acquisition of the written register.

Children who are frequently read with also develop a better overall understanding of *narrative structure*, that is, the ways that stories in books are typically structured and presented. Narrative structure includes elements such as the story setting; the introduction of characters and character goals, intentions, or problems; events around those intentions; and some kind of story resolution. For instance, Lever and Sénéchal (2011) showed that, after only an 8-week intervention, kindergarten children who were read with daily were better at retelling and constructing stories from wordless picture books compared to control children; their stories included more story elements and more statements reflecting characters' internal thoughts and emotions. Zevenbergen, Whitehurst, and Zevenbergen (2003) obtained similar results in a 30-week shared reading intervention with 4-year-olds from low-income families. Children in the intervention group, who were read with regularly, both at home and at school, afterward constructed stories with more dialogue and more references to characters' internal states than did nonparticipating children.

Finally, shared book reading tends to increase children's interest in books and reading. Debaryshe (1995) found in two studies of mostly African American children from low-income and working-class families that preschoolers showed more interest in books and reading when their mothers valued shared reading and often read with them. Baker et al. (1997) summarized multiple studies indicating that children who are read with from a young age are more interested in reading at ages 4 and 5 than are children who do not experience shared reading until their later preschool years. This impact can be lasting, affecting children's interest and the amount of time they spent in independent reading in later grades as well. They also found that warm, positive interactions during shared reading were particularly related to increased child interest, concluding that "when parents read with their children, they show them that they value reading and that reading is a pleasurable activity" (p. 75). Whether equally positive effects occur when parents and children read e-books together, rather than traditional picture books, is a question just starting to be researched, as we discuss in the Technology Toolbox.

Emergent Storybook Reading

For preschoolers who have been read with, these last four factors—understanding of basic concepts about print, knowledge of narrative structure, familiarity with the written register, and increased interest in books and reading—frequently come together in one of the earliest and most common signs of emergent literacy: children's independent attempts, long before they can actually decode print, to "read" their favorite storybooks. In fact, according to Elizabeth Sulzby, one of the earliest

TECHNOLOGY TOOLBOX:
What about E-Books and Young Children?

Books really haven't changed much since Gutenberg's invention of movable type in 1450 ushered in the era of print—that is, until recently, with the explosion of digital print. Thanks at first to the increasing popularity of the desktop computer and now of a wide variety of handheld devices, from tablets to e-readers to smartphones, one can find, borrow, buy, and read books of all kinds without ever looking at a traditional printed-paper page. Children, as well as adults, are moving rapidly toward this new reading technology; according to the Association of American Publishers, e-books accounted for 11% of their children's (including young-adult) book sales in 2013, up from only 7% in 2011 (Greenfield, 2014).

We know that shared reading of traditional print books with young children is important, but what about e-books? Are they better or worse or just the same as print books for young children's reading development? Research in this area is new and particularly challenging because the technology keeps changing, but the answer so far, as it is for many educational questions, appears to be, "It depends. . . ."

Julia Parish-Morris and colleagues (Parish-Morris, Mahajan, Hirsh-Pasek, Golinkoff, & Collins, 2013) studied middle-class parents and their 3-year-olds reading together, either traditional children's books (e.g., *Clifford, Berenstain Bears*) or similar books on the Fisher–Price electronic console system, which has readers press a button to "turn the page" of an inserted book, but also has other buttons that pronounce words or letters and activate puzzles, games, music, and so forth. The researchers found that parents reading the electronic books with their children made fewer story-related comments (e.g., "What do you think he did next?") and more behavior-related comments (e.g., "Sit still!" "Stop pressing the button."). Children who had read the traditional print book with their parents had better recall of story features and were better able to sequence story events. On the other hand, parent–child pairs who read the electronic books spent much longer reading and interacting around the books than did the traditional-print pairs. They hypothesized that the distraction of music, sounds, and games in the electronic books might have interrupted the flow of the story and thus impaired children's comprehension, but at the same time may have kept them engaged longer in the joint reading activity.

In a school rather than home setting, Segal-Drori, Korat, Shamir, and Klein (2010) studied low-SES Israeli kindergarten children who were read the same two children's books four times each. One group was read the stories by an actor in an educationally designed CD-ROM-based computer program that included "dynamic visuals," "music," and "film effects" to "bring the story to life" (p. 921) as well as special "hotspots" children could click on, after hearing a page read, that would give them extra dialogue from characters or pronounce words in a phonetically helpful way (i.e., syllabified). Other children used the same programs, but were also supported in this activity by a live instructor who stopped the program occasionally to give related instruction in word identification and phonetic pronunciation. A third group were read the stories by an instructor from a traditional print book, who also stopped at the same places in the reading and gave the same type of instruction. The children who read the electronic books with adult instruction made greater pre–post progress in word reading and concepts about print than either of the other two groups, and the traditional and electronic readers who also had adult instruction gained more than the solo electronic readers in phonological awareness. The researchers concluded that the carefully planned features of the educational electronic books may have facilitated children's learning, especially of word reading and concepts about print, but that "independent reading of an e-book, even though it is well planned for young children, might not be enough for achieving good levels of progress in emergent reading" (p. 924).

It is also important to remember that many children's e-books, especially the classics, are available free from multiple sites, including such major sellers as Amazon, Barnes & Noble, and Apple's iBook site. Two free e-book sites especially worth mentioning are *Uniteforliteracy.com*, where you can find original children's e-books, narrated in your choice of many languages, and the International Children's Digital Library (*http://en.childrenslibrary.org*), which offers e-books written/translated in multiple languages, including stories and fables from many countries. Then there are sites such as Storybird (*www.storybird.com*) and Storyjumper (*www.storyjumper.com*), which allow children to write and/or illustrate their own e-books. As we know, having "books in the home" is another important factor in children's reading development, and sites like these offer parents on a tight budget the chance to build a huge "home library" of e-books for their children, as long as they have Internet access of any kind.

Bottom line? E-books can be a great resource for reading and offering children the added possibilities of sound, music, free books, books in many languages, and even self-authored picture books. But the focus needs to remain on the words and meanings, not the bells and whistles, and they need to be used as an addition to, not as a substitute for, the vital adult–child interaction during shared reading that we know so greatly impacts children's reading development.

and perhaps the best-known scholars in this area, this kind of pretend story reading is a very normal, almost inevitable, step on the way to more conventional reading from print (Sulzby & Teale, 2003). Sulzby (1985) described a regular progression through which many emergent readers pass, starting with children (most often preschoolers) who read their book by pointing at the pictures and naming objects or making brief comments such as "Go here" or "Bad." In the next stages, children still pay most attention to the pictures, but their reading comes to resemble more and more an actual story, gradually becoming more sequential and moving from language and intonation common in oral speech to a tone and wording closer to the written register. This more story-like reading may also contain elements of the actual story, and eventually a good bit of remembered, verbatim wording from the text, but it is still cued mainly by the pictures, not the actual printed words.

Once children begin to realize that the printed words actually contain the story, many go through what seems, paradoxically, like a setback, often refusing to read because they "don't know the words" (i.e., cannot decode them). In the next stage, children begin to pick out isolated words or phrases that they can recognize in the text, often ignoring their memories of the whole story to do so, which again can look like a regression, but is usually the final stage before children accomplish a real, holistic reading of the text, at first perhaps omitting or asking about some unknown words or difficult passages, but finally becoming able to read the entire text accurately and independently. Although subsequent research in this area has focused mainly on validating and describing emergent storybook reading patterns displayed by diverse groups of children (Sulzby & Teale, 2003; Whitehurst & Lonigan, 1998), several studies have also shown correlations between levels of emergent storybook reading and literacy skills in kindergarten (De Temple & Tabors, 1996) and first grade (De Temple & Tabors; Garvin & Walter, 1991).

Direct Teaching by Parents

Parents may not only model and share reading and reading-related activities with their children, but also directly and deliberately teach their children specific reading-related skills, both before and after they enter school. They may do this through reading-related play, such as rhyming or alphabet games, or by specific instruction in reading and writing letters and words. Indeed, van Kleeck and Schuele (2010) pointed out that until the advent of public schooling in the mid-1800s, most children who learned to read did so at home, often from their mothers. Even children who attended school were usually expected to arrive there already able to read basic text.

In their 5-year study of parents' involvement in children's reading development, Sénéchal and LeFevre (2002) distinguished between *informal* home literacy activities, in which the focus is on the content or message (e.g., a parent reading a bedtime story) and *formal* home literacy activities, in which the focus is on the print itself (the same parent reading an alphabet book). Surprisingly, the frequencies of these two types of home literacy activities are not correlated. Parents who read stories and carry out informal reading activities with their children are not particularly more likely to teach them their alphabet or how to read words, whereas parents who directly taught such skills sometimes did not read books to their children. The two types of activities also may affect children's later reading skills differently. As discussed above, storybook exposure in kindergarten and grade 1 was directly and significantly related to the development of children's later reading comprehension skills, but not to the development of word reading skills. Conversely, parents' reports of direct teaching were related to their children's early literacy skills upon kindergarten entry, and these skills helped children learn to read words in grade 1. Similarly, Fernandez-Fein and Baker (1997) found that children from diverse backgrounds who were exposed at home to nursery rhymes and rhyming games scored higher on tests of phonemic awareness and word reading than those without such exposure.

Phillips and Lonigan (2009) made a similar distinction between home factors related to the code of reading (e.g., pointing out words, alphabet and rhyming games, alphabet teaching) and those related to enhanced reading experiences (e.g., shared reading, number of books in the home). They identified three distinct types of families: one cluster of middle-class families that reported relatively low levels of both types of activities, another cluster of middle-class families that reported high levels of both code- and experience-related home activities, and a third cluster of low-SES families (average annual incomes under $25,000; less than half of either of the other groups) that reported relatively high levels of code-related activities but quite low levels of experience-related activities. The researchers hypothesized that the distinction between the first and second groups might lie in the beliefs and values of the parents around reading and literacy in the home, while the third group might be composed mainly of families who thought learning to read was important for their children, but lacked the time and money to purchase books or read themselves. The researchers felt that the evidence of direct teaching by most of the parents in their study could be attributed to the increased emphasis in schools and preschools on children's acquisition of discrete reading skills at earlier ages.

Other researchers have similarly found that parents' beliefs about learning to read and appropriate reading activities with children are a strong influence on home reading activities (Curenton & Justice, 2008; Phillips & Lonigan, 2009). Lower-income parents, in particular, seem more likely to favor direct teaching of letters and words during literacy interactions (Gallimore & Goldenberg, 1993; Purcell-Gates, 1996). Although many of the studies discussed above show some positive effects of direct teaching by parents, a note of caution is appropriate. From their review of research on the motivational effects of family reading practices, mentioned above, Baker et al. (1997) concluded:

> The beliefs held by children's parents about the purposes of reading and how children learn to read relate to children's motivations for reading. Parents who believe that reading is a source of entertainment have children with more positive views about reading than do parents who emphasize the skills aspect of reading development. (p. 1)

If parents are increasingly feeling the need to teach code-related skills to their preschool children, as Phillips and Lonigan (2009) suggest, they should use games and other developmentally appropriate means to do so, and make sure that reading-related activities remain enjoyable for their children, rather than becoming times of forced drudgery, or even occasions for anxiety about not "doing it right."

To summarize, parents differ in how much and what they emphasize about reading with their young children. Parental reading practices with young children are influenced by parents' resources and their own habits of reading, as well as their beliefs about how and when children learn to read. What parents emphasize, in turn, strongly impacts the knowledge and feelings about reading that children then bring to their formal reading instruction in school.

SIBLINGS AND GRANDPARENTS

Most of the research on families and reading, like all we have discussed so far, has focused on parents and their children. Recently, researchers have also begun to look at the roles siblings and grandparents may play in children's reading development.

Simply having siblings may in some ways be a disadvantage in terms of reading development. For instance, using National Household Education survey data from over 7,000 families with preschool children, Yarosz and Barnett (2001) found that as the number of children in the household increased, parents reported reading less often with their preschoolers. Since then, several other large studies have noted similarly negative effects (e.g., Downey, 1995; Marks, 2006). It seems likely that the presence of siblings diffuses parental time and resources among multiple children (Downey, 2001). Those of you who are parents of several children will recognize this phenomenon. It is much easier to spend 30 minutes reading a story (or doing anything else) with your preschooler if there isn't an infant to feed or older children to help with their homework. It is easier to afford books at Christmas for two children than for seven.

Research on the actual reading interactions between children and siblings is rather scarce. Play among siblings can serve as a means for learning about and practicing emergent literacy skills. A number of descriptive and ethnographic studies have suggested that older siblings can serve as a literacy guide in these interactions. For example, Gregory (2001) and her colleagues have carried out descriptive and ethnographic studies with both English and Bangladeshi immigrant families in London. They observed shared book reading between older and younger siblings, and there were many instances of siblings "playing school" as well. Older siblings would pretend to be the teacher, engaging in teacher-like read-aloud behaviors and teaching the younger ones words and letters. Sometimes they saw siblings engaging in word games and the recitation of nursery rhymes. In a similar fashion, preschool children in three Dominican immigrant families studied by Rodriguez (2000) played school with their older siblings and also often watched and imitated their older siblings doing homework.

Survey data paint a similar picture of sibling interactions around reading. In a random telephone survey by Sokal and Piotrowski (2011) of Canadian parents with at least two children, one of whom was in grades 1–4, over half (51.5%)

indicated that their children had read together without a parent present at least once in the past 24 hours. This finding was not related to family income, home language, or gender of either sibling, though families with more than two children were somewhat less likely to report such sibling-shared reading. So it seems likely that intersibling reading is a fairly common practice among many different types of families.

Though even less is known about the ways sibling reading and other literate activities may impact younger children's reading development, it seems reasonable to assume that such activities would be beneficial, as they are with parents. Eve Gregory agrees, asserting that there is a *synergy* effect in such activities, from which both siblings seem to benefit. The older siblings benefit from the practice they get reading, and also from the need to be more metacognitive as they explain stories and teach their siblings; the younger siblings benefit in much the same way as they would from parental shared reading or teaching. In the context of playing school, the younger siblings may also become more familiar with the mores and patterns of formal schooling (Gregory, 2001). On the negative side, Baker et al. (1997) suggested that reading with siblings might be more conflicted and less comfortable than with parents.

In one of the few studies actually measuring the effects of sibling reading on children's reading achievement, Farver, Xu, Lonigan, and Eppe (2013) interviewed the mothers of 392 Latino children enrolled in Head Start. Many mothers who were not proficient in English were unable to help their children with English literacy activities. In this case, older siblings often helped their young siblings with literacy. The frequency with which older siblings read to preschoolers in English was powerfully related to their younger siblings' literacy achievement. The researchers concluded that older siblings who can and will read with younger children may be an important protective factor against the risks of lowered reading achievement that too often accompany poverty and English language learner status.

Research on the impacts of grandparents carrying out literacy-related activities with children is also limited. This is unfortunate because about 10% of U.S. children now live in households with at least one grandparent. Currently, 2.7 million grandparents have the primary responsibility for their grandchildren (data from U.S. Census Bureau reports, based on 2010 and 2012 figures). Again, Gregory and her colleagues have done some of the first detailed research on grandparent-facilitated literacy activities with young children in 20 Bangladeshi and Anglo families (Kenner, Ruby, Jessel, Gregory, & Arju, 2007). Grandparents frequently told stories, sang and recited rhymes with their grandchildren, read to them, and helped them with their homework. Observers noted important reading-related learning activities occurring during these interactions, focused on sound–symbol relationships and some word spelling in English, vocabulary learning in both English and Bengali, and development of narrative structure through storytelling and reading. However, no assessment data were gathered, so there is no indication of how these activities may have impacted children's actual learning.

Dunifon and Kowaleski-Jones (2007), using data from the National Longitudinal Survey of Youth on over 6,000 households with children ages 5–15, attempted to find connections between the presence of a grandparent in the home and children's reading development. They found, as has research for decades, that children who have lived more years with two married parents show, on average, better development and higher reading achievement than children living in single-parent households. The effects of adding a grandparent to that single-parent household were significant, but varied complexly by child age and ethnicity. For younger white children in single-parent households, an increase in the number of years living with a grandparent also in the house was correlated with higher scores on a measure of cognitive stimulation, whereas for black children the effects were just the opposite: the more years these single-parent children had lived with grandparents in the house, the lower their cognitive stimulation scores were. Yet, when older children took actual reading achievement tests, the results looked quite different. White single-parent children averaged the same reading scores no matter how many or few years they had spent living with a grandparent, but black single-parent children tended to get higher reading scores the more years they had lived with a grandparent in residence. Unfortunately, there were few grandparent-only and grandparent-plus-two-parent families in the dataset, so these groups were not included in the analysis. Further, the researchers noted that family income for single-parent families was generally low and varied by both ethnicity and grandparent residency in multiple ways. The researchers simply concluded that more research in this area is needed to sort out the potential impact of family income versus that of grandparent presence.

Overall, the available research on the role that siblings and grandparents can play in facilitating children's emergent literacy suggests that their influence can be positive and important. However, the impact of these extra people on children's literacy growth is likely to depend a great deal on whether they carry out the activities that we normally associate with parents, rather than siphoning off the resources that parents may have to devote to literacy learning in their young children. Clearly, more research is needed on these questions.

EFFECTS OF POVERTY ON READING ACQUISITION AND DEVELOPMENT

The effects of unequal family incomes have been interwoven in much of the research we have so far discussed about families and reading. In 2013, 22% of U.S. children (16.1 million) were living in families that earned below the federal poverty line (an income less than $24,000 for a family of four); 7 million of these children were living in extreme poverty, defined as 50% or less of the federal poverty income rate (Kids Count, n.d.). Many of these children are at risk for delayed reading development and, eventually, for inadequate levels of reading achievement. According to the National Center for Educational Statistics, in 2013, 41.9% of U.S. public school children qualified for federal free or reduced lunch benefits, meaning that they were in families earning below 185% of the official poverty line. These children scored lower on almost all measures of reading achievement. Table 1.2 shows the wide disparity in reading scores at all three grade levels on the 2013 National Assessment of Educational Progress (NAEP) between children who were and were not eligible for free or reduced lunches.

Results of the 2006 PIRLS (Progress in International Reading Literacy Study) showed the same disparity. Using data from over 100,000 fourth graders in 40 countries, Krashen, Lee, and McQuillan (2010) found that "SES has a profound effect on reading development" (p. 26); indeed, "the strongest predictor of reading achievement among ten-year-olds is SES" (Krashen, 2011, p. 19). *That* poverty adversely impacts reading and other academic achievement has been known for a long time (Coleman et al., 1966; White, 1982); *how* it impacts reading is a more complex question, because poverty can affect reading development both directly and in ways that are mediated through its negative effects on families and communities.

Direct Effects of Poverty

At its most basic, poverty can be defined as a lack of necessary material resources. Children who grow up in poverty typically experience a number of adverse conditions and events, simply because their families do not have enough money to pay for the necessities of life, many of which directly impact their overall development and, specifically, their development in reading.

TABLE 1.2. Reading Achievement among Children Eligible and Not Eligible for Free and Reduced (F & R) School Lunches in the United States in 2013

Grade level	F & R eligible			Not F & R eligible		
	Mean score	Proficient or higher	Below basic	Mean score	Proficient or higher	Below basic
4th	207	20%	47%	236	51%	17%
8th	254	20%	34%	278	48%	13%
12th	274	22%	38%	296	46%	18%

Note. Data compiled from the National Center for Educational Statistics (*http://nces.ed.gov/nationsreportcard/naepdata*).

We have already noted that children who live in poverty are likely to have many fewer books in their homes than more well-off children (Phillips & Lonigan, 2009), and that the availability of books in the home is directly related to reading achievement scores (Evans et al., 2014). Poor households are also less likely to have access to the Internet, another major source of reading materials and information. According the U.S. Census Bureau, in 2013, only 54% of households earning less than $25,000 per year owned a desktop or laptop computer, and only 48% of these households had Internet access of any kind. Compare these figures to those for middle-class households earning $50,000–$100,000 a year, 93% of which owned a computer, with 85% having home Internet access. Finally, poorer children on average have fewer toys and experiences with novel or stimulating environments (Duncan & Murnane, 2014), and are likely to spend more hours watching television (Phillips & Lonigan, 2009), especially noneducational programming, than do children in more well-off homes—all of which, as we have discussed, has an adverse impact on their reading development.

But the problems facing children living in poverty are more fundamental than a simple lack of reading-related materials and experiences. Poor children are often malnourished. In 2013, 9.9% of all children lived in food-insecure households (Coleman-Jensen, Gregory, & Singh, 2014), defined by the U.S. Department of Agriculture as lacking access to enough food for an active, healthy life at some time during the year. In 2012, 9% of children under 18 (7.1 million) had no health insurance coverage, putting them at serious risk for both current illness and longer-term health issues (DeNavas-Walt, Proctor, & Smith, 2013), and the Pew Charitable Trusts (2011) estimates that 16.5 million children go without even basic dental care each year. Lack of sufficient, nutritious food and basic health and dental care directly and adversely affect children's cognitive development, especially in the early years (Brooks-Gunn & Duncan, 1997).

Family-Mediated Effects

Poverty also affects children indirectly, through its adverse effects on their families. Inability to afford even inadequate housing causes many poor families to move frequently and to suffer periods of homelessness—some children routinely change schools two or three times within a single year. In 2011, 11% of working families did not earn enough to lift them over the federal poverty threshold. Over half of families living in poverty contain at least one working adult (Roberts, Povich, & Mather, 2013), but, ironically, getting a job can exacerbate rather than alleviate the problems poor families face. Adults in poor families are disproportionately likely to hold low-wage, service jobs, with no benefits, no paid sick or family leave, and unpredictable hours. Under these conditions, health care and dental care are typically still out of reach; quality child care is rarely available and difficult to arrange and pay for; and one car breakdown, late bus, or sick child can cause tardiness or absence that too often means job dismissal and even more difficulty getting the next job (Ben-Ishai, Matthews, & Levin-Epstein, 2014).

For all these reasons, plus the constant concern about simply having enough money for food and clothing, poverty is a major source of stress for both adults and children. The physical and psychological effects of such stress compound the problems poor families face, creating "constant wear and tear on the body, dys-regulating and damaging the body's stress response system, and reducing cogni-tive and psychological resources for battling adversity and stress" (Wadsworth & Rienks, 2012, p. 1). Such higher levels of stress also often impact family relation-ships, resulting in fewer positive and more negative interactions in families dealing with poverty (Conger & Elder, 1994; Conger et al., 2002). Depressed, worried, and overstressed parents often have little time or energy to interact positively with their children, like the single mother in Heath's 1989 case study described earlier, who so very rarely initiated or sustained conversation with her three preschoolers. Hart and Risley's (1995, 2003) classic study, also discussed earlier, found not only that parents in poverty spoke far fewer words in the home (averaging 616 words per hour, versus 1,251 in working-class and 2,153 in professional homes), but also that the types of interaction in these homes were very different. Hart and Risley (2003) provide this summary:

> The average child in a professional family [heard] 32 affirmatives and five prohibi-tions per hour, a ratio of six encouragements to one discouragement. The average child in a working-class family [heard] 12 affirmatives and seven prohibitions per hour, a ratio of two encouragements to one discouragement. The average child in a welfare family, though, [heard] five affirmatives and 11 prohibitions per hour, a ratio of one encouragement to two discouragements. . . . Extrapolated to the first four years of life, the average child in a professional family would have accumu-lated 560,000 more instances of encouraging feedback than discouraging feedback, . . . but an average child in a welfare family would have accumulated 125,000 more instances of prohibitions than encouragements. (p. 117)

Poverty also seems to be specifically related to the amount and types of read-ing done in the home. Though print and the use of print are ubiquitous features in all modern homes, parents in high-poverty homes are less likely to model extended reading or reading for pleasure (Phillips & Lonigan, 2009). For example, in the low-SES homes she studied, Purcell-Gates (1996) found that

> Some families, in fact, lived busy and satisfying lives with very little mediation by print. . . . Text at the phrasal/clausal level was most frequently read and written by the members of these families. This means that the majority of the print use in the homes involved, for example, reading container text (e.g., cereal boxes, milk

cartons), flyers, coupons, advertisements, movie or TV notices, writing grocery and to-do lists, and signing names. (p. 425)

These generally lower levels of personal reading, perhaps combined with the higher levels of stress discussed above, may help to explain why so many studies (e.g., Heath, 1983; Phillips & Lonigan, 2009; Raikes et al., 2006; Taylor & Dorsey-Gaines, 1988; Teale, 1986) have found that low-income parents are also far less likely to read with their children.

All of these family-mediated factors can have profound and negative impacts on the cognitive, oral, and reading development of children living in poverty. Unfortunately, the characteristics of the communities in which many poor children live are likely to pose additional barriers, rather than to help make up for the disadvantages faced by many of these children.

Community-Mediated Effects

For the past four decades, both income inequality and the segregation of neighborhoods and communities by income has been growing in the United States, a trend that is common, if less severe, in most of the rest of the developed world. According to U.S. Census Bureau figures, as adjusted for inflation, the income of the poorest families (the bottom one-fifth), fell by more than 25% between 1970 and 2010, while at the same time the income of the top one-fifth of families grew by 23% (Duncan & Murnane, 2014). Due to this growing imbalance, the top 20% of American households now own 84% of the wealth of this country, whereas the bottom 40% own only 0.3% of that wealth (Norton & Ariely, 2011).

In spite of, or perhaps because of, ongoing governmental efforts to provide safe, subsidized housing for families in poverty, the segregation of housing by income has likewise grown. The affluent have increasingly withdrawn to ex-urban areas or gated communities, and the poor have become increasingly concentrated in neighborhoods where only other poor people live (Reardon & Bischoff, 2011), precisely because these neighborhoods are places where people who can afford a choice do not choose to live (Kozol, 1996). Neighborhoods where poor people live have higher than average rates of violent and property crime (U.S. Department of Housing and Urban Development, n.d.), not mainly because poor people are more likely to be criminals, but because non-white-collar criminals are more likely to be poor (Lott, 1990; Western, 2007). Because poor people have less political influence, neighborhoods where most residents live in poverty often have less than adequate civic services, from police and fire protection to trash collection (Fullilove & Wallace, 2011). They are more likely to experience dangerous levels of traffic (Houston, Wu, Ong, & Winer, 2004; Males, 2009); outdoor air and water pollution from nearby industry and agriculture and aging infrastructure (Kay &

Katz, 2012); and indoor pollution from mold, insects, and perhaps most danger-ously, the lead paint dust that is common in older houses built before lead paint was banned in 1978 (Gaitens et al., 2009; Jacobs, Kelly, & Sobolewski, 2007). All of these factors negatively impact children's physical and cognitive health, and thus their reading development.

Just like the homes of families in poverty, poorer neighborhoods also have sig-nificantly fewer reading-specific resources. Neuman and Celano (2001) did one of the first and best known studies on this topic, comparing the reading resources in two high-poverty and two middle-class neighborhoods in Philadelphia, and their findings remain startling. Only 4 stores even sold books in either high-poverty neighborhood, and none of them were actual bookstores. In contrast, the two middle-class neighborhoods had 11 and 13 places to buy books, respectively, each with three or more dedicated bookstores. As a result, families in each middle-class neighborhood had access to over 2,000 different books for children and young adults, whereas those in one poor neighborhood had 358 children's titles available for purchase, and only 55 were available in the poorest neighborhood studied; neither of the poor neighborhoods offered *any* young-adult books or magazines. Neither the public nor school libraries in high-poverty neighborhoods made up for this disparity; in fact, they added to it. School libraries in the poorer neighbor-hoods contained no librarians, offered an average of 11 books per student, owned books that were both older and in worse repair, and were open an average of 3 days per week. Compare these numbers to those for school libraries in the middle-class neighborhoods, which had librarians with master's degrees, an average of 22 books per student, newer books and books in better condition, and were open all 5 days of the school week. Public libraries, though all part of the same citywide system, present a similar profile: those in "low-income communities had smaller overall collections, fewer books per child, and more limited nighttime hours than those in the middle-income communities" (p. 22). Such gross inequalities are not unique to Philadelphia; indeed, research since Neuman and Celano's original study has con-firmed that such disparities are common and, if anything, getting worse (Neuman & Celano, 2012). We might also point out that the common practice of levying hefty fines for lost, damaged, or late-returned books discourages many low-income parents from borrowing children's books from libraries.

Finally, the deep disparities between schools in poor and well-off neighbor-hoods are too well known and long-standing to require much comment here. In his 1991 book, *Savage Inequalities*, Jonathan Kozol shocked the nation with his descriptions of the truly unthinkable conditions under which poor children in the communities he visited were trying to learn: buildings with broken windows, rotting roofs, molding walls, and dysfunctional heating and plumbing; class-rooms with over 35 students each, but not enough textbooks or desks; a parade of "permanent substitute" teachers and sometimes no teacher at all; schools with shuttered libraries, unsafe hallways and playgrounds, science labs with no water, no art classes, no gym, and no paper, chalk, or pencils for the students and teachers stuck in these schools. Kozol (1996, 2000) has also written about the resilience and strength, the humor and generosity, and above all, the great potential of many of the children who go these schools—potential often unfulfilled, not because of "bad choices" or even ignorance on the part of these children, or their parents, but because of the myriad circumstances of poverty that surround and too often overwhelm them.

This discussion of poverty and its effects on reading development does not imply that we should give up on children from low-income homes, or that such children somehow cannot learn to read, and read well; indeed, the NAEP figures cited above tell us that millions of them do. It does, however, support the president's recent call to extend access to high-quality preschools to all children in the United States (The White House, Office of the Press Secretary, 2014). These "high-quality preschools," Alfie Kohn (2014) warns us, must look more like the interactive, warm, supportive environments found in the homes that best encourage children's reading development, than like the standards-driven, test-centered classrooms becoming increasingly common in public schools, especially in those that serve poor and minority children (National Association for the Education of Young Children, 2002). It also implies that, if we as a nation are serious about significantly improving reading achievement, especially that of our most struggling readers, then we will have to effectively address our increasing level of child poverty, and all the issues it brings with it.

WHAT WE CAN DO: WORKING WITH FAMILIES TO SUPPORT EARLY READING DEVELOPMENT

Get Books into Children's Hands and Homes

Many organizations and programs, both national and local, provide free or reduced-cost books to families and children who otherwise would not have them. One of the best known of these is First Book, which has distributed over 120 million books to children in poverty since its founding in 1992. A study funded by the U.S. Department of Education of over 2,500 children who received books over a 14-month period from First Book noted the following results:

> —*Children's interest in reading increased greatly*, with participants reporting a "low interest" in reading dropping from 43% to 15%, while those reporting a "high interest" more than doubled, from 26% to 55%. 63% said they were "not unhappy to have to take time away from play to read" and 80% "really like[d] to read books on their own."

—Owning more books changed home literacy practices, with 76% of the children reporting that they had "showed the book to someone at home," and almost as many (72%) saying they liked "to share reading experiences with friends, other kids, and family" and liked "to talk about" what they read. (First Book, n.d.)

Reach Out and Read (Zuckerman, 2009) represents another long-term successful attempt to get books into the hands of young children and to change the literacy behaviors of parents. In this program, children receive a book from their doctor at each medical visit from 6 months through age 5. The doctor also encourages the parent(s) to read daily with the child and provides developmentally appropriate coaching on how best to enjoy the visit's book with the child. Despite the simplicity of this program, it has been effective in increasing the likelihood that parents will engage in literacy activities and book reading with their children (Golova, Alario, Vivier, Rodriguez, & High, 1999) and has been shown to have an impact on children's developing literacy (Zuckerman)

School libraries also play a vital role in getting books to kids. Keith Curry Lance and colleagues at the Library Research Service have demonstrated through over 20 statewide studies that students in schools with larger print collections, more digital access, and increased library staff accessibility score significantly higher on state reading tests, even when students' SES, overall school funding, and community education levels are accounted for in the analyses (you can access reports of all these studies at *www.lrs.org*). Achterman (2009) found the same results in his exhaustive study of school libraries in California. Internationally, when Krashen et al. (2010) examined data from the PIRLS, they found that countries with a higher percentage of school libraries with over 500 books also had higher student reading scores, even when SES was factored into the analysis.

Help Parents Learn to Help Their Kids

Intentional efforts to share books and related activities with parents can also effectively promote family reading and reading motivation, especially in the early years. Zeece and Wallace (2009) and McNicol and Dalton (2002) describe examples of such successful programs, one designed for school libraries and one run through a large public library system.

But many programs go beyond simply sharing books to educating parents about ways to enhance their children's reading development, especially through interactive storybook reading. As mentioned earlier, many families do not have a tradition of such shared reading, and parents, even though they really want to help their children, may feel unsure of how to start one. Patricia Edwards's (1992) program, Parents as Partners in Reading, is a good example of an approach designed to help such parents. Edwards designed her program after seeing that many of the low-income African American mothers in the rural Louisiana community where she worked did not know how to read books to their children (Edwards, 1992). She recruited her first participants through what she describes as "an unlikely group of community leaders, [including] a bar owner, bus driver, grandmother, the ministerial alliance, and people sitting on street corners" (p. 352). Parents so recruited met in a local school library, where they were given book borrowing privileges, for 23 two-hour sessions, at first led by Dr. Edwards, but later by community members who had themselves gone through the program (Edwards, 1995). In the program they progressed from watching and discussing videotaped models of strategies for effective shared book reading (e.g., describing pictures, inviting text-to-life connections) to reading to each other and finally to their children, using the strategies they had learned. The program impacted not only the immediate families involved, but, as Edwards noted, parents "were discussing what they learned in the book-reading sessions with their friends, neighbors, church members and relatives," with the result that "many of the townspeople, as well as parents participating in the book-reading program, decided to return to school to earn their general equivalency (high school) diplomas" (Edwards, 1992, pp. 356–357).

Other programs have formally combined this kind of parenting information and increased book availability (often in Spanish as well as English) with adult English as a second language or basic skills classes for the parents themselves. The goal of these programs is to improve reading development in two or more generations at once (e.g., the Intergenerational Literacy Project [Paratore, 2002]; Project FLAME [Shanahan, Mulhern, & Rodriguez-Brown, 1995]). This is also the model on which the long-running federally funded Even Start program is based. All of these programs, with or without the inclusion of English language or reading classes for parents as well, are grounded in the conviction that all types of parents care about and, with support and information, can contribute to their children's learning. Evaluations of such programs have repeatedly demonstrated that most parents in these programs will spend more time reading and most children will show significant literacy gains (Paratore & Dougherty, 2011).

Bring Home Literacies into the Classroom

In some of the most successful home–school partnership programs, the emphasis is not so much on what parents can learn from teachers and educators, but rather on what teachers can learn from parents. We have discussed above that, although school-type reading and discourse around reading are not evident in all homes, all homes in our modern society do contain numerous reading-related resources, and the conversational patterns specific to all cultures can serve as springboards for significant literacy learning. For example, Heath (1982b) found that when teachers explicitly discussed various types of questions in class and incorporated into their instruction more of the open-ended sorts of questions asked by Trackton parents, as opposed to the more convergent questions common in schools and middle-class homes, children from all communities and income levels benefited. McCarthey (1999) found that "if teachers believed that students came from impoverished backgrounds, they did not build on their backgrounds, [but] when teachers were informed about and valued students' individual backgrounds, they were more inclined to adjust the curriculum to build upon students' out-of-school experiences" (p. 103).

Perhaps the studies that have been most influential in promoting this type of teacher education are those by Louis Moll and his colleagues (Moll, Amanti, Neff, & Gonzalez, 1992; also Gonzalez, Moll, & Amanti, 2005). They worked with teachers in Arizona who taught impoverished Mexican American and Native American children, encouraging them to visit their students' homes, and teaching them ethnographic methods to use in observing and talking with students' families about the many *funds of knowledge* present in these homes, ranging from carpentry and mechanical skills to knowledge of edible plants and the preparation and use of traditional medicines. Such visits helped "establish a fundamentally new, more symmetrical relationship with the parents" (Moll et al., p. 139), which in turn made parents more comfortable interacting with the teachers. Perhaps even more important, these visits also increased teachers' knowledge of and respect for the rich and varied learning contexts and resources present in students' homes and enabled them to begin incorporating these funds of knowledge into school-based projects and instruction, often inviting parents to contribute their knowledge and even teach in areas of their particular expertise. In this way, relationships between families and schools were strengthened; understanding among teachers, students, and parents was deepened; and students' learning and motivation were enhanced because they were better able to connect and use their home literacies and practices with those they were learning in school.

CONNECTING TO THE STANDARDS

Many of the ideas discussed in this section and throughout this chapter are incorporated in the standards for early childhood education programs established by the National Association for the Education of Young Children (NAEYC; 2014), the best known accrediting body for child care and preschool settings. Table 1.3 shows how these standards reinforce the vital role of families in early learning.

TABLE 1.3. Early Childhood Program Standards and Accreditation Criteria

Standard 1: Relationships

1.A.—Building Positive Relationships among Teachers and Families

1.A.01. Teachers work in partnership with families, with regular, ongoing, two-way communication.

1.A.02. Teachers gain information about the ways families define their own race, religion, home language, culture, and family structure.

Standard 2: Curriculum

2.A.—Curriculum Essential Characteristics

2.A.04. The curriculum is responsive to family home values, beliefs, experiences, and language.

2.A.08. Materials and equipment reflect the lives of the children and families as well as the diversity found in society.

2.D.—Areas of Development: Language Development

2.D.02. Children are provided opportunities to experience oral and written communication in a language their family uses or understands.

2.E.—Curriculum Content Area for Cognitive Development: Early Literacy

2.E.01 & 02. Infants and toddlers have varied opportunities to experience songs, rhymes, routine games, and books.

2.E.03. Children have opportunities to become familiar with, recognize, and use print that is accessible throughout the classroom.

2.E.04. Children have varied opportunities to be read to at least twice daily, explore books on their own, have access to various types of books, engage in conversations about books, identify the parts of books, and differentiate print from pictures.

2.E.08. Children have access to books throughout the classroom.

2.E.09. Kindergarteners have varied opportunities to learn to read familiar words, sentences, and simple books.

Standard 3: Teaching

3.F.—Making Learning Meaningful for All Children

3.F.03. Teachers and families work together to help children participate successfully in the early childhood setting when professional values and practices differ from family values and practices.

3.F.06. Teachers offer children opportunities to engage in classroom experiences with members of their families.

3.F.07. Teaching staff use varied vocabulary and engage in sustained conversations with children about their experiences.

Standard 7: Families

7.A.—Knowing and Understanding the Program's Families

7.A.02. Program staff uses a variety of formal and informal strategies (including conversations) to become acquainted with and learn from families.

Note. Adapted from the National Association for the Education of Young Children (2014). Copyright © 2015 NAEYC®. Adapted by permission.

1. What do you remember about reading in your family as you grew up? How do you think your family reading practices have affected your own reading interest and practices today? If your current reading practices are quite different from those in your family upbringing, what factors later in life do you think have influenced you? Since everyone's families have their own customs around reading, you might want to share your stories in your group or class.

2. Looking at the case study that began this chapter, what factors do you see in the account of Angie's day that will help prepare her to learn to read when she goes to school?

3. If you were giving a short presentation to a diverse group of parents about family reading practices that help prepare kids for reading, which three suggestions would you focus on, and why?

4. If you served on the School Improvement Team at a school where many students came from low-SES families, what are two things you would urge your school to do to help these children in their reading-related development, and why? Rather than proposing a new set of textbooks or a computerized phonics program, try to think "outside the box" on this question.

FURTHER READINGS

Evans, M. D. R., Kelly, J., & Sikora, J. (2014). Scholarly culture and academic performance in 42 nations. *Social Forces, 92*(4), 1573–1605.

Hart, B., & Risley, T. R. (2003). The early catastrophe: The 30-million word gap by age 3. *American Educator, 27*(1), 4–9.

Heath, S. B. (1982). Questioning at home and at school: A comparative study. In G. Spindler (Ed.), *Doing the ethnography of schooling* (pp. 102–131). New York: Holt, Rinehart & Winston.

Moll, L. C., Amanti, C., Neff, D., & Gonzalez, N. (1992). Funds of knowledge for teaching: Using a qualitative approach to connect homes and classrooms. *Theory into Practice, 31*, 132–141.

CHAPTER 2

Emergent Literacy

CASE STUDY

Ms. Johnson is concerned about Ileana, one of the 4-year-old students in her pre-kindergarten classroom. Ileana consistently uses what sounds to her like baby talk typical of a much younger child. For example, just the other day, Ileana was pretending that a container was a crib and was putting her baby doll into it, saying, "Baby go. Baby go right here. Baby little." During circle time, while Ms. Johnson was reading a rhyming book, Ileana showed almost no appreciation of the tortured and humorous rhymes that appeared in the book. Ileana often cannot answer the most basic questions about books that she reads to the class. She does not recognize the *I* or *l* or *a* in her own name. Ms. Johnson is considering how to address Ileana's needs.

From the moment babies start to make sense of their world, they embark on the development of skills that will be relevant to their later literacy. As noted in the Introduction, literacy has been an important window through which psychologists have gained insight into the mind (van den Broek & Gustafson, 1999). Indeed, in today's society, the development of literacy is intertwined with, and begins almost as soon as, general cognitive development.

Although we usually consider the term *literacy* to mean a person's ability to read and write, as we saw in the previous chapter, these skills begin to develop long before passing through a schoolroom door. Scholars who study *emergent literacy* recognize that young children bring a great deal of specific informal (and sometimes formal) knowledge about language, books, and print with them as they enter

31

school. This early knowledge forms the seed from which their formal knowledge of reading develops. Indeed, research on emergent literacy over the last 30 years has surprised us by demonstrating just how important this early knowledge is for learning to read and write.

THE FORMER READING READINESS CONSTRUCT

The importance of children's informally acquired knowledge of language and literacy has not always been recognized by psychologists or educators. Between the 1950s and 1970s, preschool and kindergarten children were generally considered too immature to begin the process of learning to read. Before the idea of emergent literacy was widely accepted, the term *reading readiness* was commonly used to refer to the likelihood of a child's being successful in learning to read when given formal instruction. As early as the 1930s (e.g., Lee, Clark, & Lee, 1934), attempts were made to develop reading readiness tests that could be given to children prior to first grade. A number of these tests were developed, marketed, and used in schools throughout the 1950s, 1960s, and 1970s (e.g., Clymer & Barrett, 1966; Harrison & Stroud, 1950; Hildreth, Griffiths, & McGauvran, 1965). Most were based on the idea (loosely derived from the work of Jean Piaget—e.g., Piaget & Inhelder, 1969; and Arnold Gesell—e.g., Gesell, 1925) that children needed to mature to a certain level of general cognitive development to be "ready" to learn to read. Children who did not pass these readiness tests were assumed simply to be not yet mature enough to benefit from reading instruction.

There were a number of problems with these tests and how schools typically used them. First, there was no uniform agreement as to which skills should be measured to determine reading readiness (Rude, 1973). Some of the skills assessed on some tests were shown by later research to actually predict later reading success (e.g., letter recognition), but many were not very relevant to reading at all (e.g., ability to draw, use scissors accurately, or copy shapes). In Table 2.1 we can see examples of the kinds of skills examined by some of these early tests of reading readiness.

There was also little recognition that virtually all young children have at least *some* of the basic knowledge needed to learn to read. Many who come to school from diverse backgrounds bring important knowledge that may not show up on standardized tests, for which cutoffs were developed using heavy proportions of children from the mainstream culture (Moll et al., 1992). There was little sense that perhaps these children's diverse literacy knowledge could be used productively to help them learn to read. Instead, the readiness concept suggested that it was simply a matter of waiting for the right time, at which point each child would be "ready" to learn to read.

TABLE 2.1. Some Skills Examined in Early Reading Readiness Batteries

Skill	Assessment battery		
	Metropolitan Readiness Tests (Hildreth, Griffiths, & McGauvren, 1965)	Clymer–Barrett Prereading Battery (Clymer & Barrett, 1966)	Gates–MacGinitie Readiness Skills Test (Gates & MacGinitie, 1968)
Vocabulary	✓		
Listening	✓		
Letter identification	✓	✓	✓
Coordination/copying	✓	✓	✓
Rhyme		✓	
Initial phoneme discrimination		✓	
Sound discrimination			✓
Blending			✓
Word recognition			✓
Matching	✓	✓	✓

Note. Based on Rude (1973).

If a child was deemed not ready, based on whichever test the school had purchased, two instructional strategies were commonly considered. Schools could wait to provide reading instruction until such time as the child tested as ready; this strategy often involved retaining the child in kindergarten or placing him or her in a "transition" classroom, in the hope that he or she would be ready sometime during the school year (Hymes, 1958). Alternatively, or sometimes in combination, intensive instruction would be provided in the readiness skills the test had identified as lacking to shorten the time until the child would be able to pass the test (Carducci-Bolchazy, 1978). Thus, in some classrooms, such children would find themselves spending their days copying basic figures, cutting out shapes with scissors, and so on, with the idea that these activities would somehow improve their readiness to read. Of course, this instructional time would have been much better spent actually engaging the child in literacy-related activities.

The *readiness* concept implied to many educators that general cognitive maturity was the main prerequisite to learning to read. Children who had problems learning to read when others their age did not were often viewed as simply delayed in their readiness. Important instructional time was often wasted, as it was hoped that they might simply outgrow the problem.

Eventually, it became obvious that none of these approaches really worked to help children get ready to read (Pikulski, 1988). By the end of the 1960s, it became obvious that scores on popular readiness tests correlated little with each other and that the tests assessed fairly different skills (Johnson, 1969). The developers themselves came to realize that the best predictors of reading readiness were underlying skills involved in reading itself (e.g., MacGinitie, 1969).

The outcome of the reading readiness approach highlights the need for a good definition and understanding of emergent literacy as the salient construct. Our definition of emergent literacy drives both research and instruction. A wrongheaded construct can lead us to wrong-headed instructional solutions.

CURRENT VIEWS OF EMERGENT LITERACY

In recent years, there has been a decided shift in both our definitions of emergent literacy and how early literacy practices are conceived. Although there is still no consensus as to what knowledge might underpin emergent literacy, ongoing research forms a basis for discussion of several approaches here.

A Cognitive Science Perspective

Whitehurst and Lonigan's work (1998, 2001) captures models of emergent literacy based primarily on a cognitive science approach to reading. They have described emergent literacy skills as comprising two basic domains: (1) inside-out skills and (2) outside-in skills. *Inside-out skills* are the skills that allow a child to translate print into the set of sounds needed to identify a word (and vice versa, for writing), those bottom-up (i.e., stimulus-driven) cognitive skills that are engaged in reading. These skills include children's ability to use lower-level letter features (e.g., the curvy features of the letter S) to identify letters and then translate them into letter sounds (e.g., the /s/ sound made by the letter S). They also include children's ability to manipulate those letter sounds and blend them together to identify a word, and might include children's ability to understand sentence grammar and the use of sentence punctuation.

By contrast, *outside-in skills* are those sources of knowledge that allow the child to comprehend the text that has been translated through inside-out skills. Outside-in skills relate to top-down skills, or conceptually driven cognitive skills that rely on preexisting knowledge that is used in comprehension. These skills include the size of children's vocabulary, both in terms of the number of words they know and the depth of that knowledge (e.g., likely word contexts and possible word combinations, lexical ambiguity, general detail of meanings). They also include the knowledge of the world that children bring to reading comprehension, how language is used in print (i.e., the *written register* discussed in Chapter 1), how it often differs from oral language, and the different types of texts and how they are most often used (e.g., stories vs. information vs. directions or informational text). All of this outside-in knowledge provides the foundation that allows children to make an interpretation of the actual print they will eventually read. Figure 2.1 provides a general overview of this model.

Researchers working from this and similar skills-based models seek to identify those skills that best predict later literacy achievement and are thus assumed to be fundamental to emergent literacy. Research is then carried out to determine how the development of these skills unfolds in learning to read and write. In this model, the instructional goal for the teacher of young children is to work to ensure that all students have sufficient levels of these identified emergent literacy skills to prevent reading failure later. Based on research demonstrating the effectiveness of direct instruction, especially in the inside-out skills emphasized in such models, good teachers will provide sequenced, specific instruction in these skills, sometimes in isolation and sometimes in carefully designed contexts, so that specific skills can be focused on and dealt with directly.

The Sociocultural Perspective

The sociocultural perspective of emergent literacy stresses the importance of parents, the family, and the literary environment in which young children develop (Razfar & Gutierrez, 2003). From this perspective, reading and writing are defined not so much as a set of specific skills to be taught and learned, but more as a set of social practices for making meaning from text, specific to particular social contexts, into which children are gradually initiated by the people around them and through which they engage in important socially defined activities (Gee, 2003). Drawing heavily on Vygotsky's (1978) theories of development and learning (see the Introduction), the sociocultural perspective emphasizes the natural literacy contexts and activities in which young children participate prior to entering school or formal literacy instruction. Researchers in this tradition focus on

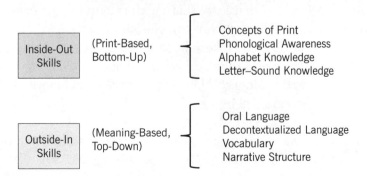

FIGURE 2.1. Model of emergent literacy. Based on Whitehurst and Lonigan (1998).

adult–child interactions around literacy, particularly in the home and community, and the functions of literacy in those interactions (Heath, 1983). They see the nonconventional understandings that young children develop through these interactions as cues to their developing hypotheses regarding reading and writing. These hypotheses become increasingly sophisticated as children interact with others around literacy materials (Braunger & Lewis, 1998).

Sociocultural researchers such as Michaels and Collins (1984) study children's own narratives to gain insight into their growing understanding of literacy-related narrative structures. They study invented spellings (i.e., the use of alphabetic signs in spontaneous writing) to gauge children's understandings of the alphabet and sound–symbol relationships because they see reading and writing as intertwined elements of literacy practices (Clay, 1975). Rather than giving children a standardized vocabulary test, they are more likely to engage children in conversation about a picture or recent event in their lives, not to evaluate whether they know a specific, standard set of words, but rather to discover what words they have learned in their homes and communities.

Indeed, sociocultural literacy researchers are particularly interested in language and literacy practices in diverse homes, cultures, and communities. They emphasize the importance of avoiding a *deficit view* of children who come from homes where these practices may differ significantly from the "standard" literacy practices taught in schools. That is, they avoid concluding that children's skills are simply deficient. They bring an understanding that school literacy practices in the United States are largely derived from white, middle- to upper-class cultural norms. Identifying variables that predict which children are most likely to become skilled readers is not seen as useful from the sociocultural perspective, since measures based on these predictors will simply identify those children whose home language and practices do or do not correspond to those of this privileged class (Heath, 1983; Michaels, 1981).

Teachers working from this perspective are not likely to start with a list of discrete skills children should master in a preplanned sequence. Rather, they begin by identifying the *funds of knowledge* that children bring with them from their homes and communities (Moll, 1992), through home visits and interviews with parents and other important caretakers. In other words, the job of the teacher is to connect instructional practices to the knowledge that children bring with them to school, encouraging and guiding children as they explore and move into the more formal literacy practices needed in school.

In many ways, the sociocultural perspective directly emphasizes what is missing from the cognitive science perspective, and vice versa. As can be seen from our description of the models above, there is no single unified model of emergent literacy that all researchers agree on. Still, research generated from these models has given us a much greater understanding of the complexity and the various sources of knowledge that children bring with them to school in preparation for formal literacy. In addition to the developing understandings of print gained at home through family-based literate experiences with family members described in the previous chapter, there are specific types of knowledge and skills included in all of these models and recognized by most researchers as key components of emergent literacy. We describe these elements in the rest of this chapter.

ENVIRONMENTAL PRINT

Environmental print is the print found in everyday life—in the home, in stores, on the road, and on the labels and logos that appear on food, packaging, signage, clothing, and billboards (Neumann, Hood, & Ford, 2013a; Neumann, Hood, Ford, & Neumann, 2013b). Environmental print is available to all children, rich and poor alike, though, as discussed in the previous chapter, there is actually less legible print and less varied print available in poorer communities (Neuman & Celano, 2001).

Environmental print is not like standard print. For one, environmental print has been designed deliberately to be attractive and draw attention, as can be seen in Figure 2.2. It is typically unique, colorful, and memorable, and mostly non-continuous; that is, it is mainly single- or multiword labels often found in signage and advertisements, rather than the continuous text found in storybooks, newspaper articles, or directions (e.g., the Walmart logo on its stores, website, and ads). Another key feature of environmental print is its functionality. A child who sees the Cheerios logo on a box of cereal each morning quickly learns that there is breakfast inside. Environmental print is usually designed to communicate its message quickly and simply, as in the case of a STOP sign.

Horner (2005) identified three types of environmental print: community signs (e.g., MacDonalds, STOP signs, Target); labels on household items (e.g., Cheerios, Coca Cola, Froot Loops); and specifically child-directed print (e.g., crayons, Lego, Barbie). The preschoolers he studied were more likely to recognize child-directed print than the other two types of print, but environmental print knowledge expands as children get older. Because of the ubiquitous nature of environmental print, preschoolers from high and low socioeconomic backgrounds often end up with similar levels of this kind of print knowledge (Korat, 2005).

Children begin to notice and interact with environmental print well before their second birthday. They begin to discriminate environmental print from other symbol systems such as numbers and pictures at around 2 or 3 years of age (Levin & Bus, 2003; Yamagata, 2007). Case studies suggest that precocious readers may begin to point out the letters and remark on the print in their interactions with adults (e.g., Lass, 1982). Other times, a caretaker might draw the child's attention

FIGURE 2.2. Examples of environmental print that children may use to begin the process of learning to read.

to a piece of environmental print and then pull apart the constituent pieces of the logo (e.g., pointing out the M in the MacDonald's sign), so that the child can begin to discern the relevance of the various parts. Sometimes this type of interaction around print will lead to informal letter instruction by the adult, who continues the interaction by supplying a letter name or sound to go with the print. Thus, adults will sometimes begin to support children's early acquisition of letter names and sounds directly through environmental print. How regularly this actually happens is unclear, and it probably varies from family to family. Purcell-Gates (1996) has suggested that, without this additional adult scaffolding, children may not be able to profit from this exposure to environmental print to begin specific early literacy learning.

The Relevance of Environmental Print for Later Literacy Learning

Given the above depiction of how environmental print might serve as an initial "hook" into literacy for young children (especially with the help of adults around them), it would make sense that children who have good environmental print knowledge might end up developing formal literacy skills earlier or better in some way. Neumann, Hood, Ford, and Neumann (2011) have proposed a model of literacy skills hypothesizing the route between sociocultural experiences with environmental print and formal reading skills, which can be seen in Figure 2.3. In this model, exposure to environmental print and the interactions that the children have around such print with parents, older siblings, grandparents, or teachers lead them to acquire a very contextualized knowledge of such print called *logographic reading* (Ehri, 1991). In logographic reading, children are able to identify logos from environmental print because of their exposure to such print and the scaffolding that the adults around them provide, but they are not yet able to read conventionally by decoding words in the logos because they do not yet have the necessary alphabetic knowledge. When information in the logos is presented in conventional black and white text, without the colors and stylized writing from the originating logos, preschoolers who are logographic readers cannot read the text from these logos or identify misspellings of them, even though they can identify the logos themselves (Masonheimer, Drum, & Ehri, 1984). This same type of logographic reading has also been observed in nonliterate adults (Cardoso-Martins, Rodrigues, & Ehri, 2003).

The premise that the logographic reading in this model helps children transition to the important process of acquiring emergent literacy skills is controversial. Does simply knowing a lot about environmental print help children acquire important features about the alphabetic principle?

Some researchers claim that the type of reading involved in identifying environmental print is useless for developing the graphemic and phonological analysis that children need to use to engage in conventional text reading (Cardoso-Martins et al., 2003; Lonigan, Burgess, & Anthony, 2000; Reutzel, 2003). Children may show excellent environmental print knowledge, but demonstrate little understanding of letter–sound knowledge, emergent writing, or word recognition skills (Blair & Savage, 2006; Korat, 2005). Thus, having environmental print knowledge by itself does not ensure the development of standard literacy skills. Still, some literacy scholars believe that it is through environmental print that children come to understand the functionality of print itself as a communication device (e.g., Goodman, 1986).

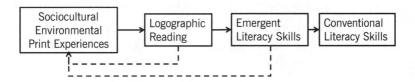

FIGURE 2.3. Model of literacy skills describing the route between sociocultural experiences with environmental print and formal reading skills. Adapted from Neumann, Hood, Ford, and Neumann (2011). Copyright 2011 by, and adapted with permission of, Sage Publications.

Classroom Practices That Use Environmental Print to Develop Emergent Literacy

Preschoolers' preexisting environmental print knowledge may, however, serve as a basis for emergent literacy learning that can be capitalized on in instruction. Cronin, Farrell, and Delaney (1999) found that having environmental print knowledge for a particular logo facilitated children's learning to read the logo words in standard print when they were subsequently given instruction. Thus, knowing the familiar red hexagonal STOP sign may help the child to learn to read the word *STOP* presented outside the context of the sign later. So, when young children have an environmental print logo in their knowledge base, even when they cannot read the print itself, they can use this knowledge to connect instruction of standard print.

Neumann et al. (2013a) turned the idea of using environmental print into a classroom strategy in which children were first introduced to familiar environmental print items. Then, the teacher would separately teach the letters that were common in the environmental print items (e.g., "Say, *m*, *i*, *o*"), and go on to point out those same letters in the environmental print words (i.e., the *m*, *i*, *o* found in Coco Puffs, Corn Flakes, Pepsi, milk). The children would then practice writing those letters. In an experimental study comparing this environmental print strategy to teaching using standard print, Neumann and her colleagues found that using environmental print as a preschool classroom strategy may produce better instructional outcomes on a variety of emergent literacy measures, such as letter–sound knowledge, letter writing, and print reading, when compared to outcomes following the strategy of introducing new letters in a standard print context. Thus, although environmental print knowledge does not automatically lead to the acquisition of conventional print knowledge, it may support the development of such knowledge when appropriately used as part of an instructional strategy.

ALPHABETIC KNOWLEDGE

Alphabetic knowledge, an important aspect of emergent literacy, consists of knowing more than recognizing, naming, and writing the letters of the alphabet. It may include knowing the "ABC song" and the ability to discern the difference between letters and other symbol systems such as pictures and numbers. It most certainly includes an understanding of letter sounds and the ability to name the letters, both upper- and lowercase, and their corresponding sounds quickly and accurately. There is a remarkable similarity across children in terms of the pattern with which they acquire alphabetic knowledge (Drouin, Horner, & Sondergeld, 2012). According to Worden and Boettcher (1990), children generally learn to recognize and name uppercase letters before lowercase letters, and they generally can name them before they can print them. Being able to generate letter sounds fluently is usually one of the last alphabetic skills to develop.

ABC Recitation Knowledge

The earliest knowledge that most children acquire about the alphabet is *recitation knowledge*; that is, being able to recite the alphabet or sing the ABC song from memory (Worden & Boettcher, 1990). Most children can recite the alphabet reliably by age 5 or so (Piasta, 2006; Worden & Boettcher, 1990), although there is a substantial group of children from low-income families that does not have even this level of knowledge by the end of preschool (Norwalk, DiPerna, Lei, & Wu, 2012); such children tend to have very low emergent literacy skills in many areas. Many parents believe that their children "know the alphabet" when they have acquired this recitation knowledge, but children with recitation knowledge may not necessarily be able to connect the sung or recited letters to their visual forms. That is, they may not have an understanding that the pronounced letter [bi:] refers to the written letter *B*. Recitation knowledge, therefore, is just a small part of the story.

Just how fundamental recitation knowledge is for acquiring other aspects of alphabetic knowledge is not clear. Some find it to be moderately correlated with other aspects of alphabetic knowledge (Worden & Boettcher, 1990), whereas others do not (Piasta, 2006). It is probably not predictive among older preschoolers from middle-class homes because most of them can already recite their ABCs.

Letter-Name Knowledge

Letter-name knowledge refers to a child's ability to name uppercase and lowercase letters when they are presented randomly and not within words or with other context cues. Letter-naming ability during preschool is often considered to be the best early predictor of children's literacy success in learning to read during the early elementary school years. According to the Early Childhood Longitudinal Study (ECLS; Denton & West, 2002), 92% of children who were proficient in letter recognition at kindergarten entry were able to read words by sight by the end of first grade, compared to only 62% of children who were not proficient. A more recent review of letter-name knowledge carried out by the National Early Literacy Panel (2008) found only moderate correlations between letter-name knowledge and later literacy skills, ranging from .48 to .54. Piasta, Petscher, and Justice (2012) suggested that children who know even 10 letters by the end of preschool are less likely to have reading difficulties later—but, as with many emergent literacy skills, preschoolers from high-poverty homes often have considerably less alphabetic knowledge compared to their middle-class counterparts (Smith & Dixon, 1995). These children may need extensive formal alphabetic instruction in preschool to catch up to their peers; not being able to recognize and name letters reliably pretty much guarantees that a child will struggle to learn to read.

Not all letter names are equally easy to learn (Phillips, Piasta, Anthony, Lonigan, & Francis, 2012). A number of cognitive factors can influence the ease with which letter names are learned. *Distinctiveness* of the letters—"the properties that make one letter easy to discriminate from its alternatives in the alphabet"—plays a role in helping children learn certain letters (Sanocki & Dyson, 2012, p. 132). Letters differ varyingly in terms of height, the presence or absence of vertically ascending or descending parts, angles, and curvature. For example, the lower case letter *j* is distinctive in that it has a descending feature that is curvy and has a dot on top. By contrast, *a, e, c,* and *o* are all curvy and short, so they might be harder for children to discriminate visually. Research (e.g., Lockhead & Crist, 1980; Nelson & Wein, 1974; Williams & Ackerman, 1971) has shown that the alphabet can be visually confusing to young children, so that the letters that are distinct from the others have an advantage. Having *uppercase knowledge* helps children learn lowercase names (Treiman & Kessler, 2004), particularly when there is visual similarity between the two forms of a letter, such as *P* and *p*, *S* and *s* (Turnbull, Bowles, Skibbe, Justice, & Wiggins, 2010).

Another factor that may influence the learning of the alphabet is the *frequency* with which letters appear in print (Smythe, Stennett, Hardy, & Wilson, 1970). For example, the letters *T* and *S* are much more likely to appear in print than the letters, *Z, Q,* and *X* (Jones & Mewhort, 2004), and children are more likely to learn these first. The repetition of letters that appear often in texts assists young children in learning certain letters of the alphabet more quickly than others.

Children may learn particular letters earlier for more sociocultural reasons, too. For example, *alphabetical order* may be important because of recitation knowledge and the fact that teachers and parents often teach the alphabet in that particular order (McBride-Chang, 1999; Phillips et al., 2012). This approach gives an advantage to letters appearing earlier in the alphabet. Children often learn the letters in their first names first, particularly the *first initial* of their first names (Justice, Pence, Bowles, & Wiggins, 2006; Treiman & Broderick, 1998). Children usually learn uppercase letters first, in part because these are what the adults around them emphasize and point out while reading (Turnbull et al., 2010).

Letter–Sound Knowledge

Letter–sound knowledge refers to children's ability to generate the sound(s) a letter makes, rather than just its name, when shown the letter in isolation, without the context of a written or spoken word. For example, letter–sound knowledge involves knowing that, whereas the name of the letter *v* is pronounced /vi/, it generally makes the /v/ sound in words. The process of learning letter–sound connections requires children to integrate the orthographic (visual) features of the written language system with the corresponding phonological (speech sound) features of the language.

Knowing letter names seems to help children with this process, especially the names of those letters that follow the *acrophonic principle*; that is, the many letters in the English alphabet that begin with the sound (called the *phoneme*) that the letter usually makes. To use the example above, in the name of the letter *v*, the first phoneme is /v/, making it easier to detect and remember. In contrast, in the name for *f*, the first phoneme is /ɛ/, not /f/, and, for *w*, the letter sound is not even within the letter name itself. Children generally find it easier to learn the sounds of letters that follow this acrophonic principle (e.g., *b, d, j, k, p, t, v,* and *z*) than of letters that don't follow this principle (e.g., *h, w,* and *y*) (Treiman, Tincoff, Rodriguez, Mouzaki, & Francis, 1998). This acrophonic principle seems to operate for the learning of letter sounds even for children having language impairments and poor phonological awareness (Treiman, Pennington, Shriberg, & Boada, 2008). The acrophonic principle shows up in children's early writing as well. For example, kindergarten children often make the mistake of spelling a word with an initial /w/ sound with a *y* because the letter is pronounced /waɪ/, with the /w/ sound first (Treiman, Weatherston, & Berch, 1994). However, British English children, who are not always taught letter names first, do not show this pattern of letter–sound learning and writing.

Practice in relating letters to their corresponding sounds also helps children establish the connection. Indeed, there is some neurological evidence that practice in learning letter–sound connections may change the brain itself, to make it later more sensitive to print in general. In a longitudinal study, Brem et al. (2010) had nonreading kindergarten children play a computer game that involved connecting letters with their sounds. Using functional magnetic resonance imaging (fMRI) and electroencephalographic (EEG) techniques, they found that after 8 weeks, these children showed greater sensitivity to print in part of the left *occipital–temporal cortex* (a part of the brain that is very active in early fluent reading) than did children who played a number-related game.

Letter Writing

Letter writing is yet another aspect of alphabetic knowledge. Conceivably, children could learn to write, or at least copy, letters without knowing anything else about them; however, both letter–name and sound knowledge seem to contribute to children's letter-writing skills (Puranik, Lonigan, & Kim, 2011). That is, children are more likely to be able to write a letter from memory correctly if they already know its name and sound.

Learning to write the letters in their own names is a first step in the process of learning to write letters for many children (Villaume & Wilson, 1989). Children who know how to write all the letters of their name in the correct order are more likely to know how to write other letters, and also more likely to know a greater variety of letter names and sounds, as well as have better phonological awareness skills (Puranik & Lonigan, 2012). So, knowing how to write their own names can be a good indicator of children's emergent alphabetic skills in general.

Writing practice may also help children develop the brain functions that optimally allow them to perceive letters as letter forms (rather than mere visual objects) more strongly. In adult readers, part of the left *fusiform gyrus* (a long narrow part of the brain at the very bottom of the cortex that is also involved in facial and object recognition) usually displays this functional specialization in connection with the activity of recognizing words (James, James, Jobard, Wong, & Gauthier, 2005). James (2010) found that providing preschoolers with practice in printing letters enhanced the signal in this brain region and maximized its response to letters.

To summarize, it cannot be emphasized enough that learning the alphabet is fundamental to the development of solid emergent literacy skills. Even though in English, there are only 26 letters (52 if you count upper- and lowercase forms), we now know that learning the alphabet is far more complicated than just learning a series of letter names. Children who do not have a solid command of all the knowledge associated with the alphabet are much more likely to struggle with literacy learning in their early years, and even later (National Early Literacy Panel, 2008). Although *some* children do learn *some* of this knowledge at home, ensuring that *all* children develop strong alphabetic knowledge, in all its forms, is probably the single most vital job of the preschool teacher. It is a major way that attending preschool contributes to later literacy learning.

Classroom Practices That Improve Alphabet Learning

Explicit teaching increases the chances of learning for preschoolers, especially for those who do not have strong literacy backgrounds. Good alphabetic instruction should integrate letter name, letter sound, letter recognition in print, and letter writing (both upper- and lowercase) for all the reasons we have indicated above. Although experimental studies examining the effects of various alphabetic teaching practices are rare, a multicomponential approach does seem to produce better results than a single-pronged approach (Piasta & Wagner, 2010b; Jones, Clark, & Reutzel, 2013). For example, Piasta and Wagner showed that children who received instruction in both letter names and sounds performed better on letter sounds later than children who were taught using letter sounds alone. Using alphabet books during shared reading is also an effective practice (Bradley & Jones, 2007).

Until recently, standard practice in most preschools has included a letter-of-the-week approach in teaching the alphabet. In this approach, teachers introduce a new letter each week, and children spend all week doing various multimodal learning activities related to that letter. The next week, a new letter is introduced and the process continues. Much has been written against the practice of using a letter-of-the-week approach; some scholars have seen it as developmentally inappropriate because it often involves teaching letters isolated from the meaningful context of words and actual texts (Bredekamp & Copple, 1997; Reutzel, 1992; Wasik, 2001; Wuori, 1999). However, if teachers incorporate activities in which they point out examples of the weekly letter(s) in multiple print materials and then have children find examples of the letter themselves in environmental and classroom print, this issue of decontextualization can be minimized. A benefit of the letter-of-the-week approach is that it ensures that all letters receive some explicit attention throughout the year. However, the letter-of-week approach has the disadvantage of focusing on each letter only once throughout a typical school year. Is this enough for children who come into school with minimal print knowledge? It is unclear.

Schwanenflugel et al. (2010) argued that perhaps a way to make a letter-of-the-week approach more developmentally appropriate is to start by teaching the easier letters first and then proceeding to the more difficult letters. They defined *easy letters* as ones following the acrophonic principle and found that children in experimental classrooms benefited from this approach compared to control children (who were generally taught in a letter-of-the-week format organized alphabetically), but only when teachers also carried out activities that emphasized a general understanding of the sound system of language (i.e., phonological awareness). Again, this finding argues for a multipronged approach to teaching alphabetic information.

Teaching letters more often, in cycles that occur throughout the year, may also yield better results. Jones and Reutzel (2012) compared a repeated cycle that introduced a new letter each day against a traditional letter-of-the-week approach. This strategy gave children more distributed practice with each letter, as it recurred numerous times throughout the year, and also enabled teachers to bring difficult letters into these cycles more often when they deemed it necessary. Compared to children receiving traditional letter-of-the week approaches, Jones and Reutzel found that this distributed practice approach reduced the number of children designated "at risk" for later reading troubles at the end of the school year because they lacked sufficient letter knowledge.

PHONOLOGICAL AND PHONEMIC AWARENESS

Besides alphabetic knowledge, *phonological awareness*, and its subcomponent, *phonemic awareness*, are the factors most commonly measured in attempts to predict which children may have difficulty learning to read because of a lack of emergent literacy skills. Phonological awareness is not merely the ability to hear and discriminate the sounds of a language, which every competent native speaker can do, typically at a very early age (Kuhl, 2004). Rather *phonological awareness* refers to children's understanding of the sound structure of spoken words in the absence of print and their ability to use that knowledge. It is a metalinguistic skill that enables children to manipulate, and to some extent analyze, the sound system of a language. It includes the understanding that words are made up of sound units such as syllables, rhymes, stressed and unstressed syllables, and individual sounds that can be blended together to make words.

Phonological awareness is a term often used interchangeably with *phonemic awareness*, but the latter actually focuses on only one type of phonological unit: the *phoneme*. A phoneme is defined as the smallest unit of speech sound that distinguishes one word from another. English has the 44 phonemes shown in Table 2.2. Phonemic awareness refers to the idea that, say, the spoken word *sun* is made up of three distinct phonemes—/s/ /u/ /n/—and includes knowing that the /s/ sound distinguishes the word *sun* from the word *fun* auditorily. Children might have some phonological awareness knowledge (i.e., they might be able to notice that the word *sun* only has one syllable) without having the phonemic awareness to be able to divide *sun* into /s/ /u/ /n/, or to replace the /s/ with /f/ to get the word *fun*. This distinction may or may not be important (Anthony & Lonigan, 2004), and perhaps only some of this knowledge is relevant for learning to read. Here we will the term *phonological awareness* to refer to this general facility with the sound system of language and *phonemic awareness* to refer to the more specific skill of identifying and manipulating single phonemes.

Development of Phonological Awareness

Phonological awareness is not a holistic skill developmentally; that is, children seem to acquire some skills before others, in a fairly predictable developmental progression (Adams, Foreman, Lundberg, & Beeler, 1998; Hoien, Lundberg, Stanovich, & Bjaalid, 1995; Webb, Schwanenflugel, & Kim, 2004). Indeed, some phonological awareness programs are organized according to this common sequence, so that children receive lessons on the earlier developing skills first and the more difficult skills later (Lundberg, Frost, & Peterson, 1988). However, children do not follow this typical developmental pattern in a strict, stage-like fashion. They can show rudimentary knowledge of the later phases of phonological awareness while they are still fine-tuning their understanding of earlier skills (Phillips, Clancy-Manchetti, & Lonigan, 2008). For example, phonological awareness tasks that rely on recognition or identification are usually easier than tasks that require production of the same knowledge (Phillips et al., 2012).

Preschoolers generally show an ability to identify large units such as syllables or words first, usually as they approach the age of 4 or so (Webb et al., 2004). In typical assessments of this skill, children are asked to clap out or count the number of words or syllables in a sentence.

TABLE 2.2. The 44 English Phonemes Children Learn to Distinguish While Developing Phonological Awareness

Vowels		Consonants	
Word	IPA	Word	IPA
beat	iː	pea	p
lid	ɪ	tea	t
get	ɛ	key	k
bat	æ	but	b
part	ɑr	duck	d
dot	ɒ	gag	g
thought	ɔː	me	m
put	ʊ	no	n
boot	uː	sing	ŋ
but	ʌ	fee	f
girl	ər	thing	θ
the	ə	seed	s
bite	aɪ	she	ʃ
cow	aʊ	cheap	tʃ
bear	ɛər	veal	v
may	eɪ	that	ð
deer	ɪr	zoom	z
boy	ɔj	beige	ʒ
boat	oʊ	age	dʒ
door	ɔːr	he	h
		low	l
		red	r
		we	w
		yes	j

Note. Based on Denes (1963). Words with target sounds in **bold** and their corresponding International Phonetic Alphabet (IPA) notation.

Then, children progress to being able to identify intermediate-sized units such as distinguishing between onsets and rimes. *Onsets* are the first phoneme(s) or consonant cluster heard in a single-syllable word; *rimes* are the ending part of the word, typically used in identifying words that rhyme (the vowel and final consonants). For example, in the word *trip*, /tr/ is the onset, and /ip/ is the rime; in the word *mist*, /m/ is the onset, and /ist/ is the rime. In an assessment of this skill, children might be asked to identify pairs of words in a group that rhyme or, in a more advanced assessment, they might be asked to produce words that rhyme with a given word. Thus, when given the trio *bat, hat,* and *big*, children who have this skill would be able to identify *bat* and *hat* as that rhyming words, or when asked for a word that rhymes with *sing*, they might produce *bring* or *king* or *string*.

Finally, children progress to identifying smaller units such as phonemes. In assessment tasks that address this skill, children are often asked to pick out two words that start with the same sound, such as *bat* and *big* from the trio above, or they might be asked to drop the /b/ sound from *bat* and say the word that results: *at*. Children who can do this consistently are deemed to have developed phonemic awareness.

Phonological Awareness and Emergent Literacy Skills

Phonological awareness has long been identified as foundational to the development of literacy skills, so it is perhaps the most closely researched aspect of emergent literacy. One recent meta-analysis by Melby-Lervåg, Lyser, and Hulme (2012) found 1,660 research articles on the relationship of phonological awareness to reading skill development! It has been widely observed in these studies that children who readily learn to read words usually have already developed good phonological awareness skills (Wagner, Torgesen, & Rashotte, 1994). Children who will later struggle in learning to read typically have very poor phonological awareness skills, often several standard deviations below the performance of typical children. In fact, Melby-Lervåg et al. (2012) found that children with *dyslexia* (the designation often given to readers who struggle the most) virtually never perform better than their age-mates on phonological awareness tasks. Thus, lack of phonological awareness is an important indicator of children who are likely to struggle later in learning to read.

However, the relevance of *specific* phonological awareness skills for learning to read remains controversial. Some claim that phonological awareness is a unitary skill and that it is this general skill that matters in learning to read; the specific subskills really do not matter much (Anthony & Lonigan, 2004). Other researchers claim that the operative skill in learning to read is being able to distinguish between onsets and rimes (Goswami & Bryant, 1990; Ziegler & Goswami, 2005). Still others claim that phonemic awareness—the ability to identify, blend, and manipulate single phonemes—is the only aspect of phonological awareness that matters for learning to read. After examining the research on this topic, Melby-Lervåg et al. (2012) concluded that, though both rime awareness and phonemic awareness were moderately correlated, the relationship between measured word reading skill and phonemic awareness is generally stronger than its relationship with rime awareness (the most commonly studied large-unit skill). In fact, the mean correlation in their meta-analysis across studies between phonemic awareness and later reading ability was .57, whereas the mean correlation between rime awareness and reading was .43. So, probably, having phonemic knowledge is an important key to unlocking print for many children.

As noted in the previous section, learning letter sounds can be an important early step in learning to read, but phonemic awareness helps with that too. As Melby-Lervåg et al. found with early reading ability, Webb et al. (2004) observed that phonemic awareness is more closely related to the ability to learn letter sounds in prekindergarten children ($r = .40$) than large-unit skills, such as syllable segmentation, which only correlated .23 with letter–sound learning. Being able to identify phonemes in speech is very helpful to applying those phonemes to learning letter sounds and, as we will see in the next chapter, using those sounds to learn how to decode words while reading.

There is probably a reciprocal relationship between phonemic awareness and learning to read. As children are taught specific letter sounds and other phonics skills in school (or elsewhere), this learning most likely acts to refine their understanding of the sound system of language, if it is not yet fully developed (Perfetti, Beck, Bell, & Hughes, 1987). So, learning words containing consonant clusters, such as the /st/ in *stop* and *best*, may cause a child to pay more attention to the separate sounds these letters make, and learning words containing digraphs, such as the /ch/ that occurs twice in *church*, may lead a child to realize that, in English, letters and sounds are not necessarily equivalent. These new insights, in turn, can then be applied to enhance the reading of other words.

Classroom Practices That Improve Phonological Awareness

Children enter preschool and kindergarten with highly varying phonological awareness skills, yet, with the downward compression of the curriculum, they are expected to begin learning to read in kindergarten (or even earlier). The wisdom of this approach can be debated, especially when so many children arrive at school so ill equipped with all kinds of emergent literacy knowledge. Still, there is little doubt that a phonological awareness program in preschool can help many children develop this important metalinguistic skill, which in turn will support them in the process of learning to read. Children can often make substantial progress in this skill, no matter where they start at preschool entry, when they receive high-quality, explicit instruction in phonological awareness (Byrne & Fielding-Barnsley, 1991; Lundberg et al., 1988).

For this reason, curriculum evaluators increasingly see phonological aware-ness instruction as an essential part of a preschool curriculum, and most preschool teachers include rhyming activities in their literacy instruction through rhyming picture books, such as those by Dr. Seuss, that young children so enjoy. When a relevant phonological skill is featured in some book or activity (e.g., rhymes in *Hop on Pop*, syllables and emphasis in marching songs), teachers will sometimes emphasize that skill in a form of implicit instruction. This is a good thing to do, but teachers often believe this approach is enough to "cover" the necessary information. However, introducing phonological awareness knowledge this way may not be enough of an instructional focus to enable many children to identify phonemes, the phonological skill most useful in learning to read.

In a large meta-analysis, the National Early Literacy Panel (2008) found that specific instruction in phonological awareness tended to improve children's pho-nological awareness skills nearly a full standard deviation, on average, compared to children who did not have such instruction. This finding indicates that many preschoolers can benefit greatly from an explicit phonological awareness program. For this reason, the National Association for the Education of Young Children (2014) has included phonological awareness activities as an indicator of preschool program quality. Still, an observation study of 11 state-funded prekindergarten classrooms found that time spent on phonological awareness activities averaged just 3% of the school day (National Center for Early Development and Learning, 2005), suggesting that perhaps phonological awareness instruction during the pre-school day is not as comprehensive as it ought to be.

This does not at all mean, however, that preschool children should be end-lessly drilled in letter–sound combinations or phonics. At the beginning of pre-school, most children cannot yet carry out activities that focus on individual pho-nemes. They may need a focus on rhyme and syllable awareness first. So, perhaps rhyming books, nursery rhymes, and songs are a good way to begin to instruct this early awareness, but they are only a start. Other activities, found in some explicit phonological awareness programs (e.g., Adams et al., 1998), include developing recognition of rhythm (and syllables) by having children move in time to a par-ticular beat while saying something like *march-ing, march-ing, skat-ing, skat-ing*, etc. Children can be introduced to initial phonemes through matching games, which involve identifying the two out of three given words that start with the same sound (e.g., *fun, fish*, and *cat*). Alternatively, they can be asked to hunt for items in the classroom (sometimes among those deliberately placed there by that teacher) that start with a particular phoneme (e.g., /f/ /f/ /f/for *fish tank*). Finally, phoneme identity can be taught similarly, by asking children to pick out or find items that end with a particular phoneme. These activities can be combined with the introduction of the letter (or letters) that makes the sound. Thus, after children identify various items that start with the /f/ sound, they can be introduced to the upper- and lowercase letters: *Ff.* Thus, the sound for *Ff* can be linked with /f/. Finally, children can then be taught how to manipulate phonemes by first blending two-phoneme words (e.g., *be:* /b/ /iː/), which require only adding one phoneme to the next, and adding another phoneme to produce three-phoneme words (e.g., *beach:* /b/ /iː/ /tʃ/), either with or without the printed letters visible. There are also a number of computer-assisted instructional programs that have been shown to effectively support the development of phonological awareness (e.g., Macaruso & Rodman, 2011). See the Technology Toolbox below for a discussion of one such study. These are just a subset of the many engaging ways that phonological awareness can be taught in preschool, and even kindergarten, planfully, explicitly, and more effectively than programs that introduce these skills implicitly or haphazardly.

Just how much focus on explicit phonological awareness practice might be necessary to develop the skill among preschoolers is, however, uncertain. An early report by the National Reading Panel (Ehri et al., 2001) suggested that perhaps brief programs that are highly focused on just a few selected phonological awareness activities might work just as well as longer and more comprehensive approaches for most children. Gillon (2004) suggests that 2 hours per week over a 10-week period may be enough to improve the reading outcomes for many children

 TECHNOLOGY TOOLBOX:
Computer-Assisted Instruction and Phonological Awareness

Computer-assisted instruction has traditionally been focused on children in early elementary school or on children struggling to learn to read. Increasingly, there is an imperative for preschool programs to enhance the instruction of emergent literacy skills to prevent the development of reading problems later. To address this need, a number of effective computer-assisted instruction programs for phonological awareness have been developed. For example, *Early Reading* (Lexia Learning Systems, 2003) is a program that contains activities that target a variety of phonological awareness skills as well as letter–sound mapping skills for preschoolers. In one such activity, the child listens to the computer present a word both aloud and on the computer screen. The child is then asked to change the item to a new word by replacing one of the letters. The child might be asked to change the word *BUG* into the word *BUS* by moving a letter tile *S* over *G* with the computer mouse. Macaruso and Rodman (2011) found that preschool children who had received at least 20 ten-minute sessions on the program demonstrated accelerated phonological awareness following the intervention compared to controls that received classroom literacy programming required by state guidelines. Such findings demonstrate the potential of technology to support the development of key emergent literacy skills.

at risk for reading struggles later. In a recent study by Carson, Gillon, and Boustead (2013), kindergarten children received phonological awareness instruction (mostly focused at the phoneme level) through games such as rhyme bingo, singing games, and odd-one-out for 30 minutes four times a week for 10 weeks as part of their classroom literacy instruction. Compared with children who received only the usual reading program, which included phonics study but not phonological aware-ness games, the children in the study group not only improved in phonological awareness, but by the end of their kindergarten year, only 6% of these children scored below age level on a test of reading accuracy and comprehension, compared to 26% of the children receiving only the regular reading program.

LOOKING BACK AND FORWARD:
ORAL LANGUAGE AND VOCABULARY SKILLS

In this chapter we have focused on what the National Early Literacy Panel (NELP; 2008) calls *code-related skills*—that is, skills that allow children to crack the code for deciphering print. Code-related skills are relatively small sets of knowledge that can be mastered rather quickly by most children in a year or 2. After all, there are only 26 letters in the English alphabet, and, as we will see in the next chapter, some scholars estimate that the number of reliable phonics rules that children need to be taught might be as small as 18 (Clymer, 1963)!

However, as the NELP (2008) notes, emergent literacy is composed of two interrelated sets of underlying abilities: (1) code-related skills and (2) oral language skills. In the previous chapter, we described how there can be fundamental differ-ences in the linguistic skills that young children bring to the task of learning to read. Although teaching code-related skills may help children learn how to read words, it does not fully prepare them for the main goal of reading: comprehend-ing text. That's where oral language skills, the other set of underlying abilities for emergent literacy, enter the picture. Oral language skills include general listen-ing abilities, comprehending and producing both simple and complex sentences, drawing inferences (i.e., determining important information not stated directly in the text), and vocabulary knowledge. Indeed, it appears that oral language skills are the major underpinnings of both reading and listening comprehension during kindergarten and preschool (Lynch et al., 2008).

In the previous chapter we discussed some of the early influences on oral language development, but, unlike the alphabetic and phonological skills dis-cussed in this chapter, oral language skills are continually developed throughout a child's lifetime, eventually requiring both the integration of vocabulary, oral and written language skills, and an ever-expanding knowledge base. Because of this extended developmental timeframe, oral language problems can be long-lasting

(Paris, 2005). Children with insufficient oral language ability, even if they learn to decode words fairly well in the early grades, may struggle in later grades as they start to read "heavy texts" or long books with well-developed themes and plots, complex sentence structures, and difficult vocabulary (Stahl, 2007, p. 56).

Vocabulary, a key element of oral language that we examine more closely in Chapter 6, may also impact the development of code-related skills, through the effects that it may have on the development of phonological awareness. A growing vocabulary presents a phonological challenge to children because, as their store of words grows, they need to change from storing words holistically to representing words at the onset–rime and ultimately at the phoneme level, so that they can discern and represent the difference between words such as *fin, fan, fun, tin,* and *bin.* This process, called *lexical restructuring* (Metsala, 1997), represents a fundamental change in the way children represent information in their mental *lexicon,* the "dictionary" of known words we all keep in our heads. It is thought that this lexical demand may be either partly or fully responsible for children's early development of phonological awareness. Indeed, the correlation between vocabulary skills and phonological awareness is a robust one (Stadler, Watson, & Skahan, 2007).

Another way in which vocabulary might affect code-related skills is by affecting later decoding. This observation from Whitehurst and Lonigan (1998) captures this point well: "A child just learning to read conventionally might approach [a] word . . . by sounding it out, [but] not infrequently, one can hear a beginning reader get that far and be stumped, even though all the letters have been sounded out correctly" (p. 849). In other words, in order to "sound out" a word successfully, young children need to be able to match the phonemes they have sounded out to the meaning of a word they know. It is only then that they truly know what they have managed to read.

Although books for early learners tend to try to use easy vocabulary, the problem described by Whitehurst and Lonigan may happen more often than you might think. For example, if we consider just the five words discussed above—*fin, fan, fun, tin,* and *bin*—it seems likely that a child with a smaller or divergent vocabulary might have trouble with the words *fin, tin,* or *bin.* Such words are used quite often in decodable texts, more than in regular books, because of their phonetic regularity, but they are not used very much in ordinary conversation. So a child might easily sound out the word *bin,* but be unable to identify it because he or she hasn't heard it used often enough to be stored in his or her mental lexicon. When children have this kind of difficulty retrieving the meaning of a particular word they have successfully sounded out, both word recognition (Nation & Snowling, 2004; Carlson, Jenkins, Li, & Brownell, 2013) and comprehension (Carlson et al., 2013; Stahl, 1999) may suffer.

Researchers are still trying to untangle the relationship between preschool oral language skills and other emergent literacy skills. Some researchers have found that, although children with good vocabularies tend to be better readers, vocabulary skills do not tell us who will end up as a good reader once code-related skills are taken into account (Muter, Hulme, Snowling, & Stevenson, 2004). Alternatively, the National Institute of Child Health and Human Development (NICHD) Early Child Care Research Network (2005) that followed 1,100 children from age 3 to grade 3 found that having good preschool oral language skills helped children learn code-related skills as well as improved later reading comprehension. As already noted, other researchers claim that preschool oral language and vocabulary skills mainly operate by helping children discriminate words by sound through lexical restructuring, which later helps them learn to read (Bracken, 2005; Metsala, 1999). Regardless of the role of oral language skills in early word reading skills, research overwhelmingly supports the role of preschool vocabulary in later reading comprehension (NICHD Early Child Care Research Network, 2005; Storch & Whitehurst, 2002). Although the picture is less clear regarding the role of oral language skills in the early process of learning to read, it is very clear that oral language skills play a vital role in reading development ultimately. Thus, oral language skills are a significant component of emergent literacy.

CONNECTING TO THE STANDARDS

At the outset of this chapter we asserted that young children bring much important formal and informal knowledge about literacy and communication with them as they enter elementary school. Attending a high-quality preschool can help young children acquire the foundational skills they need to succeed in early reading instruction later. As you can see in Table 2.3, the Early Literacy Standards from NAEYC Early Childhood Program Standards have been highly responsive to the growing research on emergent literacy. Naturally, there are also standards directed at language development that encourage teachers to provide children with opportunities to communicate and answer questions in school in their home language, and have conversations, experiences, and book readings that promote vocabulary.

We wish to point out, however, that the sociocultural influences children bring in from the home and community described in the first chapter serve as the earliest source and perhaps most continuing support for this knowledge. Consider the analogy of a bridge structure. At the bottom of the bridge, underneath the pylons and vertical piers are abutments attached to the bedrock, into which the pylons are drilled. Above ground, there are cantilevers and trusses that distribute weight across the structure. These all work together to make a bridge strong enough to withstand traffic and environmental forces over time. The sociocultural forces that influence children are analogous to the bedrock and abutments that

TABLE 2.3. Examples of Preschool (Ages 3–4) Early Literacy Standards

Topic	Standard
Book Reading	Children should have opportunities to: • Be read books in an engaging manner at least twice a day. • Be read to regularly individually or in small groups. • Explore various types of books. • Be read books several times. • Retell and reenact books. • Talk about books. • Link books to the rest of the curriculum. • Identify parts of books and print.
Writing	Children should have opportunities to write in various ways (scribbling, letter-like marks, developmental spelling). They should be given support as they attempt to write on their own, by being given access to the alphabet and printed words related to their interests. Teachers should model the use of writing.
Phonological Awareness	Children should be provided opportunities to develop phonological awareness, including: • Play with rhymes, poems, and songs. • Identification of letter names and sounds. • Manipulating words having same beginning and ending sounds. • Writing letters included in the sounds of words.
Alphabet	Children should be given opportunities to recognize and write letters.
Print Access	Children should have access to books and writing materials throughout the classroom.

Note. Adapted from the National Association for the Education of Young Children (2014). Copyright © 2015 by NAEYC®. Adapted by permission.

enable the code-based emergent literacy skills (the trusses and cantilevers) discussed in this chapter to operate in the development of reading.

CONCLUSION

In this chapter we have discussed the code-based emergent literacy skills that many researchers have identified as important foundational skills for learning to read. There are various points of view regarding how these emergent skills should to be studied and considered. We have discussed how important it is to have a good understanding of the construct *emergent literacy* and the negative consequences children experience when the need for these skills is ignored. Research on the alphabet, particularly on letter-name and letter–sound knowledge, supports the view that this is an essential emergent skill for later reading. Phonological awareness is another emergent literacy skill that has received consistent support for its foundational role in early reading. Finally, we have discussed the debates surrounding just how important oral language skills may or may not be for early reading, while emphasizing the importance these skills have for later reading comprehension.

QUESTIONS FOR DISCUSSION

1. Given what you have learned about emergent literacy, what do you think of the current trend of teaching young children to read in prekindergarten? To what evidence can you point to support your position?

2. What activities would be present instructionally in an ideal preschool program for ages 2, 3, and 4? What evidence is there to support the activities found in your ideal program?

3. Do you think that the sociocultural perspective or the cognitive science perspective provides a better account of the kinds of issues that young children face with regard to emergent literacy?

4. How well do the early learning standards listed in Table 2.3 capture what is relevant about the fundamental literacy skills needed for the formal process of learning to read? What is missing, if anything?

5. Returning to the case study presented at the beginning of this chapter, what strategies might be helpful for Ms. Johnson to use to address the emergent literacy needs of Ileana?

FURTHER READINGS

National Early Literacy Panel. (2008). *Developing early literacy*. Washington, DC: National Institute for Literacy.

National Institute of Child Health and Human Development Early Child Care Research Network. (2005). Pathways to reading: The role of oral language in the transition to reading. *Developmental Psychology, 41*(2), 428–444.

Sulzby, E., & Teale, W. (1991). Emergent literacy. In R. Barr, M. L. Kamil, P. B. Mosenthal, & P. D. Pearson (Eds.), *Handbook of reading research* (Vol. 2, pp. 727–757). New York: Longman.

CHAPTER 3

Learning to Read Words

CASE STUDY

Mr. Williams, a first-grade teacher, is concerned about Deon's progress in learning to read words. Deon is looking quite frustrated that he cannot follow the word reading activities the other children in the class seem to carry out with relative ease. Deon knows the letters of the alphabet and can connect them to at least one of the sounds associated with each letter, although even that took him weeks to master. Deon can sound out simple words like *cat*, but not longer words or more difficult words such as *chat*. He struggles to maintain the sounds while blending or he simply makes a guess, usually incorrect, because that is easier. For a word like *chat*, Deon will sound out the *c* and the *h* separately. Further, he does not seem to know what words like *chat* mean anyway, and shrugs his shoulders, puzzled, after he eventually manages the correct pronunciation with assistance. Deon never identifies groups of letters such as *-ed* and *-ing* as a unit. Mr. Williams is considering what additional kind of help he might need to provide for Deon.

We live in a sea of written words. You have to get pretty far removed from modern life to avoid items having some sort of writing on them. The presence of written words can be found well beyond the long connected texts we usually think of as the objects of literacy skills. There are stylized words on signs and in logos (*environmental print*). There are neat labels on objects describing what they are (a clunky object on the kitchen counter is labeled *Emerson microwave oven*). There are less legible handwritten items on a grocery list on the refrigerator door, indicating the need for *cashews* and *milk*. The pixelated words glowing from our electronic devices are our entry into a world of information. Words are written even where they might seem quite irrelevant—the small earpiece on a pair of glasses has the worn, barely legible phrase FRAME CHINA. The written word is ubiquitous.

Learning to read words is a central academic task that children need to master if they are to function optimally in their world. To quote Linea Ehri (2005), "When people read text, the print fills their minds with ideas. Indeed, the route to these ideas begins with individual printed words" (p. 168). Most adults read printed words with great alacrity and skill.

The goal of this chapter is to provide an overview of the research on how children learn to read words and instructional practices that have research support for various phases of word reading development.

LETTER–SOUND–MEANING CONNECTIONS

The key to reading words is learning how to map the spellings of written words onto the sounds of the words and their meanings. Let's look at the word *chick* (see Figure 3.1). Essentially, the reader has to map graphemes onto phonemes. The term *grapheme* is used instead of *letters* here because it refers to the fact that sometimes, as in the case of *chick*, several letters need to be mapped onto to a single phoneme. For *chick*, the multiletter grapheme *ch* is mapped onto the phoneme /tʃ/, the single-letter grapheme *i* is mapped onto the phoneme /ɪ/, and the multiletter grapheme *ck* is mapped onto the phoneme /k/. These relationships between graphemes and phonemes are sometimes called *grapheme–phoneme correspondences*, or *spelling–sound correspondences*. We use the term *grapheme–phoneme correspondence* here because it better reflects the linguistic basis of these relations.

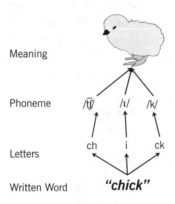

FIGURE 3.1. Reading words involves mapping letters onto phonemes so that a pronunciation can be generated that is good enough to identify the word and its meaning.

The fact that multiletter units are sometimes mapped onto single phonemes is what makes the need for phonological awareness so crucial; without an understanding of what the phonemes are, it is hard to grasp just how to map letters onto their phonemic representation. Phonological awareness facilitates the learning of grapheme–phoneme correspondence connections (Adams, 1990; Ehri et al., 2001). The effect is causal—that is, instruction in phonological awareness, by itself, has been shown to improve later decoding skills (Bradley & Bryant, 1983).

Phonics programs are instructional programs that explicitly teach the relations between graphemes and phonemes. However, once children apply their knowledge of these connections, blend them, and come up with a good-enough potential pronunciation of a targeted word, they can use it to retrieve the meanings of the word from their *lexicon* (i.e., mental dictionary).

SPELLING REGULARITY

Not all words in English map as regularly as *chick* does. We use the term *regular* in the context of reading words to refer to a word that is spelled such that all the letters can be transparently mapped onto unique phonemes. Examples of phonologically regular words are *cat, cup, sit, drop,* and *kid.* One can figure out directly what each of these words is by simply using grapheme–phoneme correspondence rules and blending the resulting sounds together.

Irregular words, by contrast, cannot be directly mapped onto phonemes—only some of their letters have direct correspondences. Examples of irregular words include *sign, island, sword, said,* and *listen.* Unfortunately for children learning to read English, such irregular spellings are more common for English than they are for languages such as Italian or German. In those languages (sometimes described as having a *shallow orthography*), the vast majority of the words can be directly mapped.

How big a problem is this irregularity when learning to read words for English-reading children? Using a large database of written English, Hanna, Hanna, Hodges, and Rudorf (1966) estimated that half of all English words have completely regular grapheme–phoneme correspondences. This regularity includes words that have relations between multiletter graphemes and single phonemes, too. Hanna et al. calculated that another 34% of English words are only irregular by one correspondence. The word *listen* is an example: Only the silent /t/ does not follow regular grapheme–phoneme correspondence rules. Presumably, using the correspondences, children would be able to approximate a pronunciation for these words and would then be able to guess them correctly by narrowing down candidates from context. Hanna et al. considered another 12% of words regular if information about the foreign origin and pronunciation of borrowed words were known (consider the word *taco* here). Of course, this kind of information might be a bit more than we would expect children to know when they are just learning to read. Taken together, however, approximately 96–97% of English words are more-or-less regular by Hanna et al.'s calculations—which does not sound too insurmountable for children learning to read.

Unfortunately, some researchers have argued that Hanna et al. probably over-estimated the regularity of English. For example, Berndt, Reggia, and Mitchum (1987) pointed out that some of the correspondences Hanna et al. viewed as "regular" had very low probabilities of occurrence in English. The *-lf* grapheme in *calf* and *half* is an example here. The *-lf* rule might subtend to only a handful of words across the language. We might not expect young children to learn those easily, and it might not be worth teaching the rule separately. Fry (2004) derived 192 grapheme–phoneme correspondence rules from a large child literature corpus that he viewed as frequent enough to merit some instructional attention.

Irregularity creates a problem for the usual way we read words. Children read irregular words more slowly and less accurately than regular words. Even skilled adults read irregular words more slowly and less accurately (Waters, Seidenberg, & Bruck, 1984). Unfortunately for children learning to read English, many words that are frequent in text are irregular. For example, *the, a, was, of, have,* and *said* are frequent, irregularly spelled words. Historically, these frequent words might have been spelling errors that got encoded as the words were originally written down. Or the spellings might have made sense originally but the pronunciations have changed without corresponding changes to the written form. Or someone might have simply borrowed the foreign spelling of a word, but used the English pronunciation of it. Regardless of how an irregular word came to be, the irregularities tended to get fossilized and maintained over time through repetition.

Because sight words are highly necessary for reading connected text, children are often taught them as a special class of words in reading instruction that uses a whole-word approach. Indeed, a quick search of the Internet using the term *sight words* will yield many lists designed for teachers to use in their classroom for this purpose. Often, one will see 100 first-grade sight words, 100 second-grade sight words, and so forth. Recent simulations suggest that the ideal number of such words to be taught using this whole-word approach strategy might be around 100 or so (Vousden, Ellefson, Solity, & Chater, 2011), not the 500–1,000 words often seen in elementary school sight reading lists (Fry, 2000).

Further, because sight words may be read differently than regular words, children's skill in reading them is often assessed separately. For example, the Test of Word Reading Efficiency (Torgesen, Wagner, & Rashotte, 1999) has two subtests: a sight word efficiency subtest consisting of a list common sight words, and the phonemic decoding subtest consisting of a list of nonwords that can be read using phonics rules. Children on this test are asked to read as many as they can in 45 seconds. Taken together, scores on these subtests are thought to comprise an estimate of children's skill in reading words.

PHASES IN LEARNING TO READ WORDS

Ehri and her colleague (1991, 2005; Ehri & McCormick, 1998) have identified characteristic changes in the processes in which young children engage while learning to read words. They grouped these changes into five phases in learning to read words. These phases are distinguished by the kind of information children use to read words, and are thought to overlap rather than proceed in a lockstep, stage-like fashion. We describe each phase in the following sections.

Prealphabetic Phase

The first phase in Ehri's stages of learning to read words is called the *prealphabetic phase*. This is akin to what we referred to earlier as *logographic reading* when discussing emergent literacy. The term *prealphabetic* is used here to convey the idea that children in this phase do not have much command of the alphabet, so do not understand how letters map onto sounds. In short, children do not yet understand how the alphabetic system works. They cannot read words in environmental print when presented outside their logographic context. They do not notice when the words within the environmental print are altered in some way. If they learn to recognize a word by sight, it is often on the basis of some highly distinctive cue, such as the double -*l* in the name *Holly*, but they know little about the connection between letters and sounds. This phase of word learning is typical of children in preschool and early kindergarten.

Children in this first phase may pretend to read a book, and do it quite convincingly at times—enough to fool parents into thinking that their child is reading. Often children will recite a book by heart, but cannot actually read the book. Close observation may show that the children are often well ahead of, or behind, the page the children think they are currently reading. When asked to point to a specific word from the page they supposedly just read, they are unable to do so. They often guess about the print on the page by looking at the picture. Usually, their guesses have little connection to actual print.

Partial Alphabetic Phase

The second phase in learning to read words identified by Ehri and her colleagues (2001) is called the *partial alphabetic phase*. Children in this phase have rudimentary alphabetic knowledge. They can discern the links between some letters and some sounds. They might, for example, notice the *t-* at the beginning of the word *this* and say the word *that*. They may combine this rudimentary knowledge with picture cues to come up with a good guess for a particular word, particularly if they are encouraged by their teachers or parents to do so. They often avoid looking much past the first few letters to come up with likely word candidates because reading is so difficult.

In this phase, children are able to engage in some sight word reading because their emergent knowledge of the alphabet gives them a hook with which to memorize them. The letters of the alphabet serve as a cue to particular sight words, but they are easily confused by other similar-looking words. Ehri and Wilce (1985) called this *phonetic cue reading*. During this phase, children often know the sounds of letters that follow the acrophonic principle, but not the others. They know little to nothing about multiletter graphemes.

Full Alphabetic Phase

In the *full alphabetic phase*, children learn to use the standard grapheme–phoneme associations needed to read words. This phase proceeds slowly and is plodding. They have many grapheme–phoneme correspondence rules (or, more colloquially, *phonics rules*) to learn, and these rules are retrieved with great effort, occupying a good bit of their working memory to decode a simple word. Direct teaching of the rules is necessary, particularly for the less frequent and/or multiletter patterns. Just how many phonics rules are worth teaching is up for debate, but Vousden (2008) suggests that perhaps around 100 rules will allow children to be able to read in excess of 90% of words, once 100 high-frequency words are acquired.

This new phonics knowledge, once finally acquired, allows them to sound out unfamiliar words. Reading words taxes children's working memory capacity. Children can now recognize similarities among words (e.g., that *mouse* and *spouse* are similar except for the initial phonemes) because their representations of the words they have learned to read have enough detail to permit this. They can eventually store them as sight words with a little practice, perhaps with as few as three or four exposures (Reitsma, 1983) or maybe even one (Nation, Angell, & Castles, 2007).

Consolidated Alphabetic Phase

In the *consolidated alphabetic phase*, children learn to link together letters that often occur together in text. This process is called consolidation or *unitization*. For example, children might unitize multiletter graphemes such as *th-*, *-ar*, *-ough*, and *-ph*; and quickly come to recognize frequently repeated sequences such as *-it*, *-at*, *-and*, and *-all* very quickly. Children also begin to use morphological information (i.e., sublexical units of word meaning) such as *un-*, *-ing*, *-ed*, *-ity*, *-tion*, and *-ly* to speed up their decoding of words (Carlisle & Stone, 2005; Nunes, Bryant, & Barros, 2012).

Changes in children's *nonword* reading (sometimes called *pseudoword* reading) provide evidence for this transition to using unitized sequences of letters. Nonword reading allows us to see what type of units children are actually using to decode words without the overt interference of other factors such as familiarity or word meaning. In the previous phase, children might read nonwords by using slow grapheme-to-phoneme translation (e.g., saying /t/ /e/ /m/ for the nonword *tem*) followed by a process of blending them together. In this phase, children can be seen to deploy larger units that allow them to pronounce nonwords such as *tem, fope,* and *huke* as a unit (Harn, Stoolmiller, & Chard, 2008; Marsh, Desberg, & Cooper, 1977).

In essence, this description of early reading follows what has been called a *small-units first* pattern (Coltheart & Leahy, 1992); that is, children gain familiarity with the simpler grapheme–phoneme correspondence rules first, taking advantage of consistent rules when initially learning to read. And then they package these simpler units into larger units. Seeing words as groups of multiletter combinations reduces the working memory load burden while reading and speeds up word recognition. Indeed, transitioning to using these larger units is important for later reading (Nunes et al., 2012). The number of words that children can recognize by sight continues to grow during this phase.

Automatic Phase

In the final *automatic phase*, children can now read words quickly and accurately. This phase is not really one of learning to read words, per se, because children now know how to read words well. In this phase, the majority of words and word patterns that children use to read are identified quickly and effortlessly. Now, word reading takes up little in terms of children's available cognitive resources. Most of the decoding strategies that children use in this phase for the occasional words with which they are unfamiliar are executed quickly. Children can now dedicate their reading to what is most important: determining the message of the text and, if reading aloud, reading with expression. In this last phase, children have begun the process of reading connected texts fluently.

Words recognized in this phase are also read autonomously. That is, word reading occurs without conscious cognitive resources being directed toward it. The reader in this phase cannot help but process print, even when he or she may wish to avoid doing so. For example, children may find their attention drawn to the conflicting *crawl* at the bottom of a television news story as they listen to the main story (Bergen, Grimes, & Potter, 2005).

Experimentally, automaticity in word reading has been measured through the use of the Stroop task (Stroop, 1935). In the traditional Stroop task, the reader is asked to name the color of a word that spells a color and is printed in different-colored ink. For example, a child might be asked to name the ink color of the word *RED* written in purple ink (i.e., the child should say, "Purple," not *RED*). Alternatively, the child might be asked to name an object that has a distracting label written on it, as shown in Figure 3.2. Autonomy is indicated when the naming of pictures or colors slows down when there is distracting print. Thus, a child who is an automatic reader will be slowed when naming a picture of a drum with the word *lock* written on it compared to naming the same picture without the distracting print. In regular reading, autonomy normally helps people read quickly and accurately because it orients their attention to print. In this special case, however, it interferes with the naming so we can directly observe the effects of autonomy.

Several studies have linked the development of Stroop interference to the development of word reading skills (Ehri & Wilce, 1979; Guttentag & Haith, 1978). Schadler and Thissen (1981) found that, among children learning to read, Stroop interference increased until they could read at a fourth-grade level. Schwanenflugel, Morris, Kuhn, Strauss, and Sieczko (2008) showed that Stroop interference emerged in young readers when the distracting words contained common grapheme–phoneme correspondences within them, suggesting that these correspondences were being automatized fairly early in the process of learning to

FIGURE 3.2. When word reading is automatic, children will take longer to name the pictures with distracting labels on them compared to *apple*, which has no meaningful text.

read. Thus, as soon as children practice decoding words using common phonics patterns, they begin to show automaticity in word reading. We think that automaticity probably becomes more complete in a wider variety of correspondences, however, during this phase.

Some researchers think that this depiction of learning to read words does not go far enough (Castles & Nation, 2006; Harn et al., 2008; Share, 1995). The concern is that this depiction, although quite correct in its general characterization of learning to read words, is basically descriptive (Harn et al., 2008). As important as accurate description is for developing theory, it does not tell us much about the underlying processes that allow the reading of words to progress from a letter-by-letter, grapheme-to-phoneme translation process to an automatic word reading process. Researchers note that in the same child, some words might be read piecemeal, grapheme by grapheme, whereas others are read quickly and accurately (Duff & Holme, 2012). Knowing how to translate graphemes into phonemes might not be enough to explain why this happens. At least two other factors may be at work: orthographic learning and word meanings.

FACTORS BEYOND PHONICS KNOWLEDGE

Orthographic Learning

One contributor to reading words might be what has been called *orthographic learning* or *orthographic processing*, defined as "the ability to represent the unique array of letters that defines a printed word, as well as general attributes of the writing system such as sequential dependencies, structural redundancies, and letter position frequencies" (Vellutino, Scanlon, & Tanzman, 1994, p. 314). Essentially, it is children's knowledge of visual spelling patterns that distinguish them from the simple retrieval of letter sounds. This type of knowledge would allow children to distinguish *rane* from *rain*, or know that *beff* could be a word in English whereas *ffeb* could not.

Evidence for the existence of this distinct kind of orthographic learning and its necessity for skilled reading comes from a group of children, labeled as having *surface dyslexia*, who have a rare but very specific difficulty representing the orthography of words (see Castles & Coltheart, 1996). Children with surface dyslexia have typical alphabetic skills. They have no difficulty learning the usual phoneme–grapheme correspondences needed to read words, such as the /b/ /ē/ /n/ of *bean*. However, they cannot distinguish between words such as *been* and *bean*, which requires representing the surface orthography of words.

There are a number of ideas regarding how orthographic learning occurs. Exposure to print is a likely contributor to the development of this kind of knowledge. Indeed, exposure to print appears to explain variance in word reading skills that is not accounted for by phonological processing skills themselves (Cunningham & Stanovich, 1998). Further, the more that children read, the more likely that they will acquire an understanding of these kinds of regularities. Thus, orthographic learning may be both a *predictor* of reading words and an *outcome* of having read lots of words.

Print exposure may be important for orthographic learning because of what has been called *self-teaching* (Share, 1995). According to this hypothesis, the activity of merely decoding a word provides young children with the opportunity to create an orthographic representation of it. Orthographic representations are developed instantaneously as children decode words. The development of orthographic learning has been demonstrated in studies that have asked children to read nonwords. A nonword is a pseudoword created by the experimenter and designed to simulate the processing of a novel word that a child might encounter for the very first time. Share (2004) showed that days after children had decoded a particular nonword even once, they could distinguish it from other nonwords that might have the same pronunciation. That is, they might be able to distinguish *yait* as a nonword they had seen once before, from *yate*, a nonword they had never seen before. Having seen *yait* before, they could also read *yait* faster than *yate*. They could spell the word *yait* when asked. Thus, the children had acquired a fairly detailed orthographic representation after only one exposure.

Another proposal regarding how orthographic learning might occur is the idea that children might acquire orthographic regularities through *statistical learning* (Pacton, Perruchet, Fayol, & Cleeremans, 2001). That is, children become sensitive to the statistical regularities of the orthography to which they are exposed. For example, we may never have been consciously aware that English words do not begin with *ff-*. It probably has never been explicitly taught to us. Yet, we know that *ffeb* is an impossible word. Examples of some of the orthographic assessments that have been used in experimental studies (Cassar & Treiman, 1997; Olson, Gillis, Rack, DeFries, & Fulker, 1991) are shown in Figure 3.3. Pacton et al. (2001) showed that a learning algorithm carried out by a computer fed words a letter at a time from a language corpus mirrored the type of learning displayed by children. The view is that children use this implicit statistical knowledge to quickly resolve the identity of letters while decoding words.

What is remarkable is how quickly children seem to acquire this kind of statistical learning. Children may begin to develop an understanding of typical letter patterns as early as kindergarten (Cassar & Treiman, 1997). However, this knowledge becomes more automatic and consolidated as children proceed through early elementary school (Schwanenflugel et al., 2006). Children appear to use this knowledge to help them read words above and beyond their knowledge of grapheme–phoneme correspondences.

Experimental Spelling Test: Pick the one that is spelled correctly	
snow	snoe
cloun	clown
deap	deep
wheat	wheet

Doublet Task: Pick the one that looks the way a word should look	
nnus	nuss
holl	hhol
gree	grii
plii	ploo

FIGURE 3.3. Orthographic learning assessments. Based on Olson et al. (1991) and Cassar and Treiman (1997).

Role of Word Meanings

So far, we have described learning to read words as a process of developing more and better skill at mapping letters and orthographic letter patterns onto a word's phonemic representation. More recently, evidence has accrued that word meanings are involved in helping children learn to read words. Evidence for the role of word meanings in reading words has been of two types. First, there are studies showing that difficult meanings affect the speed and accuracy with which young children read words. Second, there are studies showing that not knowing what a word means affects its reading.

Word concreteness is a major semantic distinction in our lexicon that affects word meaning difficulty. People can readily retrieve direct sensory referents, imagery, and contextual information for concrete words. Concrete words are words such as *market, stone,* and *flood.* When you think of the word *market,* it is quite easy to think about the smells and sounds of an outdoor farmers market. You can envision smelling the fresh bread and produce; you can hear the buzz of the crowds. Abstract words generally do not have this same ready access to this type of information, so retrieving meanings for these words is more difficult. Abstract words might include words such as *quality, effort,* and *duty.* When you think of the word *quality,* for example, it might be hard to think of a specific context for the word; you probably cannot picture it.

The concreteness of the meaning of words affects children's reading of them. Studies generally show that young children read concrete words more quickly and accurately than abstract words (Schwanenflugel & Akin, 1994; Laing & Hulme, 1999; McFalls, Schwanenflugel, & Stahl, 1996), despite controlling for factors such as word frequency and length. In teaching studies, children usually require fewer attempts to learn to read concrete words compared to abstract words (Nilsen & Bourassa, 2008). Thus, the semantic difficulty involved in retrieving abstract word meanings seems to affect how easily young readers can learn to read them.

The absence of a particular word in one's working vocabulary affects word reading also. For example, a child may not have the word *yurt* in his or her vocabulary, even though it might be more or less phonetically regular. Yet, the child might possibly encounter such a word in a social studies text while learning about the homes of nomadic peoples of Mongolia. Research suggests that young children are faster at learning how to read words whose meanings they know than words whose meanings they do not know (Duff & Hulme, 2012). Thus, it appears that, when children try to read words, they also try to retrieve their meanings to resolve that they have, indeed, decoded a particular word. You can see the puzzled expressions on children's faces when they try to read a word not in their vocabulary.

The fact that there are additional factors not discussed by Ehri involved in learning to read words (i.e., orthographic learning and word meanings) does not indicate that Ehri's description is incorrect. Indeed, Ehri's theory has stood the test of time. But perhaps it is not as inclusive as it needs to be. What research has revealed is that, to learn to read words, children have to acquire and connect three types of information: (1) they have to learn the phonemes of their language, (2) they have to understand the alphabetic system of their language and the orthographic patterns it uses, and (3) they also have to learn the meanings that their language encodes and be able to retrieve those meanings quickly. In short, children must draw connections between the *phonemes, orthography*, and *meanings*. Finally, they must automatize the connections between these three sources of information to efficiently read words.

IMPLICATIONS FOR CLASSROOM PRACTICE

At the heart of Ehri's (Ehri, 2005) theory of word reading is the idea that children learn to draw connections between graphemes and phonemes, after which they create larger units out of them. Although Ehri's theory may be only part of the story, as we have noted, understanding this development has driven educators to develop distinct practices depending on the stage children are at in their progression toward skilled reading. A skilled teacher needs to be able to recognize a given

▨ TECHNOLOGY TOOLBOX:
Using Technology for Learning to Read Words

As computer technology and artificial intelligence applications to education become increasingly sophisticated, schools are increasingly purchasing educational technology to support the mundane practice required to acquire skilled word reading. Sometimes these programs are supplemental instruction added to children's regular classroom program. These supplemental programs are directed at students' skill level and are often targeted to children who are not yet reading at grade level. Other times the programs are tightly and programmatically knit as a key aspect of the core reading program (i.e., comprehensive).

These days, the technology applications try to present an engaging, colorful set of audio and video lessons that target specific phonics skills. Often these programs have a game-like aspect to spark children's motivation. For example, Waterford Early Learning Program™ contains colorful audio–video lessons for practicing common spelling patterns for 44 sounds in the English language, along with matching decodable texts that children can read as they listen and respond. Children then move on to learn more complex spelling patterns and to read more decodable texts. They gain practice in automatic word recognition. Importantly, children can progress at their own learning pace.

Various meta-analyses have generally found small to nil effects of technological approaches on the development of word reading skills (Campuzano, Dynarski, Agodini, & Rall, 2009; Cheung & Slavin, 2013; What Works Clearinghouse, 2007). Because these programs are generally (although not always) used for children needing supplemental instruction, it can be difficult to discern the effects of the technology independent of the other interventions that children may be receiving (Cheung & Slavin, 2012). Computerized instruction is usually not the only intervention that these children receive. They often receive small-group instruction and even one-on-one instruction on top of the technological supplement, particularly in the early grades. Children in the control groups are rarely left to fend for themselves, and they may receive a double dose of some other potentially beneficial program. Also problematic is that teachers often do not use the technology with enough frequency in their daily classroom practice to provide a discernable and distinct benefit to learning to read (Cheung & Slavin, 2012).

Recently, there is an increased use of tablets and smartphones rather than computers to provide literacy instruction. Importantly, parents are beginning to download these "apps" for their children as learning tools, particularly the ones that are free (Schuler, 2009). As pointed out by Goodwin and Highfield (2012), when designed by app developers, not curriculum developers, these apps tend to emphasize drill-and-practice approaches to learning. At this point, we do not know if these apps are different in any real way in terms of effectiveness, although they are certainly more convenient. Thus, although there is promise for the use of technology in helping children learn to read words, much of that promise has yet to be realized and understood.

child's progress (or lack of it) in learning to read words. The teacher then needs to adjust his or her classroom practices accordingly. In what follows, we describe the implications of Ehri's model for instructing children in learning to read words.

Prealphabetic Phase Instruction

One main implication of Ehri's description is that, early in the process of learning to read words, there is a need for teachers to teach young children to develop an understanding and awareness of phonemes. We have discussed some of the classroom practices that might help children acquire phonological awareness in Chapter 2 on emergent literacy. Learning to both segment words into their constituent phonemes and then to blend them together are important in this instruction. Indeed, a review of high-quality preschool studies on phonological awareness, carried out by What Works Clearinghouse (2007) and as discussed in the previous chapter, concluded that phonological awareness training substantively improved phonological processing in young children. This knowledge provides an important foundation as children transition from the prealphabetic to the partial alphabetic phase.

Partial-to-Full Alphabetic Phase Instruction

In the partial-to-full alphabetic phases, it is important for teachers to provide explicit instruction in grapheme–phoneme correspondence rules, which can often be accomplished through the use of various types of phonics programs. There are two types of programs that are most often discussed here, synthetic phonics programs and analytic (analogy) phonics programs.

Synthetic phonics programs teach children grapheme–phoneme correspondence rules (or *phonics rules*, as noted earlier) separately and in isolation. Synthetic phonics programs might start with teaching children letter–sound correspondences, as well as the full array of sounds associated with the vowels and letters that have multiple sounds (e.g., *c* and *g*; Englemann & Bruner, 1969). Often they move on to frequent vowel and consonant digraphs (e.g., *oi, ea, ou, sh, ch, th*). These programs differ in the number of relations taught and how this learning is sequenced (Adams, 1990). In all of these synthetic programs, children gain practice in both identifying and blending various combinations of phoneme–grapheme correspondences. Sometimes programs also teach children to use grapheme–phoneme correspondences, along with context cues to identify words they attempt to read.

By contrast, analogy or analytic phonics programs teach children to use words they already know to identify new words as a strategy within a larger phonics program (e.g., the Seek the Word You Know strategy within the PHAST [Phonological and Strategy Training] program; Lovett et al., 2000). These programs might help children learn to recognize, for example, that they can use the word *road* (that they already know) to help them identify the word *toad*. Or they might teach words as word families (e.g., Benchmark School approach [Gaskins, 2005]; Words Their Way [Johnston, Invernizzi, & Bear, 2004]). So, they might be taught *road* in the context of the word family *toad, load, road,* and *goad.*

Some phonics programs also emphasize the use of invented spellings, particularly for kindergarten and first-grade children. Indeed, children who have practice using invented spellings tend to be able to read more real words later than children not receiving such practice (Ehri & Wilce, 1987; Sénéchal, Ouellette, Pagan, & Lever, 2012). More often than not, programs use a combination of all of these approaches.

The effectiveness of using phonics approaches has been the subject of a long and contentious debate. It is often argued that phonics programs emphasize drill-and-practice (pejoratively, "drill-and-kill") over motivation and interest in reading. The approach is sometimes associated with the use of boring worksheets that take time away from other types of instruction (Stahl, Duffy-Hester, & Stahl, 1998). It is argued that children may not transfer much of the knowledge that they learn through these programs to the actual tasks of reading longer texts. It is argued that the approach does not work well for all children.

To address the issue of effectiveness, the National Reading Panel (NRP) Report (National Institute of Child Health and Human Development, 2000) carried out a meta-analysis of experimental and quasi-experimental studies on phonics program effectiveness published between 1970 and 1999. The panel included studies in which phonics was taught systematically—that is, "explicitly teaching students a pre-specified set of letter–sound relations and having students read text that provides practice using these relations to decode words" (p. 92). The meta-analysis concluded that phonics programs had a moderate effect on improving reading skills, particularly for younger children in kindergarten and first grade. Phonics instruction was particularly helpful for struggling readers in these grades. It helped them both learn to read words better and spell better in their writing. Effects for later grades were considerably smaller, and there was no benefit for older, struggling readers. Further, no particular benefits for one type of program over another were found.

The conclusions of the NRP Report did not go unchallenged. Some argued that the focus on experimental studies left out qualitative case studies suggesting the effectiveness of other approaches for some children. Others argued that the meta-analytical approach used by the NRP overly emphasized refereed journal publications. Its stringent criteria for including experimental research ended up excluding many studies. Perhaps there is a *gray literature* of studies showing null or negative results that did not appear in print. Refereed journals do tend to prefer studies that have positive effects because null effects might occur for reasons other than true nullity. For example, the studies might have been too small and lacked statistical power. Alternatively, the interventions might have been otherwise poorly carried out, lacking sufficient intensity or fidelity. This critique would have to claim that there are a large number of null studies, given the size of the findings reported by the NRP, however.

A more recent meta-analysis by Torgerson, Brooks, and Hall (2006) made a more extensive search to uncover such unpublished experimental studies. They were able to find only a few. Further, they included some studies not available for the NRP Report. Their new analysis reconfirmed the NRP's basic findings. Similarly, other reanalyses of the NRP data have verified the previously reported effect of phonics instruction, although indicating perhaps a smaller effect than described in that report, depending on what kind of instruction to which the phonics instruction is compared (Camilli, Wolfe, & Smith, 2006; Stuebing, Barth, Cirino, Francis, & Fletcher, 2008). However, Torgerson et al. and Suggate (2010) have pointed out that the impacts of phonics instruction are relatively narrower than described by the NRP—relegated to word reading accuracy, not other skills, and benefiting children mostly between kindergarten and first grade as they are developing the alphabetic principle. Meanwhile, experimental evaluations to determine which types of phonics programs are more effective are ongoing (Di Stasio, Savage, & Abrami, 2012; Johnston, McGeown, & Watson, 2012). Thus, a variety of studies have now shown that phonics instruction does help children develop word reading skills.

Related to phonics instruction is the use of *decodable texts*. These are little books having around 50 words or so that have a relatively high percentage of phonologically regular grapheme–phoneme correspondences, compared to typical texts. Many are little picture books that might contain sentences such as "The cat sat on the mat," "The bat took the hat," and "Sam had jam from the can." This type of decodable text would reinforce the short-*a* rule, and a child reading it would get a good bit of practice with this particular rule.

The decodability of a given text is determined in relation to the phonics and sight words that children have been taught already. If children have not yet been taught the long-*e* combinations (e.g., -*ie*, -*ee*, -*ea*, -*ey*), a text loaded with words having these combinations is not considered decodable. Evaluations of reading programs using decodable texts have sometimes been found to include many words that do not match well with what has already been taught in the reading series (Hiebert & Fisher, 2007). Ideally, decodable texts should reinforce the phonics teaching that has already occurred.

In good practice, teachers might teach particular phonics patterns and then have students read a text designed around those patterns. The philosophy behind decodable texts is that they allow young readers to transfer their newly learned phonics skills to the reading of connected text. This activity will encourage children to recognize the connection between the phonics instruction and reading in something approximating normal text.

Decodable texts are designed to help children move from the partial alphabetic to the full alphabetic phase. The texts assist children in consolidating their phonics knowledge and, hopefully, this will result in their better reading skills, in general, later. Research by Juel and Roper/Schneider (1985) on the benefits of decodable texts indicates that children who practice reading with them do improve in their phonics knowledge, as indicated by the number of novel words they can read. The books also appear to change the kinds of errors that children make. That is, children's errors become more rule-governed (e.g., reading *pear* as *peer*). Reviewing the research on the use of decodable texts in the classroom, Cheatham and Allor (2012) concluded that evidence is scarce regarding whether decodable texts help children develop better general reading skills to the extent that it shows up in standardized test performance (Jenkins, Peyton, Sanders, & Vadasy, 2004).

Decodable texts are not universally endorsed. Goodman, Goodman, and Martens (2002) have criticized decodable texts for being too incredibly awkward and unlike real texts to be sensible objects of reading instruction. Indeed, we concur that it makes sense to use decodable texts only for a narrow goal of phonics practice rather than for teaching broader literacy skills such as comprehension. It is key that teachers understand that the books should be used only for this very specific purpose.

To summarize, phonics and the use of decodable texts have their place in classroom practice for helping move children from the partial to the full alphabetic phase of word reading. As Torgerson et al. (2006) concluded, phonics instruction in the early grades "should be part of every literacy teacher's repertoire and a routine part of literacy teaching, in *a judicious balance with other elements*" (p. 12, emphasis added). However, persisting in the use of phonics instruction past first (or perhaps second) grade is not recommended because, simply, it is less effective after that (Cheatham & Allor, 2012; National Institute of Child Health and Human Development, 2000; Suggate, 2010). Studies have consistently shown that the effects of later phonics instruction range from small to nonexistent. We are dismayed to occasionally see phonics programs being used throughout an elementary school when there really is little basis for it. Instructional focus must change after the first few years of school. Phonics instruction is designed for children just learning to read. Increasingly, schools are utilizing technology to allow children extra phonics pattern practice (see the Technology Toolbox, p. 69).

Finally, given research showing that word meanings have an effect on word reading accuracy and speed among young children, it would also make sense that teaching word meanings might help children improve their word reading skills, too. Research on this topic is scarce. However, one study by Duff et al. (2008) showed that among young, struggling readers who had not shown response to intervention before, adding vocabulary training to a phonics program greatly improved the number of words that they could read later on a standardized test. Further, this improvement was maintained several months later. Whether this type of intervention would show effects on word reading for more typically performing children is unknown. Regardless, as we shall soon see, vocabulary instruction will be necessary for other elements of skilled reading later, so we can think of no harm of including it more widely.

Consolidated Alphabetic Phase Instruction

The goal of the consolidated alphabetic phase is to consolidate multiletter patterns. Some of this can be accomplished through the explicit teaching of multi-letter grapheme–phoneme correspondence rules such as -ough or ph- in phonics instruction. However, instruction to develop morphological awareness is sometimes recommended for children in this phase (Bowers, Kirby, & Deacon, 2010).

Morphological instruction entails focusing children's attention on the sublevel features of language. Studying the effects of an instructional focus on morphology has allowed us to see the causal impact of morphological knowledge on word reading or spelling. It is hoped that developing an understanding of morphemes may provide less able children with another means by which to decode words.

This type of instruction can target prefixes, suffixes, base stems, or compound words. Children might be trained to distinguish, for example, which word "came from the other word" for *happy* versus *happily*, or *magic* versus *magician* (Berninger et al., 2003). Alternatively, they might be asked to generate a derivation from *happy* or *magic*. Instruction might focus on the meanings of particular morphemes, such as the idea that the *-ing* suffix shows that the action is happening currently (Apel & Diehm, 2014).

Instruction in morphological awareness has been shown to improve children's understanding of morphemic information. Importantly, this understanding seems to transfer to improved decoding and spelling. Most studies find small-to-moderate positive impacts on word decoding and spelling skills, particularly for children in early elementary school who are still in the process of acquiring decoding skills (Bowers et al., 2010; Goodwin & Ahn, 2013).

Automatic Word Reading Instruction

Finally, once children have moved from consolidating and unitizing their decoding skills, they have essentially moved to the last phase of learning to read words: automatic word reading. It is generally agreed that automaticity in word reading should come from practice with reading connected text, particularly oral reading practice (Kuhn, Schwanenflugel, & Meisinger, 2010). Through practice, children will develop both automatic word reading skills but also other skills that allow them to improve comprehension. We discuss the effects of oral reading practice later, when we discuss the development of reading fluency.

CONNECTING TO THE STANDARDS

For policy-makers, research on the importance of good word reading skills has established that they should be represented among the curriculum standards targeted at the early years of schooling. The Common Core State Standards has identified phonics and word reading skills as among the foundational skills that should be acquired by children in the early years.

As can be seen in Table 3.1, the research on the development of word reading skills has largely positioned the foundational literacy standards in the early grades. Perusing these early standards on learning to read words, one can easily discern that they move young children from the prealphabetic knowledge that they bring with them into school to the partial alphabetic phase kinds of knowledge by the end of kindergarten. These standards then direct teachers to work toward having children acquire full alphabetic knowledge in first and second grades. In grades 3–5, the standards require that children consolidate this knowledge by reading words in larger units..

CONCLUSION

The topic of learning to read words has been well studied by cognitive and educational psychologists and reading educators. It is quite possibly the topic about which we have the best evidence regarding the connection between theory and practice. Research has concluded, and we concur, that learning to read words quickly and accurately is a key skill that young children must obtain in order to read well. However, we also wish to point out that there is an optimal time and place for this type of instruction. Reading is a developmental process. The best time to emphasize skills in learning to read words is during the early elementary school years. Good classroom practices there will yield benefits that foster children's reading skills for years to come.

TABLE 3.1. Common Core State Standards (Abridged) for Reading Foundational Skills, Phonics, and Word Recognition Standards

Phonics and word recognition standard:
Know and apply grade-level phonics and word analysis skills in decoding words.

Kindergarten	• Demonstrate basic knowledge of one-to-one sound correspondences by producing the primary sound for each consonant. • Associate the long and short sounds with the common graphemes for major vowels. • Read common high-frequency words by sight. • Distinguish between similarly spelled words by identifying the sounds of the letters that differ.
Grade 1	• Know spelling–sound correspondences for common consonant digraphs. • Decode regularly spelled one-syllable words, and decode two-syllable words by breaking them into syllables. • Know conventions for representing common long-vowel sounds. • Use vowels to determine the number of syllables in a printed word. • Read words with inflectional endings. • Recognize and read grade-appropriate irregularly spelled words.
Grade 2	• Distinguish long and short vowels when reading regular one-syllable words. • Know common spelling–sound correspondences for additional vowel sounds. • Decode regularly spelled two-syllable words with long vowels. • Decode words with common prefixes and suffixes. • Identify words with inconsistent but common spelling–sound correspondences. • Recognize and read grade-appropriate irregularly spelled words.
Grade 3	• Identify and know the meaning of the most common prefixes and derivational suffixes. • Decode words with common Latin suffixes. • Decode multisyllable words. • Read grade-appropriate irregularly spelled words.
Grades 4–5	• Use combined knowledge of all letter–sound correspondences, syllabication patterns, and morphology (e.g., roots and affixes) to read accurately unfamiliar multisyllabic words in context and out of context.

Note. Adapted from the National Governors Association Center for Best Practices and the Council of Chief State School Officers (2010).

QUESTIONS FOR DISCUSSION

1. Think back to the way that you were taught to read words. What instructional practices were in effect then? Describe your experiences. How do those practices relate to the ideas discussed in this chapter?

2. Which views regarding orthographic learning seem to make the most sense to you intuitively? Why?

3. Ehri's view of how children learn to read words has sometimes been criticized as being more descriptive than theoretical. What kind of additional support might be needed so that we understand *why* children's decoding skills evolve in this way, rather than just *how* they do?

4. The reading wars ensued largely in response to the decontextualized drill-and-kill practices typical of classrooms that use phonics programs. What might be done to prevent the boredom and demotivating effects of such programs?

5. Returning to the case study presented at the beginning of this chapter, what strategies might help Mr. Williams address Deon's literacy needs?

FURTHER READINGS

Camilli, G., Wolfe, P. M., & Smith, M. L. (2006). Meta-analysis and reading policy: Perspectives on teaching children to read. *Elementary School Journal, 107,* 27–36.

Cheatham, J. P., & Allor, J. H. (2012). The influence of decodabilty in early reading text on reading achievement: A review of the evidence. *Reading and Writing, 25,* 2223–2246.

National Institute of Child Health and Human Development. (2000). *Report of the National Reading Panel. Teaching children to read: An evidence-based assessment of the scientific research literature on reading and its implications for reading instruction: Reports of the subgroups* (NIH Publication No. 00-4754). Washington, DC: U.S. Government Printing Office.

CHAPTER 4

Skilled Word Reading

CASE STUDY

Ms. Brown is concerned about a student in her eighth-grade English class, Gabriel. As a class they have been reading aloud Shakespeare's play, *A Midsummer's Night Dream*, but Gabriel refuses to participate. When she insists that he take a part, Gabriel is often completely stymied by the pronunciation of old English words in the text such as *fain, cuckold, forsooth,* and *anon*. Ms. Brown has also noticed that Gabriel's spelling on his written work is horrendous, and he often puts his head down during the 15 minutes for silent reading provided at the end of class, complaining that he is tired of reading.

The processes engaged by visual word recognition have been under intensive scrutiny since the advent of modern cognitive approaches to the study of mental processing (Gibson & Gibson, 1955; Neisser, 1967). The individual *word* would seem to be a relatively tractable unit of analysis for study, and the reading of words by skilled readers would seem to be a relatively simple skill to describe. We shall see in this chapter that the skilled reading of single words is not simple at all.

Our goal in this chapter is to provide you with an understanding of the processes involved in the skilled reading of words. We discuss how visual print is translated by our sensory and perceptual systems and how our knowledge of words acts to support the perception of letters. We describe two models that make different assumptions regarding the processes and representations involved in skilled word recognition, and then focus our attention on factors that have been shown to impact the skilled reading of words.

LETTER RECOGNITION

Most models of word reading begin with a stage describing the visual translation of print to the recognition of letters. This is a more remarkable feat than it sounds. Within a fraction of a second, skilled readers quickly recognize letters despite variations in font, case, and size. These variations generally do not interfere with the reading of words because, for the most part, print is intentionally designed to be readily legible. Pelli, Burns, Farell, and Moore-Page (2006) have noted that there is strong general consistency among traditional alphabets in terms of how speed and accuracy affect the efficiency with which letters are processed. They conjecture that most alphabets have probably evolved over time to increase reading efficiency. Of course, unusual fonts and very small font sizes can be hard to read efficiently (Cheng, 2005), but, on the whole, letters in words are readily perceived.

Letter Features

Most models of word reading begin with translating the visual features that make up letters into the recognition of letters. *Letter features* are the building blocks of letters. According to Marr (1982), the brain appears to be designed to extract certain simple shapes and forms from percepts. The brain is responsive to the letter features that relate to these "perceptual primitives." These perceptual primitives are then combined at later stages of analysis.

Given that millions of years were needed for brain evolution, it seems highly unlikely that the brain was ever designed directly to recognize print, since print is a fairly recent cultural invention, being just over 5,000 years old. Instead, recognition of letters appropriates parts of the brain used in basic object perception. The brain must be trained to recognize letters as distinct objects. A localized region of the brain, the left occipital–temporal sulcus, lateral to the fusiform gyrus, takes on the role of recognizing print in skilled readers (Dehaene, Cohen, Sigman, & Vinckier, 2005). This brain region becomes activated differentially within 150 milliseconds or so when letters are first seen (Dunabeitia, Dimitropoulou, Grainger, Hernandez, & Carreiras, 2012). It then informs other areas of the brain about the identity of the letters in the words.

To which features is the brain attuned when recognizing letters? To answer this question, researchers had people identify isolated letters under experimental conditions that make them difficult to see. In such studies, letters might be presented with very brief exposures, or under low light conditions, or with visual masks that obscure parts of the letters. Then people are asked to identify letters or to discriminate letters from nonletters. Errors in mistaking the letter *i* for *l*, compared to, say, *c*, are calculated across letters to form a *letter confusion matrix* (Grainger, Rey, & Dufau, 2008). So, for example, *H* and *N* might be confused with each other often, as might O and G, but H would hardly ever be confused with O (Gilmore, Hersh, Caramazza, & Griffin, 1979).

From these confusion matrices, researchers have inferred potential features that are used to recognize the letters of the Roman alphabet, the alphabet we use in English. For example, Fiset et al. (2008) suggest that adults use the terminations of letters primarily (e.g., the three top points of the letter W), as well as intersections (e.g., as found in the letter X), curves, slants, and the presence of horizontal and vertical lines to discriminate letters. Presumably, these same features might be ones that teachers could emphasize to help young children learn the alphabet. However, there is no guarantee that skilled readers use the same features to recognize letters that beginning readers will.

Adults seem to generate a frame of reference early in the processing of print. That is, they seem to quickly derive information regarding general font size, spacing, and weight so that these more specific letter features can be determined within certain parameters (Sanocki & Dyson, 2012). Thus, in recognizing the letter W, for example, people establish the general uniformities of the font. Then perceptual primitives are activated, such as *three top terminations, two bottom terminations, slanted,* and *not curvy.* This information is then combined to generate the recognition of the letter W. This sequence of events probably does not happen in a stage-like way, but in a cascade of partial information at each sequence that becomes accrued in a matter of milliseconds, until some threshold is passed whereby the person can identify which letter is presented.

Unfortunately, how the brain redirects the combining of these perceptual primitives so that they assemble correctly during recognition to form a single percept is unclear—i.e., people do not see W as a bunch of free-floating features, but as single visual entity. This reassembling issue is called the *binding problem* (Treisman, 1996). This binding problem exists for all feature models of object recognition, not just letters.

Word Superiority Effect

One very consistent finding is that letter recognition is quicker and more accurate when letters are embedded within a word than when they are presented by themselves or within a random string of letters (Reicher, 1969). This finding is called the *word superiority effect.* Thus, people can recognize the letter g more efficiently when it appears in the word *night* than when it appears in the random sequence of these letters: *tignh.* Information about the word can be exploited to help people to identify individual letters. Typical readers begin to show the word superiority effect at around second grade as they start to develop automatic reading skills (Juola, Schadler, Chabot, & McCaughey, 1978). Struggling readers, however, show hardly any word superiority effects, suggesting that at least part, but by no means most, of the difficulty that struggling readers are having could be orthographic in nature (Chase & Tallal, 1990; Hildebrandt, 1994).

The word superiority effect for letters is not restricted to words. It also occurs for letters within pronounceable nonwords, called *pseudowords*. So, people recognize the letter *g* more quickly when presented within a pseudoword such as *vight* than in the string of letters such as *tigvh*. This benefit has been called the *pseudoword superiority effect*. Generally, among skilled readers, the size of this pseudoword effect for letter recognition is similar to that found for words, although it is generally smaller in size among children who are in the process of becoming skilled readers (Chase & Tallal, 1990; Coch, Mitra, & George, 2012). The presence of a pseudoword superiority effect suggests that, in recognizing letters, other levels of the cognitive system become involved, such that knowledge related to similar words, such as *sight, fight, might, right, tight*, etc., is activated and combined with letter feature information to help resolve letter identity (McClelland & Rumelhart, 1981).

GRAPHEME–PHONEME CORRESPONDENCES AND MODELS OF SKILLED WORD RECOGNITION

In Chapter 3, we noted that there is probably more consistency among grapheme–phoneme correspondences for English than initially meets the eye. We showed that, once multiletter graphemes and words that are only "off" by one correspondence are taken into account, the predictability for English is much higher than is readily apparent. Further, research has shown that there is even greater consistency surrounding the pronunciation of syllables (called *rime units*) in English, such as *-ight*, than there is for single letter–sound correspondences (Kessler & Treiman, 2003). Once syllables are taken into account, the predictability of English in terms of pronunciation becomes higher yet. Skilled readers have extensive implicit knowledge of what these rules are and how to use them quickly and automatically to identify words. In reading a word, they translate letters or groups of letters into phonemes using these rules, and then they assemble them to produce a pronunciation.

However, the grapheme–phoneme correspondence rules probably will not allow readers to recognize all the words they need to know if they are reading in English. This fact has led some researchers to speculate that something other than these phonological rules for the pronunciation of words must be involved. Coltheart, Rastle, Perry, Langdon and Ziegler (2001) have suggested that a direct route to lexical information may be used for some words, rather than the route to reading words using grapheme–phoneme correspondence rules. Instead, such a route would rely on direct access to phonological and orthographic lexicons where visual and spoken word forms are stored. Figure 4.1 shows a simplified version of how this might work for an exception word such as *pint*.

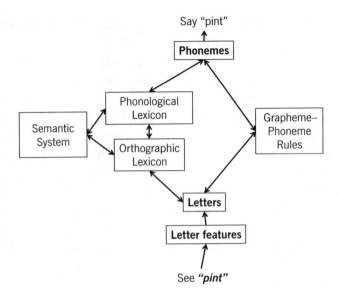

FIGURE 4.1. Simplified version of the dual-route cascaded model of word reading for reading the word *pint* aloud, developed by Coltheart, Rastle, Perry, Langdon, and Ziegler (2001).

Starting at the bottom of this figure, we can see that the reader has been presented with the simple text pint. Upon seeing this word, the letter features associated with *pint* are activated. These might include, for example, activating features for the curves in the letters *p, n,* and *t*; the downward and upward extensions in the letters *p* and *t*; and the dual bottom terminations for *n*. These features would then activate the appropriate letters (and possibly prevent the activation of letters not containing these features). These letters would then activate the two paths emanating from the letter system. Without the paths leading from Letters → Orthographic Lexicon → Phonological Lexicon → Phonemes, words like *pint* that do not follow the grapheme–phoneme correspondence rules would result in incorrect pronunciations. In this example, the activation of the Letters → Grapheme–Phoneme Rules → Phonemes route, by itself, would cause the pronunciation of *pint* to end up sounding similar to *hint*. Presumably, the lexicon contains information about the visual and spoken word forms associated with *pint* so that readers can pronounce the word correctly. To do this they use the information obtained from the path between Letters → Orthographic Lexicon → Phonological Lexicon → Phonemes to say, "*pint.*"

Why don't readers just directly use their lexicons and forgo grapheme–phoneme rules altogether? First, as we have shown in the previous chapter, knowing these phonics rules is very helpful for what has widely been called *cracking the code* of reading, that is learning the alphabetic system of print. The current view is that skilled readers continue to maintain something approximating this grapheme–phoneme rule system, supported by evidence showing that these readers continue to read words faster that have regular grapheme–phoneme correspondence relations, such as *hint*, than words that are irregular, like *pint* (Seidenberg, Waters, Barnes, & Tanenhaus, 1984). For less frequent words like *pint*, both routes are slow enough that both pronunciations become available to the reader at about the same time. Then, the reader has to discern between the conflicting pronunciations generated by the two routes. The time for this discernment slows down their reading of *pint*.

However, skilled readers tend to use the well-practiced lexical route for irregular high-frequency words such as *have*. For these words, the fact that they are irregular seems hardly to affect the speed or accuracy with which they are read by skilled readers. The grapheme–phoneme reliance theory explains this by assuming that, by the time skilled readers have assembled the phonics generated by the grapheme–phoneme route (which is thought to be comparatively slow), they have already recognized *have*. It is mainly for less-frequent words that one sees major effects of irregularity.

A second source of evidence for the existence of the two routes for word recognition is that there are some subtypes of dyslexia that seem to allow access to one route, but not the other (Shallice, Warrington, & McCarthy, 1983; Shallice & Warrington, 1980). Individuals with deep dyslexia appear to have only the lexical route. That is, they can pronounce only words that are already in their lexicon, but not items that are not in their lexicon. *Pint*, being in their lexicon, is recognized and pronounced correctly. However, they cannot generate a sensible pronunciation for a pseudoword such as *pont*. Individuals with surface dyslexia, by contrast, appear to have only the grapheme–phoneme route available to them. These individuals are likely to regularize the pronunciation of all written words. Thus, they might pronounce *pint* similarly to *hint*, but they would be able to generate a sensible pronunciation for the pseudoword *pont*.

Not all psycholinguists who study word reading accept this dual-route theory, however. Seidenberg and McClelland (1989) have argued that a parallel distributed processing (PDP) system (sometimes called the *triangle connectionist network model*) might be able to handle the effects described above more elegantly. This model does not include local lexical (word) representations, as the dual-route model does. Instead, it represents only phonemes, letter features, and letters (and semantic features in some implementations). Words are represented as a network of connections among orthography, phonemes, and semantics, connected via hidden units, as shown in Figure 4.2. (*Hidden units* are internal representations that have the effect of introducing nonlinearity to the input to better predict observed data.) In this theory, recognizing a word involves selectively activating a particular subset of these units and deactivating others.

Looking at Figure 4.2, we can see that input from print enters into the connectionist system by activating the letter features we described earlier. Then these

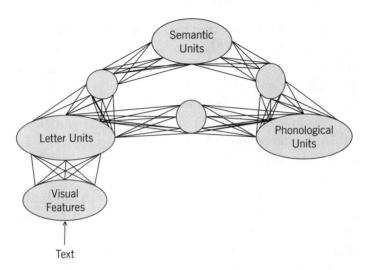

FIGURE 4.2. Triangle connectionist network model developed by Seidenberg and McClelland (1989). In this model, lexical information is distributed over orthographic, phonological, and semantic units rather than in one local representation. The blank circles represent hidden units designed to capture nonlinearities in the relationships between the named units.

features begin to activate the letter units associated with the word, which then begin to activate both the phonological units and semantic units. As the phonological and semantic units become activated, they send activation back to the lower levels (i.e., interactively). Finally, at some point the word is recognized when the network "settles on" a particular pattern of activation. The particular pattern of activity over a large number of units serves as the "representation" of the word, although no lexicon is directly represented. Seidenberg and McClelland (1989) trained a distributed computer network like this to "learn" how to pronounce words by presenting them using the frequency with which they appear in text and providing corrective feedback. This connectionist architecture produced word recognition findings similar to typical human data.

    The connectionist approach to reading words has had a number of critiques leveled against it. First, it is unclear how the model might handle the dyslexia data described above (Balota, Yap, & Cortese, 2006), which seem to be explained by the dual-route model rather naturally. Second, the connectionist model may do a poor job of describing the pronunciation of pseudowords, which would seem to be more naturally handled by the grapheme–phoneme route of the dual-route model (Besner, 1990). Further, both models need to integrate the increasing amount of neurological data regarding how the brain stages the processing of various types of information and the temporal flow of that information in the brain (Carreiras, Armstrong, Perea, & Frost, 2014).

Regardless of how this intellectual debate might ultimately pan out, it is important to note that both the dual-route and connectionist models include something like letter features, letters, phonemes, and the correspondences between them in their modeling of skilled reading. This is a conceptual point of agreement that should not be ignored, even if the models describe them somewhat differently. From an education perspective, this is probably what really matters. Indeed, simulations of word learning using these types of architectures have also replicated the benefits of phonics teaching over approaches that engage only whole-word teaching early in the process of learning to read (Hutzler, Ziegler, Perry, Wimmer, & Zorzi, 2004). It is a helpful connection between the findings of the models and those of the National Reading Panel Report (National Institute of Child Health and Human Development, 2000) that phonics instruction will facilitate the development of word recognition processes in children just learning to read.

Still, it does not escape our notice that, for English-speaking children, teachers often teach the reading of words by using mixed strategies that are very reminiscent of the dual-route approach. It is often recommended that teachers employ phonics instruction that is supplemented by whole-word teaching strategies for high-frequency irregular words (Chard & Osborn, 1999). For example, the widely used Dolch word list contains 220 sight words for teachers to teach directly outside the phonics system (Dolch, 1936). Indeed, it is our observation that this is the rule rather than the exception for teachers instructing children to read English. For languages with highly regular orthographies such as German or Italian, teachers usually teach reading using a pure phonics approach (Hutzler et al., 2004), which seems to work best for those languages. Differences in instructional history may have consequences for how skilled adults read words, but this has yet to be fully determined.

MODELS OF WORD RECOGNITION

How does knowing what the word *bird* means help readers in reading the written word *bird*? Obviously, the purpose of word reading is to initiate the processes necessary for understanding print, so meaning would seem to be of key importance. The models we have just described differ in how word meaning is accessed and whether meaning is even necessary for recognizing words.

For the triangle connectionist model, word meanings would seem to be inevitably activated when words are recognized. Activation of the semantic units is an integral part of activating letter and phonological features because they are interconnected. Traditionally, the lexicon and its operations have been deemed responsible for semantic effects (Jackendoff, 2002). In this model, however, semantic effects occur without the direct assistance of a lexicon because this model postu-lates no separate lexicon.

In the dual-route cascaded model approach, the situation regarding the role of word meanings is not as clear. Looking back at our depiction of the dual-route model in Figure 4.1, we can see that the semantic system has been segregated as distinct from the orthographic and phonological lexicons. There are routes that a reader can take so that semantic information is not necessarily invoked to rec-ognize words. For example, following the figure, the reader could go directly from Letters → Orthographic Lexicon → Phonological Lexicon → Phonemes (or, for that matter, taking the slower route via grapheme–phoneme rules). Coltheart (2004) bases the rationale for this distinction between the orthographic and pho-nological lexicons and the semantic system on neurological findings. He points out that there have been a number of patients with neurological impairments who are able to recognize written or spoken words but not their meanings, there are other patients who can access meanings of words presented auditorily, but not visually, and vice versa. Further, Evans, Ralph, and Woollams (2012) have shown that typical readers can quickly discriminate words from nonwords when nonword foils bear no resemblance to actual words (e.g., strings of consonants). When this is the case, semantic effects on word identification disappear. Moreover, fMRI studies have shown that, compared to orthographic processing, semantic retrieval is delayed by about 50–100 milliseconds, and the two processes occur in different brain locations (i.e., the left anterior temporal area versus the left posterior supe-rior temporal area; Fujimaki et al., 2009). This finding indicates that word mean-ing processes are segregated, to some extent, from other aspects of word recogni-tion. Taken together, all these findings suggest that word identification can occur without, or prior to, the retrieval of semantic information in typical readers. Still, it is reasonable to suppose that most of the time when words are being processed during reading, word meanings are being processed as well, and are certainly pro-cessed eventually.

The dual-route and connectionist models may also differ considerably on their positions as to the nature of the semantic system. The dual-route model relies on the existence of a semantic system connected to phonological and orthographic lexicons to account for semantic effects in word recognition. To our knowledge, the model itself does not make any claims about the nature of this semantic sys-tem. Given other characteristics of the model, it is reasonable to assume that the phonological and orthographic lexicons are connected to a localist semantic sys-tem of some type. *Localist* semantic memory models are those in which each word has a concept associated with it that has a unique, specific location in the seman-tic memory, called a *node*.

Distributed models are, as described above, those in which each semantic con-cept is represented as a particular pattern of activation that occurs within the semantic units in the model. Is this different from a lexicon in any practical way? It is unclear. Pinker and Ullman (2002) have argued that this depiction of the semantic system is, in fact, a lexicon. Regardless, various descriptions regarding the organization of word meanings basically boil down to belonging to either localist or distributed views.

We use a canonical finding within in the psychology of reading, the relatedness effect, to illustrate how word meanings enter into the word recognition process. The *relatedness effect* refers to the finding that presentation of a related word usually assists in the processing of an upcoming word (Meyer & Schvaneveldt, 1971). In a typical experimental trial of the effect, people might be shown a priming word, *lion*, on an otherwise blank computer screen. Half a second later, *lion* disappears and the word *tiger* appears, and the reader names it. People are usually faster to name words like *tiger* when they are preceded by a related word like *lion* than when they are preceded by a neutral stimulus (such as a string of X's or the presentation of an unrelated word, such as *truck*). In the next section, we discuss the organization and operations of the semantic system within these models.

Localist Models

The most commonly referenced localist models in the psychology of reading are the *spreading activation network* models (see Shelley-Tremblay, 2010). Spreading activation models assume that concepts are organized as a set of nodes, connected via links, and organized either by semantic similarity (Collins & Loftus, 1975) or by association (Anderson, 1983), as illustrated in Figure 4.3. In these models, reading a word causes the relevant semantic node to become activated. Activation of a node causes activation to flow from the source node, shown here as *lion*, throughout the semantic network via links emanating from this node. Activation is said to benefit the processing of other nodes in the immediate neighborhood, such as *tiger*. Activation spreads to adjacent nodes, proportional to the strength of links in the network or distance from the source node. Presumably, the processing of a word such as *graze* would benefit little, if at all, from prior reading of the word *lion* because it is many links away from *lion*.

According to Anderson (1983), the activation from a node is divided among the links emanating from it to neighbor nodes, which is proportionally less for each when there are many interconnections. This issue of multiple interconnections is called the *fan effect*. Much like the plumbing of an old house, when more people are taking a shower at the same time, there is less water pressure available to go around. Thus, again referring to Figure 4.3, when the concept *lion* is activated in the lexicon, the activation is divided up and spreads among the links leading to *hunt, mane, strong, roar, cat,* and *tiger*. Because of this *fan effect*, benefits for neighbor nodes can be somewhat reduced. In this example, the concepts of

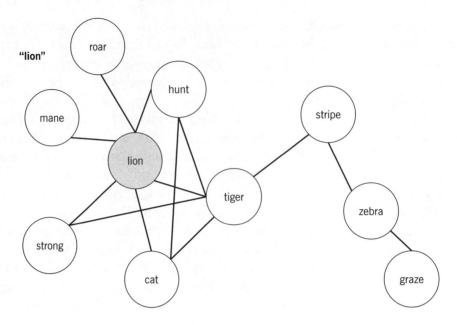

FIGURE 4.3. Simplified local semantic network for the concept *lion*. In the spreading activation network theory (Collins & Loftus, 1975), concepts are represented by nodes, shown here as circled words. Relations between concepts are represented by links between them, shown here as lines connecting the nodes.

roar and *mane* have to share activation with *strong, cat, hunt,* and *tiger* when *lion* is read, diluting their activation more than might occur in a sparser portion of the network.

The spreading activation process occurs very quickly, virtually immediately. The amount of benefit dissipates as we get further and further away from our attended node. Ultimately, in the case of our illustrated network, some minor activation of distant words such as *stripe* is possible because of the existence of a mediating link, here, between *lion* and *tiger*. Presumably, the more distant mediators *lion–cat–tiger–stripe, lion–hunt–tiger–stripe, lion–strong–tiger–stripe* would yield fewer benefits for the processing of *stripe* because of this dissipation in the network. Indirect priming can also work to accumulate effects and thereby increase the ease with which a particular word is processed. For example, the processing of *tiger* should be easily accomplished because of the activation of *lion* in our network, because of the direct link between *lion* and *tiger* and its mediating connections with *cat, strong,* and *hunt.*

Thus the processing of concepts can be assisted more broadly by the concurrent activation of a related word within the network. Activation spreads quickly within the network, reaching its maximum activation for a presented word within around 50 milliseconds (McNamara, 2005, p. 15). When the reader's attention shifts, however, activation dissipates for unattended nodes very quickly too, usually within half a second (Neely, 1991). The need to shift attention to another part of the network when an unrelated prime is presented can cause a delay in recognizing a target word, if enough time has elapsed between the presentation of the prime and the presentation of the target (Neely, 1991).

Distributed Models

In distributed models, meaning units do not correspond to specific words. In these models, meaning for a given word is captured instead by specific patterns of activation across meaning units. McRae, de Sa, and Seidenberg (1997) proposed a distributed model of word meaning wherein each meaning unit, in its distributed cascade, represents a particular semantic feature. Semantic features are considered to be elemental aspects of word meanings (e.g., *furry, large, transparent, male, animate*), much the way atoms are basic elements of molecules. The features that people think comprise their knowledge of particular words can be obtained by asking people to generate a descriptive list. So, if you ask people to list features for *lion*, they might list *furry, four-legged, pawed, mane, claws, teeth, ferocious, animate*, and so forth. In the model these feature lists are used in a distributed way; that is, they are not linked to a local word representation, per se, to serve as the semantic unit in the model for *lion* and anything else that shares these features with *lion*. For example, *tiger* will share many features listed for *lion*, except *mane*. The model can determine the interrelations among features by using a learning algorithm that includes feedback to the system. This learning algorithm codes covariation among semantic units in the network. The learning mechanism might capture the idea, for example, that if something is *furry*, then it is usually *animate*. If something is *purple*, it virtually never has a *beak*.

The model can explain the relatedness effect fairly easily. When a word is read, activation occurs within the semantic units in a way that approximates the word's meaning. Related words are said to benefit from the processing when the two words share similar activation patterns (i.e., share semantic units).

Let's take the lion–tiger example again, in which *lion* is presented and then replaced by the word *tiger*. In distributed models, when a priming word is presented, all the semantic units associated with that word become activated. In this case, the semantic units *furry, four-legged, pawed, mane, ferocious, claws, teeth*, and *animate* would all become activated and the orthographic, phonological, and semantic units for *lion* all settle, yielding the particular activation pattern across units associated with *lion*. Then *tiger* is presented. Semantic units activated by the *lion* are not immediately deactivated, but they gradually begin the process of deactivation as this new word appears. Because the target word *tiger* shares features with the prime word *lion*, the semantic units shared by the two remain active. In our hypothetical case, all the semantic units associated with *lion*, except *mane*, are shared. The activation of shared semantic units will speed up the time necessary for all the related words' semantic units to become stabilized. For *tiger*, the semantic unit *stripes* will need to become activated, as well as the orthographic units associated with *t, i, g, e,* and *r* and the phonological units. The preactivation of the semantic units shared with *lion* will begin the word recognition process by sending feedback to these orthographic and phonological units, which will speed up processing and benefit the reading of *tiger*. When the pattern of activated units associated with *tiger* becomes stabilized, the word is recognized and meaning is retrieved.

If, by contrast, the target word is unrelated (think of the word *graze* here), there are no shared units and the activation of the semantic units will have to start from scratch. In this case, recognition of *graze* will not be facilitated by the prior exposure to the word *lion*. It will be as though no priming word had been presented at all.

INDIVIDUAL WORD CHARACTERISTICS AND THEIR EFFECTS ON SINGLE WORD READING

There are a number of characteristics of individual words that make them more or less difficult to process. In this section we discuss several of these characteristics: (1) how word meaning difficulty and the age at which words were acquired developmentally affect the reading of words, (2) how the frequency of words in the language makes them more or less difficult to process, and (3) the processes engaged by recognition of homographs and morphologically complex words.

Word Meanings and Word Reading

The meanings of individual words can influence their processing. One well-known such effect is the *concreteness effect*. We might consider the term *concreteness* to refer to the dimension of words related to the imagery and sensory referents associated with them (Paivio, 1968). Concreteness (and abstractness) is, in actuality, a constellation of variables beyond imagery and sensory referents. Abstract words are learned later in development (Gilhooly & Gilhooly, 1979; Schwanenflugel, 1991), feel less familiar overall (Gernsbacher, 1984), are harder to retrieve contextual information for (Schwanenflugel, Harnishfeger, & Stowe, 1988), and are impoverished semantically (Strain, Patterson, & Seidenberg, 1995). Thus, abstract words have more difficult meanings than concrete words in a number of ways. The term *concreteness* is often used as a simpler proxy for the wordier descriptor *more familiar word meanings* in many studies of word recognition.

As we discussed in Chapter 2, children are slower and less accurate when they try to identify abstract words than concrete words (Schwanenflugel & Akin, 1994; Schwanenflguel & Noyes, 1996). It is important to note in relation to the skilled reading of words that this trend remains in skilled adult readers. The effects are found for word naming (Bleasdale, 1987; Schwanenflugel & Stowe, 1989) and lexical decision tasks (i.e., quickly distinguishing that an item presented is a word rather than a nonword or pseudoword; Schwanenflugel et al., 1988). Juhasz and Rayner (2003) have found that people are more likely to fixate on and reread abstract words, compared to concrete words, during typical text reading.

However, the "concreteness effect" may not actually relate to concreteness at all. Abstract words that have easily retrievable contexts or readily accessible emotional experiences are as easily processed as concrete words (Newcombe, Campbell, Siakaluk, & Pexman, 2012; Schwanenflugel & Stowe, 1989). The so-called concreteness effect may have more to do with the relative semantic richness of a word than its concreteness, per se (Zdrazilova & Pexman, 2013).

Concreteness effects are larger for irregular words, low-frequency words, words acquired later, and multisyllabic words—all factors that make the processing of particular words difficult (Cortese, Simpson, & Woolsey, 1997; Cortese & Schock, 2013). The finding of greater concreteness effects for words that have these features suggests that semantic information is often recruited to assist in the processing of words when processing is difficult.

The lexical processing models we have been discussing both describe how semantic information can assist readers in the processing of words. From the dual-route perspective, the effects of a word's semantic difficulty occur through greater access to semantic information via operations of lexical paths. Presumably, concrete words and earlier acquired words have greater and easier access to semantic information than abstract words do.

From the triangle connectionist model perspective, this increased rate of concrete word recognition occurs through the enriched semantic representations that concrete words are said generally to possess (Strain et al., 1995). The fact that the system is fully interactive means that information from the semantic system can send information to other parts of the system (i.e., phonological and orthographic units) to more quickly enable the settling of the units to allow for word recognition.

Word Frequency Effects in Lexical Processing

The frequency with which words appear in texts influences how easily they are processed during reading. Word frequency is defined as the relative frequency with which a particular word occurs in the corpus of a given language. High-frequency words tend to be short as a rule and are far more frequent in text compared to low-frequency words. A list of the most frequent 100 words in English, compiled from one very large corpus of the English language, can be found in Figure 4.4. As you can see, most of these words are ones you see over and over in text.

According to Brysbaert et al. (2011), 40% of the variance in lexical decision times for recognition of English words can be attributed to the frequency with which they appear in the language. High-frequency words are read more quickly and accurately than low-frequency words. Both adults and children fixate on low-frequency words longer than high-frequency words while reading connected texts (Inhoff & Rayner, 1986; Joseph, Nation, & Liversedge, 2013). Word frequency is among the most potent variables affecting word recognition speed.

The dual-route cascade model and triangle connectionist models each have mechanisms for dealing with word frequency effects. According to the dual-route model, word frequency effects are caused by activation patterns in the lexical route. Presumably, high-frequency words have greater access to the lexical route, and word recognition is completed using this route before the operations of the grapheme–phoneme rules can even enter consciousness (Coltheart et al., 2001). For the triangle connectionist models, frequency effects occur because of the way the models are trained to identify words. That is, the connections between the orthographic, phonological, and semantic units are stronger for high-frequency words than low-frequency words because they are entered in more often during the training of the network (Plaut & Booth, 2000). For the human learner, repetition leads to a cognitive optimization of these connections.

a	did	in	my	so	upon
about	do	into	no	some	us
after	down	is	not	such	very
all	first	it	now	than	was
an	for	its	of	that	we
and	from	know	on	the	were
any	good	like	one	their	what
are	great	little	only	them	when
as	had	made	or	then	which
at	has	man	other	there	who
be	have	may	our	these	will
been	he	me	out	they	with
before	her	men	over	this	would
but	him	more	said	time	you
by	his	Mr.	see	to	your
can	I	much	she	two	
could	if	must	should	up	

FIGURE 4.4. Top 100 most-frequent words used in English, according to Project Gutenberg (Hart, 2004).

Brysbaert et al. (2011) have noted that half of the word frequency effect can be attributed to words below frequencies of 2 per million. To give you a sense of what a frequency at this level might mean, a word with a frequency as few as .1 per million might be a word that an average 20-year-old has encountered 140 times already; *accordion, catamaran,* and *ravioli* are three examples of such words. Apparently, each exposure to a word throughout one's life contributes importantly to the recognition of words at these lower frequencies. In fact, Brysbaert et al. (2011) argue that the word frequency effect is really a practice effect.

There are definitely issues associated with measuring word frequency. Currently, measuring word frequency is typically carried out electronically using electronic texts. Previously, texts were keyed in by hand and researchers sampled the universe of texts until a sample of one million words was reached (e.g., Kucera & Francis, 1967). Lower frequency words were poorly estimated by such corpuses. Larger corpuses are now used. A good measure of word frequency can obtained from a corpus of 10 million words or so; such a corpus provides a more stable estimate of words at the low-frequency end of the spectrum than does a smaller corpus. (However, larger is not necessarily better because even larger corpuses tend to oversample technical words that ordinary people never see.) A good corpus will include sample sources that represent a shared history for people within a culture (Brysbaert & New, 2009).

The topic of word frequency has significance for the current educational debate about the construction and nature of texts that children read. Most children's book publishers control for word frequency (and sentence length) in their texts to make those texts easier to read, easier to comprehend, and more enjoyable. Unfortunately, these adjustments do not stop at early readers, where such changes might make sense—they continue all the way up through texts directed at college students. Adams (2010–2011) and Hayes, Wolfer, and Wolfe (1996) have documented a noticeable reduction, in a number of ways, in the complexity of texts directed at learners over the past 50 years, including word frequency, as we have become more sophisticated at controlling text. The mismatch between the complexity of texts used in schools and texts that adults will need to read in life and in the workforce is seen as a problem. The debate is whether this "dumbing down" of textbooks has had a negative impact on reading skills (and consequently, thinking skills) of the population as a whole or whether this is a good change that allows children to learn more readily from text.

There are obvious costs and benefits for monitoring word frequency in texts. Highly controlled texts may present costs in terms of children's exposure to new words. Texts relying on higher-frequency words will not introduce children to as many new words. If Henry Ward Beecher's maxim that "All words are pegs to hang ideas on" is true, then reducing this exposure will potentially restrict the kinds of ideas to which children are exposed. On the other side of the coin, there may be benefits in terms of practice for words that children are likely to encounter in text by gradually introducing words of variable frequencies (see Hiebert & Fisher, 2007). In fact, the top 300 most-frequent words in the language account for about 65% of the words we read (Fry, 2000), so to be able to read quickly and accurately, one should have considerable practice on these words early on, so as to be able to read them without hesitation. But if controlling for frequency after the elementary school years makes any sense, it is hard to see just how. Increasing the complexity of school texts in terms of word frequency and syntactic complexity has been at least part of the motivation behind the development of the Common Core State Standards for literacy.

Age of Acquisition

Age of acquisition refers to the idea that there is some consistency among children in terms of the age at which they acquire some words as compared to others. The idea that there is something special about early-learned words has been around for at least 50 years. As early as 1962, Rochford and Williams noticed that early-acquired words seemed to be those that adults with aphasia (i.e., people who have a language impairment, for various reasons, affecting the production or comprehension of speech and the ability to read or write) tended to maintain in their speech. Indeed, recent evidence has shown that the ability to remember these words applies not only to individuals with aphasia, but also to those with semantic dementia (Lambon Ralph, Graham, Ellis, & Hodges, 1998) and Alzheimer's disease (Silveri, Cappa, Mariotti, & Puopolo, 2002). Carroll and White (1973) found that early-acquired words also tended to be those that typical adults could name faster. Early acquired words show a "first in, last to go quality" and first in, fast to name quality (Hodgson & Ellis, 1998, p. 146).

Adults, surprisingly, are able to rate with some accuracy the relative age at which they learned various words: There is a good correspondence between these ratings and objective measures of when words are typically learned (Gilhooly & Gilhooly, 1980; Morrison, Chappell, & Ellis, 1997). These age-of-acquisition ratings may be a better predictor than word frequency for predicting simple lexical processing times (Morrison & Ellis, 1995; Gerhand & Barry, 1998). Distinguishable age-of-acquisition effects have been found in virtually every language for which they have been studied (Johnston & Barry, 2006).

Ideas regarding age of acquisition and word reading have not gone unchallenged. As Zevin and Seidenberg (2002) have pointed out, children may learn some words earlier simply because they are more frequently heard, so the age-of-acquisition superiority idea is really a bit circular. Johnston and Barry (2006) have argued that the age-of-acquisition effect may be really an order-of-learning effect. Some "kiddie" words may not end up being words that adults use much at all, and some relatively newly acquired adult words will be ones that they will continue to use often. It may be the trajectory of use that is more important than the age at which particular words are learned (see also Zevin & Seidenberg, 2004).

Assuming age-of-acquisition effects do actually occur in reading, how do models of lexical processing account for them? According to the dual-route model of word reading (Coltheart et al., 2001), age-of-acquisition effects would have to occur because early-acquired words have superior access to both the semantic system and the lexical route. Connectionist models can account for age-of-acquisition effects too. Modeling the acquisition of word reading using interleaved learning, in which new items are entered into the network along with previously learned items, Ellis and Lambon Ralph (2000) showed that early-learned words had a greater impact on the development of the network models than later trained words. Early-learned words seem to set the parameters for later-acquired words in network models (i.e., they create a kind of loss of plasticity within the network), so they have an enduring impact over the lifetime of the model, giving credence to the order-of-learning idea. Of course, because the learning of these distributed networks in computers is thought to simulate learning within the developing cognitive networks of their human counterparts, early words that children acquire while learning to read might have similar effects.

The idea that early-learned words may have some special status in the developing reading lexicon has also been supported by studies examining the neurological aspects of lexical processing during reading (Adorni, Manfredi, & Proverbio, 2013). For example, Hernandez and Fiebach (2006) showed that late-acquired words tended to activate the areas of the brain involved in phonological processing (i.e., posterior part of the left superior temporal gyrus) during reading, whereas early-acquired words did not, suggesting greater effortful phonological retrieval for late-acquired than early-acquired words. Further Fiebach, Friederici, Muller, von Cramon, and Hernandez (2003) found greater activity for early-acquired words in the left auditory areas, indicating a greater sensory basis for early-acquired words than late- acquired words.

Lexical Ambiguity

Let's consider the word *mug* for the moment. *Mug* is a homograph. Homographs are lexically ambiguous. A homograph is actually two or more words having identical orthographic and (usually) phonological characteristics, but with a number of distinct meanings. *Mug* is lexically ambiguous—it can refer to a heavy ceramic cup for drinking warm beverages, carrying out an assault with a robbery intent, or a face or a picture of a face (as in *mug shot*). The study of lexical ambiguity is important for research on the reading of words because it tells us something about how our cognitive system handles ambiguity in reading.

The central issue in processing homographs like *mug* is whether there is unintentional, uncontrolled, automatic retrieval of several or all meanings when we are reading a lexically ambiguous word, or of just one of them. Certainly, for the most part, we are rarely consciously aware of any kind of ambiguity while we are reading, so whatever unintended meanings are retrieved must be dealt with rather quickly by the cognitive system. The context surrounding the word usually tells us which meaning is intended by the text. The ultimate meanings we operate with must match the context. For example, we do not hang on to the crime meaning of *mug* after reading:

> Looking forward to his morning coffee, Steve brought the *mug* to his lips.

How does having multiple meanings affect the processing of homographs? It depends on the methodology used to test this question. When both meanings are similarly frequent, there is an actual advantage for ambiguous words over non-ambiguous words in single-word lexical decision studies (Kellas, Paul, Martin, & Simpson, 1991). Apparently, when deciding whether an item is a word or not, retrieving any meaning at all is enough, and having multiple meanings only helps us find one more quickly. However, studies examining eye movements during reading find that readers fixate longer on homographs when the text is not particularly biasing (e.g., "He put the remaining *straw* away") because readers must resolve the ambiguity before moving on (Rayner & Duffy, 1986). Without further information, the confusion will remain. Adult and skilled child readers will later spend extra time looking at disambiguating segments of text so that the ambiguity can be resolved, although less skilled readers do not seem to try to resolve it (van der Schoot, Vasbinder, Horsley, Reijntjes, & van Lieshout, 2009; Stites, Federmeier, & Stine-Morrow, 2013).

The processing of a homograph's multiple meanings depends on the timing of presentation. For example, in cross-modal priming studies (Seidenberg, Tanenhaus, Leiman, & Bienkowski, 1982, p. 504), a biasing sentence containing a homograph was presented auditorily, followed by a visually presented probe related to one of the meanings. For example:

> "Although the farmer bought the *straw* . . . "

After listening to this sentence, one of three visually presented probes was presented: a related word *hay*; a word related to the unintended meaning, *sip*; or a control word. Naming times indicated that, if the probes were presented immediately with the onset of *straw*, both meanings were active. That is, both *hay* and *sip* were read more quickly than the control word. However, once more time elapsed, only *hay* remained active. Meaning selection took place, and unintended meanings were no longer available. Originally, these findings were taken to mean that completely context-free, exhaustive access of meanings takes place early in processing. However, over the years, it has become evident from additional research that probes related to the contextually appropriate meaning (in this case, *hay*) show greater priming than words related to the contextually inappropriate meaning (*sip*), suggesting that some selection of meaning occurs early in processing (Lucas, 1999).

The processing of a homograph's meanings may also depend on the constraint of the contexts in which the ambiguous word appears. Some contexts are highly constraining. For example, in the sentence "Sam decided to go to a kennel where he bought a *boxer*," only the *dog* meaning of *boxer* is appropriate. In such highly constraining contexts, readers may access only the single contextually appropriate meaning (Kellas et al., 1991).

The relative frequency of a homograph's meanings, called *meaning dominance*, may also determine how a homograph's meanings are processed. Most homographs have dominant meanings. *Port* is an example: We are much more likely to think about *harbor* than *wine*. Some homographs, such as *straw* used in a previous example, have relatively balanced meanings; we are just as likely to think of *garden* as a *drink*. Research examining eye movements during reading show that for balanced homographs, readers fixate longer on the homographs than control words, indicating that readers momentarily perceive confusion because both meanings are equally probable. Later, they will fixate on information in the text that disambiguates the homograph, as noted earlier. For biased homographs, readers do not appear to notice the ambiguity as long as the dominant meaning is the one intended by the context. Readers only slow down for homographs when context indicates that a subordinate meaning was intended. This is called the *subordinate bias effect* (Sereno, O'Donnell, & Rayner, 2006).

Brain research suggests that the hemispheres of the brain may have different linguistic roles in resolving the meanings of ambiguous words. That the hemispheres of the brain cooperate to resolve ambiguity has been ascertained through studies using divided visual field presentations. A divided visual field presentation involves presenting visual stimuli only to the left or right visual hemisphere, which allows researchers to present words to only one hemisphere of the brain (Burgess & Simpson, 1988). Because of the crisscrossed way the visual system is designed, a word that appears to the left visual field is initially registered in the right cerebral hemisphere; likewise, a word that appears in the right visual field is initially registered in the left cerebral hemisphere. Further, studies using fMRI have allowed us to describe the neural correlates of ambiguity resolution in the two hemispheres (Hargreaves, Pexman, Pittman, & Goodyear, 2011). Giora (2007) suggests that, although a primary role for the left hemisphere is to process language, it may have been designed to process mainly salient, literal language, whereas the right hemisphere takes on the role of processing nonsalient, indeterminant meanings. For ambiguous words, the right hemisphere of the brain appears to play a role in keeping nondominant meanings alive until the ambiguity is resolved by structures in the left hemisphere (the left inferior frontal gyrus, possibly; Hargreaves et al., 2011).

As intriguing as this possibility is regarding how the brain resolves ambiguity, the findings that support it have recently been questioned. Harpaz and Lavidor (2012) have shown that relatively small methodological changes may affect the pattern of results related to processing of ambiguity. We will have to await further research to determine just exactly how the brain goes about resolving lexical ambiguity.

Morphological Complexity

Lexical morphology refers to the smallest basic meaning units that provide the internal structure of words. There are several types of morphology. *Inflectional morphology* modifies a word's tense or number without affecting the word's meaning or grammatical category (e.g., *walked* = *walk* + *-ed*; *walks* = *walk* + *-s*). *Derivational morphology* changes either the meaning or grammatical category of the word (e.g., *computer* = *compute* + *-er*; *computation* = *compute* + *-ation*). In compounding, two or more words are put together to form a word (e.g., *butterfly*, *blackboard*). Up to now, we have been discussing the identification of simple words. Now we discuss the identification of morphologically complex words.

One is the basic findings regarding morphologically complex words is the *stem frequency effect*: the finding that lexical decision and naming of morphologically complex words is better predicted by the combined frequency of the stem and the whole word than by the surface word itself. For example, *seeming* and *mending* have the same frequency of occurrence in the language (i.e., the same "surface" frequency). However, the cumulative frequency (i.e., "stem" frequency) of *seem*, *seemed*, *seems*, and *seeming* is higher than *mend*, *mended*, *mends*, and *mending*. Taft (2004) and others have found that inflected words with a high-stem frequency can be recognized more easily than words with a low-stem frequency. There are both surface and stem frequency effects; that is, controlling for surface frequency, there is a correlation between stem frequency and word recognition time, and vice versa.

The presence of a stem frequency effect suggests that readers decompose complex words into their constituents or parts (e.g., *mending* = *mend* + *ing*) during processing (Taft & Ardasinski, 2006). If there were no decomposition, the frequency of the stem by itself should have no effect. In fact, Solomyak and Marantz (2010) found neurological evidence for lexical decomposition early in the processing of morphologically complex words, using magnetoencephalography (MEG; a functional neuroimaging technique similar to fMRI). The morpheme frequency effect has been shown for both prefixed and suffixed words, using various methodologies, across languages, and in the lexical processing of children (Amenta & Crepaldi, 2012).

The stem frequency effect suggests the importance of having a large mental store of morpheme stems, in general. That is, knowing a lot of word stems should help children read morphologically complex words. As children proceed in school, the texts they read are more complex at various levels: structural, sentence, and lexical. In particular, there is a shift in the morphological complexity of words in the texts that children read as they proceed from texts designed for elementary school children to texts designed for middle school students (Bar-Ilan & Berman, 2007). Indeed, the majority of words in academic texts designed for advanced schooling are morphologically complex. They contain morphologically dense words, such as *economical, perception, tranquility, isolation, diagnostician,* and *migratory*. If children do not know the stem words *economy, perceive, tranquil, isolate, diagnose,* and *migrate*, then they cannot use the meanings of these words to recognize the more complex derived words (Goodwin, Gilbert, & Cho, 2013).

As we noted in the previous chapter, when children become better readers, they begin to use larger word chunks as they recognize words. One view (Rastle & Davis, 2008) is that children learn to detect the distributional probabilities of letters, which enables them to determine which letter sequences cohere. For example, *-ed,* as in *looked,* would be found together often and would cohere, whereas the *-ke-* sequence would be less frequent and would not cohere by itself. Word stems and affixes are some of these cohering letter sequences. Another view (Schreuder & Baayen, 1995) utilizes the idea that the role of morphology in language is to compute meaning. That is, children learn to relate the letter patterns of form and meaning that are systematically connected to one another. Once they recognize these larger segments, they represent these segments as meaning units and the individual morphemes begin to affect word reading.

In any case, research has shown that children having basic word reading skills will begin to show effects of morphological knowledge in their word reading. The frequency of word stems begins to influence the speed and accuracy of their reading, particularly of low-surface-frequency words (Burani, Marcolini, De Luca, & Zoccolotti, 2008). Further, morphological priming (wherein a preceding word assists in the recognition of a morphologically related upcoming word) has been observed in children as young as third grade (Quemart, Casalis, & Cole, 2011). However, morphologically complex words that shift in pronunciation between the stem and the complex word (e.g., *severe → severity*) remain a particular struggle for older elementary school readers who make many errors when reading them aloud (Carlisle & Stone, 2005).

For morphological knowledge to affect the decoding skills of children, they must have knowledge of the stems themselves. Goodwin et al. (2013) have shown that knowledge of stem words helps adolescents pronounce words derived from them. In fact, a mega-study of word recognition with over 1,000 adults found that high-vocabulary individuals (presumably, these are individuals having knowledge of many stems) showed faster and more accurate word recognition performance than low-vocabulary individuals (Yap, Balota, Sibley, & Ratcliff, 2012). Thus, a good bit of instructional focus related to decoding words in the later years should be directed toward helping children learn the meanings of new stems and how to use those stems to read morphologically complex words.

THE EFFECTS OF SEMANTIC CONTEXT ON THE READING OF UPCOMING WORDS

While we are reading, we are generally not reading single words in isolation except in rare instances. Yes, we may read single words when we are reading simple signage or labels (e.g., *Exit*), or instructionally as part of a class learning activity, but usually we are reading words to build up a mental representation of a larger text of some sort. Cognitive psychologists have focused on single-word reading in order to more easily ascertain purely lexical factors. This focus has allowed them to gain control over extraneous complications associated with larger amounts of text. As such, it has been very successful, and we have learned much. However, focusing on the reading of single words also has its limitations, as researchers in this area would certainly agree. For example, it is possible that focusing on single words has caused us to exaggerate the effects associated with single words. To take one example we discussed earlier in this chapter, we described concreteness effects as though they are integral to the reading of words. But Schwanenflugel and Shoben (1983) showed years ago that merely presenting abstract and concrete words within a supportive sentence context may actually eliminate this effect. Supportive context has a way of making difficult processing easier.

Basic Semantic Priming

We have already discussed one element of the effect of context, and we have discussed how basic models of word recognition describe the effects of semantic priming. Typically in these studies, participants are presented with one word (the prime), which is then followed up by a second word (the target). The participant needs to make some sort of response to the second word (name it, decide whether it is a word, decide whether it is from the same category, etc.). If you recall, semantic priming is said to occur when the prior presentation of a related word causes the target word to be more readily recognized.

The finding of semantic priming, originally demonstrated in a study by Meyer and Schvaneveldt (1971), is probably one of the foundational findings in the history of cognitive psychology. In that study, high school students decided whether a pair of letter strings were both words or not (e.g., *nurse–doctor* [yes] vs. *bread–doof* [no]). When semantically related word pairs were presented, this decision was 85 milliseconds faster than when they were unrelated (e.g., *nurse-table*). These 85 milliseconds of temporal benefit for related words over unrelated words have come to be called *semantic priming*. It may not seem that 85 milliseconds is very much of a benefit, but the effects of such priming are cumulative and, cognitively speaking, important.

The Meyer and Schvaneveldt (1971) study has been cited literally thousands of times by other researchers. The study provided important support for the potential of cognitive psychology approaches to uncover the basic operations underlying language processing and related topics. The original hope was that studies of semantic priming would reveal the organization and operations of the lexicon and linguistic processes—which they have done, to a greater or lesser extent. The finding of semantic priming is now considered a basic fact about language, and the existence of semantic priming itself is only rarely questioned.

One topic of disagreement surrounds the very source of these priming effects, which have been attributed to associative factors; that is, words may become related over a lifetime because of co-occurrence across contexts (e.g., *private–property*; Hutchison, 2003). Alternatively, priming effects have been attributed to "pure" semantic factors. That is, they occur because primes and targets share semantic features in common (e.g., *feather–bird*; Smith, Shoben, & Rips, 1974). Unfortunately, words that are semantically related also tend to be associated (e.g., *lion–tiger*). Generally, these effects co-occur and have been enormously difficult to tease apart (Balota et al., 2006).

If we say that two words are semantically, but not associatively, related, we usually mean that they are not primary associates (e.g., *black–white*). But we also have to rule out the possibility that they are secondary or tertiary associates. Consider the *mane–stripe* example in Figure 4.3. If we follow the path from *mane* to *lion* and then to *tiger* and *stripe*, we can see that the two words are actually more related than they initially seem. So-called *mediated priming* effects like these have been found for associates as many as three links away (as with *mane–stripe*).

Mediated priming is an interesting phenomenon in and of itself. Research has shown that the amount of priming that the target derives from the prime varies with the number of mediators. For instance, considering examples such as the ones shown in Figure 4.3, McNamara (1992) found a 15-millisecond benefit for items having two-step mediators (e.g., *mane–tiger*) and a 10-millisecond benefit for ones involving three steps (e.g., *mane–stripes*). Admittedly, such effects are very small compared to ones involving only a single step (generally in the 30- to 80-millisecond range).

These mediated priming benefits are more likely to occur when conscious strategies that might get in the way are eliminated (McNamara, 2005). Conscious strategies may get in the way here because most people do not immediately see the relation between *mane* and *stripe*. So, for example, as readers try to decide if an item is a word in making a lexical decision, they might consciously search for a connection between *mane* and *stripe* and not find one, costing time and cognitive resources. These effects are also more likely to occur when there is a strong connection between the mediator and the target word (Jones, 2012). In the case of *mane–stripe*, the mediator *tiger* is highly associated to *stripe*, making its effects more detectable.

Strategic processes that encourage readers to try to match the word to the context cannot explain semantic priming. For example, a priming effect was found in one study wherein there was only a single related pair of words in the entire experimental context, with all the rest of the trials presenting the unrelated type (e.g., *doctor–ocean*) (Fischler, 1977). Semantic priming has been found for *subliminal priming* too (Hirshman & Durante, 1992). In subliminal priming studies, the primes themselves are presented so quickly and with such limited visibility that participants have professed not to see or be able to guess any of the prime words at all, but semantic priming effects have been found in these studies anyway. Thus, the finding of semantic priming is fairly ubiquitous and hard to disrupt. Semantic priming from single-word contexts remains an important, foundational finding for the psychology of reading.

Research examining neurological correlates for semantic priming suggests that both hemispheres are involved, but that semantic processing occurs more rapidly and is more specific in the left hemisphere than in the right. Chiarello (2003) notes that, as for lexical ambiguity, the left hemisphere tends to resolve priming more quickly toward a small set of lexical expectations. The right hemisphere tends to prime in a more diffuse way. Thus, the left hemisphere deals with priming more like a fine-tuned laser, whereas the right deals with priming more like a system with a lot of static. Functional MRI studies (Rissman, Eliassen, & Blumstein, 2003; Wible et al., 2006) have suggested that the left superior temporal, lateral temporal, and inferior frontal regions are sensitive to the effects of relatedness among words in semantic priming studies, indicating that these regions are involved. The right temporal regions are also involved, to some extent (Matsumoto, Iidaka, Haneda, Okada, & Sadato, 2005; Wible et al., 2006).

Semantic Priming from Larger Units of Text

Understanding the influence of larger units of text on the processing of upcoming words is important for several reasons. Contexts vary considerably in the amount of support they provide for the processing of words. Many contexts do not provide much contextual support. Consider the sentence fragment "In the valley there were three small _____." This context does not lead us to expect any particular completion. Almost any concrete noun will do. On the other hand, other contexts provide considerable support. Consider the sentence fragment "The hikers slowly climbed up the _____." In this case, we strongly expect that *mountain* will follow, although other words are possible (*hill, stairs, path*). We can take this idea one step further. Suppose that we read this same sentence in this fuller context:

> After a treacherous hike, Bill and his friends sluggishly entered their apartment lobby. They had gotten an early start at dawn. It had been a long day for the guys. The equipment they carried was heavy. *The hikers slowly climbed up the* _____.

Now our expectations for particular words have changed. *Stairs* seems to be a more likely completion, and *mountain* now seems fairly improbable. By focusing on larger amounts of text in this way, we can learn more about how readers use context to assist their reading of words. Anticipation of particular words is fairly common, as we often find ourselves mentally finishing each other's sentences while listening, if not interjecting these anticipated words aloud (Kamide, 2008).

There are a number of effects related to those of sentence context on the processing of upcoming words. The first and most basic of these is the *sentence congruity effect*. This is similar to the relatedness effect in word priming studies. That is, words that are sensible completions to sentences are recognized more quickly than words that do not make sensible completions. For both children and adults, the processing of upcoming words is faster when the word fits the sentence as a plausible completion than when it does not (Schwanenflugel & LaCount, 1988; Stanovich, West, & Feeman, 1981).

The second effect of sentence context on the processing of upcoming words is the *contextual constraint effect*. Contextual constraint is obtained by having people generate a completion or several completions for a partial context, such as a partial sentence missing its last word, and then tabulating the likelihood that some particular word is written down. This activity is sometimes called the *cloze task*, and there are a number of variants (Taylor, 1957; Schwanenflugel, 1986). Some sentences are highly constraining, as in "He mailed the letter without a _____." Almost everyone anticipates *stamp* here. As noted earlier, some sentences are not nearly as predictable. Generally, the more predictable a given word is for the context, the faster and more easily the word is processed. This finding has been shown in studies using lexical decision or naming (Fischler & Bloom, 1979; McClelland & O'Regan, 1981; Schwanenflugel & LaCount, 1988), as well as studies monitoring brain activity (Kutas, Lindamood, & Hilliard, 1984) and eye movements during reading (Rayner & Well, 1996). People are less likely to reread highly predictable words and are more likely to skip them altogether (Rayner, Ashby, Pollatsek, & Reichle, 2004). In fact, the benefits of sentence constraint for the processing of upcoming words may be logarithmically related to the predictability of particular words in context across a number of methodologies (Smith & Levy, 2013).

Sentence constraint deals with the effects of the sentence as a whole, but there is also an effect of a lower-level kind of predictability, called the *transitional probability effect*. This term refers to the likelihood that a particular word will follow a previous word in text. It reflects low-level statistical knowledge about our knowledge of adjacent words. For example, the word *accept* is more likely to be followed by *defeat* than *losses*. So, for the sentences like "They simply will not accept _____," McDonald and Shillock (2003) found that participants fixated on high-transitional probability words such as *defeat* for less time than for low-transitional probability words such as *losses*, regardless of the larger sentence constraint. The effects of local transitional probabilities for particular words can be estimated objectively from linguistic corpuses to produce a similar effect (Wang, Pomplun, Chen, Ko, & Rayner, 2010), so these local transitional probabilities seem to represent implicit knowledge that readers acquire about the language. This benefit on initial fixation for high-transitional probability words is a smaller one compared to the more global effect of context on the processing of upcoming words, however.

Going in the opposite direction from smaller to larger segments of text, Schwanenflugel and White (1991) found that expectations built from the larger discourse might also alter the pattern of lexical processing beyond that expected based on local information alone. They found contextual benefits for both discourse-related as well as local sentence-related words. Thus, in a number of ways, studies have demonstrated that readers capitalize on various types of contextual support to assist their reading of upcoming words in text.

IMPLICATIONS FOR ASSESSMENT

The material covered in this chapter suggests that evaluation of skilled word reading should address many of the issues discussed here related to the cognitive factors underlying word reading. For example, assessments of word reading for older elementary and middle school children who have moved past basic decoding strategies might include words of various levels of semantic difficulty. That is, they might assess children's ability to read concrete and abstract words as well as words sampled from earlier and later acquisition periods. Assessments should also include a determination of whether children (1) use context to easily resolve lexical ambiguity; (2) are able to read morphologically complex words; (3) understand the phonological rules engaged by transforming one lexical variant to another, such as understanding the shift in stress that comes with transforming words such as *active* into *activity* (Jarmulowicz, Taran, & Seek, 2012); and (4) have developed the automaticity that allows them to read lists of unrelated words (i.e., children should be able to read most common words quickly and accurately).

The fact that readers capitalize on various sources of contextual support to assist in the reading of words has implications for the assessment of reading skills as well. It suggests that, to some extent, readers' skills in understanding texts can be measured by their use of context to predict particular words. In fact, some reading comprehension assessments rely on this ability to measure readers' understanding of a text. In cloze assessments and related variants, readers are given a text with words blanked out every now and then, and they are asked to produce a completion or select from among various possible completions. Correlations between cloze procedures and other means of measuring reading comprehension in adults and children are surprisingly high (in the .55–.80 range) (Greene, 2001; Deno, 1985; Taylor, 1957). This finding suggests that the use of context is a fundamental skill for reading.

CONNECTING TO THE STANDARDS

As you can see from Table 4.1, the research on the skilled reading of words has been highly influential in the formulation of objectives for the Common Core State Standards. As noted in our previous chapter, phonics and word recognition are considered foundational skills for literacy in these standards. The standards

TABLE 4.1. Common Core State Standards Related to Skilled Word Reading for Second through Fifth Grades

Grade	Standards related to skilled word recognition
2	• Distinguish long and short vowels when reading regularly spelled one-syllable words. • Know spelling–sound correspondences for additional common vowel teams. • Decode regularly spelled two-syllable words with long vowels. • Decode words with common prefixes and suffixes. • Identify words with inconsistent but common spelling–sound correspondences. • Recognize and read grade-appropriate irregularly spelled words.
3	• Identify and know the meaning of the most common prefixes and derivational suffixes. • Decode words with common Latin suffixes. • Decode multisyllabic words. • Read grade-appropriate irregularly spelled words.
4 and 5	• Use combined knowledge of all letter–sound correspondences, syllabication patterns, and morphology (e.g., roots and affixes) to read accurately unfamiliar multisyllabic words in context and out of context.

Note. Adapted from the National Governors Association Center for Best Practices and the Council of Chief State School Officers (2010). All rights reserved.

related to these skills move from the basic phonics, covered in the last chapter, to some of the more advanced skills covered in this chapter. For example, an emphasis on reading longer, multisyllabic words and words with irregular mappings begins in second grade. As children advance through elementary school, there is also a new emphasis on words with complex morphology and on their understanding of various affixes. By fifth grade, children are expected to be able to read essentially complex words with and without the help of context.

QUESTIONS FOR DISCUSSION

1. Do you think the Common Core State Standards provide enough emphasis on the foundational skills underlying skilled word reading?

2. Age of acquisition has been shown to be an important factor in the skilled reading of words. What might be the potential relationship between age of acquisition and other factors underlying the skilled reading of words, such as morphological complexity, contextual priming, and lexical ambiguity?

3. How should teachers approach instructing children to learn to read morphologically complex words?

4. Returning to the case study presented at the beginning of this chapter, what strategies might Ms. Brown use to address Gabriel's literacy needs?

FURTHER READINGS

Balota, D. A., Yap, M. J., & Cortese, M. J. (2006). Visual word recognition: The journey from features to meaning (a travel update). In M. Traxler & M. A. Gernsbacher (Eds.), *Handbook of psycholinguistics* (2nd ed., pp. 285–375). London: Academic Press.

McNamara, T. P. (2005). *Semantic priming: Perspectives from memory and word recognition.* New York: Psychology Press.

Yap, M. J., Balota, D. A., Sibley, D. E., & Ratcliff, R. (2012). Individual differences in visual word recognition: Insights from the English Lexicon Project. *Journal of Experimental Psychology: Human Perception and Performance, 38*(1), 53–79.

CHAPTER 5

Reading Fluency

CASE STUDY

Mr. Davis, a fifth-grade teacher, is puzzled by the differences among his students in their ability to read aloud. There is Abigail, who reads in a way that one can almost imagine her as an adult hired for radio ad work. She reads with beautiful intonation that communicates meaning convincingly. Her voice rises and falls in pitch; she pauses meaningfully and reaches for emphases and style that make her messages easy to understand. She reads in a manner more advanced than you might expect for an average 11-year-old. In fact, she is the lead morning announcer in the school radio club. By contrast, her best friend Heather reads painfully slowly and hesitantly, seeming to drag the text behind her. Although she can eventually pronounce all the words correctly, her reading has a broken, flat quality with numerous unnatural pauses throughout. One sentence just blurs into the next. If there is a message that the text is conveying, it is difficult to determine what it is. It is unclear whether Heather knows what it is either. Mr. Davis is unsure of how to proceed instructionally because Heather can, in fact, read all the words put in front of her, eventually. But, he wonders, does it even matter? After all, Heather can read.

For teachers of elementary school children, teaching children to read fluently is an important instructional goal. Understanding what fluency is and the psychological processes engaged by fluency is necessary for the optimal development of effective instructional practices. In the previous two chapters, we have focused on the processes engaged in the reading of single words, for the most part. Reading fluency goes beyond the ability to read single words. In this chapter, we move our focus to the larger texts more typical of ordinary reading. We discuss (1) the processes engaged in the fluent reading of connected text and the major components of fluency, (2) how good fluency helps children comprehend better, (3) where fluency fits in the development of skilled reading, and (4) the best ways to encourage its development instructionally. Although we mostly focus on oral reading fluency, we also address the transition from oral reading fluency to fluent silent reading.

WHAT IS ORAL READING FLUENCY?

A child is considered fluent when he or she can read aloud well. To be quite honest, there is no true consensus among researchers as to which elements of the reading process should be included within the concept of fluency and which elements should be considered a component of another aspect of skilled reading. However, having a good definition is important because it allows us to target just the right skills using just the right instructional strategies if a child (or adult) is having difficulty with a particular aspect of reading. Figure 5.1 indicates some of the essential elements of reading fluency according to various definitions.

Some definitions that researchers have developed are very expansive in scope. Consider this definition by Wolf and Katzir-Cohen (2001 "Reading fluency involves every process and subskill involved in reading . . . unlike reading accuracy,

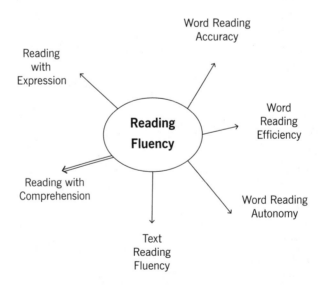

FIGURE 5.1. Essential skills underlying the development of fluent reading (solid arrow = generally agreed upon; hollow arrow = somewhat less agreed upon).

which can be executed without utilizing some important reading components like semantic processes, we argue that fluency is influenced by the development of rapid rates of processing in all the components of reading" (p. 220). To us, this definition seems a bit too expansive because it encompasses nearly all aspects of skilled reading. We do like the idea that it emphasizes rapid processing, which we think is a key piece.

Other researchers define fluency in a more circumscribed way, emphasizing only those processes involved in accurate and automatic word recognition (Hudson, Pullen, Lane, & Torgesen, 2009). In Figure 5.1, this definition is indicated by the arrows on the right-hand side of the figure leading from Reading Fluency → Word Reading Accuracy, Word Reading Efficiency, and Word Reading Autonomy. To us, this seems possibly too narrow—why not simply call fluent reading *skilled word reading*, as we have in the previous chapter? We think fluent reading is broader than that. Good word recognition skills are important, though. It is a key piece of reading fluency.

Another definition describes fluent reading as the ability to decode and comprehend text simultaneously (Samuels, 2006). This definition is indicated by the same arrows we noted above, leading from Reading Fluency → Word Reading Accuracy, Word Reading Efficiency, and Word Reading Autonomy. This definition is interesting because it connects good word reading with good comprehension. But have we gone too far this time? We feel that Paris (2005) makes some astute points that are relevant to thinking about the relationship between reading fluency and comprehension.

Paris (2005) points out that we should distinguish between constrained skills, somewhat constrained skills, and unconstrained skills. Letter knowledge, phonemic awareness, phonics, and concepts of print are constrained skills. Once children develop this knowledge, they have it and it really does not progress very much. We do not want to keep working on something instructionally that the vast majority of children have already learned. Oral reading fluency is somewhat less constrained. That is, children become fluent readers over a protracted period of time. However, the real changes in fluency that occur early in schooling and more or less level off by the time children approach middle school (as we can see very clearly in the fluency norms developed by Hasbrouck & Tindal, 2006). Comprehension, by contrast, is an unconstrained skill. Paris points out that good comprehension includes processes that develop considerably throughout a person's lifetime: vocabulary, background knowledge, reasoning skills—and would continue to accrue long after most of us would be considered fundamentally fluent as readers. Still, fluent readers usually comprehend what they read, so we need to consider how to represent this basic reality in our definition.

Other researchers eschew the emphasis on word recognition and automaticity in favor of processes involved in a good oral reading performance, called prosodic or expressive reading (Daane, Campbell, Grigg, Goodman, & Oranje, 2005; Rasinski, Rikli, & Johnston, 2009). This skill is indicated in Figure 5.1 by the arrow on the top left of this figure from Reading Fluency → Reading with Expression. But can one have a good oral reading performance without good word recognition skills? Listening to children read aloud, however, it becomes clear that a particular child might have reasonable word recognition skills and still not sound very fluent. Nonetheless, it feels true that when one listens to fluent readers read aloud, they usually do so with good expression. Expressive reading should be a key piece of reading fluency.

What is the right mix then? Kuhn at al. (2010) define reading fluency in this way:

> Fluency combines [*word reading*] accuracy, automaticity, and oral reading prosody, which, taken together, facilitate the reader's construction of meaning. It is demonstrated during oral reading through ease of word recognition, appropriate pacing, phrasing, and intonation. It is a factor in both oral and silent reading that can limit or support comprehension. (p. 242, emphasis added)

This definition is indicated in Figure 5.1 by arrows leading from Reading Fluency → Word Reading Accuracy, Word Reading Efficiency, Word Reading Autonomy, Text Reading Fluency, and Reading with Expression, and the double line between Reading Fluency ⇒ Reading with Comprehension. We feel this definition achieves the right balance between word recognition skills, on the one hand, while bringing in the idea of supporting good comprehension, on the other. It recognizes that good oral reading fluency is foundational to comprehension—frankly, it is hard to imagine having good comprehension if we consistently stumble over text. However, in this definition, fluency does not guarantee good comprehension; it merely supports it. This definition also brings our attention to the accurate, automatic, and good expressive reading of connected text that is characteristic of fluent reading. Thus it combines many of the elements of the other definitions.

Let's boil down this definition into its key components: accuracy, automaticity, and prosody. In the next few sections, we peel apart these concepts to see how they operate to produce fluent reading.

Fluency and Accuracy

In the reading context, the term *accuracy* refers to being able to read words correctly. This is a skill that children might accomplish after acquiring the basic decoding skills we described in Chapter 3. At the beginning of the process of acquiring reading fluency, children may still have a little progress to make yet in decoding skill, such as learning to read those tricky multisyllabic, multimorphemic words, as well as words with difficult or ambiguous meanings, as we described in Chapter 4. Children may still be learning how to carry out some of the more advanced aspects of decoding, while embarking on the journey of becoming fluent. For example, they might be able to read simple, controlled texts accurately and fluently. They might simultaneously be learning to decode the more advanced words characteristic of more difficult texts. They would likely stumble over texts having complex words and grammatically complex sentences. By the time we consider a child to be fully fluent, however, he or she should be able to pick up almost any nontechnical text and read it accurately.

Fluency and Automaticity

In the reading context, the term *automaticity* refers to the quick and effortless execution of processes involved in reading connected text. Automaticity and accuracy develop concurrently as young readers engage in practice. Speed and accuracy seem to be interlinked. Indeed, emphasizing reading accuracy in instruction seems to have the effect of increasing reading speed too, regardless of whether or not speed has been specifically targeted (Hudson, Isakson, Richman, Lane, & Arriaza-Allen, 2011). As the saying goes, practice makes perfect. It also makes the reading more automatic.

With regard to effortlessness, fluent readers cannot help but process print. Skilled readers find themselves reading text on the sides of passing busses, notes left carelessly around the house, and signs posting warnings such as BEWARE OF DOG without deliberately trying to do so. Researchers find that effortless automatic reading begins to occur once children develop meaningful decoding skills (Ehri, 1976; Schadler & Thissen, 1981; Schwanenflugel et al., 2008), as we noted Chapter 3. This aspect of automaticity helps readers orient their attention toward print.

Theoretically, the automatic processing of text is thought to free up cognitive resources for comprehension. While we are reading, we are using up some of our working memory resources for decoding texts, some for determining syntactic relations, and some for general comprehension of the message. Fluent readers have more resources to dedicate to processing the message of the text because they are no longer expending precious cognitive resources on decoding.

Automaticity is derived at many levels of the reading process: lexical, phrasal, and possibly even sentence levels (Logan, 1997). As we learned in Chapters 3 and 4, children begin to read by using smaller chunks such as simple letter–sound correspondences, but then move to larger units such as syllables and morphemes (Nunes et al., 2012), and eventually read whole words in some cases. This collapsing of steps in decoding is a feature of automaticity called *unitization*. Unfortunately, children who have trouble converting to the use of multiletter units for decoding tend to show poorer oral reading fluency growth later (Harn et al., 2008).

Often-repeated words and phrases can also benefit from increasing automaticity. In reading text aloud, young readers shift from reading using slow, arduous, word-by-word processing to smooth and natural readings. That is, at first, the reading sounds broken, effortful, and hesitant. The child reads primarily in groups of one or two words. Later, the reading proceeds effortlessly without these hesitations. This change probably reflects the automatized operation of lower-level transitional probability information as well as the use of general contextual constraints, as noted in Chapter 4. It may also reflect an ability to quickly derive the syntactic representation of the text, important for determining the roles of the words in the sentence (Klauda & Guthrie, 2008; Mokhtari & Thompson, 2006). This ability is important as children encounter texts with longer sentences and a greater variety of linguistic forms.

Increases in automaticity in reading a particular text accrue rather quickly with practice and eventually show diminishing returns; this process is reflective of the so-called *power law of learning* (Logan, 1997). Evidence for this power law can be seen in the cumulative effects of practice over the long term. For example, looking at the Hasbrouck and Tindal (2006) fluency norms for the end of the school year, children gain an average of 54 words correct per minute (WCPM) in terms of their reading rate between first and third grades. Between third and fifth grades they gain 32 WCPM, but between sixth and eighth grades, they gain only 1 WCPM. As noted earlier, by middle school, most children are fairly fluent.

We can also see the effects of the power law with short-term practice benefits as well. In Figure 5.2, we can see the rates from three second-grade children who read the same grade-level passage in their classroom once or twice a day over the course of a week. Some children, like Linda, do not have enough decoding skills

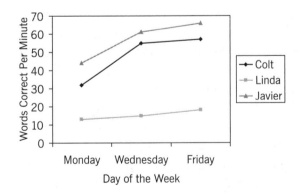

FIGURE 5.2. The progress of three children who practiced the same passage every day for a week.

to benefit from practice with such difficult text. They need basic decoding practice and are swamped by longer texts. However, for other children, like Colt and
Javier, the effects of the power law can be observed. Both children display slow
reading on a new passage at the beginning of the week, characteristic of children
of this age, which is followed by diminishing benefits from repeated practice after
midweek. Their pattern is typical of skill practice: The biggest benefits are accrued
early on, with diminishing returns thereafter.

Typically, in classroom assessment, the automaticity aspect of fluency is
measured by giving children an age-appropriate book or specially designed test
passage and then having them read it aloud for 1 minute. Teachers then calculate the WCPM for connected text reading. They tabulate the number of words
attempted up to the child's stopping point and then subtract errors such as misread
words, word omissions, word reversals, and line skipping. As you can see from this
description, this measure treats speed and accuracy in an intertwined way as an
indicator of reading fluency. WCPM is used to compare the fluency of one child
to another. Current assessments found in well-developed systems for measuring
reading progress, such as the Dynamic Indicators of Basic Early Literacy Skills
(DIBELS, specifically, DIBELS Oral Reading Fluency [DORF]; Good & Kaminski, 2010) and AIMSweb (specifically, the subscale Reading—Curriculum-Based
Measurement [R-CBM]; Shinn & Shinn, 2002; Deno, Fuchs, Martson, & Shin,
2001) all calculate WCPM as a measure of oral reading fluency. Automaticity is
the most frequently measured element of oral reading fluency. However, we think
that this really should be only part of the equation because it is missing any focus
on reading expression.

Fluency and Reading Prosody

Reading aloud with good expression (also called *reading prosody* or *reading intonation*) is an important marker of reading fluency (Kuhn et al., 2010). Reading
prosody refers to the elements of speech prosody that readers bring with them into
their oral reading. Prosody has been called the music of language (Pinheiro, Vasconcelos, Dias, Arrais, & Gonclaves, 2015). The term refers to the melodic, phrasing, and timing aspects of language that it shares with music. Indeed, prosody
may share some of the same functional neurological components of the brain—in
particular, activation of the left primary auditory cortex and the right prefrontal
cortex (Patel, Peretez, Tramo, & Labreque, 1998)—that are found to be active
when prosodic speech and melody are compared. Thus far, it appears that fluent
readers bring most elements of speech prosody with them to the reading situation.

Prosody in general has a number of psycholinguistic functions that may be
important in fluent oral reading. Prosody reflects natural informational breakpoints in speech, indicated by the occurrence of pauses or the lengthening of

syllables near the boundaries of these breakpoints, such as phrases or sentences. Prosody carves up text (or speech) in meaningful ways for syntactic phrasing (Ramus, Hauser, Miller, Morris, & Mehler, 2000).

Prosody may help to retain information in working memory so that semantic analysis can be carried out (Frazier, Carlson, & Clifton, 2006; Koriat, Greenberg, & Kreiner, 2002; Swets, Desmet, Hambrick, & Ferreira, 2007). It is possible that good reading prosody might assist comprehension by highlighting emotional interpretation and providing informational focus (Carlson, Dickey, Frazier, & Clifton, 2009; Juslin & Laukka, 2003). Prosody also carries discourse information regarding topic shifts, paragraph initiation, and conclusions (Noordman, Dassen, Swerts, & Terken, 1999; Smith, 2004; Wennerstrom, 2001). In fact, the development of reading prosody has been shown to be a unique predictor of comprehension processes in general, above and beyond accurate and automatic word reading skills (Miller & Schwanenflugel, 2006).

Reading prosody is determined by a number of speech characteristics, for example, variations in pitch (traditionally, fundamental frequency, F_0). It is also the stress and intensity or loudness (amplitude) that readers place on certain words and phrases, and it is composed of patterns of pausing that may interrupt or contribute to the rhythm and flow of the reading. These aspects of fluent reading can be observed on a *speech spectrogram*, which is a visual representation of various aspects of speech as it changes over time. Figures 5.3–5.5 present examples of a spectrogram taken from a fluent reader reading a grade-level passage. In the spectrograms we show here, the top part represents the voiced elements of speech over time, with the darkened bands formed by the energy created from spoken syllables

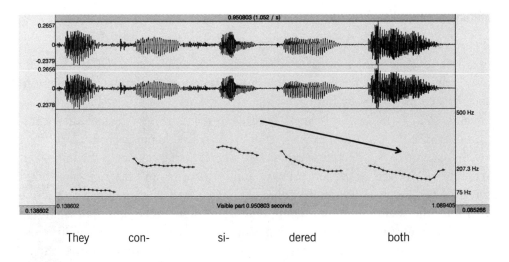

FIGURE 5.3. Example of a spectrographic pitch track from a fluent third grader reading a declarative sentence.

and words. In this case, the bottom line represents the pitch track indicated by fundamental frequency, which is used to illustrate the perceived intonation contour the child is reading aloud.

Fluent children show substantial pitch variability; that is, they do *not* read in a monotonous manner (Benjamin et al., 2013). Fluent readers show more noticeable falling pitch at the ends of declarative sentences than less fluent readers. Declarative sentences are simple statements. *They considered both* is an example of a declarative sentence. Fluent readers using American English might be expected to make a noticeable drop in pitch between *-dered* and *both* here, as the fluent third-grade reader shown in Figure 5.3 does. A less fluent reader might also make a pitch drop at the end of the sentence, but it would not be nearly as marked, appearing relatively flat.

Fluent readers also tend to show distinct pitch rises as they read yes–no questions (Miller & Schwanenflugel, 2006). Yes–no questions are those that can be answered by a simple yes or no. *Would you like to see my garden?* is an example of a yes–no question. A fluent reader reading this sentence might be expected to make a pitch rise between *my gar-* and *-den*, as the child in Figure 5.4 does, or throughout the course of the sentence. A less fluent reader would read this sentence in a rather flat, monotone way that might not sound like a question at all.

When fluent children pause during their oral reading, they do so at grammatically relevant junctures within a sentence (Benjamin & Schwanenflugel, 2010). Less fluent children make many pauses, which give their reading a very hesitant, stop–start quality. Many of these pauses seem to relate to decoding problems, as children generally pause or hesitate in some way before, within, or after a word

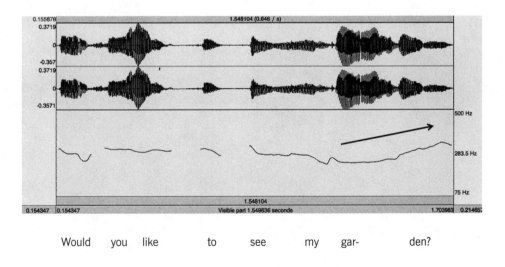

Would   you   like   to   see   my   gar-   den?

FIGURE 5.4. Example of a spectrographic pitch track from a fluent third grader reading yes–no question.

they are having difficulty decoding (Herman, 1985; Miller & Schwanenflugel, 2008). The flat lines within the top part of the spectrogram indicate pauses.

Fluent readers also assign appropriate stress patterns to syllables within words (Gutierrez-Palma & Palma-Reyes, 2007) and to particular words within sentences. While reading, the reader should give some words or phrases emphasis to focus attention on particular ideas in the passage, a feature called *linguistic focus*. Consider these two sentences: *John held up two flowers, a blue one and a yellow one. He held out one and said, "Here, take <u>this one</u>."* In this case, *this one* should receive some sort of prosodic marking such as heightened pitch or amplitude. The fluent reader pictured in Figure 5.5 displays this type of linguistic focus marking in the pitch track. There is a heightened pitch and emphasis on the word *this* and then a steep pitch decline as the child reads the word *one*. Schwanenflugel, Westmoreland, and Benjamin (2013) found that fluent third-grade children showed more pronounced marking of linguistically focused text elements through increased pitch and amplitude.

As children develop accurate and automatic word reading skills, their reading begins to incorporate many of the prosodic features we find in spontaneous speech (Miller & Schwanenflugel, 2008). Their reading prosody becomes increasingly similar to community adults reading the same passage (Schwanenflugel, Hamilton, Kuhn, Wisenbaker, & Stahl, 2004). Pitch patterns become generally less flat and more variable overall. Pause patterns become more consistent with the structure of the text. Disfluent reading, by contrast, is often monotonous and hesitant, failing to encode the communicative intent of the author.

The prosody aspect of reading fluency has been incorporated into classroom assessment through the use of rating scales, rather than the spectrographic analysis

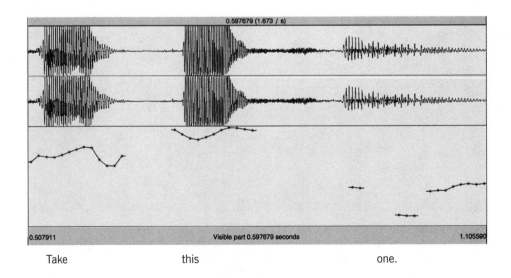

FIGURE 5.5. Example of a fluent third grader marking linguistic focus through pitch changes.

shown here. There are a number of reading fluency scales that have been created for this purpose that validly distinguish between fluent and less fluent readers. Importantly, it does not particularly matter whether the teacher emphasizes that the child should read with good expression or simply quickly—the ratings are very similar (Taylor, Meisinger, & Floyd, 2013). Basically, if children can read fluently, they will read quickly, accurately, and with good expression.

Ratings scales that measure reading expression vary in the number of reading dimensions that are rated, ranging from one (National Assessment of Educational Progress [NAEP] Oral Reading Fluency Scale; Daane et al., 2005) or two (Comprehensive Oral Reading Fluency Scale [CORFS]; i.e., Appropriate Intonation and Natural Pausing—Benjamin et al., 2013) to four elements (Multidimensional Fluency Scale [i.e., Expression and Volume, Phrasing, Smoothness, and Pace]; Paige, Rasinski, & Magpuri-Lavell, 2012). The NAEP and Multidimensional Fluency Scale are designed as stand-alone measures of fluency. The CORFS is used in conjunction with a measurement of WCPM to produce an overall reading fluency score. In that respect the CORFS is consistent with our general definition of reading fluency that we accepted above. As you can see in the next sections, the end points of the subscales included in the CORFS incorporate much of what we have described above as characteristic of fluent and disfluent reading.

CORFS

In this material we use a partial scale from Benjamin et al. (2013, p. 131).

INTONATION SUBSCALE

• 4 Rating (i.e., fluent): Makes noticeable pitch variations throughout to communicate meaning; makes appropriate and consistent end-of-sentence pitch changes. One or two exceptions may exist.

• 1 Rating (i.e., disfluent): Reads with flat or unnatural intonation throughout; does not make sentence boundaries with distinct pitch changes except occasionally.

NATURAL PAUSING SUBSCALE

• 4 Rating (i.e., fluent): Pauses may be used to convey meaning; between-sentence pauses are short, but natural. Unexpected pauses occur less than once per sentence on average.

• 1 Rating (i.e., disfluent): Reading is broken and effortful with numerous pauses throughout. Reads primarily in groups of one or two words without pausing.

Poor oral reading prosody can remain a problem for struggling readers from childhood through adulthood (Binder et al., 2013; Paige et al., 2012). In assessment, it is important to determine which component of reading fluency a particular student is having difficulty with (i.e., automaticity or expression), so that instructional efforts can be focused effectively.

THE RELATIONSHIP BETWEEN FLUENCY AND COMPREHENSION

As noted earlier, a key aspect of reading fluency is the support it provides for reading comprehension. There are strong correlations between reading fluency and comprehension. Children who have good fluency also tend to have good comprehension, whereas children who have poor fluency also tend to have difficulty building an understanding of what they are reading. During the period when children are developing fluency, correlations between fluency and comprehension are usually between .50 and .85; the correlations are toward the higher end of this range when measures of both WCPM and reading prosody are included (Benjamin et al., 2013; Deno, Fuchs, Marston, & Shin, 2001; Reschly, Busch, Betts, Deno, & Long, 2009). Students' growth rates in oral reading fluency help predict later comprehension skills (Kim, Petscher, Schatschneider, & Foorman, 2010). This finding is important because children who read with acceptable reading rates but poor expression tend to comprehend less well.

As most children become fundamentally more fluent, this correlation may weaken by the end of elementary school as the reading texts become heavier in terms of comprehension demands (Denton et al., 2011; Silberglitt, Burns, Madyun, & Lail, 2006). Despite this weakening correlation, disfluency remains a barrier to comprehension for a subset of adolescent struggling readers (Brasseur-Hock, Hock, Kieffer, Biancarosa, & Deshler, 2011; Rasinski et al., 2009).

Word Callers and Comprehension

The *word caller* concept is often used for children who show good reading fluency but comparatively poor comprehension. A word caller might be someone who reads aloud reasonably well, but when asked to summarize or answer questions about the passage just read, he or she cannot. The idea here is that children might be able to read quickly, accurately, and expressively and still might not be able to understand very much from the texts they are reading. Teachers as a group seem to believe this is a widespread problem—in one study, teachers nominated nearly a quarter of their students as word callers (Meisinger, Bradley, Schwanenflugel, & Kuhn, 2010). However, if fluency is foundational to comprehension, how can there be so many word callers?

The actual prevalence of word callers is probably much smaller than the number of readers that teachers nominated in the Mesinger et al. (2010) study. A true word caller should have average fluency at least, but substantially below-average reading comprehension skills. Meisinger, Bradley, Schwanenflugel, and Kuhn (2009) and Hamilton and Shinn (2003) found that only a tiny proportion of early elementary school children, if any, fit this pattern.

There are a few instances in which true word callers are common. Quirk and Beem (2012) were able to identify many true word callers among English learners. That these children may often be word callers makes sense if part of the issue in comprehension is vocabulary and cultural knowledge rather than fluency per se. English learners may simply not have the vocabulary and cultural knowledge needed for the texts that they are asked to read every day in school. Further, Meisinger et al. (2010) did find that the number of true word callers increased to nearly 10% among older elementary school children. Whether the number of word callers continues to increase through middle school, we cannot say. But that it might increase makes sense as other factors such as topic knowledge, vocabulary, and inference abilities become more important when reading the complex texts required in school and elsewhere for older children and adolescents.

Directionality of the Influence between Fluency and Comprehension

We have described reading fluency as a foundational skill for comprehension. What does this statement mean exactly? It means that the role of fluency in comprehension is to support comprehension as a bottom-up, data-driven process. That is, by allowing readers to decode quickly, accurately, and automatically, and allowing them to carve up the text in meaningful ways with good prosody, good fluency sets the stage for good comprehension to occur. That fluency operates in that role is shown by the usefulness of oral reading fluency assessment for predicting children's performance on state assessments of reading (Deno et al., 2001). This finding has led to a variety of quick benchmarking systems based around oral reading fluency that serve an indicator for teachers as to which of their students may need special assistance to be able to pass state assessments given at the end of year. Thus, fluency is kind of a thermometer as to the general health of reading comprehension skills. This might be expected if fluency serves as a bottom-up, data-driven process.

The relationship between reading fluency may not be as unidirectional as the preceding depiction indicates, however. Some (Klauda & Guthrie, 2008; Priebe, Keenan, & Miller, 2012) have argued that the relationship between fluency and comprehension is bidirectional—both top-down and bottom-up. That is, expectations driven by a reader's knowledge base may provide assistance in reading above and beyond bottom-up processes of fluent reading.

If we think back to what we learned in the previous chapter about the role of context, we can see how these top-down processes might work to create a reciprocal effect. Context might benefit the recognition of upcoming words through the development of expectancies from the contextual constraints provided by discourse. Word recognition might also be benefited by the reader's knowledge of sequential transitional probabilities. That is, knowing which words are likely to follow one another in a sentence can help us anticipate and quickly identify upcoming words. There are also, of course, the general word priming operations of the lexicon. Thus, having good comprehension of ongoing text might affect the speed, accuracy, and prosody involved in reading text as well.

Evidence for reciprocal effects of comprehension on reading fluency per se has been difficult to establish, however. Probably the best way to determine whether these reciprocal effects exist is to use a longitudinal design. In these designs, researchers assess children's reading fluency and comprehension skills over several time points to determine whether changes in one skill lead to changes in the other skill later on. For example, if some children's comprehension skills at a particular point in time are exceptionally good, then we should see a boost in fluency at the next time point when the fluency skills of the previous time point are controlled for. Similarly, if children's fluency skills at a particular time are good, then we should see enhanced comprehension at the subsequent time point when the previous time point's comprehension skills are controlled for. Klauda and Guthrie (2008) found a small degree of reciprocity between fluency and comprehension skills among fifth-grade children over the course of a school year, whereas Lai, Benjamin, Schwanenflugel, and Kuhn (2014) failed to find evidence of this reciprocity in second graders. Unfortunately, current research does not allow us to draw a firm conclusion regarding the reciprocity of these skills using these longitudinal designs.

Priebe et al. (2012) tackled this issue in a more fruitful way by starting with the premise that, if comprehension skills were to enhance assessed fluency, they would do so primarily on passages for which children had considerable topic knowledge. Children with good topic knowledge would be familiar with vocabulary, which might help with the decoding of difficult words. They would have more knowledge of the organization of ideas, words, and transitional probabilities in that segment of the lexicon, potentially allowing them to benefit from priming operations that would, in turn, allow them to read words faster. They could derive more detailed expectancies from context. All of these processes might help children read more fluently.

To test this hypothesis, Priebe et al. (2012) selected children who had similar general fluency, reading comprehension, and vocabulary skills, but who varied on passage topic knowledge. They then asked the children to read passages for which they did or did not have topic knowledge. There might be some children, for instance, who have unusual expertise in dinosaurs, whom we could observe reading a dinosaur passage aloud. We could then compare these children reading the dinosaur passage against, say, children who have unusual expertise regarding snakes. Priebe et al. found that having topic knowledge significantly increased fluency (and improved comprehension), but only for children who had generally poor decoding skills. The view is that these children used their knowledge about the topic to compensate for their poor decoding skills, possibly by allowing substantial correct guesses. Using ongoing comprehension to benefit fluency, then, may be relegated to poor readers having special knowledge.

FLUENCY IN DEVELOPMENTAL CONTEXT

Quite possibly the best articulated view of the development of reading is Chall's (1996) stage model of reading, as we described in the Chapter 1 overview, which, to some extent, inspired the organization of this book. In this model, fluency appears as a major development in a third stage of reading development. By this point, children have gained familiarity with emergent literacy skills (Chall's Stage 0), as we described in Chapter 2. They have learned how to link phonemes to basic letter patterns and blend them to decode basic words (Chall's Stage 1), as described in Chapter 3. It is only after children gain some skill with these that they begin to develop fluency (Chall's Stage 2).

Chall's observation was that once children can read most texts with some fluency, they can now begin to use their newly freed up cognitive resources to learn from those texts. Their reading is no longer muddied by the basic retrieval of processes related to the task of discerning the words within the text. This earlier learning has now been consolidated, and we might argue, automatized. Chall described this distinction between the first three stages and later ones as the transition between "learning to read" and having "reading as a tool for learning, as texts begin to contain new words and ideas beyond their own language and their knowledge of the world" (Chall & Jacobs, 2003, p. 15). Put more simply, it is the distinction between *learning to read* and *reading to learn*.

This distinction between learning to read and reading to learn has been critiqued by opponents of this developmental view as a depiction of a hard and fast distinction between developmental periods. The distinction has been critiqued on three grounds. One possibility is that the Chall viewed the structure of reading skills themselves as changing as children get older, following the acquisition of fluent reading. A second possibility is that Chall was recommending that teachers forgo comprehension emphasis in the instruction of early reading until children are fluent readers. Proponents of the developmental description presented by Chall insist that she meant neither of these things. Unfortunately, she died in

1999, so we can only discern her views from her writings, but both critiques are worth considering here.

Is there really any evidence that the structure of reading skills changes noticeably between the advent of fluency and later reading progress? Are there really late-emerging reading processes that cause some children to suddenly develop reading problems where none were evident before? In fact, Chall and Jacobs (2003) did allude to this possibility when they described a "fourth-grade slump" in reading skills. To address this issue, researchers have looked for changes in the patterns of influences on the reading skills in younger versus older children. For example, Harlaar, Dale, and Plomin (2007) studied genetic contributions to reading in younger versus older children. Genetic influences explain, at least to some degree, why children differ in their reading abilities. These types of influences are determined by comparing twins to other siblings. If there is a shift in the structure of reading as children get older, we might expect there to be greater genetic influence in one phase over another. However, these researchers found substantial genetic stability in reading skills instead. This stability would argue that the structure of reading does not really change developmentally.

Further, there is a small group of children who do display *late-emerging reading disability*. These are children who seem to be doing fine in the acquisition of reading skills but who suddenly seem to hit a wall, psychometrically speaking, at about fourth grade. The existence of such children might also suggest a developmentally related change in the structure of reading skills. Compton, Fuchs, Fuchs, Elleman, and Gilbert (2008) tracked the reading skills of a large group of children over several grades and found about 3% of them qualified as having this kind of late-emerging reading disability. However, when they examined the skills of these fourth graders more closely, they learned that the students' reading problems did not suddenly emerge at fourth grade. Such children had listening comprehension problems and slower fluency growth that had emerged as early as first grade. Again, listening comprehension and fluency are not literacy skills new to fourth grade, although they may gain in importance around that time.

Others place the source of the fourth-grade slump on the texts children now have to read (Best, Floyd, & McNamara, 2004). As children get older, the texts get more difficult and become more informational than narrative. Because the amount of complex informational text children read increases at around fourth grade, comprehension issues become more evident, and some children struggle. So, does the structure of reading skills change at fourth grade? No, but the comprehension demands probably do.

A second concern regarding the Chall developmental theory — the possibility that she advocated that teachers forgo comprehension instruction in the early grades until children are fluent readers (Houck & Ross, 2012)—seems doubtful to us. Instead, she was probably advocating that teachers let go of their instructional emphasis on decoding as children become fluent in favor of comprehension instead. If this latter point is true, then we should find that shifts in instructional focus away from decoding would be advantageous for the development of reading skills. Indeed, some recent research by Sonnenschein, Stapleton, and Benson (2010), examining the effects of instructional focus on the development of reading skills, suggests that persisting in an instructional focus on decoding skills long after most children have acquired them may be detrimental to good reading skill progress. Further, fluency instruction does not have to be mutually exclusive of an emphasis on comprehension. Stahl (2007) describes how both can ensue while maintaining an effective classroom focus on fluency.

A third critique of the Chall developmental theory is probably more on target. Chall suggested that, in the early phases of learning to read, instruction should emphasize texts with familiar settings and concepts. Certainly, the Common Core State Standards, with its emphasis on informational text, introduces children early to the idea that reading can serve as a means to learn new things. If the Chall view regarding the focus on familiarity and easy text is correct, we may find that children fail massively to make good reading progress. At a basic level, some findings suggest that fourth graders can read informational text as fluently as narratives without negative impact on comprehension (Hiebert, 2005; Cervetti, Bravo, Hiebert, Pearson, & Jaynes, 2009). There is little evidence that using instructional texts containing unfamiliar materials for fluency practice is particularly problematic for building fluency. Indeed, some effective programs for targeting reading fluency in the elementary years, such as the Quick Reads (Hiebert, 2002) program, are built around informational texts.

TRANSITION TO SILENT READING

When we talk about reading fluency, the emphasis is usually on *oral* reading fluency, as we noted at the outset. To a large extent, oral reading is a transitional phase on the way to silent reading fluency. Indeed, it has been our observation that, once children are truly fluent readers, their interest in reading aloud declines and they prefer silent reading. However, as we describe in this section, there is something important about having a phase dedicated to oral reading fluency.

The potential importance of having a phase dedicated to oral reading emerges as a by-product of a surprising finding regarding silent reading reported by the National Reading Panel (National Institute of Child Health and Human Development, 2000). As part of its examination of classroom practices related to reading fluency, this panel reviewed existing experimental studies examining the common practice of including sustained silent reading in elementary school children's ultimate reading skills. *Sustained silent reading* refers to the practice of providing

10–20 minutes of self-chosen recreational reading time to be carried out during the school hours. The designated purpose of sustained silent reading is to improve, among other things, fluency, vocabulary, and reading comprehension skills. It is hoped that these hours spent reading during school time will encourage children to read afterward and come to appreciate the value of reading for a lifetime. However, the National Reading Panel Report concluded, "The NRP did not find evidence supporting the effectiveness of encouraging independent silent reading as a means of improving reading achievement" (pp. 3–4).

This conclusion has been sustained by more recent evaluation of the practice, which found that children often act as though they are reading during sustained silent reading, when they are not (Hiebert & Reutzel, 2010). That is, children may have their eyes on text, as the teacher requires, but they are actually just daydreaming. Some children will be completely off-task during this time, distracting others (Bryan, Fawson, & Reutzel, 2003). Further, the self-selected book aspect of sustained silent reading assumes that most children can read books independently. This assumption is probably not true before second grade or so, in general, at least for books children might actually *want* to read on their own. Often, if left to their own devices to choose books, children will select books that are too difficult to read by themselves (Donovan, Smolkin, & Lomax, 2000).

As with any practice that is beloved by many educators, the conclusion that sustained silent reading is ineffective did not go down without a fight. Proponents continued to advocate sustained silent reading time during the school day as an important part of classroom practice (Krashen, 2005; Garan & DeVoogd, 2008). For example, in a harsh critique of the panel report, Garan and DeVoogd (2008) pointed out that the panel did not find sustained silent reading to be ineffective, but, rather, that it was no better than control practices. They argued that the evidence reviewed by the panel was flawed, even by its own experimental standards, and that it relied on a small number of flawed studies in its analysis. They decried the fact that the standards imposed by the report excluded the findings of "literally hundreds of correlational studies that find that the best readers read the most and poor readers read the least" (National Reading Panel Report; National Institute of Child Health and Human Development, 2000, Chapter 3, p. 21). Stahl (2004) pointed out that the panel also ignored studies showing that increasing the amount of reading materials for children can "dramatically increase reading achievement" (p. 206). Given this state of affairs, what other kinds of evidence do we have about the relative effectiveness of oral versus silent reading?

Research suggests that there may be a particular role for oral, as compared to silent, reading for younger, and perhaps less skilled, readers. It turns out that low-skilled and beginning readers understand what they are reading better in the oral than the silent mode (Holmes & Allison, 1985; Miller & Smith, 1985). That is, children who are asked to read something aloud are more likely to be able to answer questions about what they are reading than the same children when asked to read something similar silently.

The oral reading advantage may be fundamental during the early phases in the development of reading skills. Prior et al. (2011) showed that oral reading comprehension was superior in first through fifth graders, but silent reading was superior by seventh grade. Eventually, silent reading fluency becomes uniquely and statistically related to comprehension, above and beyond the effects of oral reading fluency, as children's reading skills develop (Kim, Wagner, & Lopez, 2011). This finding means that eventually silent reading is a better predictor of good comprehension once children have gained good oral reading fluency. In fact, being able to take advantage of silent reading practice seems to require good oral reading fluency. In a longitudinal study of early elementary school children, Kim et al. (2011) found that children who become fluent readers earlier make the transition to good comprehension during silent reading sooner.

So, theoretically, what is it about oral reading that makes it more advantageous for young readers? One theory by Prior and Welling (2001) is that oral reading may support the internalization of the cognitive processes surrounding reading that have their origins in the interpersonal relationships children have around books with parents and other adults. Figure 5.6 shows how this may work. Prior to school entry, parents and other adults may read aloud to children, and the social interactions surrounding reading take precedence. It is on their parents' laps reading books that children learn some of the basics about the general features of books and the alphabet, and they learn about the entertainment and/or informational value of books. Indeed, Bus and van IJzendoorn (1995) have shown that children who have positive interactions around books with their caregivers tend to become skilled readers years later. Eventually, children begin the process of reading aloud themselves, usually to a supportive adult, who provides assistance when some knowledge gap needs to be filled. That is, the child is still highly dependent on the adult for good reading to occur. Once children achieve sufficient ability to read on their own, they attempt to read aloud alone. This reading aloud may serve

Adult reads aloud to child.   Child reads aloud to adult.   Child reads aloud alone.   Child reads quietly alone.

FIGURE 5.6. The Vygotskian framework for the transition between oral and silent reading (Schwanenflugel & Ruston, 2007, p. 11).

as a transition phase between the social dependence of reading to an internalization of reading processes. Then, finally, children are able to read silently. The social origins of reading have gone underground.

Another theory is that oral reading may boost the phonological memory code (i.e., the little voice in our heads) involved in reading. As we indicated in Chapter 3, the phonological code is necessary for carrying out basic decoding (e.g., allowing for the maintenance of sounds to permit blending) and for capturing the meaning of the message (Gathercole & Baddeley, 1993). The oral reading allows the young reader to maintain the slow unfolding of the text's message until it can be understood. This boost in the code may be needed particularly when the text is difficult. Even adults seem to switch to the oral reading mode when processing is very difficult (Hardyck & Petrinovich, 1970). Further, oral reading may help children read by enhancing their own attentional focus on the text (Prior et al., 2011).

Regardless of which of these views is correct (and, perhaps, they may both be correct at some level), they both propose that oral reading is a fundamental transitional phase for learning to read well. Going back to the topic of sustained silent reading that we introduced at the outset of this section, current research is focused more on how to carry out sustained silent reading more optimally. For example, Kragler (1995) suggests a technique called *mumble reading* that allows children to utilize some of the elements of oral reading during silent reading time: Students mumble the text softly to themselves during "silent" reading. Teachers can use technological solutions to some of the problems of sustained silent reading, such as providing audio-recorded stories that children can follow in the text or, if tablets are available, provide those that are equipped to deliver technological assistance if children are having difficulty reading a particular word. More recently, programs that monitor children's eye movements and comprehension while providing daily silent reading practice have been found to be successful in improving children's reading (Reutzel, Spichtig, & Petscher, 2012). Whether these latter programs follow the spirit of sustained silent reading, we cannot say, but they do seem to assist in the transition to silent reading fluency.

BILINGUALISM AND READING FLUENCY

We have discussed how reading fluency is an important indicator of the general state of reading skills among young readers. However, does reading fluency play a similar role among children whose dominant language is not English? Other linguistic skills surely have a role to play. We focus here on what we know about the development of reading fluency in English language learners (ELLs) living in the United States.

As noted earlier, one reason that reading fluency has been emphasized in both assessment and instruction is its strong correlation with reading comprehension. As with native speakers, there is a good, although weaker, correlation between reading fluency and reading comprehension in ELL children (.40–.60 for ELLs, compared to .50–.85 for non-ELLs; Crosson & Lesaux, 2010; Quirk & Beem, 2012). Thus, disfluent readers who are bilingual tend to comprehend what they read less well than fluent bilingual readers. The impact of oral reading fluency on reading comprehension is reasonably moderated by English oral language competencies such as vocabulary and listening comprehension (Crosson & Lesaux, 2010). That is, bilingual children who have good English vocabulary and listening comprehension tend to read more fluently and understand what they are reading than bilingual children who do not. As noted earlier, Quirk and Beem (2012) noted a distinct gap between ELL children's normative reading fluency and their comprehension skills. They identified as many as 55.5% of second- and third-grade ELLs as word callers. These were children whose normative fluency is greater than .67 *SD*s above their reading comprehension scores. In other words, these are children who seem to be able to read fluently, despite their relative lack of understanding of the language. This lack of understanding contributes to their lack of comprehension while reading. These findings support the view that oral language is an important foundation that allows fluency to serve as the bridge to comprehension.

Identifying which ELL students need special education services can be particularly problematic, and such children often get overlooked because of their language background. Oral reading fluency assessment can be an important component when determining whether a particular child needs such services. Al Otaiba et al. (2009) found that both ELL children who never qualified for English language services and those who graduated from English as a second language (ESL) programs tended to read below grade level. Further, both groups showed slower growth in fluency when compared to national norms. Linan-Thompson, Cirino, and Vaughn (2007) suggest that this discrepancy between ELLs and the normative growth rate may be particularly useful in specifying which ELLs will and will not need special education services later. Bilingual children with small growth rates will be likely to need special reading instruction later. Therefore, just as with native English-speaking children, lack of growth in reading fluency in bilingual children indicates a likely basic problem in learning to read.

IMPLICATIONS FOR INSTRUCTION

Classroom instruction that focuses on the development of reading fluency is important because of the impact that fluency has on reading comprehension, as noted earlier. Importantly, because fluency is only one element of skilled reading, teachers need to find the most efficient way to carry out fluency instruction, and, as such, it is often combined with emphasis on other aspects of reading as well, such as decoding skill building or comprehension instruction.

Most fluency instruction adheres to the idea that reading practice will generate fluent reading and an automaticity of skills. A review carried out by Kuhn and Stahl (2003) found that repeated reading practice was an instructional component of the majority of effective interventions designed to assist children in developing fluency. In repeated reading, children are given a particular text to practice reading aloud; they may end up reading the same text anywhere from 3 to 15 times in a single week, given the length of books with which young children are usually provided. For example, Stahl and Heubach (2005) developed fluency-oriented reading instruction in which children read the same text every single day several times and at home for a week. Then they would move on to another text the following week. The repeated reading practice would be carried out beginning with the teacher reading a grade-level text aloud and children following along silently in their books. The next day, teachers might carry out an echo reading of the text; that is, teachers would read a few sentences aloud and then the child would echo these segments back, until the text was completed. The next day, the teacher and the children would carry out a choral reading of the text, reading the text aloud together. The following day the children might engage in partner reading: Two children take turns reading pages of the text; one child might help with the remaining decoding difficulties of the other. The last day of the week, teachers would carry out some activity involving the book that would require children to refer back to it. Each night of the week, the children were asked to read the passage aloud to a family member at home. As you can see, this approach involves many repeated readings of the book. The view behind repeated reading practice is that it leads to the development of automaticity for the practiced texts.

One issue with repeated reading is whether the automaticity that children might accrue from reading the same text over and over again generalizes over the long haul to new passages. To be sure, one might expect that most children would gain facility with a particular text (as the example in Figure 5.2 shows), but that is not particularly interesting. The real issue is whether that improvement carries over to texts on which children have not practiced. This potential issue has led to the development of a wide reading approach to fluency practice. This approach also involves substantial practice in reading text aloud, but teachers increase the number of texts that children read (Kuhn, 2005). For example, in the Kuhn et al. (2006) study, the wide reading approach utilized the same basic practices of Stahl and Heubach's (2005) repeated reading approach, but children read three passages in a week rather than the same one over and over again. Children might complete perhaps one to four readings of a given passage rather than the 10 or so of simple repeated reading approaches. However, with wide reading approaches, children will have the benefit of being exposed to more and different texts over the school year.

Several studies comparing repeated and wide reading approaches carried out by Kuhn and her colleagues (Kuhn, 2005; Kuhn et al., 2006; Schwanenflugel et al., 2009) have found a slight advantage for wide reading over repeated readings on fluency development. There was also a slight advantage for reading comprehension and reading motivation developed from wide reading practice (Schwanenflugel et al., 2009). These findings make sense given the broader vocabulary and ideas to which children have been exposed with the wide reading approach.

Regardless of how it is carried out, the most important aspect of fluency practice is, in fact, practice. Practice is particularly important during children's skill building in the elementary school years (and perhaps even after; Chard, 2011). Many classrooms do not place nearly enough emphasis on eyes on text, let alone oral reading practice. Donahue, Finnegan, Lutkus, Allen, and Campbell (2001) documented that, on average, fourth-grade children read about 10 pages of text during the school day (approximately 8–12 minutes of reading). More recent figures from high-poverty schools participating in comprehensive schoolwide literacy intervention indicated that children still spent only 18 minutes out of a 90- to 120-minute literacy block with their eyes on text (Brenner, Hiebert, & Thomkins, 2009). To a great extent, the limited amount of time that teachers spend on actual reading during their literacy period is the problem that sustained silent reading time in schools is designed to address.

Even outside of school, the differences between skilled and less skilled readers might be traced back to practice. Anderson, Wilson, and Fielding (1988) found that time spent on outside book reading was the best predictor of a student's reading proficiency. They found that a mere 12 minutes of outside reading per day distinguished readers in the top quartile from those at the bottom (although the very best readers read a great deal more than that). Clearly, gaining more reading practice is something that all schools aim to achieve.

CONNECTING TO THE STANDARDS

Given the importance of reading fluency, as we have indicated in this chapter, it is not a surprise that reading fluency has been recognized for its foundational role in literacy and incorporated as a curricular goal for schools. As you can see from Table 5.1, the Common Core State Standards include several standards surrounding fluency. These have been highly influenced by the definition of reading fluency we have ascribed to above as well as the research literature on the psychology of reading fluency. As you can see, they recognize the role of reading accuracy, rate and expression. They recognize the foundational role of reading fluency for comprehension.

TABLE 5.1. Common Core State Standards Related to Reading Fluency

Fluency (general standard):
Read with sufficient accuracy and fluency to support comprehension.

Grade	Specific standard
1–2	• Read grade-level text with purpose and understanding. • Read grade-level text orally with accuracy, appropriate rate, and expression on successive readings. • Use context to confirm or self-correct word recognition and understanding, rereading as necessary.
3–5	• Read grade-level text with purpose and understanding. • Read grade-level prose and poetry orally with accuracy, appropriate rate, and expression on successive readings. • Use context to confirm or self-correct word recognition and understanding, rereading as necessary.

Note. Adapted from the National Governors Association Center for Best Practices and the Council of Chief State School Officers (2010). All rights reserved.

QUESTIONS FOR DISCUSSION

1. Given what you have learned about oral reading fluency, what definition of oral reading fluency makes the most sense to you? Why?

2. Benchmark assessments of oral reading have been critiqued as being unhelpful for providing information about children's reading skills in a manner that is useful to teachers. Is this critique fair, given what you know about the development of oral reading fluency? Should assessment of oral reading prosody become part of standard assessment of reading skills?

3. Do you think that reading prosody is an indicator of comprehension or a contributor to it?

4. Do you think that the fourth-grade slump is real or merely an artifact of the way that we teach children to read currently?

5. What do you think about the use of sustained silent reading practices in first- through third-grade classrooms? Keep or discard?

6. Consider the case study at the beginning of this chapter. What do we know about the development of reading fluency that will help us derive fundamental instructional practices to promote fluency in young readers?

FURTHER READINGS

Kuhn, M. R., Schwanenflugel, P. J., & Meisinger, E. B. (2010). Aligning theory and assessment of reading fluency: Automaticity, prosody, and definitions of fluency. *Reading Research Quarterly, 45*(2), 232–253.

Reschly, A. L., Busch, T. W., Betts, J., Deno, S. L., & Long, J. D. (2009). Curriculum-based measurement of oral reading as an indicator of reading achievement: A meta-analysis of the correlational evidence. *Journal of School Psychology, 47,* 427–469.

CHAPTER 6

Vocabulary

CASE STUDY

Ms. Carter has a sweet, quiet little guy, Raymond, in her prekindergarten class. She has noticed that Ray is often hard to understand. He will tend to use the most basic of terms to describe things, talking in short, sometimes meaningless, sentences. For example, the other day, she wrote some of these down: "I hold it." "I would for my [unintelligible]." "[Unintelligible] want our hanging." "I want sit right here." "We play race." He sometimes misuses common words. For example, he said, "I want bigger." Sometimes Ray ends up grabbing for things he wants or exhorts "Excuse me!" over and over again.

Like Ray, his parents also have a calm, quiet demeanor. During their parent–teacher conference, they did not say much but listened attentively. It is clear that they take excellent care of Raymond, though, and it is commendable that they both showed up for his conference.

During circle time, Ray seems unable to understand the books that Ms. Carter reads to him, and he is able to answer only the most basic questions. Ms. Carter is concerned about Raymond's language skills, given the demands of the kindergarten literacy curriculum next year.

According to the National Reading Panel, the term *vocabulary* "refers to the words we must know to communicate effectively. In general, vocabulary can be described as oral vocabulary or reading vocabulary. *Oral vocabulary* refers to words that we use in speaking or recognize in listening. *Reading vocabulary* refers to words we recognize or use in print" (National Institute of Child Health and Human

Development 2000, p. 34, emphasis added). Note that this definition makes the fundamental distinction between oral and reading vocabulary. Early in the process of learning to read, this distinction may be important. Children can recognize many words that they may not be able to read. Ultimately, words that are present in our oral vocabulary should also be ones that we are able to read. However, most of us as adults encounter many more words in print than we typically hear in everyday life, so we may also come to recognize new words while reading that we cannot quite pronounce. Throughout this chapter, we assume that having a large vocabulary is a good thing in general.

We have already discussed the importance of vocabulary for reading. In Chapter 2, we discussed how vocabulary represents one of the major outside-in emergent skills described by Whitehurst and Lonigan (2001) that young children bring to the task of learning to read. In Chapter 3, development of vocabulary was described as assisting in the restructuring of phonological information in the growing lexicon (Metsala, 1997). We noted that, when we lack vocabulary, the words we are lacking are more difficult to learn to read accurately (Duff & Hulme, 2012). In Chapter 4, we pointed out that individuals with large vocabularies generally have faster and more accurate word recognition performance as well (Yap et al., 2012). Thus, we have already established vocabulary as important for reading. By the end of this chapter you should be able to articulate in greater detail how knowing words helps readers to read better.

The study of vocabulary depends heavily on what we mean when we say that we know a word. What do we mean when we say that we *know* a word? The fairly simple description given by the National Reading Panel (National Institute of Child Health and Human Development, 2000) is one operative way of considering vocabulary. However, *knowing a word* is a multifaceted skill. There are many aspects associated with the concept *word*, and these aspects can serve as criteria for determining whether someone knows a word.

Not surprisingly, this topic has been given considerable attention by researchers studying the development of vocabulary in a second language. Often nonnative speakers use a particular word in an awkward way that indicates that their understanding of it is incomplete. In Table 6.1, we can see what Nation (2001) posits as the kinds of knowledge that one needs to know to truly know a word. Note that each of these aspects of knowing a word has a receptive element (i.e., understanding the word during reading and listening) as well as an expressive element (i.e., using the word in speaking and writing in an appropriate way). Presumably one might be able to understand a particular word while reading without knowing exactly how and where to use it. Generally, it is assumed that words enter into the vocabulary in the receptive domain before we attain expressive use of them.

Let's consider this statement by 4-year-old Paul, uttered while his mother was transporting him by car: "Mom, you recognize when we rode the bus the other

TABLE 6.1. Aspects of Knowing a Word

Dimensions of knowing a word		
Form	Spoken	Knowing what the word sounds like.
	Written	Knowing what the word looks like.
Meaning	Conceptual and referential	Knowing what is included in the concept.
	Associative	Knowing a word's associates and synonyms.
Use	Grammatical	Knowing the grammatical contexts in which the word occurs.
	Collocational	Knowing what other words co-occur with the word.
	Constraints on use	Knowing how often we hear, read, or use this word.

Note. Based on Nation (2001).

day?" Paul can pronounce *recognize* well enough to be understood, although he most likely cannot read or write it yet. Paul is missing some of the conceptual and referential elements of *recognize* that relate current sensory input to past events. He has some knowledge about the general cognitive verb domain in which *recognize* fits and the some of the key associations therein (i.e., relating to the past), but may not yet have the associative understanding that *recognize* is not a direct substitute for the word *remember*. He probably does not have adult-like associations with the word. He uses *recognize* appropriately as a verb, but does not quite understand that the collocation pattern, *recognize when*, is atypical here. He may not yet understand the constraints on use that make *remember* the more general and frequent term to describe past memories. Thus, whereas at some levels we can say that Paul knows the meaning of the word *recognize*, on other levels, he clearly does not.

We need to consider more carefully the very gradual nature of the development of word knowledge. According to Zareva (2012) and Shore and Durso (1990), we should consider that for a subset of words, speakers might have what researchers have called *frontier knowledge*. With frontier knowledge, a person knows that something is a word with a meaning he or she can sense in a tip-of-the-tongue-type fashion, but the person knows little else about it. Thus, a listener or reader might be able to identify the word as an English word, but be vague beyond that. He or she might have the wrong conceptual knowledge associated with it (i.e., for *abattoir*, "to strike repeatedly"); might not know what part of speech to which the word belongs; have only a vague sense of some of its conceptual features (e.g., for *lackadaisical*, "don't care"); or might know what part of speech to which the word belongs but not its conceptual features (e.g., for *solstice*, "a type of day").

Sampling words using an English language word frequency corpus, Zareva (2012) found that approximately 10% of words formed frontier words for native-speaking college students, but even for advanced language learners of English, 20% of words or more were frontier words. Often, English learners simply misinterpret the meanings of frontier words altogether. Because this problem occurs for native college speakers, we might safely assume that, for children, especially those who are learning English, words at the frontier level might represent a sizeable chunk of their emerging vocabulary too.

Does frontier knowledge constitute meaningful vocabulary knowledge? That's for you to decide, but at some minimal level, these words are a meaningful part of children's vocabulary. According to the *partial knowledge claim* (Yurovsky, Fricker, Yu, & Smith, 2014), frontier word knowledge may act to benefit acquisition ultimately because it represents an initial step in the learning of new words. The idea of frontier in this context—as partial vocabulary knowledge—assumes that this initial vocabulary knowledge serves to benefit vocabulary growth by providing an initial hook that helps children gather knowledge about meanings later. Presumably, with exposure, familiarity with the word form increases and different aspects of meaning are revealed when the word is presented different contexts. The association between the word form and its meaning is strengthened.

The plausibility of the partial knowledge claim comes from an experimental study by Yurovsky et al. (2014). In that study, adults had to learn the relationship between pseudowords that served as novel vocabulary (i.e., words made up for the experiment) and some potential referents. The experimental presentations were designed to partially mimic what goes on when a child is presented with a context containing a number of novel words and a variety of referents in a scene. In each trial there were several words and several potential referents, making the task of mapping words to their referents difficult. When the participant guessed the referents for the novel words incorrectly, some missed words were reexposed in subsequent blocks. In these subsequent blocks, participants showed faster learning for these previously missed words than they did for a brand new set of items presented for the first time. This superior learning for the previously missed items is expected if the participant had experienced some partial learning on the initial trial, even though he or she had gotten the item wrong. Moreover, one fascinating finding of the study was that developing partial knowledge not only helped the learning of the particular repeated items, but also the learning of brand new items presented in the subsequent sets. In fact, the same basic process has been found for toddlers learning new words. Thom and Sandhofer (2009) showed that teaching toddlers some words in a domain facilitated the learning of other words in the domain. Thus, the partial knowledge gained early in the learning of a new word may serve to assist in the learning of those new words. Further, partial learning of these words assists in disambiguating to-be-learned items around them.

DIMENSIONS OF VOCABULARY KNOWLEDGE

A distinction is often made between two dimensions of vocabulary knowledge: vocabulary breadth and vocabulary depth. *Vocabulary breadth* is used to refer to the dimension of vocabulary size. The term *vocabulary depth* refers to the idea that some words might have only partial knowledge associated with them, whereas others have greater detail. In learning vocabulary, a child may have a large breadth in terms of the number of lexical entries in his or her lexicon, but these words have only partial knowledge connected to them (i.e., low depth). Alternatively, he or she may have comparatively few entries (i.e., small breadth) compared to other children, but have greater detail (i.e., great depth).

Usually, measures of vocabulary breadth and depth are strongly correlated (Quian, 1999). Breadth and depth of vocabulary knowledge may have distinct implications for reading, however. For example, Oullette (2006) found that, for fourth-grade students, vocabulary breadth was more important for predicting decoding skills, whereas depth of vocabulary knowledge was more important for predicting reading comprehension skills.

Measuring Vocabulary Breadth

Vocabulary breadth is the element most often measured in studies that measure vocabulary. Standardized tests of vocabulary are most often used, and they almost uniformly measure vocabulary breadth. These standardized tests are designed to identify vocabulary problems quickly. From our experience, schools often administer them as part of their general testing regimen. In federal interventions designed to improve children's language or school readiness skills, standardized testing is the norm (e.g., U.S. Department of Health and Human Services, Administration for Children and Families, 2005).

A number of available standardized tests of vocabulary have a long history of use. The Peabody Picture Vocabulary Test (Dunn & Dunn, 1981) is a commonly used receptive vocabulary test. It simply asks children to point to one of four pictures that matches a word spoken by the tester. The Expressive Vocabulary Test (K. T. Williams, 2007) is a commonly used test of expressive vocabulary. It requires children to provide a name for a picture presented by the tester. For both of these assessments, the more words that the child knows, the greater breadth of vocabulary he or she is assumed to have. Standardized assessments of vocabulary have been sharply critiqued, however, for being culturally and racially biased (Restrepo et al., 2006; Pae, Greenburg, & Morris, 2012).

Another measure of vocabulary breadth that does not rely on the assumptions of standardized assessment is language sampling. This measure obtains an estimate of vocabulary breadth by using the words a person deploys in everyday speech.

Typically, in language sample assessments, children (or adults) are given some sort of prompt designed to evoke speech—a wordless picture book to narrate, an intriguing topic to discuss, or a set of provocative pictures to describe (e.g., a child in a dentist's chair). Speakers are asked to describe what is going on in their own words. Then the number of unique words the speaker produces is compared against the total number of words that he or she produces in the sample. The resulting calculation is called *lexical diversity* (Malvern, Richards, Chipere, & Durán, 2004). Lexical diversity is thought to provide an estimate of children's active vocabulary; that is, words they may know well enough to use in everyday speech (or writings) (Malvern & Richards, 2002). In both child and clinical samples, lexical diversity is moderately correlated with standardized expressive vocabulary scores (Malvern et al., 2004; Silverman & Ratner, 1997). Lexical diversity has the advantage of removing background knowledge and cultural differences that may bias scores on standardized assessments (Lai, 2014), and of using a familiar medium (e.g., conversation) without necessarily biasing against different cultural upbringings.

Language samples may have different problems than standardized assessments for estimating vocabulary size. When we obtain a language sample in one setting, we naturally exclude all the words that a participant may know that do not pertain to that topic. Further, the words participants use to discuss something at one time point may not necessarily be the same words they use at another. Meara and Olmos Alcoy (2010) have observed that this problem can be likened to the one that population biologists have when they try to estimate the number of different animals living in a particular forest. Simply counting the animals is not straightforward: The animals hide and are never seen (i.e., not counted), or they reappear more than once, causing the researchers to overcount them. They simply do not line up and wait to be counted reliably.

Other estimates of vocabulary breadth rely on dictionary sampling (e.g., Johnson & Anglin, 1995). For example, a researcher may decide that he or she will sample every 60th word or every 7th word in a particular dictionary. Then participants are asked to define a word, provide an association or two, or simply self-report their knowledge (i.e., "I know/don't know this word"). However, dictionary sampling has its own problems: How large is the dictionary? Do we sample from one that is massive or a smaller one directed at the particular population we have in mind (e.g., children, foreign language learners)? Do we include technical words? Homonyms? Words with derivational affixes? Finally, in this regard, it is important to remember that the job of the lexicographer who develops dictionaries is different from the job of the language learner: Most language learners do not have the goal of developing as large a vocabulary as possible. Learners aim to communicate and understand satisfactorily the language that appears around them. Regardless, it is important to remember that no matter how we estimate children's relative vocabulary size, it is, indeed, an estimate with its own advantages and disadvantages.

Measuring Vocabulary Depth

Other kinds of assessments target depth (sometimes called *quality*) of vocabulary knowledge. Asking children to define words is a way to target depth of vocabulary knowledge. In this type of assessment, the child is presented with a word and asked to define it in his or her own words. A child with limited depth of knowledge for the word might provide a vague or brief answer. Those with greater depth of knowledge may reference the word's general semantic category and provide several distinguishing features in their definitions. More recently, automated approaches to scoring definitions have been developed that determine the degree of match between the words in a target definition and the words in the vocabulary learner's responses (Frishkoff, Collins-Thompson, Perfetti, & Calan, 2008). This match has been shown to capture changes in depth of vocabulary learners' knowledge with learning (Frishkoff, Perfetti, & Collins-Thompson, 2011).

Definitions have their own limitations for measuring vocabulary depth. Formal definitions require providing superordinate category information and distinguishing details. For example, an appropriate definition for *wolf* might be, "It is an *animal* that looks a lot like a dog but is wild and has big teeth" (Ordóñez, Carlo, Snow, & McLaughlin, 2002). Definitions may not be a very good measure for determining the depth of vocabulary knowledge among early elementary school children or younger, because they are usually not yet familiar with formal definition forms (Snow, 1990). They might say, for example, for *wolf*, "It's mean and nasty"—true, but not really a definition. Further, this means of obtaining people's understanding of vocabulary ignores the classic problem that meanings have fuzzy boundaries in the sense that, for many words, a simple list of distinguishing features will not distinguish what is and is not a referent of the word

Another way to measure depth is to determine the speaker's patterns of associations (Wilks & Meara, 2002). Speakers might be asked to generate associates for sampled words, and these associations can be compared against other perhaps more sophisticated users of the language. For example, we might compare the associates produced by second-language learners to native speakers of the language. For native speakers, associations tend to cluster around a small number of commonly agreed-upon associative hubs. This fact has been interpreted as indicating that there is stability among semantic connections between words in the lexicon of native speakers (Schmidt, 1998). Speakers with less vocabulary depth might be expected to lack this agreement. For example, Zareva, Schwanenflugel, and Nikolova (2005) found considerably little agreement between second-language learners and native speakers in terms of the commonality of the associations they produced, even when they produced the same number of associates.

Another way to consider using associations to evaluate vocabulary depth is to examine the type of associations that are produced for new words (Meara, 1981).

Early word knowledge is characterized by the presence of *syntagmatic associations*, that is, associations based on the ways words are used that preserve the order in which they typically occur. These might include associations for *parrot*, for example, such as "parrot talked" and "green parrot." By contrast, associations from the same grammatical class as the stimulus word are considered *paradigmatic*. Thus, for *dog*, the associations "dog cat," "dog wolf," and "dog pet" are all paradigmatic associations. These paradigmatic associations tend to be linked with deeper lexical knowledge, although not always (Wolter, 2006).

In summary, vocabulary breadth and depth are both important dimensions of vocabulary knowledge. There are multiple ways of assessing each dimension. When evaluating studies of vocabulary knowledge, it is important to consider just what dimension of that knowledge is being evaluated.

HOW MANY WORDS DO CHILDREN KNOW?

As noted above, the seemingly simple concept of *knowing a word* is actually complex and has its limitations. However, let's brush these concerns aside for the moment to peruse some various estimates of vocabulary size at various stages of development. It is important to recognize that all of the estimates we present below are exactly that—estimates.

Perhaps the easiest group to estimate would seem to be toddlers who, after all, are just beginning to learn and use language. Perhaps the most widely cited study on the topic of toddler vocabulary growth is one by Hart and Risley (1995, 2003). Researchers in this study visited the families monthly from the time children began talking until they were 36 months old and recorded everything that was said between the family members and toddlers in the home during the hourly visit each month. The speech of the children and the family members was transcribed, and vocabulary was calculated based on the number of different words that the individuals uttered. The study focused on class differences in vocabulary, so they studied children from 13 upper-middle class, 23 middle-/working-class, and 6 poverty/welfare families. They found that, by the time children were 36 months old, the vocabulary produced by the upper-middle-class children (1,116 words) was higher than the vocabulary produced by the middle-/working-class children (749 words) and the children living in poverty (525 words). Importantly, the study found that children's vocabularies mirrored the number of different words used by family members in speaking with the children and the cumulative number of words parents addressed to children. The researchers estimated that by age 3, children in upper-middle-class homes might be exposed to as many as 30 million more words in the home than children living in poverty!

This study, as groundbreaking as it was, had obvious problems, the most glaring being the small number of children from high-poverty families followed. These families may or may not have been representative of their socioeconomic class. Further, the number of words children produced in the recorded interactions did not necessarily represent the number of words the children actually knew receptively; receptive vocabulary most certainly would have outstripped the expressive vocabulary produced in the limited setting of the home. It is also possible that the lower-class families were more circumspect around the upper-middle-class researchers who were visitors to their home. (Imagine the reverse awkwardness of poverty participants marching into the homes of wealthy families to record their interactions.) Finally, Dudley-Marling and Lucas (2009) have objected to the deficit-oriented conclusions drawn by Hart and Risley in the sense that they pathologized the language, culture, and interaction style of poor families.

Mayor and Plunket (2011) took a different approach to the growth of vocabulary size by mapping a well-established, validated parental report of toddler vocabulary, called the MacArthur–Bates Communicative Development Inventories (CDIs; Fenson et al., 2007), against several systematically kept diaries of particular children's speech (e.g., Robinson & Mervis, 1999). By doing this, they were able to derive an estimate of the total size of vocabulary at various ages. Table 6.2 presents the vocabulary size of the typical child at the 25th, 50th, and 75th percentile ranks and the number of words they are likely to produce between the ages of 16 and 30 months. By 30 months, children in the top quartile were estimated to have approximately twice the vocabulary of children in the bottom quartile. This vocabulary advantage was established early.

TABLE 6.2. Estimates of Toddler Vocabulary Size in Words for Expressive Vocabulary

Age in months	Percentile rank		
	25th	50th	75th
16	18	46	98
18	30	84	187
20	78	194	408
22	121	389	710
24	221	500	914
26	308	775	1,258
28	512	833	1,203
30	873	1,353	1,704

Note. Estimated by Mayor and Plunket (2011, p. 784).

There have been a number of attempts to estimate the vocabulary size of typical elementary school children. Possibly the best known study is one by Anglin
(1993), who used a dictionary sampling method to identify a sample of main dictionary entries that children might know. Children were first asked to tell the
interviewer what a particular word might mean. If the child could not do that, he
or she was asked to use the word in the sentence. If the child could not do that,
he or she was asked to choose from among four multiple-choice answers the one
that provided the meaning of the word. From this, Anglin estimated an average
vocabulary size of 10,398 for first graders, 19,412 for third graders, and 39,994 for
fifth graders. Of these words, approximately half could be defined at each grade,
another 12–14% could be used in a sentence, and approximately another third
could be identified only through multiple-choice selection. He suggested that
these estimates meant that, in general, children learn approximately nine words
per day throughout elementary school, which is similar to another estimate by
Nagy and Herman (1987) of eight words per day throughout elementary, middle,
and high school years. A daily vocabulary growth of eight to nine words per day
represents a very rapid rate of vocabulary growth indeed!

Note, however, that these are not universally agreed-upon numbers. If one
focuses on words or root words, a slower rate of growth seems apparent. For example, Beck and McKeown (1990) estimated that only two to four root words are
acquired per day during elementary school. Biemiller and Slonim (2001) carried
out an extensive study restricted to the development of word-root words only; that
is, basic words with prefixes and suffixes removed. Approximately half of the words
children know are root words (Anglin, 1993). They sampled root words from the
Living Word Vocabulary (Dale & O'Rourke, 1981) and asked children to indicate
what words presented in a simple sentence meant. For example, children might
be shown: "The material was translucent. What does *translucent* mean?" From
their responses, Biemiller and Slonim estimated the vocabularies of normative
children (high-poverty, working-class, and middle-class children attending public
schools) and advantaged children (upper-middle-class children attending a university school). The estimates of vocabulary size determined by Biemiller and Slonim
can be found in Table 6.3.

Biemiller and Slonim identified two trends in the acquisition of root words.
First, before grade 2, normative children were estimated to have average growth
rates of about 2.2 root words per day, whereas the advantaged children had somewhat faster growth rates of 2.4 root words per day. However, by the end of elementary school, the growth rates of the advantaged and normative groups had
switched: The growth rate was now 2.9 root words per day for normative children,
whereas growth was now only 2.3 root words per day for the advantaged children.
Essentially, the less advantaged children began to catch up to their advantaged
peers. Second, they pointed out that there is a dramatic increase in root word

**TABLE 6.3. Estimated Root Word
Vocabulary Size for Children in Grades K–7**

Grade	Population group	
	Typical	Advantaged
K	2,924	3,173
1	2,669	4,295
2	5,175	6,157
3	5,759	7,397
4	6,794	7,164
5	8,411	8,685
6	8,737	9,492

Note. Based on Biemiller and Slonim (2001).

vocabulary that begins in second grade. This is a period in which children are beginning to read more complex materials and experience tremendous cognitive as will as linguistic growth, a phenomena sometimes called the *five-to-seven shift* (Sameroff & Haith, 1996).

Why does having a correct estimate of vocabulary growth during the school years actually matter? It matters because, if children's vocabulary growth is rather slow when left to their own devices, vocabulary programs in schools might actually have a noticeable impact on vocabulary size. That is, such programs might be able to accelerate the learning of new words among children who have poor vocabularies, so that they can eventually catch up to the linguistic skills of their peers. If, on the other hand, vocabulary growth is rapid, then it is hard to see how the 350–500 words we might teach with a typical vocabulary program implemented during the school year might have much of a noticeable impact on ultimate vocabulary size. Essentially, disadvantaged children might never catch up. Thus, researchers such as Hart and Risley (1995) are pessimistic about the prospects of children catching up, whereas researchers such as Biemiller are more sanguine about it (Biemiller, 2003).

Finally, to end on a happy note, it appears that our vocabulary sizes continue to expand throughout our lifetime, even after we leave school. In a large meta-analysis of studies comparing younger and older adults, Verhaeghen (2003) found a consistent benefit of age on standardized tests of vocabulary. Older adults between the ages of 62 and 80 scored approximately .80 *SD*s higher than younger adults in the 18- to 35-year range. Put in standard score terms, this would amount to a benefit of 12 points on a scale where the mean is 100 and the *SD* is 15, reclassifying the average adult from "average" to "bright" (Wechsler, 1939). This benefit of age is particularly apparent for expressive vocabulary, and it occurs even after the education level is taken into account. In fact, vocabulary skill remains one true bright spot in the general decline of cognitive skills often observed in studies of aging.

VOCABULARY DOMAINS OF DEVELOPMENTAL IMPORTANCE FOR SCHOOL-AGE CHILDREN

From what we have described above, it seems that all words are alike—that is, a word is a word is a word—and that all are equally likely to be attained or absent in a child's vocabulary. There are distinctions between words that make some words learned earlier or better in some way than others. In this section we focus on three that have implications for word learning in children: word concreteness, cognitive verbs, and academic vocabulary.

Concrete and Abstract Words

There is a considerable amount of evidence that the concreteness conveyed by words represents a fundamental semantic distinction among them. For example, in factor analytic studies that consider correlations among various semantic qualities, concreteness consistently emerges as an important variable that distinguishes among words (Clark & Paivio, 2004; Di Vesta & Walls, 1970; Rubin, 1980). As noted in Chapter 4, abstract words are words that evoke less imagery and have fewer sensory referents than concrete words. Put simply, children acquire abstract vocabulary later than concrete vocabulary as a trend.

A perusal of early infant language corpuses (Gentner, 1982; Nelson, 1973) shows that none of children's first nouns are abstract. This tendency for concrete words to enter into children's vocabularies sooner continues through elementary school. For example, Brown (1957) compared high-frequency words used by first-grade children to discern whether children possessed a bias toward using concrete nouns and verbs. Of the high-frequency words used by kids, 75% of the nouns and 67% of the verbs were concrete, whereas only 28% of high-frequency nouns and 33% of high-frequency verbs used by adults were concrete. Similarly, Schwanenflugel (1991) examined the acquisition of a sample of similarly frequent abstract and concrete nouns for adults and matched them against the Rinsland (1945) word count taken from children's conversations, letters, and stories. Figure 6.1 shows that the discrepancy between concrete and abstract nouns is fairly persistent developmentally. By second grade children have acquired approximately 85% of frequently occurring concrete nouns, but do not acquire a similar level of abstract nouns until the end of middle school. Thus, from an instructional point of view, it can be assumed that if a word is abstract, it is probably a lexical

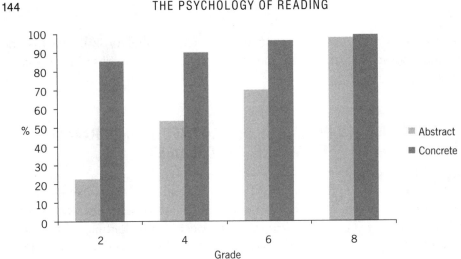

FIGURE 6.1. Percentage of high-frequency abstract (light bar) and concrete (dark bar) nouns acquired by children in grades 2–8 (based on Schwanenflugel, 1991).

gap that instruction can fill. Certainly, the lack of abstract vocabulary or the partial knowledge of it can impede children's reading of such words, as indicated in Chapter 4.

Cognitive Verbs

Cognitive verbs refer to mental states about thinking and knowing—for example, *know, recognize, remember, forget, guess, understand, believe, estimate,* and so forth. The understanding of such verbs has a very long developmental trajectory. Although young children use cognitive verbs practically from the onset of speech, they use them in a narrow, formulaic way (Shatz, Wellman, & Silber, 1983), as in "Know what?" They may not use cognitive verbs to refer unambiguously to mental states until around age 4 (Moore & Furrow, 1991). Elementary school children appear to have many cognitive verbs in their vocabulary, but this aspect of the lexicon reorganizes during this period to reflect an increased understanding of the constructivist nature of the underlying activities to which the words refer (Schwanenflugel, Henderson, & Fabricius, 1998). The growth of this domain continues well into the adolescent years for more advanced verbs, such as *wonder, guess, infer,* and *hypothesize* (Wing & Scholnick, 1986; Astington & Olson, 1990). In adults, the constructive nature of cognitive verbs dominates their organization. Thus, we see words such as *wonder, guess, infer,* and *hypothesize* as having a basic constructive nature, which is distinct from less constructive words such as *see, recognize,* and *memorize.* Children might not appreciate the constructive nature of many of the cognitive verbs that they use.

Cognitive verbs are the language of school and, as such, have obvious importance to schooling. Because they are important for describing the mental states of story characters, cognitive verbs are fundamental for understanding stories. When parents read with children in joint storybook reading, they frequently point out the mental states of characters using cognitive terms (Dyer, Shatz, & Wellman, 2000). Ornaghi, Brockmeier, and Gavazzi (2011) showed that experimentally enriching stories with many cognitive verbs and discussing the terms resulted in an increased understanding of cognitive verb vocabulary and a deeper understanding of their own and others' beliefs among preschoolers. In general, the presence of cognitive verbs in storybooks supports the development of an understanding of the inferred mental states of book characters (Adrián, Clemente, & Villanueva, 2007). Thus, in this way, early storybook reading with young children works to foster the development of emergent literacy skills by increasing the focus on mental state terms.

Academic Vocabulary

Academic vocabulary refers to words used in academic language. Nagy and Townsend (2012) define academic language as "the specialized language, both oral and written, of academic settings that facilitates communication and thinking about disciplinary content" (p. 92). These words are typically not used in social settings and everyday communication. In the context of reading, academic vocabulary includes the words found in print and digital media where disciplinary ideas are communicated.

Academic vocabulary has several distinctions that make it different from regular conversational or even storybook vocabulary. Academic vocabulary tends to be more often derived from German or Latin origin (Bar-Ilan & Berman, 2007). The words tend to be more morphologically complex, using derivational affixes and morphological transformations (e.g., such as the nominalization that occurs when turning a verb or adjective into a noun: *evaporate* into *evaporation*, *humid* into *humidity*) that are acquired rather late developmentally (Nippold & Sun, 2008). They are more likely to be nouns, particularly abstract nouns, and they tend to occur within complex, elaborated noun phrases, such as *correctly balanced indoor humidity* (Fang, Scheppegrell, & Cox, 2006). The words are more likely to be abstract. All of these features conspire to make academic language particularly difficult.

Interventions that focus on academic vocabulary have been mostly successful with moderate effect sizes (Nagy & Townsend, 2012). Most involve identifying some subset of words within texts that the students are learning from, providing some instruction regarding meanings and their relationship to the larger topic. They usually include subsequent opportunities to practice the words in some way (Brown, Ryoo, & Rodriguez, 2010; Lesaux, Kieffer, Faller, & Kelley, 2010).

WHY DOES HAVING A GOOD VOCABULARY MATTER?

Having a good vocabulary appears to have a number of general cognitive consequences that enable ideal cognitive functioning. In this section, we outline four major ways in which vocabulary operates to maximize cognitive functioning.

Vocabulary Helps Us Construct and Remember Cognitive Distinctions

Having a good vocabulary helps people construct cognitive distinctions in the world a bit more easily. This point has been recognized for a very long time. Here, we are reminded of the words of the famous 19th-century preacher and essayist, Henry Ward Beecher (1813–1887), who famously noted, "All words are pegs to hang ideas on."

As this quote would imply, vocabulary knowledge and topic knowledge are closely related (Bedard & Chi, 1992). One quick way to determine how much knowledge someone has regarding a topic is to simply have him or her list the vocabulary from the topic and provide organizational links between concepts (Nesbit & Adesope, 2006). Further, examining the availability and organization of specific vocabulary within a culture can provide insights into the cognitive importance of a domain for its users (Berlin, Breedlove, & Raven, 1973; D'Andrade, 1995). For example, Dougherty (1978) noted that for the category *trees*, most Americans make only gross lexical distinctions between various types of trees (e.g., *tree*, *pine*, *palm*), whereas the average Tzeltal Mayan child is able to make linguistic contrasts for over a hundred different plants, trees, and grasses. Tzeltal Mayan children are more often left to their own devices to forage in the forest, so having these labels can come in handy for remembering important distinctions. None of this is to say that one cannot conceive of distinctions that one does not have a word for, but that having a word will probably make that distinction an easier one to make or remember. The idea that labels have an important connection to knowledge is codified in the common practice in classrooms for teachers to teach the meanings of domain vocabulary as key part of teaching about a domain itself.

Vocabulary Size Is Related to Intelligence

Vocabulary may be generally important for intelligence. It is well established that standardized tests of vocabulary are positively correlated with verbal IQ. As Sternberg (1987) puts it,

> Vocabulary is probably the single best indicator of a person's overall level of intelligence. Stated in another way, if one wants a quick and not-too-dirty measure of a person's psychometrically measured intelligence, and thus has time to give just

one brief test of it, vocabulary is generally the best predictor of overall score on a psychometric IQ test. (p. 90)

There are numerous examples showing that the correlation between standardized tests and IQ is strong, indeed. According to Dumont and Willis (2007), the correlation between the standard scores on the Peabody Picture Vocabulary Test–III (PPVT; a test of receptive vocabulary) and the Wechsler Intelligence Scale for Children—Third Edition (WISC-III, a widely used IQ test) ranges from .82 to .92, depending on age. K. T. Williams (2007) reported a .72 correlation between standard scores on the Expressive Vocabulary Test and the WISC Verbal IQ. Correlations between the PPVT-III and the Kaufman Brief Intelligence Test for adults range from .62 to .82 (Dumont & Willis, 2007). As noted by Campbell, Bell, and Keith (2001), we probably do not want to substitute vocabulary testing for diagnostic IQ testing in schools, however, because of the problems with standardized tests of vocabulary that make them unsuitable for estimating minority children's IQ.

We can use children's early vocabulary skills to predict their later IQ, to some extent, anyway. Marchman and Fernald (2008) found that the CDI measure of toddler vocabulary correlated .53 with IQ scores at age 8 in an upper-middle-class sample of children, even when other measures of toddler cognitive skills were taken into account.

Taken together, Sternberg's assertion, noted previously, is largely correct. The reasons behind these high correlations are less clear and currently rather speculative. Sternberg (1987) argued that the same basic cognitive processes are involved in both IQ and vocabulary: Both skills are related to the ability to pick up information from one's surroundings. Further, Marchman and Fernald (2008) argue that having early skills in categorizing and interpreting speech labels may be foundational for a range of intellectual achievements later.

Vocabulary Helps Children Make the Phonological Distinctions Necessary for Spelling and Decoding

As we noted in Chapter 2, vocabulary appears to be integral in prodding children to reorganize their lexicon to reflect phonological contrasts. These phonological contrasts will be key to their "cracking the code" and for learning to spell out words. The existence of the phonological contrasts will enable the development of phonological awareness.

Children acquire a phonological system based on generalizations they develop over their lexicon. When particular consonant and vowel sounds appear in many words in their vocabularies, children are able to more accurately represent and reproduce these sounds. Children with larger vocabularies have more robustly generalized phonological systems. They represent and produce both frequent and less frequent phonological patterns (i.e., single sounds and syllables) accurately, and they can retrieve them quickly—both frequent and less frequent contrasts exist in their vocabularies and the phonological generalizations can be made. For children with smaller vocabularies, less familiar phonological patterns are less well represented and more fragile. To a great extent, their vocabularies may not contain the needed phonological contrasts. As a result, Edwards, Beckman, and Munson (2004) found that children with small vocabularies had difficulty accurately reproducing nonwords made up of less frequent phonological language patterns. This issue will surface later when such children need to acquire cognitive control over these patterns to use them to gain literacy.

Vocabulary Helps Children Comprehend What They Read Better

It makes intuitive sense that if children are reading some text and they encounter many words they don't know, this lack of vocabulary will impede their comprehension. If you have ever tried to read a jargon-filled textbook in an area with which you are unfamiliar, you can recognize the lack of comprehension and confusion that can result. Indeed, research has consistently found that there is a strong relationship between vocabulary knowledge and reading comprehension. Studies have found correlations between standardized assessments of vocabulary (which, as we have indicated earlier, are measures of vocabulary size) and reading comprehension skill in the .35–.55 range in elementary school children (Muter et al., 2004; Ouellette, 2006; Share & Leiken, 2003). Ouellette (2006) found that the depth of vocabulary knowledge, however, is particularly important for determining reading comprehension skills beyond receptive knowledge. When he included all sources of vocabulary knowledge (receptive, expressive, and depth) as predictors, he found a correlation of .76 between vocabulary skills and reading comprehension skills among fourth-grade children. Thus, both size and depth of vocabulary matter for good understanding of text. However, the mere existence of this correlation does not tell us exactly how vocabulary knowledge supports comprehension. It may seem obvious that we cannot comprehend sentences if we do not know the meaning of many of the words, but this relationship between vocabulary and comprehension can occur for a variety of reasons. There are at least four hypotheses regarding how vocabulary knowledge might support reading comprehension. Two hypotheses, the lexical quality hypothesis and the instrumentalist hypothesis, attribute the superior comprehension displayed by individuals with stronger vocabulary skills directly to vocabulary per se. Two other hypotheses, the aptitude hypothesis and the knowledge hypothesis, describe vocabulary benefits to comprehension as an indirect product of factors related to vocabulary skills.

The *lexical quality hypothesis* (Perfetti, 2007) attributes the better comprehension skills found in some readers to the general quality of their word representations.

Lexical quality includes not only breadth and depth of vocabulary, but also precision of words' orthographic, phonological, and morphosyntactic features. This hypothesis claims that some children have incomplete, low-quality information regarding these lexical features. Such children might, for instance, confuse the meaning of *wail* with *whale* by confusing the orthographic qualities associated with these two words. Among children with comprehension issues, these lexical features are considered less tightly bound together in a word's representation. Lacking precision regarding word qualities is considered a major impediment for deriving meaning from text during comprehension. For example, these incomplete lexical representations will activate context-inappropriate words that are similar to the word (as in *wail* vs. *whale*). Inefficient retrieval will occupy cognitive resources that would normally be utilized for generating inferences and integrating new information during reading. Indeed, Hamilton, Freed, and Long (2013) found that vocabulary skills were related to the readers' ability to integrate new nouns into the ongoing representation of the text while reading.

The *instrumentalist hypothesis* (Anderson & Freebody, 1981) posits that having a large vocabulary might affect reading comprehension in a causal way. It is sometimes stated that if a child does not know the meaning of, say, one out of 20 words that he or she is reading, the child will experience comprehension difficulty. This difficulty can be attributed to the mere lack of vocabulary. The prediction is that teaching vocabulary should improve reading comprehension directly, causally, and in a general way. Indeed, for teachers, this is probably the most important hypothesis because it determines the relative value of teaching vocabulary directly or not. If teaching vocabulary improves children's reading comprehension substantially, then it makes sense to include it as an important element of the curriculum (Stahl & Fairbanks, 1986).

A recent meta-analysis of studies examining the effects of vocabulary instruction on reading comprehension by Elleman, Lindo, Morphy, and Compton (2009) provides some support for the instrumentalist hypothesis. This meta-analysis indicates that teaching vocabulary does improve the comprehension of texts to which those words pertain. As might be expected from the instrumentalist hypothesis, gains in instructed vocabulary were moderately correlated (.43) with subsequent gains in reading comprehension. Unfortunately, the positive effects of vocabulary instruction were limited to only the texts that contained those instructed words; instruction did not transfer to general reading comprehension skills. For the teacher, this means that the benefits of vocabulary instruction will be a passage-by-passage matter, not the broader transferred effect for which one might hope. Importantly, these benefits from vocabulary instruction are much larger for children experiencing reading difficulties. For them, this meta-analysis found that vocabulary instruction was essential for improving reading comprehension.

The *aptitude hypothesis* (Anderson & Freebody, 1981) points out that readers with high IQs also tend to have large vocabularies, as we also noted earlier. They have an unusual ability to make and remember verbal distinctions, as required by a large vocabulary, are those who also tend to understand what they read better. Indeed, the correlation between verbal IQ and vocabulary is very high, making the operation of one factor difficult to discern from the operation of the other (Sattler, 1988). Consequently, standardized assessment of vocabulary is often used as a proxy for general verbal IQ in studies of reading (e.g., Hecht, Burgess, Torgesen, Wagner, & Rashotte, 2000). Thus, the effect of having a good vocabulary on reading comprehension might be merely an indirect result of being generally smart verbally.

Related to this idea is the *knowledge hypothesis*. This view states that vocabulary is a good reflection of a person's general conceptual knowledge (Anderson & Freebody, 1981). Indeed, we can often determine a person's knowledge of a domain by simply measuring his or her vocabulary in it (De Marie, Aloise-Young, Prideaux, Muransky-Doran, & Gerda, 2004). It is hard having knowledge of a domain without having knowledge of the vocabulary within it. People with greater knowledge in a variety of domains also tend to have better vocabularies. At some point, having broader general knowledge becomes isomorphic with higher IQ, because high-IQ people pick up knowledge around them faster and more generally. People with stronger knowledge bases also tend to comprehend what they read better because they have a range of knowledge that they can bring to the task of comprehension. Broader vocabulary and good comprehension skills potentially result from this larger knowledge base.

MEANS FOR LEARNING NEW WORDS

As noted earlier, vocabulary learning in children occurs at a rapid pace—and this process requires some explanation. Some have claimed that the ability to rapidly pick up new words emerges once a toddler has acquired approximately 50 words (Golinkoff, Hirsh-Pasek, Mervis, Frawley, & Parillo, 1995). The generalization of new words to various contexts and shapes is fairly inflexible prior to this learning spurt. When the child realizes that words can be generalized beyond their original or narrowly prescribed referents, he or she generalizes the meanings of words along categorical lines to items that fall within the same basic category as the original referent. Once this understanding is obtained, a word spurt occurs wherein children switch from learning just a couple of words every few weeks to approximately 5–10 new words per day (Mervis & Bertrand, 1995).

The concept of a *word spurt* requires that there be something of an inflection point in word learning rate during toddlerhood at which word learning suddenly becomes more rapid. Some studies have failed to find such an inflection point, suggesting that it is perhaps more reasonable to assume that word learning rate is rather constant over early childhood (Ganger & Brent, 2004). Others note that a given child may experience a number of detectable spurts, which may or may not be not clearly linked to any particular developmental or linguistic phase (Dandurand & Shultz, 2011). Regardless, researchers agree that children's vocabularies increase rather rapidly when provided with sufficient linguistic and environmental input. There are a number of mechanisms that children appear to use to increase their vocabulary as rapidly as they appear to do.

Mutual Exclusivity and the Novel Name–Nameless Category (N3C) Process

The term *mutual exclusivity* refers to the idea that children acquire a potential meaning for a new word by making the assumption that, if they already know a label for an object, they can reject a new vocabulary word as a potential additional label for that object (Markman, Wasow, & Hansen, 2003). Children seem to assume that vocabulary terms are mutually exclusive; that is, they prefer that each type of object have only one vocabulary term associated with it. They also prefer to assign new vocabulary (i.e., novel name) to objects of which they do not know the name (i.e., nameless category). When presented with a new vocabulary word, they tend to pin this new word onto this nameless object. This has been referred to as the novel name–nameless category (N3C) principle (Mervis & Bertrand, 1994, 1995).

The N3C principle shows up again in other difficulties preschoolers have in word learning. For example, the N3C interferes in learning distinct meanings for homonyms. Homonyms (i.e., words with ambiguous/more than one meaning; e.g., *bank*) require that the word learner apply a second distinct meaning to a known word, which young children are loathe to do because they use the N3C (Casenhiser, 2005). However, they eventually do manage to learn such words. Further, bilingual children may need to forgo or substantially weaken these principles altogether to learn a second language in which having dual labels for objects is the norm (Davidson & Tell, 2005; Houston-Price, Caloghiris, & Raviglione, 2010).

This set of principles has been discussed mainly in the context of word learning in toddlers and preschoolers, but a perusal of Figure 6.2 should convince you that the N3C can be used by adults too. The vocabulary word in question here is *cherimoya*, a fleshy soft, sweet fruit indigenous to South American Andean regions. Obviously, adults do not need to assume that objects have only one word associated with them, yet, given a choice, they use the N3C. Looking at the picture array in Figure 6.2, you most likely assumed that *cherimoya* represented the word for the picture in the middle. You have begun to add a new word to your vocabulary and have developed at least partial knowledge of it.

Find the *cherimoya*.

FIGURE 6.2. When provided with an unknown word (*cherimoya*), listeners have a tendency to pin the word on an object for which they do not have a name—for most of us, the item in the middle. This is called the *novel name–nameless category* (N3C) principle. Apple photo by Abhijit Tembhekar; cherimoya photo by Hannes Groba; banana photo by Evan-Amos. Used by permission. (*http://creativecommons.org/licenses/by-sa/3.0/legalcode*)

The N3C can be incorporated as a classroom strategy for introducing new vocabulary as well. For example, in the PAVEd for Success prekindergarten and kindergarten vocabulary program, teachers present pictures of objects representing new words in the context of pictures containing items whose names are familiar to young children, similar to Figure 6.2; that is, depicting one unknown item among a pair of known items (Hamilton & Schwanenflugel, 2011). Then children are simply asked to identify the picture that represents the new word, in this case, *cherimoya*. Children automatically select the picture that represents the unknown word. This can be the first step of many in moving new words into children's vocabularies.

Joint Attention

Joint attention refers to times when a child and adult's attention are focused on the same thing. Joint attention includes a variety of behaviors (Tomasello, 1995). It can include joint gaze on an object or scene between the child and the adult. The child or adult might point out something while catching each other's eye in reference to it. The child might hold something up, (perhaps) looking for a label or some comment from the adult who is engaging with a child. It can include simply talking about the same understood topic. Joint attention is one of the primary ways that children learn new words while interacting with their parents during play and storybook reading (Farrant & Zubrick, 2012). Typically, parents provide vocabulary through these joint attention processes, as we learned in Chapter 1. These joint attention behaviors give children the means to nonverbally (or verbally) query for new words. Indeed, infants who carry out joint attention activities with great frequency display accelerated vocabulary growth in general (Brooks & Meltzoff, 2008; Farrant & Zubrick, 2012).

Use of Linguistic Context

Linguistic context provides another means for learning new words. The term *linguistic context* refers to all the verbal and written sources, both explicit and embedded, whereby unknown words become available for learning by children and adults as part of everyday interactions with them. This type of learning is often called *incidental word learning* because it occurs outside of direct, formal vocabulary instruction.

Young children often learn new words incidentally by participation in spoken contexts. They infer meanings of unknown words from adult talk as they are offered up in conversation. Often adults will highlight new words by using fixed frames (e.g., "This is a/an _____"), presenting the new word in the final position of a sentence (e.g., "He's going up, up, up the mountain, very *steep*"), or by using emphatic stress (e.g., "It's *beneath* the table"; Clark, 2010). Usually, children will show evidence of their knowledge of the new words by repeating the introduced word in their own speech within the next turn or two (Clark, 2007).

For older children and adults, reading is a main vehicle for learning new vocabulary. This incidental word learning is thought to accelerate once children gain facility with reading (Biemiller & Slonim, 2001). The learning of new words during reading has been thoroughly studied. Indeed written materials can be rich in new vocabulary and tend to contain words not often used in conversation. Estimates of vocabulary learning from reading text containing some unknown words indicate that children learn somewhere between 11 and 22% of new words they encounter in text (Swanborn & deGlopper, 1999).

Word learning from reading text occurs more rapidly for older children and skilled readers. A high-skilled reader is likely to learn more than twice as many words than a low-skilled reader (McKeown, 1985).

Having a high density of unknown words within a text impedes word learning, probably because this high density impedes text comprehension, as noted earlier. Swanborn and deGlopper (1999) estimated that if there are only one or so unknown words per 150 words in running text, the probability of learning that single word is approximately 30%, whereas having 1 unknown word per 10 running words reduces the learning dramatically to approximately 7%. Readers gain this new word knowledge gradually rather than gaining full knowledge of word meaning all at once (Schwanenflugel, Stahl, & McFalls, 1997).

Not all contexts are equally helpful, however. Beck, McKeown, and McCaslin (1983) described contexts as ranging from *directive* (i.e., providing the reader with explicit and detailed information about unknown words) to *nondirective* (i.e., providing the reader with information that is neither helpful nor unhelpful) and even *misdirective* (i.e., provides information that leads the reader to infer an incorrect meaning). So, what kinds of clues do contexts provide to help readers infer the meanings of unknown words?

Ames (1966) developed a classification scheme related to the context clues available in texts that might assist adults in understanding unfamiliar vocabulary. A context clue can be defined as "any piece of text that led to constraints on the possible meanings for a target word" (Parault Dowds et al., 2014, p. 9). These context clues were derived empirically by inserting a pseudoword substitution for every 50th word in randomly selected magazine pieces and having adults introspect about what they thought the meanings of the pseudowords were. From this, Ames developed a classification scheme of 14 context clues that participants appeared to use to determine the meanings of the words. More recently, Parault Dowds et al. (2014) refined this system to cover the kinds of context clues available in books designed for children. They perused 24 popular children's books to discern available context clues that could be discerned reliably. They identified the 15 clues shown in Table 6.4.

Because these context clues are available in text and it appears that both children and adults use context to discern the meanings of new words, it might make sense that instruction on context clues would improve vocabulary skills. That is, knowing which context clues to attend to should help children determine the meanings of new words. It would provide a guide to teachers on which clues to point out and instruct.

Fukkink and deGlopper (1998) found that context clue instruction is helpful generally in their review of a dozen studies examining the issue. Indeed, urging children to carry out contextual analysis to infer the meanings of new words within the classroom setting has been shown to be effective in improving children's vocabulary skills (Hairrell, Rupley, & Simmons, 2011). However, most classroom studies evaluating the instruction of contextual analysis to learn the meanings of unfamiliar vocabulary usually either teach the general rule that context can be helpful or they just teach some subset of possible clues (Baumann, Edwards, Boland, Olejnik, & Kame'enui, 2003). Unfortunately, we still do not know which clues are most beneficial to teach or the best ways to teach them. Clearly more work is warranted.

Dictionaries

In teaching vocabulary, it is a popular exercise in schools to have children look up a word in a dictionary and then write a sentence incorporating the new vocabulary word. Alternatively, children are given a vocabulary list with dictionary definitions and asked to do the same. Or simply, if they do not know the meaning of

TABLE 6.4. Context Clue Classification System for Children's Narrative and Expository Text

Context clue	Description
Cause and effect	A cause-and-effect situation described in the text, such as A caused B or B is a result of A, can be used to infer target meaning.
Compare or contrast	The reader can compare or contrast the target word with another word, phrase, or analogy found in the text to derive the meaning of the target word.
Definition or description	The target word is explicitly defined or described in the text.
Feature (for nouns)	Features of the target word, such as properties, functions, or locations of the target concept, can be used to constrain possible meanings for the target.
Language experience or familiar expression	The target word is part of an expression or idiom used in oral language.
Main idea	The text main idea can be used to constrain some aspects of the target word's meaning.
Phrase/clause/ grammatical use	The grammatical use of the target word in a phrase or clause can be used to constrain aspects of the word's meaning.
Picture	A picture near the target word can be used to constrain some aspects of the word's meaning.
Presentation	Typographic aids (e.g., a bold font) or other presentation clues (e.g., quotations around dialogue) can be used to constrain aspects of the target word's meaning.
Prior knowledge	The text activates prior knowledge or schema, which can be used to constrain aspects of the target word's meaning.
Question–answer	A question-and-answer pattern in the text can be used to constrain aspects of the target word's meaning.
Setting	The setting described by the text can be used to constrain aspects of the target word's meaning.
Synonym/antonym	There is a synonym or antonym for the target word within one or two paragraphs of surrounding text.
Mood/tone	The tone or mood portrayed in the text can be used to constrain aspects of the target word's meaning.
Words connected or in a series	The target word is used in a series of words or in connection to another word, which can be used to constrain aspects of the word's meaning.

Note. Adapted from Parault Dowds, Haverback, and Parkinson (2014, p. 22). Adapted by permission.

a word, they ask their teacher, who encourages dictionary use by saying, "Go look it up." These all seem reasonably good practice on the surface, but they are not.

In what is now a classic study on the topic, Miller and Gildea (1987) examined thousands of sentences written by fifth and sixth graders after they had tried to learn the meanings of new vocabulary by examining dictionary definitions. In general, they found that children could not make sense of dictionary definitions. They suggested that children go through a process such as the following: A child might read a definition. He or she would then pick out a familiar word or phrase from it and substitute the vocabulary word in a sentence where the phrase might otherwise fit. To illustrate with an example they provided, a child was given the word *meticulous*, which was defined as "*very careful or too particular about small details. Adj.*" She selected the one phrase she truly understood in this definition: "*very careful.*" She then considered the times she was very careful and wrote, "I was meticulous about falling off the cliff." Obviously, something has gone very awry.

It might seem that a children's dictionary would do much better in providing appropriate word definitions. After all, major publishers have been designing children's dictionaries for a long time. Some of these dictionaries can now be easily accessed online. So, we looked up *meticulous* again in the online Merriam-Webster Word Central dictionary, a children's dictionary site. *Meticulous* was now defined as "*extremely or overly careful in thinking about or dealing with small details.*" Note how similar this definition is to the paper dictionary definition by Miller and Gildea over 25 years ago. We think we can assume that the results for children's learning of new vocabulary would be fairly similar as well.

We think that it is reasonable for teachers to include dictionaries and definitions as part of their curriculum. These days, online dictionaries or other electronic tools make it easy to look up a word, and word learners can use them successfully in an on-demand way (Dalton & Grisham, 2011; Dang, Chen, Dang, Li, & Nurkhamid, 2013). Should teachers decide to present dictionary definitions in their own teaching, however, they will need to modify the definitions to make them user-friendly and more meaningful in terms of vocabulary gains. McKeown (1993) suggests that a good definition entails information regarding *when* speakers tend to use a particular word, a *prototypical use* for the word, and the use of *understandable* terms within the definition. Further, the definition should direct children to the *whole* definition, not just part of it. For example, for *improvise*, the dictionary definition "*to make, build, or provide on the spur of the moment or from materials found nearby*" might be modified to "*to make something you need using whatever is available at the moment*" (Gardner, 2007, p. 368). This latter definition seems to have a better likelihood of being understood by elementary school children than the standard definition. Indeed, studies have shown that providing child-friendly definitions results in improvements in vocabulary learning (McKeown, 1993). Moreover, using both child-friendly definitions as well as presenting the words in meaningful contexts results in improved vocabulary learning, compared to either context or definitions alone (Gardner, 2007; Nist & Olejnik, 1995). Thus, child-friendly definitions are a worthwhile element of a set of classroom strategies aimed at improving children's vocabularies (Wilkinson & Houston-Price, 2013).

Morphology

Much of the vocabulary growth that occurs around the fourth grade can be attributed to the introduction of words that have some degree of morphological complexity (Nagy & Anderson, 1984; Bar-Ilan & Berman, 2007). Indeed, teaching children how to deal with this morphological complexity can go a long way toward giving children the tools they need to ferret out the meanings of unfamiliar words. In Table 6.5, we show the most common affixes found in books written for children, according to White, Sowell, and Yanagihara (1989). These affixes can be used productively to derive at least some aspect of the meanings of morphologically complex words. White et al. pointed out that the first 9 or 10 prefixes and suffixes accounted for the vast majority of affixes used in children's printed materials.

To use affixes productively, the child needs to be able to (1) identify a group of letters as a common affix; (2) be able to "peel off" the affix and recognize the underlying root word (i.e., seek the part you know); (3) understand the basic meaning or meanings of the affix; and (4) derive a guess at how the affix might change the meaning of the root word. Thus, given the word *lecturer*, the child needs to (1) discern that *-er* might be operating as a suffix here; (2) peel off *-er* from the root word (*lecture* + *-er*); and (3) discern that *-er* has the meaning of *one who* (fill in the verb) to venture a guess that it might mean *one who lectures*. White et al. (1989) found that teaching children to apply these procedures improved third graders' ability to derive the meanings of unfamiliar multimorphemic words, compared to control children who had not been taught this way. Recent meta-analyses confirm across studies that morphological instruction carried out in various ways has a general beneficial effect on vocabulary building (Bowers et al., 2010; Goodwin & Ahn, 2013), particularly for children experiencing literacy difficulties (Goodwin & Ahn, 2010). As we noted in Chapter 4, having this knowledge also helps children decode words more quickly and accurately as well. Thus, there appears to be little downside to adding some instruction regarding morphological awareness to the list of elements that we may wish to teach in elementary school reading instruction.

TABLE 6.5. Most Common Affixes in Children's Word Corpus

Rank	Prefixes	Suffixes
1	un-	-s, -es
2	re-	-ed
3	in-, im-, ir-, il- (not)	-ing
4	dis-	-ly
5	en-, em-	-er, -or
6	non-	-ion, -tion, -ation, -ition
7	in-, im- (in)	-ible, -able
8	over-	-al, -ial
9	mis-	-y
10	sub-	-ness
11	pre-	-ity, -ty
12	inter-	-ment
13	fore-	-ic
14	de-	-ous, -eous, -ious
15	trans-	-en
16	super-	-er
17	semi-	-ive, -ative, -itive
18	anti-	-ful
19	mid-	-less
20	under-	-est

Note. Based on White, Sowell, and Yanagihara (1989).

CLASSROOM PRACTICES FOR LEARNING NEW WORDS

We have already identified several effective classroom practices for learning new words. We have discussed how children's *use of the N3C* can be capitalized on to foster initial vocabulary knowledge. We have discussed how using reading materials containing the appropriate amount of new words can increase the number of new words entering into children's vocabularies, particularly if they are urged to carry out *contextual analysis.* We have discussed how *user-friendly definitions* can be used to increase children's vocabulary. We have shown that teaching children how to carry out *morphological analysis* can be a tool to gain partial knowledge of the meanings of new words. Next we describe additional practices that have been identified as successful classroom strategies for increasing children's vocabularies.

Interactive Storybook Reading

One leading recommendation for enhancing children's vocabularies is to carry out interactive storybook reading (Wasik, Bond, & Hindman, 2006). In interactive storybook reading teachers use questioning, pointing, and other sorts of techniques designed to engage children actively and linguistically during teacher read-alouds. In carrying out interactive storybook reading, teachers provide some kind of feedback and assistance in helping the children to address comprehension and, sometimes, difficult vocabulary. The questions take into account the cognitive level of the children in the room. Often teachers carry out questioning around some sort of an acronym that directs children to various types of information associated with the reading, such as CROWD (Whitehurst et al., 1994):

Completing (a sentence).
Recalling (information from the story).
Open-ended (predictions or descriptions of what is going on in the story).
Wh-questions (related to the story).
Distancing (relating book to experiences outside the story).

Typically, teachers carry out these read-alouds for groups of children who cannot read books for themselves, generally preschoolers and kindergarteners, using picture books. Interactive storybook reading sessions are often designed to supplement the storybook reading that may or may not be occurring in the children's homes. The read-alouds are often carried out in small-group classroom settings, but they can also be conducted in large classroom settings as well. To be interactive, teachers need to ask children questions before, during, and after the reading. Much research has been carried out on interactive storybook practices and their effectiveness. In general, these practices seem to have a moderate effect on children's standardized vocabulary test scores and oral language skills when carried out by classroom teachers (Mol, Bus, & de Jong, 2009). In general, the more often teachers reference difficult vocabulary in these interactive storybook discussions, the more likely children are to experience gains in vocabulary (Wasik & Hindman, 2014).

More recently, researchers have experimented with carrying out interactive storybook reading using a variety of electronic storybook platforms, such as DVDs, apps on phones, and apps on tablets. Increasingly, electronic storybooks targeting very young children, including toddlers and preschoolers, are being developed through these platforms because delivery through phones and so forth allows parents to keep their children occupied by engaging in a culturally valued activity (i.e., book reading) (Rosin, 2013). These electronic approaches to interactive storybook reading involve an e-reader who reads the story aloud to the child, stopping occasionally to ask him or her a question. For example, in one study by Smeets and Bus (2012), a child was read a story in which a bear is said to fan a fire, and the child was asked a question about fanning (e.g., "In which picture does Bear fan the fire?") by the app. The child then selected the picture containing a bear fanning a fire and received feedback such as "Good job! Here you see Bear fanning the fire; the fire is growing." Answering such questions sprinkled throughout the texts improved children's vocabulary learning compared to a simple listening-only control. Thus, these kinds of electronic interactive storybook readers can be expected to increase as educators and publishers gain an appreciation for how best to design these applications to increase their educational value.

Repeated Reading

Quite possibly the simplest classroom strategy shown to increase the learning of vocabulary is the straightforward repeated reading of books. In a way, this is the opposite of interactive storybook reading because, in this case, we are relying on simple repetition of the text to promote word learning, not the interaction around the meanings of the text and particular word meanings. Vocabulary acquisition through repeated readings probably occurs for the simple reason that storybooks often contain words that are used infrequently in children's conversations with others (Beals & Tabors, 1995). Each reading gives the child another opportunity to ferret out the relationship between the words and the pictorial and textual context.

To a great extent, many parents, even middle-class parents, rely on repetition of storybooks over time to accomplish what a quick definition or interaction around the meanings of particular words could accomplish in a single reading (Evans, Reynolds, Shaw, & Pursoo, 2011). Some researchers have characterized this as a missed opportunity, which it probably is. However, many parents are likely to read some books to children over and over again. Research has shown that with each verbatim repeated reading of a storybook, children do make some modest gains on learning the meanings of the difficult words within that book (Evans & Saint-Aubin, 2013; Sénéchal, 1997). Although we can hardly say that repeated readings represent the best way to encourage vocabulary learning, it is a potential element in vocabulary learning for beleaguered teachers and parents who can sometimes only muster up the energy to read books to children in a straightforward way.

Teacher–Child Conversations

Vocabulary skills have been shown to be related to opportunities to engage in conversation (Snow & Blum-Kulka, 2002). In schools, even in preschool settings, conversations between teachers and their students are relatively infrequent, and children with low verbal skills are likely to be conversationally ignored (Kontos & Wilcox-Herzog, 1997). For example, one study of 119 preschool classrooms found that teachers spent 30% of their time interacting with the class as a whole, but only 10% with individual children (Layzer, Goodson, & Moss, 1993). Wilcox-Herzog and Kontos (1998) found that 81% of the time teachers did not talk to children even when they were within 3 feet of them. Verbal interactions between preschool teachers and children currently tend to be related to concrete, routine matters (Dunn, Beach, & Kontos, 1994). Indeed, in one study of professional development targeting strategies for improving vocabulary practices in preschool classrooms, professional development regarding the amount and quality of small-group–teacher conversations was the least implemented strategy used by teachers for improving children's vocabularies (Schwanenflugel et al., 2009).

Ruston and Schwanenflugel (2010) found that a relatively brief training of adults to implement a linguistically and cognitively complex conversation intervention with pairs of children had an effect on improving children's vocabulary. These adult "talking buddies" were trained to bring rare words into conversations with children and to recast children's sometimes simple phrasings into ones involving rare words (e.g., Child: "Larger!" Adult: "Should it be more *humungous?*"). They were trained to expand on children's simple sentences (e.g., Child: "I beating you!" Adult: "You are beating me"). They were shown how to create open-ended questions that encouraged talk (e.g., Child: "I know my house nasty." Adult: "Why is it nasty?"). After 10 weeks of this short-term, pull-out intervention (50 minutes per week), children's standardized expressive vocabulary test scores improved substantially over a matched group of children who remained in their classroom. Thus, such an approach is a promising potential implementation within the school setting.

Fostering Word Consciousness

Finally, if not obvious before, all of these strategies involve creating an atmosphere in classrooms where word consciousness is the norm. *Word consciousness* is defined as "the knowledge and dispositions necessary for students to learn, appreciate, and effectively use words" (Scott & Nagy, 2004, p. 201). Vocabulary researchers urge teachers to take word consciousness into account throughout their day, rather than treating vocabulary as an isolated skill to be taught and then moved away from as another skill is taught. Word consciousness requires an emphasis on vocabulary instruction in all curricular areas, including creating an affective as well as a cognitive stance toward words—that is, an eagerness to learn and use new words and the love of a perfect new word (Graves & Watts-Taffe, 2008). Teachers can encourage children to hunt for words that are rare and interesting and support them to write using complex sentence phrasing and rare words. Teachers are urged to treat the use of words as interesting objects of study and descriptive language as something to be treasured and enjoyed.

CONNECTING TO THE STANDARDS

The Common Core State Standards explicitly address standards surrounding vocabulary acquisition and use. The standards begin in kindergarten and continue throughout schooling. As children progress through school, there is more emphasis on metaphorical and figurative language, and the use of source materials to discern the meanings of new words. These standards, as they apply to elementary school children, can be found in Table 6.6.

TABLE 6.6. Common Core State Standards for Language Addressing Vocabulary Acquisition and Use (Abridged) for Elementary School Children

Anchor standard: Determine the meaning of unknown and multiple-meaning words and phrases by using context clues, analyzing meaningful word parts, and consulting general and specialized reference materials.

Kindergarten	Determine or clarify the meaning of unknown and multiple-meaning words and phrases based on *kindergarten reading and content*.
Grades 1–5	Determine or clarify the meaning of unknown and multiple-meaning words and phrases based on *grade-level reading and content*, choosing flexibly from an array of strategies.

Anchor standard: Demonstrate understanding of figurative language, word relationships, and nuances in word meanings.

Kindergarten	With guidance and support from adults, explore word relationships and nuances in word meanings.
Grade 1	With guidance and support from adults, demonstrate word relationships and nuances in word meanings.
Grades 2–3	Demonstrate understanding of word relationships and nuances in word meanings.
Grades 4–5	Demonstrate understanding of figurative language, word relationships, and nuances in word meanings.

(continued)

TABLE 6.6. *(continued)*

Anchor standard: Acquire and use accurately a range of general academic and domain-specific words and phrases sufficient for reading, writing, speaking, and listening at the college and career readiness level; demonstrate independence in gathering vocabulary knowledge when encountering an unknown term important to comprehension or expression.

Kindergarten	Use words and phrases acquired through conversations, reading and being read to, and responding to texts.
Grade 1	Use words and phrases acquired through conversations, reading and being read to, and responding to texts, including using frequently occurring conjunctions to signal simple relationships (e.g., *because*).
Grade 2	Use words and phrases acquired through conversations, reading and being read to, and responding to texts, including using adjectives and adverbs to describe (e.g., "When other kids are happy, that makes me happy").
Grade 3	Acquire and use accurately grade-appropriate conversational, general academic, and domain-specific words and phrases, including those that signal spatial and temporal relationships (e.g., "After dinner that night we went looking for them").
Grade 4	Acquire and use accurately grade-appropriate conversational, general academic, and domain-specific words and phrases, including those that signal precise actions, emotions, or states of being (e.g., *quizzed, whined, stammered*) and that are basic to a particular topic (e.g., *wildlife, conservation*, and *endangered* when discussing animal preservation).
Grade 5	Acquire and use accurately grade-appropriate conversational, general academic, and domain-specific words and phrases, including those that signal contrast, addition, and other logical relationships (e.g., *however, although, nevertheless, similarly, moreover, in addition*).

Note. Adapted from the National Governors Association Center for Best Practices and the Council of Chief State School Officers (2010). All rights reserved.

As can be seen in these standards, the first anchor standard in this table places emphasis on various ways that children can derive the meanings of new words and various meanings of words that they already know. This standard points to processes such as the use of context, affixes, root words, as well as standard reference materials such as glossaries and dictionaries. This standard is supported by much of the research we have described here. The second standard reflects an emphasis on the semantic relations that exist between words and their contexts. It highlights distinctions among words in a domain sharing similar meanings and domains that children might find challenging (e.g., cognitive verbs). The standards focus attention on relations among words within the lexicon (e.g., taxonomy, antonymy, and partonomy relations). As children get older, figurative meanings are emphasized.

1. How might we emphasize vocabulary depth instead of breadth in classroom instruction?

2. Given the research on the number of words elementary school children learn per day, do you think it is worthwhile to emphasize the explicit teaching of vocabulary in the classroom?

3. The Common Core State Standards have an increased emphasis on the reading of informational text. What implication might this emphasis have for the teaching of vocabulary in schools?

4. Returning to the case study presented at the beginning of this chapter, what have we learned that is relevant to thinking about Raymond's language issues?

FURTHER READINGS

Anderson, R. C., & Freebody, P. (1981). Vocabulary knowledge. In J. T. Guthrie (Ed.), *Comprehension and teaching: Research reviews* (pp. 77–117). Newark, DE: International Reading Association.

Nagy, W., & Townsend, D. (2012). Words as tools: Learning academic vocabulary as language acquisition. *Reading Research Quarterly, 47*(1), 91–108.

Nation, I. S. P. (2001). *Learning vocabulary in another language.* New York: Cambridge University Press.

CHAPTER 7

Theoretical Models of Reading Comprehension

CASE STUDY

Ms. Richardson is worried about the reading comprehension of Emily, a girl in her fifth-grade classroom. Recently, she asked her class to read a particular story in their basal reader and answer the comprehension questions at the end. Emily was able to do this as long as the questions did not involve combining information from various parts of the story and did not contain words such as *analyze, consider,* and *evaluate.* Ms. Richardson assigned writing a summary of the story for homework. Emily's homework showed that she approached this assignment by selecting a sentence or two from each part of the story. She had merely copied a few sentences, or fragments of them, from the beginning, middle, and end. Oddly, the sentences she chose to copy were not the most important ones, so her composition did not read like a real summary. Ms. Richardson thinks that Emily is missing the big picture and is worried about how Emily will fare in middle school where the texts are longer and more complex. Ms. Richardson is considering strategies for helping Emily with her comprehension.

Good comprehension is the ultimate goal of reading. Improvement in comprehension is the gold standard against which all reading instruction should be evaluated (Kuhn et al., 2006). Before we embark on describing the research related to reading comprehension, we should consider what is meant by the term *reading comprehension* itself. Surprisingly, a solid, well-supported definition of reading comprehension is hard to come by. This problem has been recognized for quite a long time. For example, nearly 40 years ago, Durkin (1978) pointed out that defini-tions of reading comprehension had been rarely provided in research on reading comprehension instruction, and she characterized her own efforts to uncover such a definition as "fruitless." Twenty years later, in his highly influential book *Com-prehension: A Paradigm for Cognition*, Kintsch (1998) stated: "The terms *under-standing* and *comprehension* are not scientific terms but are commonsense expres-sions. As with other such expressions, their meaning is fuzzy and imprecise. . . . What seems most helpful here is to contrast understanding with perception on the one hand and with problem solving on the other" (p. 2). Yet, an alternative mean-ing to differentiate the colloquial meaning from a scientific one was never really offered. The book title itself implies that *comprehension = cognition*.

A few years later, the influential National Reading Panel Report (National Institute of Child Health and Human Development, 2000) did not offer a direct definition of the construct of reading comprehension either, but did offer the observation that reading comprehension had come to be viewed as

> intentional thinking during which meaning is constructed through interactions between text and reader (Durkin, 1993). According to this view, meaning resides in the intentional, problem-solving, thinking processes of the reader that occur during an interchange with a text. The content of meaning is influenced by the text and by the reader's prior knowledge that is brought to bear on it (Anderson & Pearson, 1984). Reading comprehension was seen as the construction of meaning of a written text through a reciprocal interchange of ideas between the reader and the message in a particular text. (p. 4-39)

Although this excerpt contains important ideas about comprehension, it is not a definition by itself. What is notable to us is the general lack of definition provided by researchers studying this topic.

As in all domains, a well-grounded definition and delineation of the cognitive construct we are trying to understand is important. Having a well-defined con-struct increases the potential that we will have more precise instruction as well as more valid assessment. One of the benefits of having a well-grounded definition is that assessments guided by it will not be seen as tangential to instruction, but rather as a helpful guide to understanding the precise nature of student difficulties. Box 7.1 discusses the problems that a lack of a well-agreed-upon definition can have on assessment.

For now, we content ourselves with the brief definition provided by Kintsch (1988): "Discourse comprehension . . . involves constructing a representation of a discourse upon which various computations can be performed, the outcomes of which are commonly taken as evidence for comprehension" (p. 163). What Kintsch means here is that reading comprehension involves developing a representation of the text (discourse) that is the end result of performing a variety of cognitive activities (computations) on the information provided in the text. This is still vague, we recognize, and possibly not all that helpful. But this definition will become clearer once we understand what various theories have to say about how comprehension takes place. In this chapter, we outline four influential theories of reading comprehension. These theories can provide the theoretical domain for the characterizing and studying reading comprehension.

BOX 7.1. Reading Comprehension Assessment Issues

Test developers have identified a need for a well-defined construct of reading comprehension (Rupp, Ferne, & Choi, 2006). Currently, test developers who design comprehension assessments find themselves dealing with issues related to test format, instead of the alignment of the test with theory and instruction (Svetina, Gorin, & Tatsuoka, 2011). Formatting issues are ubiquitous in reading comprehension assessment. Here is a sampling.

Multiple-choice tests may not assess actual comprehension. Instead, multiple-choice tests tend to elicit strategies such as lexical matching (Buck, Tatsuoka, & Kostin, 1997). For example, to answer a comprehension question about a passage on frogs, such as "Why are frogs are going extinct?," a child might simply search for the words *frogs* and *extinct* within the text, selecting the option that best matches the surrounding text, without understanding, or perhaps even reading, the passage at all.

Other tests have *stop-rule* problems (e.g., the Neale Analysis of Reading Ability). Tests that use stop rules have children read stories of increasing difficulty aloud and then answer questions about them. When a certain number of oral reading errors are made, testing stops and a comprehension score is calculated based on only the questions that the child has answered up to that point (Spooner, Baddeley, & Gathercole, 2004; Cain & Oakhill, 2006). Because passages can be difficult in different ways for different readers, due to prior knowledge effects, the child might have been able to answer questions from later passages, but he or she will not have the opportunity.

Cloze or maze tests (e.g., as found on some benchmarking systems for reading comprehension) ask children to select or generate a possible completion for sentences within a passage where a word has been deleted. Scores children receive on these tests tend to reflect their familiarity with syntax or their comprehension of single sentences, rather than their comprehension of the larger text (Shanahan, Kamil, & Tobin, 1982).

For purely format-specific reasons, children can score well on some test types but poorly on others (Keenan, Betjemann, & Olson, 2008). This issue leads many researchers and teachers to question the utility of such tests for understanding and remediating student differences in comprehension.

THE SIMPLE VIEW OF READING

The *simple view of reading* (henceforth, the *simple view*; Hoover & Gough, 1990) "does not reduce reading to decoding, but asserts that reading necessarily involves the full set of linguistic skills, such as parsing, bridging, and discourse building; decoding in the absence of these skills is not reading" (p. 128). Thus, the two skills involved in reading comprehension, according to this view, are (1) decoding, which requires the efficient use of word recognition skills from print (discussed in previous chapters)—having these skills allows the child to access the mental lexicon and derive word meanings from it; and (2) linguistic comprehension, which involves taking lexical information and deriving discourse (text) representations from it. The linguistic comprehension skills referred to by this model are amodal, that is, they apply similarly to children's listening and reading comprehension skills. This model points out that neither decoding nor linguistic comprehension is sufficient by itself, but rather that good reading comprehension requires both skills such that:

Reading Comprehension = Decoding × Linguistic Comprehension

Using a large dataset, Hoover and Gough (1990) found that including this multiplicative relationship statistically as a predictor went beyond the simple additive effects of decoding and linguistic comprehension in predicting differences among children in their reading comprehension. The multiplicative function between decoding and linguistic comprehension significantly improved their ability to predict reading comprehension skills among English–Spanish bilingual students in grades 1–4. In fact, including these multiplicative effects produced multiple correlations that were very high indeed, from .84–.91! It seems hard to imagine a model that would do better than that.

Figure 7.1 illustrates a general schema for considering four types of readers predicted by the simple view, including three ways that poor reading comprehension can result. In Case A, a child might have poor decoding skills but sufficient linguistic comprehension. In this case, a child might not be able to decode fluently and accurately, and this would limit his or her comprehension in a bottom-up way. This issue might be found among children who are diagnosed as classically dyslexic—those who have difficulty retrieving and manipulating the letter–sound skills needed for decoding print, but who otherwise exhibit typical listening comprehension and communication skills.

In Case B, a child might have poor linguistic comprehension but sufficient decoding skills. This pattern might be found among children who are hyperlexic; that is, children who have unusually good decoding skills for their age but who

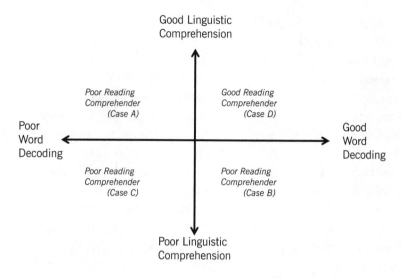

FIGURE 7.1. The simple view of reading (based on Hoover & Gough, 1990).

lack commensurate linguistic comprehension and communication skills (Worthy & Invernizzi, 1995). This pattern is perhaps most evident among children who are learning to decode words in a second language before they have developed an adequate understanding of the structures and vocabulary of that language. This pattern might also be found in so-called *word callers* described in our chapter on reading fluency.

In Case C, a child might have two problems: both poor decoding and poor linguistic comprehension skills. These are the all-around poor readers. The multiplicative function described by the simple view would predict that such children would have very poor reading comprehension, indeed.

Finally, Case D illustrates a child lacking neither of these skills. Children in this quadrant have adequate to good decoding skills and adequate to good listening comprehension skills. Such children usually have good reading comprehension.

Evaluation of the Simple View

A great deal of research has been done that supports these predictions generated by the simple view of reading. For example, Nation and Snowling (1997) found that elementary school children with poor passage comprehension demonstrated the same deficit even when passages were read aloud to them. Catts, Adlof, and Weismer (2006) identified a subgroup of children with poor passage comprehension despite adequate decoding and found that these children became more identifiable as they got older when the demands of the texts become heavy. These children appeared to have general issues with drawing inferences from text, whether written or spoken. Catts et al. (2006) have identified children who have adequate decoding despite poor listening comprehension, and, as predicted by the view, these children too have reading comprehension difficulties.

Another type of evidence for this view is the finding that there is a decline in the correlation between word decoding and comprehension skills as children approach middle school, which also might be expected as the demands on comprehension become stronger. Similarly, as we discussed in Chapter 5 on reading fluency, there is also a general decline in the relationship between fluency (which involves fast and accurate decoding) and the comprehension that occurs as children move through schooling. As a result of these factors, the variance in reading comprehension explained by individual differences in listening comprehension increases over time (Tilstra, McMaster, van den Broek, Kendeou, & Rapp, 2009). Also, as would be predicted from the model, factors that affect word decoding (e.g., letter knowledge, phonemic awareness) appear to be largely different from those that predict comprehension (Carver, 2000; Muter et al., 2004; Protopapas, Simos, Sideridis, & Mouzaki, 2012).

A basic argument against the simple view is that it is *too* simple, which is perhaps not surprising. Researchers have responded to the simple view by suggesting various additions to the model. These arguments generally present evidence that our ability to predict individual differences in comprehension skills can be improved by adding some new factor, beyond just decoding and listening comprehension. For example, Joshi and Aaron (2000) have suggested that a general component of processing speed should be added to the simple view. Others have suggested that simple naming speed (time taken to name pictured objects) would adequately account for speed differences (Johnston & Kirby, 2006). Some have argued that perhaps a fluency component needs to be added (Tilstra et al., 2009; but see Adolf, Catts, & Little, 2006). Connors (2009) called for adding attentional control as a new component within the model. Ouellette and Beers (2010) suggested that vocabulary should be treated separately within the model. Kirby and Savage (2008) note that reading comprehension strategies are not considered within the model. Essentially, then, a predominant empirical response to the simple view has been to make it more complex.

To a great extent, some of the strongest concerns with the simple view have come from reading educators. One of the issues they raise is that the simple view seems to suggest that decoding and comprehension might be treated separately in instruction as distinct skills, although Hoover and Gough (1990) would deny this. Stuart, Stainthorp, and Snowling (2008) think that the simple view encourages teachers to carry out comprehension instruction and decoding instruction as part of their daily reading programming because children will need both to read well ultimately. Pressley et al. (2009) point out that, in practice, the simple view has the effect of encouraging teachers to emphasize the drill-and-kill decoding practice in the early grades, while ignoring comprehension instruction altogether, since comprehension demands are light in the texts typically used in these grades. We think it is fair to say that the basic success and understandability of the simple view has often resulted in the teaching of decoding skills in isolation from the skills needed for comprehension of complex texts than might have otherwise occurred. Whether the teaching of isolated skills is a good idea or not remains a strong issue of contention among reading educators (Goodman & Goodman, 1979; Stanovich, 1994), and we do not intend to try to resolve that question here.

Other reading educators have complained about the lack of centrality and detail about comprehension instruction provided by the model. For example, Hoffman (2009) argued that the view treats the comprehension side of the equation too monolithically. It ignores the challenges that some genres (e.g., informational vs. narrative texts) might pose to children, and the unique difficulties children have when reading beyond their decoding level. He points out that the view ignores differing purposes and motivations people have for reading various texts (e.g., skimming, entertainment, deep reading). Others have suggested that the simple view is too simple to serve as any kind of guide for instruction at all. Harrison (2010) went so far as to suggest that the simple view is so simple that it is useful only as an "elevator pitch" to politicians about the value of reading research for instruction (p. 207).

Regardless of its limitations, the simple view has helped us clarify the deeply entangled relationship between lower-level decoding processes and higher-level comprehension processes. Other models we describe next have focused more heavily on the comprehension side of the equation. Each of these models has given us deeper insight into the workings of reading comprehension side than the simple view does.

SCHEMA THEORETIC VIEW

The schema theoretic view (henceforth, *schema theory*) did not start out to be a model of reading comprehension, but rather as a more general psychological model "for representing how knowledge is stored in human memory" (Anderson & Pearson, 1984, p. 259). The term *schema* was first used in 1923 by Bartlett (cited in Anderson & Pearson), and is close cousin to Piaget's (1970) term *scheme*, but it was not until psychologists first started commonly using computers to model human thought in the 1970s that schema theory was fully articulated, and shortly thereafter began to be used in the field of reading (Anderson & Pearson). Although many scholars worked on and articulated schema-related theories of reading (e.g., Adams & Collins, 1977; Rumelhart, 1980), Richard Anderson and David Pearson's chapter in the first *Handbook of Reading Research* is generally recognized as the classic version of this view, and it is their model that we describe here.

What Are Schemas?

A *schema* is a knowledge structure that organizes and summarizes what a person knows about a specific topic. It contains both memories of that person's experiences related to the topic and also what he or she has learned about the topic through other means (e.g., conversation, reading, and schooling). Figure 7.2 is a diagram of some elements of the *dog* schema for Nancy (one of the authors, who is a lifelong dog enthusiast). This example demonstrates several key points about schemas.

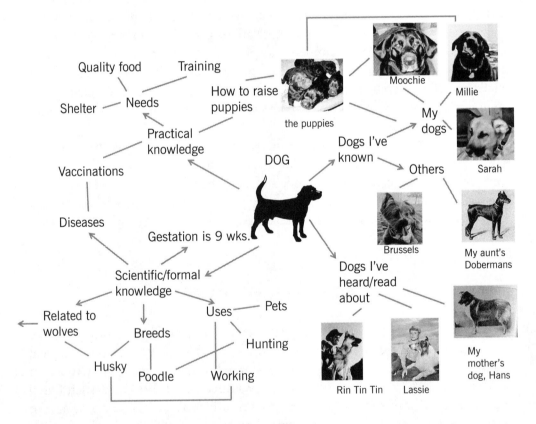

FIGURE 7.2. Nancy's schema of *dog*. All images by the author except the following, which are in the public domain: dog silhouette, Doberman pinscher, collie (Hans), Rin Tin Tin, and Lassie.

Adult Schemas Are Very Complex

This diagram contains only a very small part of Nancy's stored knowledge about dogs—you can see how it could keep going and going, listing more dogs she has known, more practical or formal knowledge she has learned about dogs through reading or being told about them, and so forth. If somehow we could accurately diagram this whole schema, the web of nodes and interconnections would become incredibly tangled. Of course, this schema is also connected to many of Nancy's other schemas (note the arrow pointing out from *related to wolves*). It is estimated that the average adult mind has 80–100 billion neurons, and each of these neurons can connect to 100,000 other neurons, resulting in up to 10 thousand trillion possible connections, many of which change daily as we experience and learn more (Lieff, 2012). Yet as humans, we keep all these connections, and the connections within and between a myriad of other schemas, relatively straight in our minds.

Schemas Have Both Hierarchical and Overlapping/Connecting Organizational Structures

According to Adams and Collins (1977), schemas have both hierarchical and overlapping/connecting organizational structures. An example of a hierarchical structure in Figure 7.2 is the way that *DOGS* leads to *Dogs I have known*, which then goes to *My dogs*, and then down to individual dogs, about each of which Nancy also has a schema, though there isn't room to show all of these in the figure. In the same way, *formal knowledge* Nancy has about dogs includes their various *Uses* as *Pets, Hunting,* or *Working* dogs, knowledge about many different *Breeds* of dogs (only a couple could be shown here), and that dogs are *related to wolves*. At the same time, there are interconnections across the various categories of knowledge: *Huskies* are a breed of dog, but they are also *Working* dogs and the dogs most closely related to wolves. Nancy's formal knowledge about dog *Diseases* is connected to her practical knowledge about which *Vaccines* they need to get. Much of her practical knowledge about *How to raise puppies* comes from her personal experience of raising a litter (*the puppies*), and two of these puppies were *Moochie* and *Millie*. Again, only a few of these connections could be shown here——for example, there should be lines from *Pets* to all the dogs Nancy has had and known; from *Millie* to *Diseases*, since she has had quite a few; and so on.

One key assertion of schema theory is that the organization and connections in a schema are just as important as the actual bits of knowledge (or *nodes*) in it. In other words, a heap of disconnected facts and experiences, with no organization, would not be a schema, or even any kind of useful knowledge at all. Fortunately, humans from infancy up seem to have an innate drive to organize their knowledge into structures, and to make these structures as coherent and useable as possible (Anderson & Pearson, 1984; see also Piaget, 1970; Sharps & Wertheimer, 2000).

Schemas Contain Different Types of Knowledge from Different Sources

Two main types of knowledge that schemas contain are knowledge *about* things, which can be learned in many ways, and knowledge *of* things, that is, memories of actual experiences that somewhat resemble film clips, but with added smell, taste, touch and emotional content. We have tried to show this in Figure 7.2 by using images for the experiential knowledge (*of*) and only words for the more semantic (*about*) knowledge, but of course, in real schemas, there are images associated with semantic knowledge, and, since humans are language users, we inevitably associate words with our experiences (Vygotksy, 1978). Note that books, movies, and even narrative accounts can be seen as experiences in their own way. For instance, long before she got her first dog at age 20, Nancy had been told stories about her mother's dog, Hans; had played often with her aunt's Doberman dogs; and had read Lassie books and watched *Rin Tin Tin* on television; so she already had in her *dog* schema some ideas of the possible pleasures of owning a dog, not in terms of a mental list (that would be knowledge *about*), but in terms of experiences she had imagined and emotions she had felt when hearing, reading, or watching these stories. Such vicarious experiences are particularly relevant when we consider why people read, especially for pleasure.

A third type of knowledge, *procedural knowledge*, or knowledge of *how* things are done, can be gained either from personal experience or from more abstract learning, though it is likely there are differences in the quality of knowledge developed in each way. Some scholars have characterized schemas about procedures as *scripts* that "describe an appropriate sequence of events in a particular context," almost like the script of a play that tells actors what to do (Schank & Abelson, 1975, p. 151). In Figure 7.2, the node *How to raise puppies* probably connects with a collection of scripts for doing specific tasks such as *weaning puppies* or *housebreaking puppies*. An example of another script that many people have is a schema of *What to do at a restaurant* (which may have subscripts for different types of restaurants, from fast food to elegant dining), complete with *roles* such as waiter and customer, *actions* like ordering and paying, and *items* such as menus and tables (Schank & Abelson).

Schemas Are Individual, but Joint Members of a Group Usually Share Elements of Their Schemas

Obviously, no one other than Nancy could have exactly the same schema as the one partially diagrammed in Figure 7.2, because no one else has had identical experiences, and it is likely no one else shares the exact same knowledge she has learned about dogs. However, we would expect to see many of the same elements, especially on the *knowledge about* side, in the schemas of other people living at this time in the United States, where Nancy lives, and even more shared elements, on both sides, in the *dog* schemas of her mother or son. On the other hand, a native Alaskan who ran sled dogs in Alaska would have a different and much more elaborated set of elements clustered around *Huskies* as *Working* dogs, including a script for *How to drive sled dogs*, knowledge of what to feed them, and so forth. We consider in greater depth how schema theory helps us understand the effects of culture on learning and reading later in this chapter.

Schemas and Reading

According to schema theoretic views of reading, readers use schemas at all levels of reading, from recognizing the forms of letters to predicting what types of words will fit the syntax of sentences in their language (Adams & Collins, 1977). The ultimate goal is comprehension, defined as "activating or constructing a schema that provides a coherent explanation of objects and events in a discourse" (Anderson, 1994, p. 473). All of these activities happen simultaneously and interactively; in other words, the reader does not first recognize and comprehend words, then combine the meanings of words into understandable sentences, sentences into paragraphs, and finally, the separate meanings of paragraphs into a comprehensible whole story or argument.

Instead, as soon as a reader begins to read a text, he or she is searching mentally for an overall schema to use to help make sense of that text. If the reader has difficulty locating an appropriate schema, either because the reader lacks knowledge in the area or because the writing is vague or unclear, comprehension will suffer, even if the reader knows all the words in the text. Consider the following passage from a longer text used by Bransford and Johnson (1972) in a series of experiments on comprehension:

> The procedure is actually quite simple. First, you arrange the items into different groups. Of course one pile may be sufficient depending on how much there is to do. If you have to go somewhere else due to lack of facilities that is the next step; otherwise, you are pretty well set. It is important not to overdo things. That is, it is better to do too few things at once than too many. In the short run this may not seem important but complications can easily arise. A mistake can be expensive as well. (p. 722)

This passage was deliberately written to be vague, and although the words and sentences are not complex, most people found it quite difficult to comprehend; that is, unless they were told ahead of time that the passage was about *washing clothes.* When the appropriate schema was called up in this way, the passage became very easy to comprehend.

According to this theory, some problems in comprehension arise from either failing to find a useful schema or adopting an incorrect schema from the start. For example, most people reading the following passage would assume that it was about a prisoner contemplating escape:

> Tony slowly got up from the mat, planning his escape. He hesitated a moment and thought. Things were not going well. What bothered him most was being held, especially since the charge against him had been weak. He considered his present situation. The lock that held him was strong but he thought he could break it. (Anderson, 1994, p. 472)

However, Anderson, Reynolds, Shallert, and Goetz (1977) found that wrestlers and people interested in similar sports tended to interpret the same passage as referring to a wrestling match. If the passage had been really about a prisoner, such an initial choice of schema could seriously impair comprehension. Perhaps more important, though, this example shows how two widely differing interpretations of a text can both be justified—an assertion that directly addresses whether a test or a teacher can say there is a "correct" interpretation to a poem or a "right" theme to be found in a work of fiction. Notice also how the initially accessed schema changes the meaning of certain words in the passage: A *charge* is either a wrestling move or a legal accusation, and a *lock* is a wrestling hold or a metal object. No "actual" meaning of these words constrains the meaning of the passage; rather, the schema the reader uses to interpret the passage dictates the meaning these words will convey.

The schemas a reader accesses while reading are also invaluable for filling in places where the writer has assumed knowledge on the part of the reader. As we discuss more thoroughly in the next chapter, this process, called *inference*, is inevitably necessary in reading; no writer can include all the knowledge necessary to understand a text. Schemas greatly assist this process because each schema has certain "slots" that are typically filled, elements that readers familiar with that schema will search for in the text or supply from their own knowledge, if those elements are missing. As an example, let's consider a text related to a restaurant schema referred to earlier.

> Richard was tempted not to leave any tip at all. His food had taken over 40 minutes to come, it was cold when he got it, and there was butter on his potato, although he had specifically requested sour cream. As the final straw, after he had waited 15 minutes with an empty glass, he actually had to ask the hostess for another glass of water. In the end, he left a small tip, but told himself that he would never eat there again.

Did the phrase "leave a tip" immediately signal to you that this scene was occurring in a restaurant? Think of all you must draw from your schema about restaurants to comprehend this passage. Richard obviously fills the "customer" slot, and the person filling the "waiter/waitress" slot is also a key to this passage, even though he or she is never mentioned. You have to draw on your restaurant script, or schema, to know that a tip is money left for a wait-staff person for good, or at least adequate, service, and to know that bringing food before it gets cold, getting orders correct, and refilling empty glasses of water without being asked are all actions servers are expected to do. To catch the more subtle elements of the final sentence, you may have to realize that people (perhaps especially men) are often embarrassed not to leave a tip in a restaurant, even if the service is bad, something younger readers may not know. This, in turn, indicates that the inefficient server may be causing the restaurant to lose business. On the other hand, Richard may be a rather spineless character, not very good at standing up for himself. Effective readers will consider all these potential implications as they prepare to read on in the text, but can do so only because of prior knowledge drawn from a well-instantiated restaurant schema. Of course, this passage could also be from the beginning of a mystery in which Richard's waitress has just been kidnapped. Kidnapping is not a part of the typical restaurant schema, and mystery writers often use such schema violations to heighten the tension and sense of unpredictability that mystery fans enjoy.

In addition to enabling comprehension, schemas affect what readers learn and remember from texts. They do this in part by focusing readers' attention on the elements in the text that are either important or in some way challenge or upset the typical schema of the text. For example, if you were tested tomorrow on your recall of the short passage above, you might not remember that the man's name was Richard; his name is not important to comprehending the passage, nor does it violate a typical restaurant schema. You might also not remember that he waited exactly 15 minutes before asking the hostess to refill his water. However, you would probably remember that he waited a long time, and that his food was cold and his order not right, since they are elements important to comprehending the text.

A number of experiments have shown that importance is not a set quality of a text element, but rather is judged by readers relative to the schema they are using when reading. Some studies have demonstrated that the importance of, and thus memory for, a text element can be increased by priming the reader with a related question prior to or during reading (e.g., Rothkopf & Billington, 1979), as in the familiar test-prep strategy that recommends reading the questions before the passage. Other studies have shown that importance, and recall, of text elements can be heightened or lowered by providing readers with a schema prior to reading. For example, Pichert and Anderson (1977) asked people to read the same passage about a house from the point of view of a potential buyer or a potential burglar.

They found that those who read as buyers were likely to recall elements such as a leaking roof, whereas those who read as burglars remembered things like the three 10-speed bikes in the garage.

But attention does not explain all of the effects of schema on memory; in fact, sometimes a strong schema can induce readers to "remember" elements that were not in the text at all (Anderson, 1994). For instance, if asked to retell the story a week after reading about Richard in the restaurant, you might state that "the waitress did not do her job well," although no server gender is actually mentioned in the passage. Studies have shown that when expected schema slots, such as the identity of the server, are not filled by the elements in the text, readers tend to fill them with "default" elements drawn from their general schemas; so if your default image of a server in a restaurant is a waitress, that may be what you remember. You might even falsely state that Richard wanted his coffee cup refilled because in your schema of restaurant eating, coffee refills are much more significant than water refills. This sort of memory distortion is a schema-related effect all too familiar to police who collect eyewitness reports and judges who caution jurors not to rely on them too much in court proceedings (Greenberg, Westcott, & Bailey, 1998).

On the positive side, it appears that an effective schema can be a framework that helps readers recall text elements after reading a passage. This effect was perhaps best demonstrated by an experiment done by Anderson and Pichert (1978), following the original house study cited above. In this new experiment, people were initially asked to read the same passage taking one of the same two viewpoints, and then to recall all the details they could, with the same results as in the first experiment described above. Then they were asked to assume the opposite viewpoint and, without reading the passage again, to remember all the details they could about the house; that is, the home buyers were now asked to imagine themselves as burglars and write down as much as they could remember about the house, and the erstwhile burglars were now asked to think of themselves as potential homebuyers. Remarkably, each group now recalled additional details about the house that they had not remembered at first—details mostly more relevant to the new schemas they had been asked to activate. Clearly, the new schema had enabled them to recall additional details from the passage. Both of these studies by Anderson and Pichert highlight the importance of a reader's ability to use prior knowledge not only to understand but also to remember the contents of a text, both of which factors are usually considered important in reading comprehension (Anderson & Pearson, 1984).

Finally, before leaving this model, we want to mention a type of schema that is particularly relevant to reading comprehension: a schema for a particular text form or genre. The best known of these is probably the common narrative schema known as a *story schema* or *story grammar* (Mandler & Johnson, 1977; Rumelhart, 1980; Stein & Glenn, 1979). These contain the well-known elements of a setting, a protagonist(s) (and possibly other characters), a problem or conflict, one or more events/attempts to solve the problem, and an ending or resolution. Readers use their story schema to guide their understanding of the text in an ongoing way. The reader essentially looks for and expects to find information about the protagonist, identifies the problem or conflict that the protagonist is having, evaluates the attempts toward resolving that problem that are presented in the story, and recognizes the resolution to the story as the problem is solved.

To consider the elements of a story schema, it might be helpful to think about a simple story that you might tell a 4-year-old, say, *A Fire Engine Named Fred.* In such as story, typically we might expect that Fred would be the protagonist. Perhaps Fred was a bored little fire engine that hardly ever got to leave the firehouse (problem). We could imagine that the protagonist might engage in several unsuccessful attempts to fix this problem (setting off false alarms, convincing the fire chief to use him in a parade, etc.). We might anticipate that there will be a resolution (that Fred actually gets to help put out a real fire). Although such stories might not constitute great literature, they do capture the basic elements of the story schema.

Reviews of multiple studies by Dimino, Taylor, and Gersten (1995) and Stetter and Hughes (2010b) have confirmed that a command of this basic story schema greatly facilitates narrative comprehension and production in students at multiple ages. Further, teaching this schema to readers with learning disabilities, second-language learners, and others who struggle with comprehension is an effective instructional intervention.

The emphasis newly placed on expository text at all grade levels by the Common Core State Standards has led to an increase in research on the effects of *expository text structures* on comprehension. Based on work by Meyer and colleagues (Meyer, Brandt, & Bluth, 1980; Meyer, 1985), it is clear that expository structure schemas show more variation than traditional story grammars, including differing structures for descriptive, sequence-directive, cause–effect, problem–solution, and compare–contrast expository texts. However, both Meyer's earlier research and multiple studies since then show that, just as for story grammars, readers who understand these structures show greater comprehension of expository texts and that, likewise, teaching these structures to students who are unfamiliar with them results in increased comprehension (Akhondi, Malayeri, & Samad, 2011; Meyer & Ray, 2011; Williams et al., 2014).

Schema theory, as you can see, focuses most of its attention on the structure of knowledge and the use of that knowledge by the reader in understanding the text. This is a top-down, knowledge-driven approach to addressing issues of comprehension. In the next model, attention is focused on how readers develop a representation of the text from the bottom up, constructing and integrating lower-level text information with their prior knowledge.

CONSTRUCTION–INTEGRATION MODEL

The construction–integration model (henceforth, the C-I model; Kintsch, 1988, 2004) takes a multilevel approach to understanding reading comprehension. Specifically, it describes the reader as building and managing different levels of cognitive representations of a text in an ongoing way. There is "a linguistic level of representation, conceptual levels to represent both the local and global meaning and structure of a text, . . . and a level at which the text itself has lost its individuality and its information content has become integrated into some larger structure" (p. 163).

The C-I model describes comprehension as occurring in two general phases to obtain new levels of text understanding. The first of these is a *construction phase*, a bottom-up process that captures information from surface text information (*surface code*) to build an initial representation of the text. The *surface code* level captures the exact wording and syntax of the text. This surface representation is very temporary and is quickly dismissed in favor of a level of representation that captures the basic ideas present in the text, called the *textbase*. To develop this textbase, the reader derives a set of basic ideas that correspond to the text by forming a set of propositions. A *proposition* is thought to be the simplest representation of a unit of meaning in a text. It represents a very simple, stripped-down idea from the larger context (Bovair & Kieras, 1985). After reading the sentence *Ann wore green beads*, you might split this idea up into a number of propositions (that distinguish text ideas from the surface code), each representing a simpler idea: Ann *wore* (Ann, beads), and beads (green). Text propositions can also cause the reader to retrieve information strongly associated with those propositions from long-term memory. For example, if you are reading a passage entitled "Mardi Gras," you might retrieve the strongly associated information from long-term memory that Mardi Gras involves beads. These propositions from memory also get entered into the textbase along with information derived from the text. The reader also draws some minimal inferences (or ideas developed from the text that are not represented directly within it). For example, if the next sentence started with *She*, you might draw the basic inference that *She* referred to *Ann*. These too get entered into the textbase along with constructed propositions gained from reading the text and those from prior knowledge. The resulting textbase representation from the construction phase of the model consists of a set of overlapping propositions that interconnect ideas in the text.

It is important to notice that the representation of the text that is developed during this construction phase goes beyond the text. It can include information that is merely associated but irrelevant to the text. It can include incorrectly drawn inferences. It is, in essence, sloppy. Generally, as people are building this knowledge net, they work with a limited set of propositions at a time, in cycles, due to the constraints of working memory. Let's work through the textbase construction process in greater detail so you can see how the construction process works for a very simple text, *Chris is a chef. He cooks at a sorority.*

The propositions shown in Table 7.1 hypothetically comprise the textbase generated by a reader for this simple passage. How one derives the particular list of propositions is beyond the scope of what we wish to present here, and we have deliberately simplified the process. However, a proposition can represent a key concept, a relationship, or a simple sentence. Suffice it to say that the end result of this construction phase should be to describe how ideas are potentially interconnected within the textbase. Let's walk through the textbase that our reader has generated during the construction phase.

First, we note that the textbase contains several associations that our hypothetical reader has retrieved from long-term memory. After the first sentence, our reader has retrieved the association from prior knowledge that chefs work in restaurants (proposition E below), that they cook (D), and that the name *Chris* is usually connected to someone who is male (F). However, it is possible that Chris is female or that he works somewhere else. Importantly, the association that chefs

TABLE 7.1. Hypothetical Propositional Analysis Based on the Construction–Integration Model for a Simple Text

Textbase for *Chris is a chef. He cooks for a sorority.*		
Reference letter	Proposition	Construction
A	(CHRIS)	Chris exists and named entities are important.
B	(CHEF)	Nouns can have their own proposition.
C	BE (A, B)	Connect A with B in the network.
D	BE (B, PERSON)	Connect the knowledge base association that chefs are people D with B.
E	COOK (B, RESTAURANTS)	Connect knowledge base association that chefs cook in restaurants E with B.
F	BE (A, MALE)	Connect name gender association from knowledge base F with A.
G	HE (A)	Connect G with A as pronoun assignment inference.
H	(SORORITY)	Nouns get their own propositions.
I	COOK (C, H)	Connect I with C, H (indirectly with A and B and D).

Note. Based on Kintsch (1988).

cook in restaurants (E) happens to be irrelevant for this passage. The construction phase is indiscriminate in this way—it simply retrieves information from long-term memory that is closely associated with text concepts, relevant or not.

Note that during the construction phase, our hypothetical reader has also drawn a reasonable, basic inference that assigns the pronoun to its antecedent (G). In this case, our reader has correctly inferred that HE refers to CHRIS. The inferences the reader draws from the text get entered into the textbase.

Finally, note that there is overlap among these propositions, which can be seen for CHRIS and CHEF, in particular. These two are linked and referred to often with other ideas in the textbase, although they appear only once in the surface text itself. The textbase that our reader has created here contains a number of direct and indirect interlinkages between text ideas, CHRIS, and CHEF. For the network of propositions that has been constructed by our reader for the textbase, the concepts CHRIS and CHEF are central.

The second phase of the C-I model is an integration phase wherein the fragmented and inconsistent textbase representation is combined to construct a coherent, abstract representation of the text, called the *situation model*. This situation model represents the text in an abstracted way that is now several levels away from the specifics of the text itself. The integration phase resolves inconsistencies that are developed during the sloppy, association-driven construction phase through a process of spreading activation and inhibition. Related propositions are strengthened and activated. Inconsistent or seldom-mentioned propositions disappear.

Returning to our text, after integration, CHRIS (A) and CHEF (B) have become highly activated because of their centrality to the network. Note that CHRIS and CHEF are strongly activated, even though they are mentioned only once in the text directly, the same as the word SORORITY (H), but because of how they are represented in this network of interrelated propositions, they gain in importance over SORORITY through this integration process. In fact, this is one of the basic rationales for the notion of propositions and their textbase representation. The textbase can represent the fact that even though something is presented only once in the surface level representation of the text, it can have undue centrality in comprehension.

Propositions that are mentioned recently or often are carried over in working memory as people go on to process more text. During this phase, unrelated or contradictory propositions are eliminated and deactivated. Proposition E will disappear altogether from our final integrated representation of this passage. This integrated model of the text, the situation model, is now a complex, holistic representation of the text.

The situation model can go well beyond the text itself. It can carry with it the reader's goals for reading the text, his or her feelings about it, and its connections to prior knowledge (Kintsch, 2010). Importantly, it integrates the new text with the reader's knowledge base. Our reader might update his or her notions of a CHEF in long-term memory to indicate that chefs might also cook for sororities. It is really in this integration phase that true comprehension is said to take place.

Evaluation of the C-I Model

The C-I model makes a number of predictions that have been supported by research. First, the model predicts that readers will more likely recall propositions that are interconnected with other propositions in the situation model (Kintsch & van Dijk, 1978). In our case, propositions A, B, and perhaps C are likely to be recalled.

The model predicts that having prior knowledge related to a text should improve comprehension because this information is available as readers construct the textbase (Dooling & Christiaansen, 1977; Rawson & Kintsch, 2004). In our case, if Chris had actually cooked at a restaurant, this prior knowledge would have been helpful.

The model also predicts that readers should recall more topic-related information when this topic is cued in some way (Rawson & Kintsch, 2004). Topics can be identified by their interconnection with other ideas in the text. From the C-I model point of view, topic-related information helps readers draw connections between ideas in the text and between the text propositions and the topic itself in the textbase. After the integration phase, having topic information available would have the effect of strengthening the interconnections among certain topic-related text propositions while reading, making them easier to recall. For our text, it will be helpful to have knowledge that sororities are often places where people eat and, thus, a chef might be required to cook for all those people. If a child did not know how sororities worked or what a sorority was, the text would be more difficult to understand and recall.

The C-I model also predicts that some texts will take longer to read and understand than others because they are denser propositionally. Texts with lots of descriptive information might look like this. Our text is very simple, so its representation is simple too. Research has shown that the more propositions there are in a passage, the longer it takes readers to read, even when two passages have the same number of words (Kintsch & Keenan, 1973).

The C-I model also predicts that people will generally lose both surface and textbase information captured in the construction phase once integration has occurred; they should retain information from the situation model instead. Indeed, readers do generally recognize situation model information better than textbase information (Radvansky, Gerard, Zacks, & Hasher, 1990; Mulder & Sanders, 2012). Older adults are particularly reliant on the situation model in their memory for text compared to young adults, who do often retain some information regarding the textbase (Radvansky, Zwaan, Curiel, & Copeland, 2001).

Further, the model also predicts that people initially construct a textbase as described by the model, which then gives way to the formation of a situation model. Evidence for this comes from Till, Mross, and Kintsch (1988), who examined changes in the patterns of contextual benefits to the processing of text-related words over time. These researchers found that words related to all meanings of ambiguous words are activated when people encounter them as they are constructing the textbase (e.g., the word *BANK* will retrieve both the RIVER and BUILDING meanings in an associative way; see also Tanenhaus et al., 1979). However, as the integration process takes place, meanings unrelated to the situation model become deactivated. Subsequent work has also found that these text-based, lexical effects on subsequent text processing occur rapidly, whereas the discourse-level effects of the situation model on processing are relatively slower to emerge (Huang & Gordon, 2011). Words related to inferences developed for the creation of the situation model become activated, suggesting that the situation model is all that remains.

The C-I model has a number of limitations, however. First, the C-I model may overemphasize propositional overlap in representing the organization of particular ideas within the situation model. That is, just because a particular proposition has been represented a number of times within the textbase and carried over to the situation model does not mean that the idea is necessarily central to the developing representation of the text. Fletcher and Bloom (1988), for example, think that evidence favors the use of logical relationships by readers, such as causality, in developing the representation of the text.

Some have suggested that there are other levels of analysis missed by the C-I model. Graesser, Millis, and Zwaan (1997) and Graesser and McNamara (2011) consider the C-I model limited in its depiction of comprehension. They have suggested that a genre level and communication level may be necessary to describe comprehension patterns. The *genre level* represents the type of text that it is; that is, whether the text is a story, editorial, instructional document, descriptive text, joke, poem, or newspaper article, for instance. If a reader correctly identifies the signals that each of these genres provide, it helps him or her comprehend the text (Williams et al., 2005). For example, the words *Once upon a time* signal a story. Words such as *alike, both, compare, but, than, contrast* can signal an instructional document. The *communication level* refers to the reader's understanding of the writer's goals, attitudes, and intended audience. Note that these are aspects that are captured relatively easily by comparison within the schema theoretic view.

Gibbs (1994) has questioned whether there is an initial textbase representation at all, which later gives way to a situation model over time. He suggests that representations formed initially might be constructed directly within a situation model, rather than only later after the textbase has been formed.

Implications of the C-I Model for Instruction

The C-I model does not directly address instructional strategies, but it is fairly easy to infer from the model what might be important to emphasize in instruction. One can infer that basic language skills, prior knowledge, working memory, inference skills, and integration skills are all key to good comprehension (Caccamise & Snyder, 2005). Basic language skills are influential in the creation of the surface code. Prior knowledge, working memory, and minimal inference skills are important for the development of the textbase. Broader inferential and integration skills are important for the development of a situation model. Improvements in these skills should be included within our pedagogical goals for children, according to this model.

The model also makes suggestions about the characteristics of the texts that we should use for novice readers. We can infer from the model that, in selecting texts, teachers should attend to the sentence-by-sentence coherence of the passages and the general considerateness of texts in terms of cuing prior knowledge. Research suggests that considerate texts, from a C-I standpoint, are easier to learn from than inconsiderate texts. An inconsiderate text is one in which the inferred information has not been made explicit and that relies heavily on prior knowledge that the reader does not have. Revising texts using the C-I model improves the learnability of material in inconsiderate texts (Britton & Gülgöz, 1991). Novices to a topic (which include children) particularly benefit from having well-structured texts in which fewer inferences are needed and the necessary prior knowledge is already indicated clearly in the text (McNamara, Kintsch, Songer, & Kintsch, 1996). Box 7.2 discusses the issue of readability and reading comprehension models.

The C-I model would also imply that there is value in having children develop summaries after reading (Kintsch, 2010). A good summary should capture the basic elements of a completed situation model. Writing summaries gives children practice in creating situation models, and this practice should improve comprehension. It is well documented that children have difficulties in writing good summaries (Winograd, 1984). Indeed, much research has shown that there is a tendency of children to hang on to the lower, more verbatim levels in text memory rather than creating a situation model (Brainerd & Reyna, 1990). Franzke, Kintsch, Caccamise, Johnson, and Dooley (2005) showed that having eighth graders practice writing summaries improved their general comprehension of texts.

DIRECT AND INFERENTIAL MEDIATION MODEL

The direct and inferential mediation model (DIME) takes a component skills approach rather than the comprehension levels approach of the C-I model. The

DIME model hypothesizes that comprehension is a function of an organized set of cognitive skills, specifically background knowledge, inference capabilities, strategy use, reading vocabulary, and word reading/fluency skills. Cromley and Azevedo (2007) suggest that research on reading comprehension can be adequately captured by the DIME model, shown in Figure 7.3. Let's take a walk around this figure to understand the kinds of research that led to the conceptualization of this model.

BOX 7.2. READABILITY AND MODELS OF READING COMPREHENSION

Many texts designed for young readers are constructed using readability formulas, which emphasize word frequency and sentence length, primarily. Replacing less frequent, situation-specific vocabulary with basic high-frequency terms may not adequately cue children's prior knowledge. Chopping up long sentences into short ones eliminates connectives (e.g., *and, but, therefore, because*), and children have to infer connections that have been eliminated, which they may fail to do. Connectives help children relate ideas within text and cue activation of previously constructed propositions. Further, the formulas ignore the impact of readers' prior knowledge on comprehension altogether. Armbruster, Osborn, and Davidson (1985) posit that texts created from readability formulae may actually make the texts harder for children rather than easier. This problem is illustrated in this simple science text with a first-grade reading level that was probably constructed using a readability formula: "A cell is made of living stuff. A cell can grow. It takes in food. It changes the food into more living stuff" (Armbruster et al., 1985, p. 20).

The construction–integration model (Kintsch, 1998) has inspired the development of readability tools. For example, Brown, Snodgrass, Kemper, Herman, and Covington (2008) created a readability tool called *computerized propositional idea density rater* (available at *http://ail.ai.uga.edu/caspr*) that estimates the number of propositions in a text by simply counting verbs, adjectives, adverbs, prepositions, and conjunctions in a passage. The tool will give teachers a rough idea of how densely written and difficult a particular passage is likely to be.

Coh-Metrix (*www.cohmetrix.com*) is another, albeit more elaborate, online readability tool (Graesser & McNamara, 2011) that provides readability information along five dimensions: narrativity (i.e., whether a text has story-like characteristics), syntactic simplicity, concreteness, referential cohesion, and deep cohesion. It analyzes aspects of text cohesion, such as the overlap among ideas and other issues that might affect understanding, as well as some aspects of genre and pragmatic communication. Coh-Metrix has been used successfully to evaluate the readability of children's textbooks and student writing (Graesser, McNamara, & Kulikowich, 2011; McNamara, Graesser, McCarthy, & Cai, 2014).

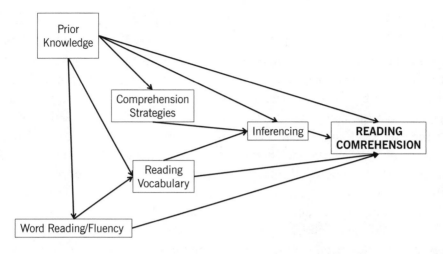

FIGURE 7.3. Interrelationship among components of the DIME model (Cromley & Azevedo, 2007). Copyright 2007 by the American Psychological Association. Adapted by permission.

First, consider the links between the knowledge base and other aspects of the model. Research supports the direct Prior Knowledge → Reading Comprehension link. Prior knowledge is an element in both the schema theoretic and C-I models. Further, preteaching background knowledge has been shown to be effective in improving children's comprehension of text (Dole, Valencia, Greer, & Wardrop, 1991). Knowledge base has been shown to influence the use of comprehension strategies (i.e., Prior Knowledge → Comprehension Strategies). For example, asking questions is one comprehension strategy. Apparently, adults who have some knowledge about a topic are better at asking questions about texts related to the topic than those without such knowledge (Miyake & Norman, 1979). Prior knowledge also influences the ability to draw inferences about a passage (i.e., Prior Knowledge → Inferencing). For example, Tarchi (2010) found that prior knowledge of a topic played an important role in allowing middle school children to draw the inferences needed for science and history text comprehension. This issue is particularly relevant for science texts in which there is a lot of unfamiliar vocabulary (i.e., Prior Knowledge → Reading Vocabulary). Finally, Priebe et al. (2012) found that, among struggling fourth graders having similarly low levels of decoding skills, children with prior knowledge for the passage made fewer reading errors than their peers who did not have this prior knowledge (Prior Knowledge → Word Reading/Fluency). Thus, as you can see, having appropriate prior knowledge is rather fundamental to this model, as it is to the schema theoretic and C-I models.

The DIME model posits that comprehension strategies have an effect on reading comprehension. Proficient readers carry out strategies that can help them understand the text (Comprehension Strategies → Reading Comprehension). They pause to consider the meaning of the text, reread difficult parts, skim for key words, utilize key aspects of the text (e.g., genre) to direct their understanding, and so forth. For example, León and Carretero (1995) reported that high school students taught to use genre-specific strategies (e.g., identifying informational text subgenres such as compare–contrast, problem–solution) while reading showed both superior recall and better organization in their recall compared to students not receiving this instruction. Further, the DIME model also says that using a strategy can lead to improvements in inferencing skills (Comprehension Strategies → Inferencing). For example, Gambrell and Koskinen (2002) found that teaching children to use visualization while reading (i.e., "Make a picture in your head") vastly improved their abilities to draw accurate predictive inferences about upcoming events in a story, compared to control children.

Finally, the DIME model claims that providing children with decoding instruction will tend to improve their vocabulary over time (White, Graves, & Slater, 1990), which will eventually work to improve children's reading comprehension skills. Being able to decode unfamiliar words is helpful in developing orthographic representations that can serve as the basis for vocabulary development from reading (Word Reading/Fluency → Reading Vocabulary). We have already discussed evidence for the remaining links in this model in prior chapters. In particular, in Chapter 6, we described how vocabulary knowledge helps children understand what they read better (Reading Vocabulary → Reading Comprehension). In Chapter 5 we described the impact of reading fluency on comprehension (Word Reading/Fluency → Reading Comprehension). It makes sense that being unable to retrieve the meanings of words in the passage, either because one is lacking the word in one's vocabulary or because one is unable to decode them, will significantly impede comprehension.

Cromley and Azevedo (2007) examined the ability of the DIME model depicted in Figure 7.3 to account for reading comprehension in ninth-grade students. Taken together, the DIME model accounted for 66% of the variance in individual differences among students in reading comprehension scores. Reading vocabulary and prior knowledge had the largest impact on students' reading comprehension, whereas inferencing skills, reading strategy knowledge, and word reading/fluency skills accounted for less. The impact of word reading/fluency skills was direct on reading comprehension, however. Students who had greater reading strategy knowledge were better able to draw appropriate inferences, and the benefits on comprehension were mainly derived from this skill. Note that ninth graders might be generally far along in the development of inferencing, strategy, and fluency skills.

Evaluation of the DIME Model

To date, the DIME model has been tested primarily on older readers ranging from middle school through college. In these groups, the DIME model appears to work reasonably well, and it provides a good account of individual differences in reading comprehension skills (Smith, 2014; Cromley & Azevedo, 2007; Cromley, Snyder-Hogan, & Luciw-Dubas, 2010). How this model will fare with younger readers is unknown.

Further research has suggested that the relative importance of individual skills in the model might depend on the particular requirements of specific passages (Cromley et al., 2010). Technical texts such as biology and chemistry texts might engage prior knowledge and inferential skills more heavily than domain-general texts might.

Finally, we think that the model does a good job of enumerating the skills that are engaged in the comprehension of connected text, but we note that it does not really provide a description of how those skills operate together to build a representation of the text. That is, it tells us *which* skills are involved but not *how* they work together to come up with a particular interpretation of a text. Still, the model is in its infancy compared to the other two models we have discussed, so only time will tell whether this is a good way to conceive of reading comprehension skill.

Implications of the DIME Model for Instruction

The DIME model may have an advantage over the other two models from the point of view of instruction. Note that much of the evidence we have described for the DIME model emerges from studies examining the effects of instruction on particular links in the model. In each case, the DIME model describes how instruction on components of the model results in improvements in reading comprehension skills. In this respect, the DIME model provides clear and consistent instructional guidance for teachers regarding how to best improve children's understanding of text. It also tells us where our instructional impacts will be greatest for reading comprehension: Teachers should (1) provide instruction on vocabulary, (2) help children develop a knowledge base for the passages they will read, and (3) provide instruction on genre-specific inferencing skills for texts engaging difficult topics.

CONCLUSION

As you can see from our discussion of the basic models of reading comprehension presented in this chapter, one model has a strong bottom-up emphasis, whereby the flow of information emerges largely from lower-level decoding processes to comprehension (the simple view). Another model has a strong top-down emphasis (schema theoretic view), which gives little to no attention to the bottom-up processes that are required to decode text. Yet other models have both top-down and bottom-up emphases (C-I and DIME) to describe the interaction between these processes to produce good comprehension.

To return to our original question regarding the definition of reading comprehension, we can see that our definition might be different depending on the model we select. From the simple view, our definition would emphasize the relationship between listening and word reading skills in producing good comprehension; good comprehension would be an interaction of word reading and listening skills. From the schema theoretic view, we would say that good comprehension emerges from the reader's successful use of prior knowledge to construct a coherent and useful meaning for the text. From the C-I model, our definition would emphasize the products that result after we have integrated the outcome of our lower-level reading processes; comprehension is said to be the construction of a successful situation model. From the DIME point of view, our definition would emphasize the optimal outcome that interactions between lower-level and higher-level reading skills can provide. Instruction of these skills can foster optimal outcomes for children.

We might point out here that there are strong points of commonality among these theories too. For example, all theories would claim, directly or indirectly, that readers bring information used in listening comprehension into their reading comprehension. All models treat the basics of reading and listening comprehension as the same activity. All theories would claim that prior knowledge and vocabulary are important for comprehension. All theories would claim that comprehension occurs because of an interaction between the text and the reader.

QUESTIONS FOR DISCUSSION

1. At the beginning of this chapter we discussed the need for a definition of reading comprehension. Now that you have read this chapter, can you suggest a potential definition?

2. Which theory of reading comprehension do you feel does a better job of capturing the empirical research on reading comprehension? Why?

3. Which theory of reading comprehension provides teachers with better guidance regarding the instruction of comprehension? Why?

4. Returning to the case study at the outset of this chapter, what recommendations might you now make to address Emily's reading comprehension issues?

FURTHER READINGS

Anderson, R. C., & Pearson, P. D. (1984). A schema-theoretic view of basic processes in reading comprehension. In P. D. Pearson, R. Barr, M. L. Kamil, & P. Mosenthal (Eds.), *Handbook of reading research* (pp. 255–291). New York: Longman.

Cromley, J. G., & Azevedo, R. (2007). Testing and refining the direct and inferential mediation model of reading comprehension. *Journal of Educational Psychology, 99*(2), 311–325.

Hoover, W., & Gough, P. (1990). The simple view of reading. *Reading and Writing: An Interdisciplinary Journal, 2*, 127–160.

Kintsch, W. (2004). The construction–integration model of text comprehension and its implications for instruction. In N. Onrau & R. B. Ruddell (Eds.), *Theoretical models and processes of reading* (Vol. 5, pp. 1270–1328). Newark, DE: International Reading Association.

CHAPTER 8

Components of Reading Comprehension

CASE STUDY

Dr. Harada had asked Jay to stop in during office hours to discuss his failing midterm grade in freshman economics. When he arrived, Jay was pretty discouraged. He told Dr. Harada that he just couldn't understand the textbook. Looking at the most recently assigned chapter, Dr. Harada asked him which concepts he was having trouble with, and Jay replied, "I'm not sure; just all of it, I guess." Dr. Harada then asked what he usually did when he had trouble reading a textbook, and Jay said that his books in high school had not been this hard. With this textbook, even though he often went back and read the whole chapter over again, lots of times he still just didn't "get it."

He said he also felt at a disadvantage because so many of the other students, all intended business majors like himself, had obviously taken an economics course in high school, but his high school had not offered one. When Dr. Harada asked him what had led him to major in business, Jay said his parents had thought it would help him get a good job, like his father's, in middle management in a large company. Jay himself had not yet held a job. His parents had handled all the financial aspects of applying for student aid and paying for tuition and room and board in the dorms, and had deposited a small amount for spending money each month in a checking account they had opened for Jay, the first he had ever had. Dr. Harada realized that Jay had never seen a W-2 form or signed a lease or even had to shop for groceries for himself. He didn't know how much his father earned or how his family budgeted their income. Jay said that he had always thought it would be exciting to own his own business, with the chance to make it big like Mark Zuckerberg or Bill Gates, but Dr. Harada realized that Jay had a long way to go.

PRIOR KNOWLEDGE

In one way, we have been discussing the effects of prior knowledge on reading throughout this book. In Chapter 1, we considered how young children's prior understanding of the purposes of reading and their concepts about print impact their subsequent acquisition of reading ability. In Chapters 3 and 4 on word reading, we discussed the influences of children's prior understandings of letters on the development of the alphabetic principle. Fluency depends greatly on the number of automatically recognized words stored in prior knowledge. Vocabulary knowledge is so closely intertwined with other types of prior knowledge that it is difficult to separate them; when one learns a new word, clearly one learns something about the concept the word represents, and similarly, as discussed in Chapter 6 on vocabulary, the vast majority of the words in the average high school student's vocabulary are learned through reading (Nagy & Herman, 1987). Later in this chapter we discuss how knowledge of reading strategies and purposes affect readers' ultimate ability to understand text. However, when we discuss the impact of prior knowledge on reading comprehension, we usually do not mean this kind of knowledge about reading, per se, but rather what is often called *background knowledge*: knowledge about the world, and particularly, about the topics treated in a specific text a reader is trying to comprehend. It is in this sense that we use the term *prior knowledge* in the rest of this discussion.

In the case study at the beginning of this chapter, one of the reasons Jay is having trouble understanding his textbook is that he has very little prior knowledge about economics. All of the theories of reading we have considered recognize the importance of prior knowledge for reading comprehension. Hoover and Gough's (1990) simple view of reading subsumes the influence of prior knowledge under listening comprehension. The schemas at the heart of Anderson and Pearson's (1984) schema theoretic view of reading comprehension are defined as constructions of prior knowledge in the mind. In Kintsch's (1988) C-I model of reading, some of the propositions used to create the initial textbase are drawn from prior knowledge, and the final step of the model involves integrating the situation model of the text into the reader's existing knowledge base (Kintsch, 2010). That prior knowledge strongly impacts reading comprehension is a finding so frequent and robust in research on reading that it is basically beyond question (Dochy, Segars, & Buehl, 1999); indeed, many would agree with Allington and Cunningham (2006) that "the most important factor in determining how much readers will comprehend . . . about a given topic is their level of knowledge about that topic" (p. 52). Therefore, in this section, we look beyond the main effects of prior knowledge already discussed in Chapter 7 to address additional ways in which prior knowledge can impact reading comprehension.

Effects on Processing Speed and Efficiency

Prior knowledge not only provides the background we use to contextualize and understand what we read, it can impact the actual processing of the text we read. Kaakinen, Hyönä, and Keenan (2003) found that readers reading previously unseen texts on a familiar subject read faster and more efficiently, with fewer eye movement regressions, than they did when reading an equally difficult text on an unfamiliar subject. Recht and Leslie (1988) compared the effects of prior knowledge of baseball on good and poor middle school readers' comprehension of a written description of a half inning in a baseball game. They found that readers with greater prior knowledge of baseball demonstrated better comprehension of the text, regardless of their tested reading ability. In fact, poor readers with high baseball knowledge comprehended the text just as well as good readers with high baseball knowledge and much better than good readers with low baseball knowledge, as demonstrated by their ability to identify important ideas and construct a coherent summary of the text. Willingham (2006) suggests that this improved performance occurred because readers familiar with baseball were able to *chunk* actions in the text when dealing with them in working memory; for example, they could simply note that the fifth batter stuck out twice and then walked on the fourth ball, instead of having to deal with each sentence as a separate concept, such as "The batter swung once and missed. Then the pitcher missed the plate. On the next throw, the pitcher again failed to throw over the plate. On the fourth throw, the batter swung and missed . . .," etc. The advantages of chunking in any kind of information processing are well known, and, as Willingham points out, particularly applicable in reading comprehension because

> most of the time . . . it is not enough to understand each sentence on its own—we need to understand a series of sentences or paragraphs and hold them in mind simultaneously so that they can be integrated or compared. Doing so is easier if the material can be chunked because it will occupy less of the limited space in working memory. But, chunking relies on background knowledge. (p. 34)

Effects of Inconsistent or Incorrect Prior Knowledge

However, prior knowledge is not always helpful in comprehension; in some cases, prior knowledge can *interfere* with text comprehension. For example, Lipson (1982) found that third graders were better at comprehending and remembering information in leveled science and social studies texts when that information either agreed with their prior knowledge, as measured by a pretest, or was entirely new. When a pretest showed that they had incorrect knowledge, both average and poor readers usually failed to comprehend contradictory information in the text. Indeed, on a post-reading comprehension measure, these readers often maintained that the passage had said whatever they had originally believed. Thus, they "comprehended" a meaning that was actually not in the text. Alvermann, Smith, and Readance (1985) found that having sixth graders deliberately activate prior knowledge prior to reading science passages about snakes and sunlight turned out to be a disadvantage when the passages contained counterintuitive information, such as "In space, the sun's heat cannot even roast a potato" (p. 429). Students who engaged in activities to call up their prior knowledge on these topics actually did worse on post-reading measures of comprehension than students who read the passages without any pre-reading activities. Kendeou and van den Broek (2007) found even worse results in a study of undergraduates' comprehension of physics texts. In their study, undergraduates holding common misconceptions about physics not only comprehended texts containing correct explanations less well, they rarely even noticed the contradictions between the texts and their own (incorrect) prior knowledge, unless the texts were structured to specifically describe and refute their incorrect beliefs. Even under these conditions, though, they still demonstrated less understanding of and learning from these texts than those who read them without previous misconceptions. Studies like these, common both to reading research and research on misconceptions in science education, show that prior knowledge, usually so helpful, can also have a negative impact on comprehension.

Effects of Prior Knowledge on Reading Comprehension Assessment

Because prior knowledge so strongly affects reading comprehension, it can make assessing general reading comprehension skill much more difficult. Most test makers today try hard to avoid using questions that draw on prior knowledge that is likely to differ greatly among various groups of people. This was not always the case: For instance, there was a question on the SAT reading test in the 1970s that required readers to know the meaning of the word *regatta* (Beaver, 1996). But even with the best efforts, it turns out to be almost impossible to eliminate the effects of prior knowledge on reading comprehension assessments. For example, Johnston (1984) found that comprehension of a sample test passage for Illinois eighth graders on the Civil War, a topic from the eighth-grade curriculum with which obviously none of them had personal experience, was still affected by individual differences in prior vocabulary knowledge. In addition, he found that students answered questions central to the meaning of the text better when they could *not* refer back to the passage, and this effect was strongest for those with the most prior knowledge. Taking this issue a step further, Keenan and Betjemann (2006) found that children could correctly answer most questions on the popular Gray Oral Reading Test (GORT) at a rate higher than chance *without* reading the passages, thus demonstrating that they were drawing, at least in part, on prior knowledge to answer these questions. In two studies of undergraduate reading, Shapiro (2004) tried two strategies often used in research to counteract possible effects of prior knowledge on comprehension: use of texts on imaginary topics or texts in areas where readers are likely to be novices. In her first experiment, she had students read a passage about the history of a completely fictional country, yet she found that students' general domain knowledge in history still significantly affected their comprehension scores. In the second experiment, she had undergraduates who had just enrolled in a course on cognition read advanced texts on human memory, and found again that, even though all participants were novices in the field, differences in prior knowledge significantly predicted comprehension results. It may be that prior knowledge and reading comprehension are so interrelated that there is really no way to measure "general" comprehension ability, completely apart from prior knowledge. Based on this conclusion, Shapiro suggests that studies of comprehension should always include a measure of prior knowledge used as a covariate in analyzing any results. Johnston, applying similar thinking to education, suggests that schools and teachers must use caution in interpreting or acting upon any student's score on a single reading comprehension test, since that score may be strongly influenced by whether the student had accurate prior knowledge of specific passage topics.

INFERENCES

One of the main reasons prior knowledge is so important to comprehension is that it is what allows readers to make inferences from and about the text. In Chapter 7, we learned that there was unanimity among theories of reading comprehension that comprehension involved more than simply assembling the meanings of the words directly written in the text. To understand a text, readers must go considerably beyond the words alone. In fact, no text could be nearly explicit enough to include all the information that a reader would need to know to comprehend a passage. Written language is simply a brief sketch of the intended message, and it is assumed that readers bring both knowledge and skills other than decoding to assist their comprehension. They draw inferences about importance from their prior knowledge, and they draw connections between ideas. Essentially, drawing inferences helps readers fill in information that is not explicitly stated in the text. Being able to draw inferences is central to reading comprehension and a causal contributor to good comprehension (Paris, Lindauer, & Cox, 1977).

Recall the very simple text we discussed in Chapter 7: *Chris is a chef. He cooks at a sorority.* Let's just call this the *Chris Text*. Even for this very simple text, the reader could bring in knowledge that:

- Chris is probably male.
- *He* in this case probably refers to *Chris*.
- Chefs cook.
- Chefs usually work in restaurants.
- The term *sorority* refers to both a place and an organization.
- Sororities (the place) have houses with kitchens.
- Sorority houses have a larger number of residents than normal houses.
- These residents need to eat.
- So, sororities (the organization) serve meals.
- Providing such meals requires a professional who knows how to cook for large groups of people.
- Chefs are professional cooks.
- So, chefs can satisfy this need to eat.

Note that none of this information is included directly in the Chris Text. It would be tedious and long if it included all of this information. Thus, understanding even the ridiculously simple Chris Text requires quite a bit of prior knowledge.

This section focuses on the ability to draw appropriate inferences to complete the process of comprehension during reading. Put simply, *inferencing* is the ability to put two or more pieces of information from text and/or prior knowledge together to derive a third piece of information not stated explicitly in the text. Readers must make inferences to form a coherent representation of the text. Without forming inferences, comprehension will fail.

To a great extent, authors must guess which bits of knowledge their readers are likely to know, and which they need to include explicitly in the text. They assume that readers will be able to resolve some ambiguities inherent in the text through their inferencing skills. They take a gamble on which pieces of information they need to include and what the reader will be able to infer. But there is no guarantee that the reader will be able to infer what is required to understand the text; one mark of good writing is that the author tends to guess correctly about what must be stated in the text and what most readers can infer. In this section, you will learn about three different forms of inferences: *referential* (or pronoun) inferences, *bridging* (sometimes called *coherence*) inferences, and *elaborative* inferences.

Referential Inferences

Pronoun resolution is important to the creation of a comprehensible representation of a text. It is a key device for creating clarity. Even in the Chris Text, to create an understandable representation of text, the reader must infer that *He* refers to *Chris*. Determining the antecedent, or referent, of a pronoun is a frequent occurrence while reading. Pronouns represent approximately 1 out of every 10 running words (Säily, Nevalainen, & Siirtola, 2011), and readers attempt to deter-mine the referent for each of them immediately upon encountering one in text (Arnold, Eisenband, Brown-Schmidt, & Trueswell, 2000). Being able to infer the antecedent to a pronoun, then, is fundamental to good reading comprehension; in fact, good authors go to great pains to make the antecedent for each pronoun clear and as unambiguous as possible. In English, readers can often use pronoun gender, subject–object information, and number to help them determine the *ante-cedent* (i.e., the word to which the pronoun refers) of a pronoun. Not all pronouns have all these features, however. Many English pronouns, such as *I, me, we, us, you, they, and them*, are ambiguous with regard to gender. Others, like *you* or *it*, are ambiguous in terms of whether they refer to the subject or the object of the sen-tence. *You* is even ambiguous with regard to number (but neatly disambiguated in the Southern dialect by the second person plural, *y'all*). Some pronouns are ungen-dered (*it, anything, everything, nothing, something*), referring to things rather than persons. Pronouns are ubiquitous in English; beyond the ones just mentioned, *all, any, anyone, anybody, both, each, either, everyone, everybody, few, he, him, her, most, many, neither one, no one, none, nobody, one, some, someone, somebody, several*, and *she* are all pronouns. Readers can rely on the knowledge that plural pronouns (e.g., *most, many, they*) will have plural antecedents, and singular pronouns (e.g., *she, it, one*) will have singular antecedents. In the Chris Text, *Chris* is the only referent for *He*. He is singular (there is only one Chris), and Chris is the subject of the sen-tence. The match-up is easy. Assuming that there is no *referential ambiguity* (i.e., more than one possible referent for the pronoun), the gender and number of the pronoun in this example provide enough information to allow the reader to easily select the appropriate antecedent, or referent. Because there is no real alternative, this identification of the referent occurs just about immediately when the reader encounters the pronoun (Arnold et al., 2000).

Sometimes, though, readers have to narrow down potential referents for pro-nouns in a passage—they need to infer the most likely referent for pronouns that occur. As mentioned above, good writers try to avoid creating this situation, but they also want to avoid constantly repeating nouns. For example, in the case study at the beginning of this chapter, the third sentence, "He told Dr. Harada that he just couldn't understand the textbook," would be boring, and even confus-ing, to read if it said, "Jay told Dr. Harada that Jay just couldn't understand the textbook." But in its current form, it does require the reader to infer that the "he" who couldn't understand the textbook was Jay, not Dr. Harada. Both Jay and Dr. Harada are individual males, and thus "he" could refer to either, so how does a reader make this type of inference? When inferring the antecedent of the pro-noun, the reader has to link the pronoun to some relevant piece of information in recently processed text. The pronoun must refer back to something that is in the reader's evolving text representation—the *situation model*, to use Kintsch's (1988)

C-I model terminology. If more than one concept is currently active within this representation, pronoun gender, subject–object information, and number can be helpful for narrowing down the set of active concepts, but often, as in the example above, these are not enough. When this information is available, it can facilitate the matching of a pronoun to its antecedent (Foraker & McElree, 2007).

The use of a pronoun in a passage implies that the writer believed that the reader would have no difficulty locating the antecedent of the pronoun in memory. Pronoun assignment needs to be carried out for a good representation of the passage to be developed. Thus, normally, the referent of a pronoun is a salient, focused feature of the ongoing discourse. Focused entities in the ongoing discourse are more active in working memory (Grosz, Joshi, & Weinstein, 1995). People use salience to narrow down the possibilities for pronoun matching. If the pronoun refers to one of these focused elements, the reader can easily resolve the identity of a focused antecedent, link the pronoun to the antecedent, and integrate the pronoun into the ongoing discourse representation (Garrod & Sanford, 1994; Foraker & McElree, 2007). Contrast the example situations below, one in which the pronoun refers to an item within focused attention and one in which it does not:

> It was the new foreman who unrolled the latest blueprint.
>
> (a) He pointed at the drawings on the paper. (focused)
>
> (b) It curled at the edges of the paper. (unfocused)
> (From Foraker & McElree, 2007, p. 361)

For this simple discourse, *foreman* is in focus. *Foreman* is the subject of the sentence, which puts it in focus anyway, and this focusing effect is heightened by the use of a linguistic device called *clefting* (in this case, *it was the*). Clefting helps direct the reader's attention toward *foreman*. Thus, for (a), when reading the pronoun *he*, the reader experiences no difficulty in resolving its identity, and the pronoun–antecedent link can be integrated with the ongoing discourse representation. If, instead, the reader reads (b), the reader will have more difficulty identifying an antecedent for *it* because *blueprint* is not the focus at the moment.

Generally, *subjects* of sentences are focused elements in a discourse (Hobbs, 1979), and readers have a preference to assign upcoming pronouns to it. Consider: *Tom helped Sam with his homework. He later went to the gym.* Obviously both Tom and Sam could have gone to the gym, but the reader generally assigns *he* to *Tom* because *Tom* is the subject of the sentence. Related to this preference is the first-mention bias in assigning pronouns. *First-mention bias* is the tendency for readers to consider the first out of two or more elements in a sentence to be the more salient one. Subjects tend to be the first mentioned, so they benefit from this bias. Early mention is one way that writers communicate the saliency of potential items in a text, and readers use first mention to assign pronouns (Arnold et al., 2000).

The semantics of verbs may play a role in assigning pronouns as well. Some interpersonal verbs carry an implicit causality bias with them. *Implicit causality bias* is the preference of readers to assign causes of events to either a subject or the object of a clause (Cozijn, Commandeur, Vonk, & Noordman, 2011). The protagonist of verbs having this bias is brought into focus. Sentences with verbs like *impress, frighten, defeat,* and *disappoint* cause the subject of the sentence to become the focused element, whereas verbs such as *criticize, doubt, trust, fear,* and *sue* cause the object of the sentence to be the focused element. Consider the sentence, *Harry felt sorry for Dan because his girlfriend broke up with <u>him</u>.* Here *him* gets assigned to *Dan,* not *Harry* because *Dan* is the implicit causality focus of the verb *felt sorry for.* Skilled readers are particularly likely to use this focusing effect from implicit causality to resolve the pronoun identity quickly (Long & De Ley, 2000).

Readers usually try to connect the pronoun to a referent from the immediate textual context. Sometimes this is not possible. Sometimes pronouns seem to appear out of the blue. Take for example, *The last film I bought was* Star Wars. *<u>They</u> are coming out with a new <u>one</u>."* The information on which resolution of the pronoun *they* rests has not appeared explicitly in the text, but the reader still needs to infer to whom the pronoun *they* refers. *They* is an *unheralded pronoun,* that is, a pronoun that lacks an immediate antecedent (Gerrig, Horton, & Stent, 2011). Textual analyses have demonstrated that there are a nontrivial number of these unheralded pronouns in text (Gerrig, 1986), and research suggests that unheralded pronouns occur because the writer has assumed a common ground with his or her readers, that is, prior knowledge to which they can both refer. The pronoun *they,* in this case, refers to the shared cultural knowledge that *Star Wars* and other movies are made by a large industry. Most unheralded pronouns are plurals like this one (Gerrig, Horton, & Stent, 2011). Surprisingly, unheralded pronouns do not appear to cause processing problems for readers as long as the referent can be reasonably inferred from this shared knowledge (Sanford, Filik, Emmott, & Morrow, 2008). Usually, the shared prior knowledge assumed in such cases is generated from information that is within the focus of the text (Greene, Gerrig, McKoon, & Ratcliff, 1994). So, focal information is still being used in assigning pronouns, but the referent is associated with prior knowledge, rather than specific text, related to that focal information. Further, the information from which we are deriving the prior knowledge tends to be recent. It is probably for this reason that unheralded pronouns are not often a problem for readers.

Still, shared prior knowledge is harder to come by with children, which suggests that the use of unheralded pronouns in texts designed for children comes with a risk. Looking at common children's texts, it would seem that children's authors understand this. They appear to reduce their use of pronouns of any sort, giving children's books a kind of stilted quality. Take the following example:

Peter Rabbit lost his appetite. Now when Peter Rabbit loses his appetite, something is very wrong indeed with him. Peter has boasted that he can eat any time and all the time. In fact, two things that Peter thinks most about are his stomach and satisfying his curiosity, and nearly all the scrapes that Peter has gotten into have been because of these two things. (Burgess, 1920, pp. 1–2)

Note that *Peter* is repeated over and over when simply *he* or *him* might do. For adults, this kind of repetition feels confusing because it violates our sense, mentioned earlier, that we do not rename entities that are focal in our discourse representation. (This confusion has been demonstrated and is called the *repeated-name penalty*; Gordon, Grosz, & Gilliom, 1993.) However, renaming the subject in children's texts over and over again is very common (Arnold, 1998).

Is there any justification for avoiding pronouns with young children? Maybe. Most 5-year-olds are able to use gender and number to identify pronoun antecedents (Arnold, Brown-Schmidt, & Trueswell, 2007). However, children this age still have difficulty in determining antecedents for ambiguous pronouns and are unable to use some of the cues that adults normally use to infer the correct antecedent (Arnold et al., 2007). This finding suggests that teachers should be attentive to the fact that young readers may have difficulty identifying the antecedents of pronouns in texts that they are reading.

Bridging Inferences

Bridging inferences are those inferences that are needed to form a consistent and intelligible mental picture of a text. Bridging inferences map the content of the currently read text onto either something that has been recently read or some relevant prior knowledge that has been encoded within the evolving situation model. Bridging inferences are created to maintain coherence and used to resolve incongruities or ambiguities in a text. Often these ambiguities arise because readers try to connect incoming information directly to something stated previously when the text does not fully specify the intended connection between ideas in a text. Consider this simple text:

Steve's Car

Steve's car died suddenly, so he carefully pushed it off the road. Maybe the transmission was broken.

In this example, readers have to make a number of inferences. First, they need to infer the connection between pushing the car off the road and the car dying. The word *so* signals that there might be a connection between the two ideas. Like pronouns, *so* is a cohesive device that indicates that the two ideas might be caus-ally related. Our language is filled with words and phrases that signal the reader to infer links between ideas in a text, such as:

Listing: *first, second, third; to begin, to conclude*

Causal links: *so, therefore, as a result, consequently*

Similarity: *In the same way, similarly, correspondingly, like*

Contrast: *instead, in contrast, conversely*

Reinforcement: *also, furthermore, in addition, in the same way*

But often the text does not fully provide these cohesive devices. In our case, the reader needs to infer the connection between the transmission being broken and the ideas expressed by the previous sentence. For this, the reader will need to retrieve information from prior knowledge to connect the ideas. He or she will need to create a plausible explanation as to why an action, event, or state is explic-itly mentioned in the text (Graesser, Singer, & Trabasso, 1994). If the reader of this text is lucky, he or she possesses the knowledge that a broken transmission might cause a car to die suddenly. Bridging inferences can be classified in two ways, then: either as those that use cohesive devices or as those that use prior knowledge. Our Steve's Car text requires one of each.

Research has shown that inferences required for formulating a coherent mental model of the text are generated *during* the comprehension of text, that is, immediately. The inferences generated during the reading of a text include refer-ential inferences, as noted in our section on pronouns, causal antecedent infer-ences (Magliano, Baggett, Johnson, & Graesser, 1993), such as the one described for Steve's Car, themes and generalizations (Ritchey, 2011; Zhang, 2005), as well as inferences regarding characters' goals and emotions, as these tend to drive the storyline of a narrative text (Gernsbacher, Goldsmith, & Robertson, 1992; Long & Golding, 1993).

One can see from the Steve's Car text just how important prior knowledge is to the process of drawing a bridging inference. Readers who have knowledge relevant to the text will comprehend it better due to their knowledge (Chiesi, Spilich, & Voss, 1979). They will be better able (and more likely) to fill in the little gaps in the text that could impede comprehension (Magliano & Millis, 2003; Oakhill, 1984).

The advantage of prior knowledge obviously creates a problem for low-knowledge readers, including younger children in general. Children may have to rely on coherence devices to generate inferences; presumably they can be taught to use these (McNamara & Kendeou, 2011). Young readers benefit considerably from having highly coherent texts written with lots of such devices embedded and with the necessary prior knowledge filled in (Beck, McKeown, Sinatra, & Loxterman, 1991). They also benefit from book illustrations that contain or pre-serve the information necessary for drawing such inferences (Pike, Barnes, & Barron, 2010).

Even when children can find the information needed for drawing an infer-ence in their knowledge base, though, there is no guarantee that they will do so. Research suggests that young children are less likely to use their prior knowl-edge spontaneously to draw necessary bridging inferences. To investigate whether children of different ages would use prior knowledge to create inferences, Barnes, Dennis, and Haefele-Kalvaitis (1996) taught children knowledge about a ficti-tious world, "Gan," about which neither early elementary nor high school students could possibly have prior knowledge. After ensuring that the teens and younger children had learned this information to a similar level, both groups were read a story. Story comprehension required that the children use this taught information for creating bridging inferences. Researchers found that high school students were more than twice as likely to draw upon this new knowledge in creating inferences than younger elementary children. The primary cause of the failure to draw the appropriate inferences was not any inability of the younger children to integrate sources of information, but rather their failure to retrieve the prior knowledge upon which the inferences were based.

Thus, young children tend to have a harder time in making the bridging inferences necessary for comprehension of a text for two reasons. First, they often lack the prior knowledge upon which such inferences would be based. Second, they may not retrieve relevant information from prior knowledge even when they do possess it. Both types of difficulty are linked to Anderson and Pearson's (1984) schema-driven theory of comprehension, as explained in Chapter 7. Moreover, children's tendency to not draw certain types of inferences necessary for compre-hension seems to be stable. That is, children show similarity in their inferencing abilities across written, televised, and aurally presented stories (Kendeou, Bohn-Gettler, White, & van den Broek, 2008). To a great extent, basic difficulties with inferencing account for a good bit of the variance in individual differences in comprehension among children (Cain & Oakhill, 1999).

Elaborative Inferences

An important distinction needs to be made between those inferences that are coherence-based (the two main types we have discussed up to this point) and those that are merely elaborative. *Elaborative inferences* go beyond those inferences required for maintaining a simple cohesive text representation; rather, they serve to enrich the mental representation of the text. As would be suggested by schema theory, these enrichments invariably come from the reader's prior knowledge and therefore can be highly individual.

Let us return to Steve's Car to consider the kinds of elaborative inferences that a reader might draw. We might infer that the car was old, that it was small and light, and that Steve was driving the car, alone. We could infer that the car stopped in the middle of the street, that other cars needed to navigate around him, and that this required care on his part while pushing it to the side of the road. We could potentially infer that the car ended up parked close to the curb, but not really off the road per se. We might predict that Steve learned about the status of his car from a mechanic somewhat later. None of these inferences are required for basic comprehension of the text, but it is certainly possible that you generated some of these thoughts while reading it.

One type of elaborative inference that has been studied extensively is the predictive inference. When readers make *predictive inferences*, they activate information about future outcomes or events that might be expected on the basis of the situation model that they generate as they read and construct their evolving representation of the text. Teachers are often urged to teach children to use effective predictive inferences to improve their comprehension, as in the prediction strategy noted in the next section of this chapter (Duke & Pearson, 2002). Interestingly, however, unless the preceding context is strong and predictive, it seems that adult readers do not usually generate such predictive inferences during comprehension (McKoon & Ratcliff, 1986). Consider the following passage from Cook, Limber, and O'Brien (2001):

> *Introduction*: Mark had been putting off painting the building for weeks. Finally he couldn't stand the flaky chipping paint or his nagging any longer. He went into the storage room and got out all of the supplies he would need. He decided to start on the back of the building first. He walked around the building and set everything up on the farthest corner.
>
> *Low Constraint Context*: The building was only one story, so he decided to start at the top and work his way down. The scaffolding he was using was a little wobbly, but he didn't think it would be a problem.
>
> [or]
>
> *High Constraint Context*: The building was fifteen stories high, so he decided to start at the top and work his way down. The scaffolding he was using was a little wobbly, but he didn't think it would be a problem.
>
> *Continuation*: He had been painting away happily for about an hour when he heard a loud noise. He turned around sharply when he heard the noise. Just then, Mark lost his balance and fell.
>
> *Target Word* (i.e., the word the reader is supposed to predictively infer): *dead*.
> (p. 232)

Research has shown that only when readers are provided with a highly constraining context do they generate target elaborative inferences. For example, in this Cook et al. passage, participants were quicker to recognize the inference word *dead* only when it was presented following the high-likelihood context, not the low-likelihood one. Lassonde and O'Brien (2009) also have shown that, as contextual constraint increases, the activated inferential information becomes increasingly more specific. Thus, in the high-likelihood condition context above, *dead* will be activated but *hurt* will not be. Readers are also more likely to generate predictive inferences when the key information needed for the inference resides within current working memory (Linderholm, 2002) and when readers are encouraged to adopt a strategy of prediction (Allbritton, 2004). These findings suggest that elaborative inferences occupy valuable cognitive resources, so readers do not usually engage in them unless they are pressed to do so.

There are individual differences in the degree to which readers generate elaborative inferences. For example, it has been shown that readers differ from one another in terms of the standards of coherence they use while reading a text. *Standards of coherence* are "criteria that readers incorporate while reading to achieve their intended depth of comprehension" (Clinton & van den Broek, 2012, p. 651). Readers with high standards of coherence are more likely to generate elaborative inferences—they tend to go beyond the minimal amount of inferencing needed to simply establish coherence (van den Broek, Bohn-Gettler, Kendeou, Carlson, & White, 2011). They actively search for information from prior knowledge to add to their understanding of the text. They strive for deep understanding. As a result, such readers tend to learn more from text than readers with low standards of coherence do (Clinton & van den Broek, 2012).

As discussed further in the next section, readers' goals may also play a role in how much elaborative inferencing they do. Readers generate more elaborative inferences while reading texts on topics for which they have high interest (Clinton & van den Broek, 2012). For example, if you are interested in space travel, you are more likely to use your prior knowledge to elaborate on a text about the Apollo moon mission program than you would on another text about dish washing, a topic probably equally familiar, but much less interesting to you. Readers also carry out more elaborative inferencing when they are reading texts to perform well on a test rather than to be merely entertained (van den Broek, Lorch, Linderholm, & Gustafson, 2001), because creating a strongly coherent representation that is firmly integrated within long-term memory is prerequisite for good test taking. Both of these circumstances, known to increase elaborative inferences, help explain why, as we explore in Chapter 9, motivation to read can strongly impact reading comprehension.

Finally, for a look at how neurological studies have contributed to our understanding of the cognitive processes behind reading comprehension, see Box 8.1.

BOX 8.1. Neurological Contributions to Reading Comprehension

As is evident from all of the theories we discussed in Chapters 7 and 8, reading comprehension involves a great deal more than just understanding words and sentences. Clearly, a great variety of cognitive processes are recruited to contribute to good comprehension. Correspondingly, neurological studies have uncovered a rich language network of brain structures that are engaged by reading comprehension.

Adult readers recruit a general set of brain regions associated with language to accomplish comprehension (e.g., the left inferior frontal gyrus, the middle and superior temporal gyri, the inferior temporal gyrus, the angular gyrus, and inferior frontal cortex; Bookheimer, 2002; Maguire, Frith, & Morris, 1999; Robertson et al., 2000). Indeed, reading comprehension and listening comprehension tend to recruit similar brain areas while processing (Buchweitz, Mason, Tomitch, & Just, 2009; Jobard, Vigneau, Mazoyer, & Tzourio-Mazoyer, 2007), another piece of evidence in support of the simple view. However, reading may activate a somewhat broader set of brain areas than listening does, particularly in children for whom reading is demanding (Berl et al., 2010).

Brain researchers have done a number of studies investigating how our brains recognize/construct coherence when reading, because coherence is a uniquely discourse-oriented process that is distinguishable from sentence- and word-level processes. One methodology used by researchers compares the brain regions activated by adult readers while reading coherent texts with those activated by incoherent (i.e., scrambled or unrelated) texts. From a C-I model point of view, lack of coherence in a text poses a problem for readers as they try to form a situation model, and this particular difficulty in the formation of a situation model should be distinguishable in brain activity. And in fact, this is what they see: Coherent texts appear to engage the dorsomedial prefrontal cortex and the posterior cingulate cortex to a greater degree than do incoherent texts in adult readers (Ferstl, Neumann, Bogler, & von Cramon, 2008).

Other neurological studies (e.g., Yarkoni, Speer, & Zacks, 2008) have found brain activation patterns to be staged in the manner predicted by the C-I model. For example, comparing immediate and later patterns of brain activity, Yarkoni et al. found changes in the timing of localized brain activation patterns during comprehension, such that the posterior parietal cortex is more active during the construction phase of comprehension, whereas the frontotemporal regions are more involved in situation model maintenance. Related to the development of a situation model, some researchers have suggested that the right hemisphere of the brain might be associated more closely with extracting the global gist of passages (i.e., situation model creation) while comprehending text (e.g., Robertson et al., 2000). More recently, however, research has suggested that activation of various language regions of the brain in both hemispheres might be the norm (Ferstl et al., 2008; Yarkoni et al., 2008). Another discourse pattern that has been investigated in studies examining brain activity during comprehension is the formation of an event structure while reading a story. The importance of determining of an event structure for understanding might be expected from a schema theoretic view. If you recall, the schema view claims that as readers are reading stories, they are constantly trying to construct a pattern of events leading to a particular goal, rather than simply storing information in a linear fashion. Organizing stories into events tends to be cued by words that describe changes in a character's location or goals, such as *after he had left the town* or *once she had finished her work* (Zwaan, Radvansky, Hilliard, & Curiel, 1998). Brain research has shown that when readers segment the story into series of events, there are increases in neural activity in specific areas of the brain at event boundaries. Using fMRI techniques, Speer, Zachs, and Reynolds (2007) found a network of brain regions that responded to event boundaries as people read short stories—the posterior medial cortex, anterior and superior temporal gyri, and right middle frontal and subcallosal gyri. Apparently, these brain regions are the same as those that respond to event boundaries as subjects view movies of everyday events. This finding suggests that information about event structures is used to interpret both types of information sources.

Finally, as we have seen in this chapter, another fundamental process to reading comprehension is drawing inferences. Both the C-I and DIME models directly discuss the role of inferences in text comprehension. Accordingly, we should find activity in particular brain regions associated with inferencing when we compare brain activity during the reading of short stories that describe explicit events with ones requiring readers to draw inferences. Virtue, Haberman, Clancy, Parrish, and Jung Beeman (2006) observed that the superior temporal gyrus and inferior frontal gyrus are heavily recruited when individuals generate inferences. In particular, the superior temporal gyrus appears to be more active during the early stages of inferencing when readers are selecting information for inference generation, whereas the inferior frontal gyrus is more active during the later integration phases of inferencing (as might be predicted by the C-I model) (Virtue et al., 2006).

The results from brain imaging studies have found general support for the kinds of activities proposed by current theories of reading comprehension. Right now, studies investigating processes engaged by young children just learning to read complex texts are few. We can expect this area of research to grow considerably over the next decade as investigators discern how the brain carries out the complex tasks involved in reading comprehension.

STRATEGIC COMPREHENSION

Although only the DIME model, among the four we described in Chapter 7, explicitly includes comprehension strategies, researchers have long recognized that good readers selectively employ a number of specific strategies to help them comprehend challenging texts (Brown, 2008; Duke & Pearson, 2002; Pressley, Johnson, Symons, McGoldrick, & Kurita, 1989). Efforts to identify and fully describe these strategies have extended for over 50 years (e.g., Robinson, 1961), with the hope that if struggling readers could be taught to use the strategies that good readers develop naturally, they could improve their reading comprehension. The distinction between a *reading skill* and a *reading strategy* has been debated for nearly as long and is still somewhat unresolved (Afflerbach, Pearson, & Paris, 2008), but a generally recognized distinction is that a *skill* may be employed tacitly, without deliberate thought or intention, whereas a *strategy* is a "deliberately controlled process" (Afflerbach et al., p. 371) employed by a reader when attempting to understand a text that he or she cannot comprehend automatically and easily. Because strategies are seen as more deliberately and consciously used, they can also be employed more flexibly and adapted to varying texts and purposes, as compared to skills, which are employed automatically and thus in a more rote-like fashion (Dole, Duffy, Roehler, & Pearson, 1991). This distinction is one reason that, although many scholars list *drawing inferences* as one comprehension strategy, we have treated it separately. As explained in the section above, drawing inferences is something all readers do while reading, and often do automatically and unconsciously. It is only when readers are making difficult pronoun or bridging inferences, or deliberately accessing prior knowledge to make elaborative inferences, say in preparation for a test, that inferencing rises to a conscious level.

Another source of some confusion in this field is that over time, different researchers have identified different sets of strategies as important for comprehension and have also used somewhat different terminology for similar strategies. These differences have masked what is actually substantial agreement among scholars regarding at least six important general comprehension strategies, as shown in Table 8.1, which lists the strategies identified and terminology used for them in seven seminal articles on comprehension strategies and strategy instruction published from 1961 to the present.

Six Generalized Comprehension Strategies

Activating Prior Knowledge

As discussed above, using prior knowledge to fill in assumptions and enable inferences is an essential component of reading comprehension. Good readers search for and use prior knowledge in their efforts to comprehend both narrative and

TABLE 8.1. Comprehension Strategies Identified in Selected Programs and Reviews

Source	Generalized comprehension strategies						
	Activating prior knowledge	Questioning	Summarizing	Visualizing	Using text structures	Comprehension monitoring	Miscellaneous strategies
Robinson (1961) SQ3R (later PQ4R)	Survey	Question	Recite		Survey		Review
Palincsar & Brown (1984) Reciprocal Teaching	Predicting	Questioning	Summarizing			Clarifying	
Pressley, Johnson, Symons, McGoldrick, & Kurita (1989)	Activating prior knowledge	Question generation and answering	Summarization	Mental imagery	Story grammar		
Dole, Duffy, Roehler, & Pearson (1991)		Generating questions	Summarizing		Determining importance	Monitoring comprehension	
Duke & Pearson (2002)	Prediction/prior knowledge	Questioning	Summarization	Visual representations	Use text structure	Think-aloud	
Guthrie, Wigfield, Barbosa, et al. (2004) Concept-Oriented Reading Instruction (CORI)	Activating background knowledge	Generating questions	Summarizing	Organizing information graphically	Learning story structures	Monitoring comprehension	Searching for information
Brown (2008)	Predict, Connect with prior knowledge	Self-question		Visualize		Clarifying	

Note. If a specific instructional program is identified with a cited article, that program is listed with the citation in *italics*.

expository text, but younger or less able readers often do not. For this reason, most experts feel that struggling or novice readers can benefit from learning strategies for accessing any prior knowledge they may have related to the topic(s) of a text. *Prediction* is the most commonly recommended strategy for accessing prior knowledge when reading narrative texts (Duke & Pearson, 2002). As good readers approach at story, they develop expectations of what the story will be about, and as they read, they are constantly making mental guesses about what will happen next, especially when the story is suspenseful or exciting. A number of studies have verified that helping novice or struggling children learn to make predictions both prior to and during reading not only aids comprehension but increases their interest in reading the story, especially when they compare their predictions to actual story events as they read further (Duke & Pearson, 2002; Hansen & Pearson, 1983).

Informational texts require readers to use different strategies to activate prior knowledge. *Surveying* or *previewing* is probably the most often recommended strategy for this purpose, and not much about this strategy has changed since Robinson taught college students in 1961 to look at main and subordinate headings and any illustrations and read the summary, if available, before reading a chapter in their textbooks. Previewing a text in this way not only calls up relevant prior knowledge but offers students an *advance organizer* for the text, a kind of "ideational scaffolding" (Ausabel, 1978, p. 253) into which the knowledge to be learned can be fit (Duke & Pearson, 2002). More formally, students may be asked to engage in K-W-L group discussions[1] (Ogle, 2009) or draw concept maps of their prior knowledge on a topic before reading a text. Interestingly, Gurlitt and Renkl (2010) found that students who engaged in scaffolded mapping activities, completing concept maps on which instructors had pre-drawn key elements and relationships, actually learned more from subsequent reading than those who generated a personal concept map from scratch. Such scaffolded mapping activities might help because they again offer a useful advance organizer to students, or because they lessen the chance that students would access inappropriate or even incorrect prior knowledge—which, as discussed previously, is always a potential problem in activating prior knowledge. Another explanation for the usefulness of such scaffolded maps might be that the pre-drawn elements from the instructor provided students with background knowledge they themselves did not have.

Questioning

Questioning is perhaps the most agreed-upon strategy for comprehension; almost all research in this field has noted the efficacy of asking and answering questions

---

[1]*K* stands for "what we know"; *W* stands for "what we want to find out," and what the students eventually learn is recorded under *L*.

prior to, during, and after reading. When done before reading, generating questions about the text is often combined with previewing or prior knowledge activation strategies and serves many of the same purposes, as well as helping the reader identify a purpose for reading, an element of strategic comprehension discussed later in this chapter. Generating questions while reading is perhaps the single strategy most prevalent in good readers and absent in poor ones. Teachers are all too familiar with the phenomenon of readers who "allow text to 'wash over them'" (Keene & Zimmerman, 1997, p. 6) as they read, instead of actively participating in the process of understanding" (Lloyd, 2004, p. 115). Generating questions and looking for answers is a distinguishing characteristic of readers who are engaged in a *deep processing* (Alexander, 2005) of text (Dole, Duffy, et al., 1991; Brown, 2008), and multiple studies have shown that helping students learn to pose good questions as they read enhances their comprehension and engagement (Dole et al.; Singer & Donlan, 1982). Activities in which peers pose and respond to each other's text-based questions have also demonstrated positive effects on comprehension (Lloyd, 2004; Palincsar & Brown, 1984).

Most questioning strategies involve asking and hopefully finding answers to questions about the author's meaning (e.g., Pressley et al., 1989; Raphael & Au, 2005). However, encouraging students to ask evaluative questions regarding the author's intentions, accuracy, and reliability may also be important, particularly to encourage critical reading, which is so important in later grades and adulthood (Lloyd, 2004; McDaniel, 2004). For example, in a decade of studies on their *questioning the author* strategy, Beck, McKeown and colleagues (e.g., Beck, McKeown, Sandora, Kucan, & Worthy, 1996; Beck & McKeown, 2001; McKeown & Beck, 2004) have found that presenting the text as "the product of a fallible author" empowers struggling readers to think of themselves as evaluators and "revisers" of texts, and thus to "grapple" with difficult-to-comprehend ideas with less self-consciousness and fear of failure (McKeown, Beck, & Worthy, 1993, p. 562).

Summarizing

Equal in longevity and popularity to questioning is the strategy of teaching students to summarize texts after reading them. Many scholars in this field have recommended summarization as an important aid to comprehension, including the authors of the National Reading Panel report (National Institute of Child Health and Human Development, 2000) and the Carnegie Corporation Writing to Read report (Graham & Hebert, 2010). One advantage of this strategy is its flexibility. Both narrative and expository texts can be summarized, as can larger or smaller portions of a text. Summarizing after each paragraph or section of a text, as suggested in the *Recite* element in Robinson's original (1961) SQ3R strategy, can help readers construct meanings for complex texts a little at a time. This process, also known as *paraphrasing*, has been shown to be effective in fostering comprehension, especially for struggling students (Gajria, Jitendra, Sood, & Sacks, 2007).

Summarization of longer passages or compete texts is a much more complex task that seems to show a developmental trajectory (Brown, Day, & Jones, 1983). Most children can summarize simple narratives or stories (Kintsch, 1990), but many high school and even college students find it difficult to summarize longer expository texts (Hill, 1991). Yet research clearly shows that learning to write such summaries is worth the effort. Summarization of extended texts passages encourages deep processing and results in better learning because it calls for readers to engage the text using complex cognitive operations: They must select what is important to include or can be left out, condense subordinate details into superordinate concepts, and finally integrate all this material into a single coherent representation of the original text (Dole, Duffy, et al., 1991)—sort of a mega-version of Kintsch's (1988) situation model of a text. Both paraphrasing and summarizing can also serve to prompt comprehension monitoring, another vital comprehension strategy, discussed shortly.

Visualizing

The idea of *visualizing* as a strategy for promoting reading comprehension has been investigated in three rather different ways. Researchers such as Oakhill and Patel (1991) and Gambrell and Jaywitz (1993) studied the effects of teaching children to make mental images of events, characters, or settings, primarily while reading narrative texts. Pressley et al. (1989) characterize the effects of such mental imagery strategies as being relatively small but reliable. For example, Pressley (1976) taught 8-year-olds to read part of a story and then stop and try to picture the event they had just read about, starting with sentences and working up to larger portions of text. He found that children learned the process quite easily and were better able to remember stories they had read. Gambrell and Bales (1986) found that visualizing also helped children detect inconsistencies or missing information in stories. In their study, children learned to do this in only 30 minutes of training, but were then better able to identify problems in texts than were children who were not trained in the process.

Pressley et al. (1989) also describe the use of constructed mental images as mnemonics to help readers recall salient aspects of a text. Such images might be created by a teacher or researcher and just shown to students, or the students themselves might make them up. In either case, these images are artificial constructs, typically using plays on words as mnemonic devices, rather than realistic representations of textual elements. Two studies by Joel Levin and colleagues illustrate both types of mnemonic imagery. In Levin, Shriberg, and Berry (1983), eighth-grade students were given information outlining the advantages of fictitious towns and were then shown pictures in which these attributes were somewhat comically represented. For example, the key attributes of the town of Fostoria were incorporated into a cartoonish drawing where the attributes are shown all covered in frost—*frost* being the key word intended to help students recall the name *Fostoria*. Students who were shown such drawings remembered a significantly greater proportion of town attributes than those who did not see these pictures. In a second study by Peters and Levin (1986), students of the same age read passages about interesting Americans and then used an associated keyword (e.g., *mad* for Joseph Maddy, founder of the first national music camp) to construct an image relating each person's name and accomplishments. Upon being given each name, good readers using this strategy were able to accurately recall many more accomplishments than were equally skilled readers who had not been taught the strategy; the effect was weaker, but still significant, for poorer readers. These and similar studies are open to the criticism that recall of relatively trivial facts is rather peripheral to true comprehension. However, constructing such images does require careful observation of details in the text, and, as Pressley et al. noted, the great popularity of such strategies among students must indicate that they find some value in them (perhaps because school-based tests so often require the recall of trivial details?).

Certainly the most studied type of visualization-based strategy involves the development of graphical representations, rather than mental images or pictures, of texts. Since this strategy is most often used as a way to represent text structures, both narrative and expository, we discuss it in combination with structure-related strategies next.

Using Text Structures

Research on the relevance to comprehension of story grammars (Mandler & Johnson, 1977; Stein & Glenn, 1979) and common expository text structures (Meyer, 1985; Meyer & Ray, 2011) has already been described in Chapter 7 in our discussion of schema theory. Good readers consistently use their knowledge of common text structures to help them comprehend both types of text.

The elements of story grammars (setting, problem, goal, etc.) are part of the prior knowledge that experienced readers use to understand narratives. Although a few studies have shown benefits from simply teaching children about the common elements in story grammars, more often teachers use a *story map* (Beck & McKeown, 1981), a diagrammatic representation of the elements and sequence of this typical narrative structure, to help novice or struggling readers understand stories better (Idol, 1987; Davis & McPherson, 1989). At first, the teacher or maybe the class as a group will work together to fill out a story map; then, as readers become more familiar with the structure, they may fill out a blank map individually as a strategy to help them comprehend a particular story. Use of story

grammar strategies has been shown to improve narrative comprehension in students at many levels and ages, including those with specific disabilities related to
reading (Dimino et al., 1995; Duke & Pearson, 2002; Hagood, 1997; Stetter &
Hughes, 2010b), and even to help students better comprehend word problems in
mathematics (Xin, Wiles, & Lin, 2008).

Just as for narratives, readers who are more knowledgeable about expository
text structures achieve greater comprehension when reading expository texts (Williams et al., 2014). Successful readers use knowledge of text structure to identify
which information in the text the author sees as most important, to organize this
information as they read, to hypothesize about author intent and biases, and to
construct a mental or even written summary of parts or all of the text, as discussed
above (Dole, Duffy, et al., 1991; Duke & Pearson, 2002).

Instructional studies over the past 40 years have clearly shown that helping
struggling readers better understand and attend to text structure can improve their
comprehension of expository texts. At first, such efforts were limited to explaining
text structures to readers (Slater, Graves, & Piché, 1985) or reminding readers to
attend to cues such as headings and boldface text (Robinson, 1961). Taylor and
Beach (1984) extended this work by teaching seventh graders to successfully write
summaries of unfamiliar texts using these features. However, researchers quickly
realized that, as mentioned in Chapter 7, expository texts vary in structure much
more than narratives, so that instruction might be more effective if it targeted specific text structures. In recent work (Meyer & Wijekumar, 2007), Bonnie Meyer,
one of the pioneers in this field, has identified five common expository text structures that represent a reasonable consensus of the research in this area: *description,
sequence, comparison* (often called *compare–contrast*), *cause and effect,* and *problem
and solution.* Much of the ongoing research in this field has used visual representations, such as concept maps and graphic organizers, as tools to help readers understand and use these common structures (e.g., Armbruster, Anderson, & Meyer,
1991; Defelice, 2010; Gersten, Fuchs, Williams, & Baker, 2001; Oliver, 2009), and,
as mentioned above, the most recent studies have shown particular success with
scaffolded strategies using partially completed maps or computer-assisted mapping
(Marée, van Bruggen, & Jochems, 2013; Wijekumar et al., 2014).

Interestingly, "the research suggests that almost any approach to teaching the
structure of informational text improves both comprehension and recall of key
text information" (Duke & Pearson, 2002, p. 217). One reason for this effect might
be that, as J. P. Williams (2007) points out, these are argument structures used
generally and universally in thought, not just in written text; thus in learning
these structures, readers may also be improving their general reasoning abilities.
Alternatively, perhaps by attending to these structures in specific texts, readers
are learning more about the structure and content of knowledge in the relevant

domain (Duke & Pearson), or maybe it is simply the increased attention readers must focus on the text in order to discern or map its structure that increases their comprehension. Most likely, it is some combination of these factors, perhaps unique to each situation, which results in the positive effects of structure-based strategies on expository reading comprehension.

For a discussion of the way culture affects readers' prior knowledge, use of text structure, and other aspects of comprehension, see Box 8.2.

BOX 8.2. Culture and Comprehension

We have talked about the effects of culture on reading in many places throughout this book, but this chapter seems like a good place to highlight this issue because our discussions of prior knowledge and inferences—and schema theory in the previous chapter—are so relevant for understanding the effects of culture on reading comprehension.

The most obvious way in which culture affects comprehension is that people from different cultures possess different prior knowledge. In some cases, people from one culture may simply lack the knowledge needed to interpret something written from the viewpoint of another culture. For example, children raised in the city may have great difficulty comprehending a story set on a farm, not because they lack general comprehension skills, but because they don't have the knowledge base to infer, for instance, that a hailstorm is a potential disaster to a wheat farmer or why farm children often have to help milk cows even before they go to school. (Hail flattens wheat, making it subject to rot and impossible to harvest mechanically, and cows must be milked at the same time morning and evening to yield the most milk.)

In many cases, however, people from different cultures have schemas about the same concept, but those schemas may be very different, leading again to failures of comprehension. For example, Anderson (1994) wrote about how, in one of his studies, participants from India misunderstood a passage about an American wedding that said the bride wore her grandmother's lace-over-satin wedding dress. They inferred that the bride was poor, and felt it was sad that she had to wear an old, out-of-style wedding dress. In the same study, American participants were confused by a passage about an Indian wedding that stated that the bride's parents were concerned because the groom's family might demand a motor scooter. Because they lacked prior knowledge about the custom in India of giving a dowry to the groom's family, the Americans could not make the necessary inference to comprehend the passage.

It is fairly easy to see how such clear differences in background knowledge could lead to problems in comprehension. But cultures differ in more subtle ways as well. Even cultures that share a country and a language may differ greatly in the way in which they use that language, the patterns of discourse that are embedded in their schemas about how people talk and write. In another study, Anderson and colleagues investigated how African American and European American eighth graders interpreted a passage about two boys "playing the dozens," a form of bantering exchange of ritual insults enacted mainly in the African American community. An excerpt from the passage appears below:

> I was really ready for lunch. I got in line behind Bubba. . . . For a little action Bubba turned around and said, "Hey, Sam. What you doin' man? You so ugly that when the doctor delivered you he slapped your face!" Everyone laughed, but they laughed even harder when I shot back, "Oh yeah? Well, you so ugly the doctor turned around and slapped your momma!" It got even wilder when Bubba said, "Well, man, at least my daddy ain't no girl scout!" We really got into it then. After a while more people got involved—4, 5, then 6. It was a riot! (Reynolds, Taylor, Steffenson, Shirey, & Anderson, 1982, p. 358)

African American students correctly interpreted this passage as referring to a teasing exchange between friends, whereas European American students misunderstood it to be about a serious fight, and when asked to recall as much of the passage as possible, often recalled events, such as the boys getting in trouble for fighting at school or even continuing their fight after school, that had not actually been described in the passage.

Cultural groups may even use different text structures. Urbach (2010) writes about Aisha, an African American first grader who told stories during story time that enthralled her peers, but "did not fit the expected school-based narrative structure" (p. 399). When Urbach analyzed one of Aisha's stories using Stein and Glenn's (1979) traditional story grammar, it appeared "hard to follow. [It] did not have a clear beginning, middle, and end" (p. 400), and was rated as on only a preschool developmental level. Yet when Urbach analyzed the same story using McCabe's (1997) *stanza analysis*, based on a story structure common in many nonwhite cultures that involves a series of events that are topically, rather than sequentially, associated, Aisha's story was revealed as having a strong thematic structure and employing sophisticated tools such as repetition and expressive phonology to emphasize her points.

In both of the studies described above, though they were done nearly 30 years apart, cultural differences in language patterns and use led to difficulties in comprehension and also to potential misjudgments about members of a minority culture. Studies like these should make us more open to multiple interpretations and structures of texts, and also more cautious about judging the meaning or quality of texts drawn from another culture using our own cultural schemata.

Comprehension Monitoring

The ability and disposition to monitor whether one is, in fact, understanding what one is reading is both the hallmark of a good reader and necessary for the effective use of all the other comprehension strategies; a reader must first recognize the need for a strategy before he or she will employ one (Paris, Lipson, & Wixson, 1983; Yang, 2006). Like many elements of reading we have discussed, the ability to monitor one's comprehension seems to develop with age and increased reading skill (Baker, 1984; Garner, 1980; Ehrlich, Remond, & Tardieu, 1999). Thus, a younger or less skilled reader, when assigned to read a passage for a test, will most often read it only once, without identifying or going back over any difficult parts, and assume that he or she has gained all the understanding needed from it (Brown, Campione, & Barclay, 1979; Oakhill, Hartt, & Samols, 2005). On the other hand, older and better readers will read difficult passages more slowly, stopping to check comprehension and employing varying comprehension strategies as needed, and then often reread difficult passages to make certain they have understood them (Kucan & Beck, 1997).

Comprehension monitoring has been most often studied by measuring readers' ability to detect anomalies in words or phrasing in constructed texts, like those marked in italics in the following excerpt from Oakhill et al.'s (2005) study of comprehension monitoring in 9- and 10-year-olds.

> He left his plane and began to walk across the sand. For hours Danny walked, hot, dusty and thirsty. He kept going by telling himself *he would something on soon see the horizon*, but the desert was unchanging. At last there was something ahead of him—a gleam of sunlight on metal or glass. He staggered towards it until he was *sert* enough to see, quite clearly, his own plane. (p. 665)

Other times, readers are asked to judge the coherence of passages containing two or more contradictory sentences, like those marked with an asterisk in this passage, also from the Oakhill et al. study:

> Moles are small brown animals and they live underground using networks of tunnels. *Moles cannot see very well, but their hearing and sense of smell are good. They sleep in underground nests lined with grass, leaves and twigs. Moles use their front feet for digging and their short fur allows them to move along their tunnels either forwards or backwards. They mainly eat worms but they also eat insects and snails. *Moles are easily able to find food for their young because their eyesight is so good. (p. 677)

A possible critique of such research is that the contexts are rather artificial; readers rarely run into passages with scrambled words or phrases or such blatantly contradictory sentences as those in the passages above (Dole, Duffy, et al., 1991). Fortunately, research in actual classrooms has both confirmed the importance of comprehension monitoring and suggested ways in which readers might be taught to engage in monitoring more often and more effectively. Kucan and Beck (1997) concluded from their review of think-aloud research that both teacher and student think-alouds around reading facilitated students' comprehension monitoring and thereby improved their comprehension. Comprehension monitoring is one of the six key cognitive strategies emphasized in Guthrie and colleagues' Concept-Oriented Reading Instruction (CORI) program, proven to help students better comprehend and learn from content-area reading in social studies and science (Guthrie et al., 1998; Guthrie, Wigfield, Barbosa, et al., 2004). One of the most successful ways to help readers learn this strategy is by having students help each other monitor comprehension (Lloyd, 2004); for example, this technique is used in Palincsar and Brown's (1984) reciprocal teaching approach, one of the best-known and most successful programs for comprehension strategy instruction. In this program, students learn to monitor comprehension through a process called *clarifying*, in which they are taught to pose questions regarding difficult text elements to each other in small groups. Reciprocal teaching has repeatedly been proven to increase both students' reading comprehension and their ability to self-monitor their comprehension, and it continues to be used in research and classrooms spanning different ages, subjects, and even languages (e.g., Choo, Eng, & Ahmad, 2011; Gruenbaum, 2012; Klingner & Vaughn, 1996; Rosenshine & Meister, 1994; Reichenberg & Kent, 2014; Slater & Horstman, 2002; Spörer, Brunstein, & Kieschke, 2009).

Summary: The Strategic Reader

We have reviewed the evidence for six strategies known to impact reading comprehension: *activating prior knowledge, questioning, visualizing, summarizing, using text structures,* and *monitoring comprehension.* Good readers often develop these strategies naturally; indeed, these strategies were originally identified through observation studies of what good readers did when reading challenging text. However, we have also described and cited multiple studies showing that novice and struggling readers can learn to use these strategies with good results. Although learning even one of these key strategies can positively impact readers' comprehension abilities, Guthrie, Wigfield, Barbosa, and colleagues' CORI (2004) and Palincsar and Brown's (1984) reciprocal teaching are examples of the greater benefits of instruction that teaches strategies as part of a meaningful whole, in the context of reading and comprehending a variety of texts. This greater benefit is related to the goal of strategy instruction, which is not that readers should be able to name and describe specified strategies, per se, or even that they can use the strategies when cued to do so (Duffy, 1993). The ultimate goal of strategy instruction is that readers become *strategic* (Paris et al., 1983).

Strategic readers begin with a purpose for reading and recognize that different goals require different types of reading (Taraban, Rynearson, & Kerr, 2000). As an adult, you read a grocery list, a novel, a rental contract, and an academic text in very different ways, and the strategies you use depend in part on your purposes for reading. For important texts, strategic readers are not satisfied to read superficially or attain just a shallow comprehension (Cain, Oakhill, Barnes, & Bryant, 2001); they typically engage in what Alexander (2005) calls *deep processing* of text, seeking not just comprehension, but also "the personalization or transformation of text" (p. 422)—that is, to experience a story or integrate information from a text into their own knowledge base so they can use it in the future (see also Pressley et al., 1992). As Wolfe (2002) says, "An effective strategic reader will constantly coordinate strategies, modifying, adjusting and checking, until meaning is created" (p. 8).

WHAT WE CAN DO: CLASSROOM PRACTICES THAT FOSTER READING COMPREHENSION

Help Students Access or Develop Necessary Prior Knowledge

As we have been discussing, prior knowledge is the foundation of comprehension, but students are often asked to read texts for which they lack adequate prior knowledge. For example, *Sadako and the Thousand Paper Cranes* (Coerr, 1977) is a novel about a 12-year-old Japanese girl who is diagnosed with leukemia, caused by the atom bomb dropped near her home in Hiroshima 10 years earlier, at the end of World War II. The novel is relatively short (80 pages) and written at about the fourth-grade reading level, so it is often assigned in upper elementary classes. Even though the reading level and length are appropriate, most students at this age will need help to activate and/or acquire the prior knowledge needed to understand Sadako's story and appreciate how it has come to be seen as an iconic anti-war narrative. Class discussions about what it's like to be sick, and especially to be in the hospital, far from home, may draw on students' own experiences or those of people they know. Information about childhood leukemia, appropriately formatted for children, is available from the Childhood Leukemia Foundation. Children can be encouraged to talk with their grandparents or other older relatives about World War II and the decision to drop the bomb; though most of these relatives were not alive at that time, they have lived through the Cold War and read or heard or watched movies about World War II, and so will have information and ideas to share about the issues involved. Students can bring what they learn from relatives back to share with the class in written or other forms, creating a rich pool of shared information and opinions that can be augmented by additional readings from the school library or websites such as Wikipedia for Kids (*www.wikiforkids.ws*), Ducksters for Kids (*www.ducksters.com/history/world_war_ii/ww2_atomic_bomb.php*), and an interview done by children of a survivor of the Hiroshima bomb posted on the Scholastic website (*http://teacher.scholastic.com/activities/wwii/interview/trans.htm*). The process of gathering and discussing information and ideas from these or many other possible sources will not only prepare students to comprehend Sadako's story better when they read it, but also help them begin to understand the deeper themes it portrays and the difficult decisions and the suffering of the innocent that are part of every war.

Help Students Realize the Need for, and Give Them Practice in, Making Inferences

In this era of standardized testing, children seem especially likely to believe that every question can be answered by finding the correct phrase in the text, even though most questions beyond the purely factual require some level of inference to answer. One way to help students realize this is to talk about the different levels of inference needed by different types of questions. For example, Raphael and colleagues (Raphael & Au, 2005; Raphael & Pearson, 1985) developed a program called QAR (Question–Answer Relationship) to help elementary school children draw inferences by teaching them that the answers to questions they may have while they are reading, or questions on worksheets and tests, may be located in four different ways. Some questions have answers that are "right there"; these are the answers that really can be found just by looking for the right sentence or phrase in the text. Others require students to "think and search"; these answers are in the text, but the reader will need to combine information from two or more sentences to get the answer (much like the *referential* and some of the *bridging inferences* described earlier in this chapter). To answer many questions, students must use their own prior knowledge along with the text (as in some *bridging* and *elaborative inferences* described earlier); Raphael and Au call these "author and me" QARs. Finally, there are questions whose answers must come mainly from reader's prior knowledge because very little about them is actually in the text; these are called "in my head" QARs and most closely resemble the *elaborative inferences* described earlier. The QAR program has helped students in a number of studies become more skilled at drawing inferences to answer questions both to enhance their own reading and to score better on tests of reading comprehension.

Help Students Learn and Practice Other Key Comprehension Strategies

There has been some debate in the field as to whether teachers should name and teach various comprehension strategies explicitly, or only model them as the need arises in the context of student's own authentic reading. The problem, of course, is that if strategies are taught in isolation from real reading, too often students end up being able to name and describe all the steps for each strategy, but they never actually use them when they read (Duffy, 1993). On the other hand, no teacher has the time to wait until the need for a certain strategy comes up in each student's own reading and then teach it to each student individually. The solution seems to be for the teacher to first explicitly describe and model the strategy, often through a think-aloud process, perhaps inviting more advanced students to model the strategy as well. The teacher would then work with the whole class or a smaller group of students to use the strategy on an appropriate text, followed by additional group and then individual guided practice, as the teacher gradually releases responsibility for when and how to use the strategy to the students. The final step occurs when students use the strategy as needed on their own, coordinating it with other strategies they have learned. This *gradual release-of-responsibility* model (Pearson & Gallagher, 1983) is incorporated into the *Transactional Strategies Instruction* (TSI) program developed by Pressley et al. (1992) and based strongly in Vygotskian (1978) learning theory, which they describe as "an interpersonal and interdependent way of promoting the long-term goal of developing active, strategic readers" (p. 523). TSI has been successfully used at both elementary and secondary levels in regular classrooms and also to work with readers who are struggling and/or have learning disabilities (Brown, 2008; Casteel, Isom, & Jordan, 2000; Hilden & Pressley, 2007).

Another useful instructional practice is to encourage students to share the strategies they have used after reading a difficult class-assigned text. The point of such a discussion is not to have students identify and assert their use of the generalized, "official" strategies listed above, but rather to have them describe their own strategic thinking and actions as they worked to comprehend the text. Such open class discussions of strategic reading have several clear benefits: (1) They model the message that comprehending such texts is not automatic, even for good readers, but that reading of difficult tests is a strategic, effortful process for everyone; (2) they encourage students to be more metacognitive, that is, to reflect on their own reading practices and how they might be enhanced; and (3) they enable students to "swap" strategies in an informal context, to hear about reading strategies they may never have considered and perhaps even decide to try a strategy recommended by a peer. As college faculty, we have promoted such discussions in both undergraduate and graduate classes and found that students appreciated and enjoyed them, with many adding new strategies to their repertoires as a result.

CONNECTING TO THE STANDARDS

Given the centrality of comprehension to reading, it is not surprising that 7 of the 10 Common Core Curriculum's College and Career Readiness Anchor Standards for Reading directly address issues we have discussed in this chapter and the previous one. Table 8.2 lists these standards.

TABLE 8.2. Connecting to the Core: Common Core College and Career Readiness Anchor Standards Specifically Related to Reading Comprehension

Read closely to determine what the text says explicitly and to make logical inferences from it; cite specific textual evidence when writing or speaking to support conclusions drawn from the text. (www.ccss.ela-literacy.ccra.r.1)

Determine central ideas or themes of a text and analyze their development; summarize the key supporting details and ideas. (www.ccss.ela-literacy.ccra.r.2)

Analyze how and why individuals, events, or ideas develop and interact over the course of a text. (www.ccss.ela-literacy.ccra.r.3)

Analyze the structure of texts, including how specific sentences, paragraphs, and larger portions of the text (e.g., a section, chapter, scene, or stanza) relate to each other and the whole. (www. ccss.ela-literacy.ccra.r.5)

Delineate and evaluate the argument and specific claims in a text, including the validity of the reasoning as well as the relevance and sufficiency of the evidence. (www.ccss.ela-literacy.ccra.r.8)

Analyze how two or more texts address similar themes or topics in order to build knowledge or to compare the approaches the authors take. (www.ccss.ela-literacy.ccra.r.9)

Read and comprehend complex literary and informational texts independently and proficiently. (www.ccss.ela-literacy.ccra.r.10)

Note. Adapted from the National Governors Association Center for Best Practices and the Council of Chief State School Officers (2010). All rights reserved.

1. Think about a time when you have had difficulty comprehending a text. Which of the factors described in this chapter made understanding that particular text more difficult for you?

2. We have discussed six general reading strategies known to increase comprehension on average, but certainly no reader uses them all equally, nor does any reader use all of these strategies on a single text. Part of being a strategic reader is knowing which strategies work best for you, so think about which of these strategies you may have used in reading this book. Are there other strategies, beyond those we have mentioned, that you have also found useful? If there is time, share and compare these strategies with your classmates or colleagues.

3. In the case study presented in this chapter, Jay is probably not the only freshman in Dr. Harada's class who did not take an economics course in high school and who has had little personal experience in the economic system. In what ways might Dr. Harada help such students build the background knowledge they need to understand the ideas in his text and his course?

4. Jay is also unlikely to be the only student in Dr. Harada's class who came to college without any developed strategies for reading difficult texts because high school was pretty easy for him. What could Dr. Harada do to help students like Jay to both understand the textbook better so they can pass his class and also begin to become more strategic readers, so they can learn more successfully throughout college?

FURTHER READINGS

Dole, J. A., Duffy, G. G., Roehler, L. R., & Pearson, P. D. (1991). Moving from the old to the new: Research on reading comprehension instruction. *Review of Educational Research, 61*(2), 239–264.

Duke, N. K., & Pearson, P. D. (2002). Effective reading practices for developing comprehension. In A. E. Farstrup & S. J. Samuels (Eds.), *What research has to say about reading instruction* (Vol. 3, pp. 205–242). Newark, DE: International Reading Association.

Wolfe, A. (2002). Confessions of a just-in-time reader: Reflections on the development of strategic competence in reading. *Language Learning Journal, 26*(1), 4–10.

CHAPTER 9

Motivation to Read

CASE STUDY

Ms. Garvey has just given her sixth-grade students 30 minutes to read and answer some comprehension questions on Sandra Cisneros's short story "Eleven," a Common Core State Standards suggested text for the middle grades.

Julie slips a small piece of paper under her copy of the story. She starts to read, but whenever Ms. Garvey isn't looking, she slips the paper out and writes a note to pass to her friend sitting behind her. The two of them pass notes back and forth the whole half hour, so when Ms. Garvey announces that there are 5 minutes left to complete the questions, Julie hasn't even finished the story. She hurriedly writes some answers that look OK to her on the worksheet and turns it in just in time.

Linda, using the test-taking strategies that she has been taught, reads the questions first and then skims through the story, searching for the correct answers and then copying them onto her worksheet. She is pleased when she finishes before anyone else, and so is Ms. Garvey, who whispers "Good work!" to her as she turns in her worksheet.

Brittany doesn't even pick up the story. She has struggled with reading all her life, and hardly ever tries to read her assignments any more. It was kind of a relief when she was diagnosed with a learning disability last year. Maybe her special education teacher will read the story to her later and help her with the worksheet; if not, she'll just get another zero.

Shondra takes her time reading the story, feeling glad when, at the end, Mrs. Price figures out that the ugly sweater doesn't belong to Rachel, but a little sad that the incident has spoiled Rachel's birthday. As she answers the comprehension questions, she wonders about how Phyllis felt having to claim the ugly sweater, and raises her hand to ask Ms. Garvey if there is more to the story. She's a bit disappointed when she finds out there isn't, but she finishes the worksheet and has time left to start another chapter in her library book.

Delores is nervous when she sees that the story is three pages long. She starts to read, intrigued by the fact that the author has a Hispanic surname, but the reading isn't easy for her, and she soon realizes she won't be able to finish in time. After about 10 minutes, she goes up to Ms. Garvey's desk and asks permission to go to the nurse because she feels sick. Ms. Garvey frowns because Delores has missed a lot of class, but gives her permission, reminding her that she will still need to finish her work at home tonight. That's all right with Delores; she is actually kind of interested to see how the story turns out, and she knows her older sister will help her if she needs it.

Ms. Garvey sighs, looking around the classroom as students are turning in their papers. Except for a few like Shondra, her students just don't seem very motivated to read.

Psychologists have recognized the importance of motivation to read since they first began to study reading. In 1908, Edmund Burke Huey, author of perhaps the first book on the psychology of reading, wrote:

> Drill on form "benumbs" by its monotony and repetition. The child does not want to learn reading as a mechanical tool. He must have a "personal hunger" for what is read. He must come, too, to his reading with personal experience with which to appreciate it. (pp. 305–306)

Researchers and educators have increasingly come to realize that knowing how to read is only half the battle; readers also need to be motivated to *seek meaning* in order to read successfully (Afflerbach, Cho, Kim, Crassas, & Doyle, 2013; Conradi, Jang, & McKenna, 2014).

Understanding motivation is a vital part of understanding the psychology of reading for two reasons. The first is simply because people who read more tend to read better (Krashen, 2009; Allington, 2014). The amount of reading a person does is one of the strongest and best-supported correlates of reading achievement at all levels (Anderson et al., 1988; Alexander, 2005; Cipielewski & Stanovich, 1992; Garan & DeVoogd, 2008). This relationship has been repeatedly demonstrated, both nationally (National Endowment for the Arts [NEA], 2007; National Center for Education Statistics [NCES], 2013) and internationally (Clark & De Zoysa, 2011; Organization for Economic Cooperation and Development [OECD], 2010). It holds true in diverse populations of readers, including English language learners (Krashen, 2009), young teens (Howard, 2011), developmental college students (Paulson, 2006), and even adults who are deaf (Parault & Williams, 2010). In addition, the amount of variance in reading skills explained by time spent reading significantly increases with age, going from 12% in early childhood to 34% in college students (Mol & Bus, 2011). The amount that one reads predicts growth in reading skill (Guthrie, Wigfield, Metsala, & Cox, 2004), especially in comprehension (Krashen, 2006), and students given time to read connected, authentic texts in school make greater gains in tested reading achievement than students offered only traditional, skills-based instruction such as phonics worksheets or repeated reading (Schwanenflugel et al., 2009; Shany & Biemiller, 1995; Shin, 2001). In their 2005 meta-analysis on independent reading time in school, Lewis and Samuels found "in 79% of the student samples that had some form of independent reading experience, reading ability scores improved in relation to their pretest scores or in comparison to a nonreading control group" (p. 12), concluding that the "evidence reveals not only a strong positive correlational relationship between reading time and reading achievement, but some probability of a causal relationship as well" (p. 21).

In Chapter 1, we discussed the importance of access to reading materials in the home and its connection to preschoolers' development of early reading knowledge and skills (Debaryshe et al., 2000). Access continues to be a key factor in reading development throughout the school years; children who have more access to books, whether at home or in libraries, score higher on tests of reading achievement, even when the results are controlled for home or community SES (Evans et al., 2014; Krashen et al., 2012). But no amount of access to reading materials will benefit someone who won't read, so motivation is a key mediator between opportunity to read and reading development. Simply put, children who choose to read become better readers. For instance, in a longitudinal study of over 1,500 students from fifth through eighth grades, Retelsdorf, Köller, and Möller (2011) found that both reading enjoyment and self-efficacy predicted tested reading performance, and reading interest also predicted reading growth over the 3 years of the study. Actually, causation between motivation to read and reading ability appears to be bidirectional and reciprocal (Morgan & Fuchs, 2007), as it is between enjoyment and learning in general (Blunsdon, Reed, & McNeil, 2003). That is, people who read better tend to enjoy reading more, and people who enjoy reading tend to read more and get better at it (Guthrie & Wigfield, 2000; Morgan & Fuchs; Stanovich, 1986).

The other reason motivation is vital to understanding the psychology of reading is that motivation affects not just the *quantity* but also the *quality* of a person's reading. We have all had the experience of reading something that did not interest us, perhaps a required novel or an assignment in a textbook (though not this one, of course!), and having our attention wander from the reading so much that we found ourselves at the bottom of a page with no recollection at all of what we had just "read." This common phenomenon is perhaps an extreme example of the type of *surface-level processing* described in Chapter 8. Clearly, simply to read the words in a text is not enough; to gain from that reading, the reader must be motivated to understand what is read.

As we discuss in more detail later in this chapter, readers who doubt their own ability to comprehend or see no value in what they are reading tend to read, if they do so at all, on a merely surface level, reading the words and taking perhaps the literal meaning from those words. In contrast, motivated readers tend to process what they are reading actively and deeply (Guthrie & Wigfield, 2000). As discussed in Chapter 8, *deep processing* involves integrating the text into one's personal schemas through strategies, used consciously or subconsciously, such as visualization, questioning, and comparison with other texts and knowledge held. Deep processing during reading leads not only to better comprehension and recall of the text being read, but also to greater overall learning, in terms of both reading skill improvement and knowledge development (Alexander, 2005; Willingham, 2003). These connections are confirmed by multiple studies showing significant, direct connections between reading motivation and comprehension (Anmarkrud & Bräten, 2009; Clark & De Zoysa, 2011; Guthrie et al., 2007; Guthrie, Klauda, & Ho, 2013; Park, 2011).

Unfortunately, multiple studies over decades have also confirmed that personal motivation to read, though it starts quite high in young children, often declines significantly as children move through elementary school (McKenna, Kear, & Ellsworth, 1995; Scholastic, 2015; Wigfield et al., 1997), with further declines common upon entry to middle and high school (McKenna, Conradi, Lawrence, Jang, & Meyer, 2001; Oldfather & Dahl, 1994; Gottfried, Fleming, & Gottfired, 2001). Paris and McNaughton (2010) suggest that this steady loss of motivation to read may be due to demotivating practices common in many schools, including decontextualized instruction and increasing emphasis on external evaluation and sanctions.

EXPECTANCY × VALUE IN READING

So far we have been discussing motivation to read as though it were a unitary concept, a single quality that one either has more or less of at any given time. But motivation to engage in any task, including reading, is actually a complicated interaction of a number of different factors, influenced by characteristics of the task, the context, and the person's task-related values and beliefs as developed through past experiences and learning (Guthrie & Wigfield, 2000; Conradi et al., 2014).

To frame our discussion of these many factors as they relate to reading, we use an adapted version of one of today's best-accepted motivation theories, Eccles and Wigfield's *expectancy–value* model of motivation (Eccles, 2005; Wigfield & Eccles, 2000; Wigfield, Tonks, & Klauda, 2009). Their model draws in part on earlier work by Lewin (1938), Atkinson (1964), and others. It describes people's motivation to achieve tasks that require some degree of intentional effort (e.g., *not* motivation to breathe or eat chocolate cake) as related to their *expectancy* of being able to achieve the task and the *value* success would have for them. Notice that this model of motivation emphasizes the subjective perceptions and beliefs of the individual, not necessarily some measurable reality of the situation (Eccles). In terms of reading, this means that even if children *really* could read a text, if they *believe* they cannot read it, they will not be very motivated to try. For example, a second grader with good reading skills might still be unwilling to try even relatively easy chapter books, such as Osbourne's *Magic Treehouse* series, because he or she is intimidated by the lack of pictures. Likewise, it doesn't matter that much whether a book is *really* well written or has literary value; if a child *perceives* it as interesting or of value, he or she will be more motivated to read it; Pilkey's *Captain Underpants* books are very popular among early elementary readers (Williams, 2008), even though few would call them great literature.

Table 9.1 provides an organized picture of 10 factors that can contribute to readers' expectancies of success and perceptions of value in reading. This model includes several factors not found in Eccles and Wigfield's original model of general motivation because these factors have been shown specifically to impact reading motivation. Also, in line with recent findings by Nagengast et al. (2011), using PISA data from over 57 countries and nearly 400,000 students, we have reinstated the interactive symbol "×" that was used by the earliest researchers (e.g., Atkinson, 1964; Feather, 1959); that is, we are using an expectancy × value model. We use the × not to imply (as some early researchers did) that motivation can be exactly or mathematically calculated using these factors, but rather to clarify that expectancy and value interact in forming motivation, such that if one factor is essentially zero or even negative, little or no motivation will exist, even if the other factor is quite high. For example, a student who knows very little English may not be motivated to try to read a novel in English, even if it is required for a class grade (high value), because the student is sure he or she won't be able to read it (no expectancy of success). On the other hand, an accomplished teen reader could easily read the currently popular vampire novels (high expectancy), but will not be motivated to do so if he or she dislikes horror stories (low, even negative, value). Finally, it is important to acknowledge that expectancy and value overlap in some ways. For example, someone can have both intrinsic interest and utility value for reading a particular text; in fact these two constructs are often somewhat correlated in research (Guthrie & Wigfield, 2000). The boundaries of these categories,

TABLE 9.1. Expectancy × Value in Reading Motivation

EXPECTANCY Do we expect to be able to read the text successfully?	VALUE Does reading the text have value for us?
Self-Efficacy: We are more motivated to read if we feel competent in reading.	**Intrinsic Interest:** We are more motivated to read texts that are engagingly written or about topics that personally interest us.
View of Ability: We are more motivated to read when we believe our skill will improve with practice and effort.	**Utility Value:** We are more motivated to read when reading will help us achieve other goals we value.
Locus of Control: We are more motivated to read when we feel in control of when and what we read.	**Self-Concept:** We are more motivated to read when reading enhances, rather than threatens or contradicts, our self-concept.
Support: We are more motivated to read difficult texts if we believe help will be available if we run into problems.	**Relational Value:** We are more motivated to read when reading enhances our relationship(s) with people we care about.
Time: We are more motivated to read if we believe we will have enough time to read.	**Cost/Risk:** We are *less* motivated to read when cost (time, effort, or risk of failure) seems high compared to possible benefit.

Note. From Knapp (2015) based on Wigfield and Eccles (2000).

like all human categories, are somewhat artificial, arbitrary lines drawn across an actually seamless reality; nevertheless, they are useful for discussion.

EXPECTANCY OF SUCCESS IN READING

The term *expectancy* refers to whether a reader believes he or she will be *able* to read and understand a particular text in a particular situation. Research has identified five major factors impacting expectancy of success in reading.

Self-Efficacy

Self-efficacy can be defined as our beliefs about our competence or ability to complete tasks in a given domain, also sometimes called *ability beliefs* or *competence beliefs* (Wigfield & Eccles, 2000, 2002). Self-efficacy beliefs are affected by a number of factors (Bandura, 1994). Perhaps the strongest influence is often personal experiences of failure and success, especially in moderately difficult tasks, but self-efficacy can also be influenced by vicarious experiences—that is, by seeing other people similar to us succeed or fail at a task. For example, we may feel more nervous about our own driving right after seeing an accident occur. Social persuasion, derived from comments by other people about our abilities, can also powerfully impact our self-efficacy. Self-efficacy can even be influenced by emotions and moods; the negative impact of strong test anxiety on performance is an example of this effect.

Self-efficacy in reading, then, refers to a person's judgment of his or her ability or competence in reading. Research in reading self-efficacy has focused mainly on the effects of success and failure experiences in reading. This research suggests that early experiences may be the most powerful, in part because young children have a very limited set of prior experiences to draw upon and in part because early experiences of success or failure in reading may influence later reading behaviors (Becker, McElvany, & Kortenbruck, 2010). For example, Morgan, Fuchs, Compton, Cordray, and Fuchs (2008) found that as early as midway through first grade, children who were quite successful at reading tasks believed themselves to be more competent, whereas those who had experienced repeated failure already perceived themselves as less competent in reading. Teachers likewise rated successful children as more intrinsically motivated to read, while they rated children who frequently failed as already task-avoidant in reading. Chapman and Tunmer (2003) and Quirk, Schwanenflugel, and Webb (2009) found that early skills in word reading and fluency impacted second-graders' later beliefs about their reading competence. Children who had good basic reading skills early on demonstrated stronger positive beliefs about themselves as readers later, whereas children who had poor basic reading skills ended up with negative views of themselves as readers. Elementary-aged children tend to base their judgments of self-efficacy in reading mainly on skill and fluency in word identification (Guthrie et al., 2007; Knapp, 1999), but as children get older and throughout adulthood, they begin to base their self-efficacy judgments more on reading comprehension (Shell, Colvin, & Bruning, 1995).

Children's self-efficacy is also influenced by the verbal evaluations they receive from others. Children whose reading is frequently criticized by their teachers, parents, or peers are likely to develop low self-efficacy in reading, as are children who consistently receive low grades in reading (Durik, Vida, & Eccles, 2006). Conversely, children whose reading is praised may develop higher self-efficacy, as long as they perceive that praise to be honest and deserved (Guthrie & Wigfield, 2000).

Research strongly supports the reciprocal impact of self-efficacy beliefs on reading achievement, even as early as second grade (Quirk et al., 2009). Students with higher self-efficacy in reading are likely to read more, choose more challenging reading materials, use reading strategies more effectively, and persist even when reading tasks are difficult (Durik et al., 2006; Guthrie & Wigfield, 2000;

Schunk & Zimmerman, 1997). All of these reading behaviors, in turn, enhance their reading skills, making self-efficacy one of the key factors in the influence of motivation on reading achievement.

View of Ability

View of ability refers not to a person's view of his or her own abilities (that's self-efficacy), but rather to a person's beliefs about the nature of ability itself: whether it is something fixed and innate or something that can be substantially increased through effort. Carol Dweck and her colleagues (Dweck & Leggett, 1988; Dweck & Master, 2009) have pioneered research on this aspect of motivation, looking primarily at students' views of intelligence. They found that some students have an *entity* view of intelligence; that is, they see intelligence as mainly fixed. They believe that a person is either smart or not, and if not, there is not much the person can do about it. Other students have an *incremental* view of intelligence, seeing it as something that develops, so they believe that they can get smarter through effort and practice. Students who hold an incremental view of intelligence are more likely to focus on learning because, by learning, they feel they can get smarter. Students with an entity view of intelligence, on the other hand, are most concerned about looking smart in school or at least not looking stupid. Their concern can get in the way of actual learning, as when a student is confused but unwilling to ask a question for fear of looking less intelligent. Young children tend to hold an incremental view of ability, believing that effort and ability go together. They have had many experiences of working at something like running or throwing a ball and getting better at it because practice at this early age nearly always leads to improved performance. However, by the time they are in first or second grade, most students begin to hold an entity view of ability that tends to get stronger as they get older. Due perhaps to the increased opportunities school offers for social comparison, students at this age often begin to believe that putting in less effort is a sign of greater ability because needing to expend a lot of effort on something implies that one's natural ability is low (Stipek, 1993).

People can hold entity or incremental views in many fields besides intelligence. For instance, we often hear people talk about someone being a "born athlete" or "born musician." Many people hold entity views in specific academic areas. For example, some students avoid math classes or tasks involving math because sometime during school they were told (particularly if they are girls), "It's OK—not everyone can be good at math" (Rattan, Good, & Dweck, 2012). Students can also hold entity views of reading ability, believing that some students are just "good readers," whereas others are not. Just as in other areas, entity views in reading can contribute to lower motivation for learning. For example, Baird, Scot, Dearing, and Hamill (2009) found in a study of over 1,500 6th to 12th graders that students diagnosed with a learning disability were more likely to hold entity views of ability. Those holding entity views exerted less effort in reading, believing that effort was useless and would only further reveal their lack of ability. Pepi, Alesi, and Geraci (2004) similarly found that third graders with reading disabilities who held incremental ability views were able to learn more from comprehension strategy instruction than those who held entity views. They suggested that interventions for struggling readers should be carefully designed to reinforce incremental, rather than entity, views of reading ability. Berkeley, Mastropieri, and Scruggs (2011) demonstrated that the right kind of instruction could effectively encourage incremental views, even in struggling students. In their study, two groups of middle-school students with mild learning disabilities received the same strategy instruction, but students in one group were also taught to attribute success in reading to effort and effective use of strategies rather than to innate ability. Both groups of students initially improved in reading comprehension compared to students who received no special instruction, but the group who had been taught new attributions retained a much larger advantage in comprehension after 6 weeks, and only they showed changes in their beliefs about the sources of reading ability.

Locus of Control

Another factor in Wigfield and Eccles's (2000) expectancy–value model of motivation, *locus of control*, is actually a combination of two of Weiner's (1985) classic dimensions of casual attribution: *locus of causality* and *controllability*. Locus of causality measures whether a person believes the cause of a success or failure was due to something inside him- or herself or to some external factor. For example, children who believe they passed an Accelerated Reader test because they read and understood the book are attributing their success to an internal cause, but if instead they think they passed because the test was easy, they are making an external attribution. However, as we saw in the previous discussion of view of ability, attributions to uncontrollable internal causes, such as innate ability, are not very motivating, especially for challenging learning tasks. Attributions to internal, controllable factors such as effort, strategy use, or lack of practice are much more motivating, even in the face of initial failure. Essentially, we are more motivated when we feel a strong personal locus of control because we believe that we have significant control over the tasks we perform and our success at them.

The perception of a strong personal locus of control, sometimes called *agency* or *autonomy* (Deci & Ryan, 1987; Guthrie & Wigfield, 2000), is not simply a personal trait or characteristic. Rather, it varies for any given task, influenced not only by our own beliefs and past experiences, but also by the characteristics of the task and situation. It is stronger when we can choose the nature and difficulty level of our tasks, and when we feel that our success does not depend on luck or someone else's favor. Unfortunately, typical schools and classrooms do not tend to foster this sense of agency and control; instead, too often students feel, as deCharms (1977) described it, like *pawns*,

> a person who feels that someone other than himself is in control of what he does. He feels that what he does is imposed on him, what he does he is forced to do. The results of his actions are not really his and he need take little responsibility for them or pride in them. (p. 297)

Teachers who respect students' experiences, offer students bounded choices (Gambrell, 2011), and share influence on classroom goals and procedures with students help them feel more like *origins*, that is,

> a person who feels that he directs his own life. . . . He takes pride in his successes but realizes that he is also responsible for his failures. He owns his actions and their consequences and takes responsibility for them. (deCharms, 1977, p. 297)

Students who feel more like origins than pawns in the classroom are not only more motivated to learn, but also feel less aggressive and more competent, both cognitively and socially (deCharms; Ryan & Grolnick, 1986).

Research, specifically in reading, has repeatedly validated these general findings. For example, Turner (1995; Turner & Paris, 1995) found that even first graders were more motivated by *open* literacy tasks in which processes and goals were partially self-determined (e.g., after reading *Clifford's Birthday Party* [Bridwell, 1988], choosing to work in a group to make Clifford's birthday cake following the written directions or to read more Clifford stories independently) than by *closed* tasks, in which the desired end and acceptable process to that end were both controlled by the teacher or textbook (e.g., answering comprehension questions and identifying vocabulary in the story on a worksheet). Grolnick and Ryan (1987) found that students who read social studies texts under noncontrolling conditions enjoyed the process more and also understood and remembered more concepts from the text. Similarly, Wigfield, Guthrie, Tonks, and Perencevich (2004) report that students who formuated their own personal questions during hands-on science activities were more motivated to search for answers by reading science-related books than students who were simply given questions and assigned those books to read. Cappella and Weinstein (2001), studying students who entered high school several grade levels behind in reading, found that one of the factors that differentiated between the majority who continued to fail and often left school and the 15% who improved to at least average levels and ultimately graduated, was the students' sense of an inner locus of control. Finally, numerous studies have found that students who are allowed to choose what they want to read are more motivated to read, spend more time and effort reading, and also understand what they read better (Gambrell, 2011; Krashen, 2006).

Time

Though not originally included in Wigfield and Eccles's (2000) expectancy–value model, research has shown that *time* to read is an important element in reading motivation. As discussed at the beginning of this chapter, time spent reading is an essential component of reading development, and multiple studies have shown that providing students with time for self-chosen reading in school is an effective way to promote reading growth (Krashen, 2009). For example, Allington and Johnston (2000) found that teachers in classrooms where students showed above-average gains in reading allocated, on average, three times as much class time to independent reading than did teachers in classrooms where students showed only average reading progress. These less effective teachers commonly allocated more time to pre- and post-reading activities like vocabulary review, answering comprehension questions, or completing worksheets than to actually letting students read. Foorman et al. (2006) found similar results when they studied classroom reading activities in over 100 primary classrooms in high-poverty schools. They found that only time allocation for the reading of connected text consistently differentiated between more and less effective teachers; no other differences in time allocation, including time spent on alphabetic, word, or phonetic instruction, were related to variations in students' reading growth.

Yet, Hiebert (2009) suggests that many students may lack motivation to read books or other extended texts because they have little opportunity in school to do the sustained kind of reading that promotes deep engagement. Personally, we can imagine nothing more frustrating than starting a really good book and being dragged away from it after reading for only a few minutes, but this seems to be a common happening in school. In fact, Brenner et al. (2009) found that in third-grade Reading First classrooms in Mississippi, students read connected text for only 18 minutes on average out of a 90-minute or longer reading instructional block. This finding echoes others over the past 40 years: In 1977, Allington noted that the early remedial and struggling readers he observed read on average only 43 words in context during a typical small-group teacher-led reading lesson. Gambrell (1984) calculated that students in school read individually only about 14 minutes on average each day. Foertsch (1992) found that over half of students taking the NAEP in 1988–1990 reported reading 10 pages or fewer for school each day. A decade later, Donahue et al. (2001) found almost identical results.

Extensive time in school for free voluntary reading (Krashen, 2011) may help motivate students to read for a number of reasons. It increases students' sense of autonomy (discussed above) and engages their intrinsic interest (discussed in the next section). It also gives them time to experience what Csikszentmihalyi (1990) has called *flow*, "the state in which people are so involved in an activity that nothing else seems to matter; the experience itself is so enjoyable that people will do it . . . for the sheer sake of doing it" (p. 4). This certainly describes the reading experience of avid readers, and such experiences are, by definition, highly motivating.

Another time-related issue is the interaction of timed testing and reading motivation. Teachers we work with frequently describe poor readers who are so discouraged by standardized tests that they "make Christmas trees" on the bubble-in answer sheets or otherwise completely disengage during testing. Fuchs, Fuchs, Mathes, Lipsey, and Roberts (2001) concluded from a large meta-analysis that learning disabled and other low-achieving readers scored considerably lower on timed tests than they did on parallel tests that did not restrict time. Interestingly, Perlman, Borger, Collins, Elenbogan, and Wood (1996) found that when 59 fourth graders with learning disabilities were told they could have extended time on a standardized reading test, they scored significantly better, even though all but one actually finished the test within the publisher's standard time limit. This finding suggests that it was the emotional or motivational effects of knowing they had a time limit, rather than the time limit itself, which had lowered their previous test scores. Though we found little research in this area so far, given the ubiquity of timed testing in education today, the question of how time limits impact achievement motivation on reading tests and for reading overall seems ripe for investigation.

Support

Another factor added to the expectancy side of the expectancy × value model of reading motivation described here is *support*. Support in reading can be as simple as helping students find engaging books. It can be showing a willingness to value what students like to read and listen when they talk about it. Alexander (2005) suggests that resistant readers and even highly competent readers can benefit from this sort of support, and those who find reading to be hard work may benefit from encouragement to read more strategically, so they can learn to "work smarter rather than harder" (p. 428). In a large evaluation study Guthrie et al. (2013) found that CORI, a content-reading program that offers multiple supports for strategic reading, positively impacted students' reading engagement and motivation, as well as their comprehension.

Readers who struggle the most may benefit from more extensive support through *scaffolding*, defined as providing external support that enables novices "to complete tasks more complex than they would otherwise be able to carry through . . . while learning strategies and patterns that will eventually make it possible to carry out similar tasks without external support" (Applebee & Langer, 1983, pp. 169, 171; see also Wood, Bruner, & Ross, 1976). For example, in the Reading Apprenticeship program, adults partner-read student-chosen books with delayed readers over a period of 10–12 weeks, assisting them to decode difficult words, defining unknown vocabulary, and modeling comprehension strategies (Knapp & Winsor, 1998). In a summary of eight studies of this intervention, Knapp (2013b) found that through such scaffolding, struggling elementary readers gained not only in reading fluency and comprehension, but also in reading motivation as reported by the children, their parents, and their teachers. Computers and other devices are also being used with increasing success to scaffold reading for struggling readers, including English language learners. Digital devices can now pronounce unknown words with a touch or a click, offer instant definitions and visual representations of unfamiliar vocabulary, and, if necessary, read aloud any text that is just too frustrating to the reader. According to Stetter and Hughes (2010a), research in this area indicates that such digital readers can offer struggling students effective support and even learning opportunities in word identification and vocabulary. Evidence for their effectiveness in supporting comprehension is not as clear. Using such digital scaffolding to remove barriers caused by problems in decoding or vocabulary should enhance struggling readers' motivation to read (Morgan, 2013), and studies by Higgins and Raskind (2005) and Young (2013) offer some anecdotal evidence for this hypothesis, but much of the needed research in this area has yet to be carried out.

Summary of Expectancy in Reading

Our feelings of self-efficacy, views of ability, perceptions of agency and control, and beliefs that we will have sufficient time and support all influence our expectancy of success in any particular reading situation, and thus our motivation to engage in that reading. However, the impacts of these five factors are not simply additive, with so much self-efficacy combining with a certain amount of control and support to reach some total level of expectancy sufficient to motivate reading. Rather, these factors interact in complex ways. For example, we know that the combination of low self-efficacy and an entity view of ability—a person's notion that some people will just never be good at reading, and that he or she happens to be one of them—is both very common and very damaging for many struggling readers. However, research suggests that even gifted readers' high sense of self-efficacy can be threatened by seemingly minor failures if they hold an entity view of ability (Fletcher & Speirs Neumeister, 2012; Roberts & Lovett, 1994).

In another example of such interactions, Guthrie et al.'s (2007) findings suggest that locus of control and support may be more important to some readers than to others. In their study, some fourth graders, particularly avid readers, felt very strongly about choosing their own books, but others felt that parents or teachers made better choices for them. Similarly, reading with others was preferred by many fourth graders, but particularly avid and confident readers often chose to read by themselves, apparently finding the independent control experienced when reading alone to be more important than the support of a partner.

It is also important to recognize that reading success can be differently defined in different circumstances. Success in reading a novel for pleasure just means understanding enough to enjoy it, whereas success in reading a car repair manual involves gaining enough information to fix the car. On the other hand, as suggested in both the schema theoretic (Anderson & Pearson, 1984) and C-I (Kintsch, 2004) models of reading covered in Chapter 7, success in reading a textbook requires not only understanding the text in depth, but also remembering it and integrating it with other knowledge to pass a test or write an essay. So, although we know that these five factors influence readers' expectancy of success, we still have much to learn about their interactions in different readers and different contexts.

FACTORS IMPACTING VALUE IN READING

Expectancy refers to readers' beliefs about whether they will be *able* to read a particular text in a particular situation. *Value* is about whether and how they *want* to read it. Guthrie and colleagues (Guthrie & Cox, 2001; Guthrie & Wigfield, 2000) describe the reader who values reading for enjoyment and meaning as an *engaged* reader. Their work supports the idea that increasing reading engagement, both inside and outside the classroom, increases reading ability because it affects both the quantity and quality of reading. Only students who learn to value reading will become lifelong readers, continuing to read at a significant level once they leave school (Cramer & Castle, 1994). Unfortunately, we are seeing increasing numbers of *aliterates*, people who can read but choose not to (Asselin, 2004), in our schools and society (National Endowments for the Arts, 2007). We even see a substantial number of aliterates among preservice and inservice teachers (Applegate & Applegate, 2004; Nathanson, Pruslow, & Levitt, 2008)—which is particularly disturbing given that teachers serve as models for children. Though in schools we tend to focus much more on increasing students' reading skills, and thus their expectancy for success in reading, helping students come to value reading is clearly a related, and at least as important, goal.

Intrinsic Interest

Intrinsic interest in an activity arises from the enjoyment one anticipates or experiences in doing it; Ryan and Deci (2000) describe it as "a natural wellspring of learning and achievement [and] a critical element in cognitive, social, and physical development . . . a significant feature of human nature that affects performance, persistence, and well-being across life's epochs" (pp. 55–56). Certainly, intrinsic interest is one of the most powerful factors impacting motivation to read. Intrinsic interest motivates most recreational reading and, as discussed above, recreational reading is associated with a number of desirable academic and personal outcomes. Such interest can arise from a fundamental enjoyment of reading itself, as it does for students who have developed the "reading habit" (Sanacore, 2000), who take a book with them everywhere and both encourage and frustrate their teachers by sneaking chances to read during lectures or other classroom activities. For most readers, though, intrinsic interest is generated by particular texts or reading activities.

Students are often intrinsically interested in texts associated with popular movies (e.g., the *Hunger Games*) or other desirable activities, such as "hands-on" science investigations (Guthrie et al., 2006). Interesting or unusual illustrations or text formats (e.g., *Eyewitness Books*, graphic novels, or comic books; Schneider, 2014) or even the opportunity to read digital text on electronic devices, rather than traditional print on paper (Jones & Brown, 2011) can all increase intrinsic interest. Reader-chosen book award lists, such as the American Library Association's Teen's Top Ten and the Children's Book Council's Children's Choice Awards, demonstrate that well-written texts, with vivid prose, compelling characters, or exciting plots also spark readers' interest across age groups. But intrinsic interest is most commonly stimulated when the topic or genre of a text is related in some way to a reader's own life or personal interests (Gambrell, 2011).

We have all seen the motivating power of this kind of intrinsic interest. The nonreading sports fan will ask to read a biography of his or her favorite basketball player. The struggling reader who loves teen romances will eagerly await the next installment in a favorite series. Guthrie and Wigfield (2000; see also Ivey & Johnston, 2013) call these *interesting texts* and advocate for their use in classroom reading instruction because students spend more time reading personally interesting texts and also tend to learn more from them. Students show greater comprehension and recall of personally interesting texts (Guthrie et al., 2007), and these effects are even stronger for poor readers than for good readers (Logan, Medford, & Hughes, 2011). Alexander (2005) points out that intrinsically interesting texts are especially important in motivating beginning readers, for whom reading is still very effortful. A book that engages this kind of intrinsic interest can be the gateway into reading for a novice or struggling reader; many of us can still remember the first real book that grabbed our interest in this way.

Utility Value

An activity with *utility value*, also called *instrumental value*, is not seen as desirable in itself, but rather as a means to some other desirable end. Everybody does things every day based on this sort of motivation: We do assignments to get grades, we do laundry to have clean clothes, we work to get a paycheck. Some motivation theorists call this *extrinsic motivation*, but classic extrinsic motivation—motivation that is imposed from without in order to avoid punishment or gain rewards—is actually only one kind of utility value. Extrinsically imposed rewards and punishments, though very commonly used in education, are probably the least useful means of sparking motivation for learning, in part because externally motivated students tend to look for the shortest, easiest route to their goals (Corpus, McClintic-Gilbert, & Hayenga, 2009), doing the minimum, memorizing, or even cheating, rather than taking the time to understand what they are studying. Utility value that does not arise from an extrinsic source, but is based on a learner's own recognition of the potential usefulness of the knowledge to be gained, is much more conducive to learning (Ryan & Deci, 2000).

Reading, like other activities, is often motivated by utility value, and readers can be motivated by both kinds of utility value just described. Sometimes readers read simply to satisfy some outside requirement, like a teacher's assignment. Other times, they read to gain information they see as personally useful, such as a teen reading auto repair manuals to fix up a car; or to develop valued knowledge or skill, as a teacher does in reading about new ways to motivate students. Readers who voluntarily read to gain personally valued knowledge or information have not been studied very much (Guthrie et al., 2007), but Becker et al. (2010) found that they looked a lot like intrinsically motivated readers, in that they tended to read more deeply, more often, and for longer time periods, and thus developed better reading skills.

On the other hand, reading motivation based on desire for external rewards, such as grades or prizes, or in response to external pressure from parents or teachers, tends to be associated with a number of negative consequences (Becker et al., 2010; De Naeghel, Van Keer, Vansteenkiste, & Rosseel, 2012; Guthrie & Wigfield, 2000; Paris & McNaughton, 2010). Readers who are motivated by such external factors tend to choose easy books and use mainly surface-level reading strategies, so this kind of motivation negatively impacts growth in reading skill, especially in terms of comprehension. Although incentives or pressure may increase amount of reading in the short term, they do not tend to increase later time spent reading because once the grade is earned or the prize won, externally motivated readers have no further reason to read.

Of particular concern is that this kind of external motivation may actually lead to decreases in intrinsic motivation. This phenomenon is well documented in general motivation research (Deci, Koestner, & Ryan, 1999; Kohn, 1993), but whether incentives for reading undermine intrinsic motivation is a question still hotly debated (Marinak & Gambrell, 2008). Several recent studies suggest that one very common reading incentive program may at least sometimes have this effect (Berridge & Goebel, 2013; Pavonetti, Brimmer, & Cipielewski, 2002; Thompson, Madhuri, & Taylor, 2008).

Self-Concept

Self-concept is our own mental representation of ourselves, our personal response to the question "Who am I?" Alternative terms sometimes used for this idea are *self-image* or *self-schema*. Self-concept is also often confused with *self-efficacy* and *self-worth*, but it is somewhat different from either. Self-efficacy, as we have already discussed, refers to our beliefs about our ability or competence to do tasks in a specific area. *Self-worth*, also called *self-esteem*, is a judgment, rather than a perception; it is our judgment of our own merit or value (Harter, Whitesell, & Junkin, 1998). Our self-worth is based on how far our self-concept is from our *ideal self*, the person we would most like to be (Rogers, 1959). Too much distance between our self-concept and our ideal self, particularly in areas that are important to us or important to our society (Harter et al.; James, 1890), constitutes a threat to our sense of self-worth (Rogers).

   Self-concept is a much broader term than any of these, encompassing not only competence and worth but many other characteristics (Conradi et al., 2014). For example, reading self-concept, our particular area of interest, can include not only perceptions of how well we read (e.g., "I'm a good reader"), but also ideas about how and what we read, how important reading is to us, and how we compare to other readers, as seen in Figure 9.1.

   Children's self-concepts develop and change as they mature, based on their experiences, messages from significant others, and their increasing ability to measure themselves against other people in a process known as *social comparison* (Harter, 2008; Stipek, 1981). Most very young children have an unrealistically positive self-concept in many areas, due in part to their past successes in mastering early life skills. As children enter school, the challenges they encounter and the normative comparisons between themselves and others fostered by the school environment can lead to a decline in self-concept across many areas that also affects their overall sense of self-worth (Stipek & Daniels, 1988; Wigfield, Eccles, & Pintrich, 1996). This effect is particularly noticeable in the area of reading. Most children begin school with a strong desire and belief that they can learn to read, but children who initially encounter difficulties may lose this optimism very quickly. In a longitudinal study of 60 children, Chapman, Tunmer, and Prochnow (2000) found differences in reading self-concept after less than 2 months in kindergarten

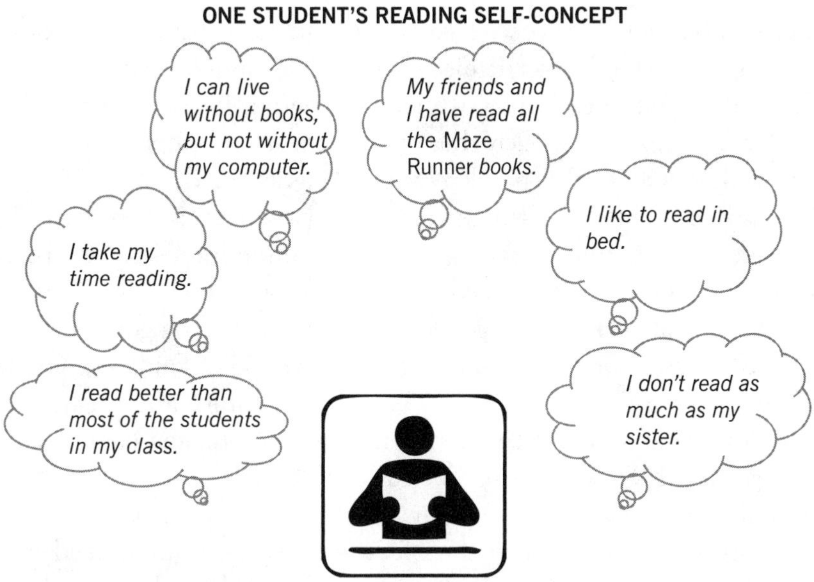

ONE STUDENT'S READING SELF-CONCEPT

I can live without books, but not without my computer.

My friends and I have read all the Maze Runner books.

I take my time reading.

I like to read in bed.

I read better than most of the students in my class.

I don't read as much as my sister.

FIGURE 9.1. An example of a student's reading self-concept.

between children who were learning successfully and those making less progress in reading. By second grade, those children who had initially shown a more negative reading self-concept in kindergarten read fewer and less difficult books and reported less liking for reading. They also had a lower academic self-concept in general. Chapman and Tunmer (2003) suggest that the extreme importance of reading, in both our schools and our society, may explain why difficulties in reading impact overall academic self-concept so early and so easily.

Failure in such an important area as reading is almost always experienced as a serious threat to self-worth, stimulating both emotional and behavioral defenses. A common defense is avoidance; because they feel threatened, struggling readers tend to avoid occasions for evaluation of their reading and reading itself when possible, leading, of course, to even less progress in reading (Stanovich, 1986). Hall (2010) found that struggling middle school readers refrained from engaging in behaviors they admitted would improve their reading, such as using comprehension scaffolds, asking questions, and participating in discussions, due to their fear of being identified by others as poor readers. Johnston (1985) found similar effects even in adults who had voluntarily come to a university reading clinic in order to improve their reading.

Struggling readers may also try to protect their self-worth by devaluing the importance or desirability of reading, declaring that "reading is stupid," or perhaps deciding that reading is only for "nerds." They may then turn their efforts toward another area, such as music or athletics, in which they feel they have a better chance of succeeding. However, because reading is so central to school success, this devaluing can extend to academics in general, leading to apathy or even rebellion and disaffection from school as whole (Covington, 1992; Weinstein, Gregory, & Strambler, 2004). It seems likely that the current strong emphasis on evaluation in schools will only make this problem worse (Wigfield & Cambria, 2010).

There is also evidence that boys may feel a particular conflict between motivation toward reading and other recognized masculine interests. One problem is that in school boys are so often asked to read books with protagonists and themes that do not resonate with their gender. Though male protagonists outnumber females in children's books by a ratio of 1.6:1 (McCabe, Fairchild, Grauerholz, Pescosolido, & Tope, 2011), the mostly female elementary and English teachers in schools don't tend to assign the nonfiction or action-related books that appeal more to boys (Smith & Wilhelm, 2002; Taylor, 2004).

Cultural and language minority students can face similar issues. They often have difficulty even seeing themselves in the books commonly read in school (Sciurba, 2014). Despite decades of attention to the problem, there is still a dearth of children's literature that portrays minority characters in a nonstereotyped, positive fashion (Brooks & McNair, 2009; Nilsson, 2005; Sabis-Burns, 2011). In 2014, less than 3% of children's books published in the United States were about African American characters, and the ratios for Asian, Hispanic, or Native American characters were even lower (Cooperative Children's Book Center [CCBC], 2014). As a result, minority students are often identified as reluctant readers (Greenleaf & Hinchman, 2009), although they may in fact be very eager to read texts with characters and themes that reflect their cultural heritage (Fader & McNeil, 1968; Moje, Overby, Tysvaer, & Morris, 2008).

A more fundamental problem is that both boys and minority students may feel that learning and liking to read conflict directly with valued gender or ethnic roles. Multiple studies have found that many boys identify reading as an essentially feminine activity (Smith & Wilhelm, 2002; Watson, Kehler, & Martino, 2010; Young, 2000), perhaps because the overwhelming majority of elementary school teachers in the United States are female, and this disproportion is greatest at the lowest grade levels, where children are first learning to read (*www.mensteach.org*). Combined with the fact that fathers are less likely to read themselves (National Endowment for the Arts, 2015) and less likely to read to their sons (Leavell, Tamis-LeMonda, Rubel, Zosuls, & Cabrera, 2012), the result is that young boys are left with few models of masculine readers.

For cultural minority students, schools all too often require assimilation to white cultural norms as a condition of success (Ogbu, 2003). These students may see success in reading as *acting white* (Fordham & Ogbu, 1986), and thus betraying their own heritage in order to succeed in school. Kohl (1992) recounts two examples of minority students facing such dilemmas. One was a Hispanic immigrant who refused to learn English because he was afraid that if he did, his culture and language would be lost to the next generation. The other was an African American college student who refused to read Conrad's *Heart of Darkness* in his English class because of its racist themes and imagery—historical elements that Kohl, as the teacher, had not even recognized until they were pointed out to him. Native American students likewise experience conflicts between ethnic identity and the reading demands of schooling. A long and sometimes violent history of cultural suppression in government efforts to educate Native American students has left many of these students with both lowered reading achievement and the conviction that learning to read and write English is only for white people (Reyhner & Jacobs, 2002). For all the marginalized groups described here, motivation to read is negatively impacted by issues regarding culture and gender identity and resistance—issues that school and teachers rarely seem to help them to navigate successfully.

Relational Value

Our motivation to engage in activities and tasks that enhance our relationships with people we care about, called *relational value*, is another aspect of motivation evident in several of the previous examples. It has long been known that relationships powerfully impact motivation in many areas. In their self-determination theory of motivation, Deci, Vallerand, Pelletier, and Ryan (1991) list the *need for relatedness* as one of the three basic psychological needs shared by all humans. Wigfield and Eccles (2000) acknowledge the role of socialization influences on motivation, and Guthrie and Wigfield (2000) wrote specifically about the importance of this kind of social motivation in reading. Research has identified at least three groups of people known to influence students' reading motivation: family members, teachers, and peers (Klauda & Wigfield. 2012).

We discussed the impact of families on young children's desire to read in depth in Chapter 1, but there is good evidence that family influences continue to impact motivation all the way through adolescence. Older elementary school children report that their parents, especially mothers, supported and encourage reading in a number of ways, including continuing to read aloud to their children, reading frequently themselves, talking with their children about reading, suggesting things to read, and giving books as presents. A composite measure of this support was the strongest predictor of children's reading motivation in a study by Klauda (2009), and the second strongest predictor of reading frequency, after reading skill. Strommen and Mates (2004) found similar results in a study of sixth to ninth graders; avid readers, but not disengaged readers, reported having parents who read for pleasure themselves, discussed books, and suggested books to them. Findings from a nationwide survey of teens in Australia likewise highlighted the impact of ongoing support from families on adolescents' motivation to read, concluding that "parents who maintain encouragement beyond their child's acquisition of independent reading skills can influence their children to become lifelong readers" (Merga, 2014a, p. 160).

Qualitative and mixed-methods studies of older adolescents have found that having a parent who reads and discusses or recommends books influences whether and what teenagers read (Klauda, 2009), with avid readers especially saying they were motivated to read specific books their parents were reading or had read in their youth (Chandler, 1999; Cherland, 1994). Though in several of these studies mothers were still cited as more frequent and stronger influences on reading, Hamston and Love (2003) found that 11- to 17-year-old male committed readers experienced and particularly valued increased sharing and discussion of multiple sorts of reading materials, including informational and Internet-based reading, with their fathers as they got older (see also, Merga, 2014a). These boys also mentioned multiple other family members whom they considered to be influences on their reading habits, including mothers, grandparents, aunts, and uncles. Clearly, the role of family relationships and interactions in reading motivation remains strong well past early childhood.

Alexander (2005) asserts that if children are to become lifelong readers, they need adults who can and will introduce them to the habits and pleasures of reading. Teachers know they are often called upon to fulfill this role, especially for children whose parents are not frequent readers. In an early national survey covering 84 potential reading-related topics, teachers identified creating interest in reading as their top concern (O'Flahavan et al., 1992). One of the most important ways teachers can influence reading motivation is by creating classrooms in which the motivating factors we have already discussed are prominent: access to interesting books on many topics and levels, frequent student choice of reading materials, and significant time for reading within the school day (Gambrell, 1996). McKool and Gespass (2009) found that teachers who were avid readers themselves were significantly more likely to offer time for sustained reading in class, discuss books students were reading, and read aloud to students, and were three times more likely than teachers who did not report reading for pleasure to recommend specific books to students. Unfortunately, they also found that nearly half of the 65 teachers they studied reported reading for pleasure less than 10 minutes a day on average, a finding that duplicated results from Applegate and Applegate's (2004) study of preservice teachers.

Studies like these suggest that teachers' own feelings about reading, and their willingness to share those feelings, can enable them to play an even more personal and relational role in promoting motivation to read. Gambrell (1996) suggests that teachers "become reading models when they share their own reading experiences with students and emphasize how reading enhances and enriches their lives"

(p. 20), and her assertion is borne out in research. Knapp (1998) found that most children as early as second grade knew whether their teachers enjoyed reading and could give concrete examples of how they knew. Fourth graders that Edmunds and Bauserman (2006) interviewed frequently named their teacher as the person who had introduced them to books they personally liked, especially in narrative fiction, and also often identified a teacher as someone who had gotten them "excited about reading" (p. 420). Teachers' reading aloud to students of all ages has been shown to impact not only reading motivation, but also comprehension and critical reading abilities (Ivey & Broaddus, 2001; Trelease, 2013). As Atwell (2007) emphasized, there is great power in teachers' and students' sharing of books, and recommending, talking, and writing about books to and with each other, because for many students, this is their only gateway into "the reading club" (Smith, 1988).

As children grow older, their peers begin to play an increasingly important role in their motivation to read. Adolescents who are motivated readers are more likely to have friends who are also readers, with whom they discuss books and share recommendations (Hughes-Hassell & Rodge, 2007; Partin & Hendricks, 2002). Support from friends has been found to impact reading motivation from fourth-grade through high school (Klauda, 2009; Klauda & Wigfield, 2012; Partin & Hendricks). However, most adolescents report little encouragement from friends to read. On average, teens report that only 10–20% of their friends read much for pleasure (Hughes-Hassell & Rodge; Merga, 2014b), and because they don't frequently talk about books, many teens say they simply don't know if their friends read much or not (Clark, Osborne, & Akerman, 2008). Girls seem significantly more likely than boys to report reading or talking with friends about what they are reading (Baker & Wigfield, 1999; Klauda & Wigfield; Merga; Moje et al., 2008), but only about one-quarter to one-third of even girls report such interactions. Nevertheless, friends appear to be an important source of book recommendations for both boys and girls, surpassing parents or teachers from late elementary through high school (Cherland, 1994; Edmunds & Bauserman, 2006; Moje et al., 2008; Smith & Wilhelm, 2002)

Adolescents' perceptions of their overall peer groups' attitudes toward reading can also impact reading motivation, either positively or negatively. A recent survey of over 500 teens in Australia found that students who rarely read and reported less liking for reading were also more likely to agree with the statement "It is not cool to read books" (Merga, 2014b, pp. 475–476), while 77% of all those responding felt that their classmates had a negative or neutral attitude toward recreational reading. For both questions, boys were again slightly more likely to give negative responses than girls. However, in a finely-grained mixed-methods study of primarily Hispanic students at three urban middle schools, Moje et al. (2008) found that reading could be a source of social capital in some cases, and that even boys' peer groups interacted around nontraditional texts such as gaming manuals and car and bike magazines. They suggest that one reason many adolescents seem unmotivated to read in school is their preference for texts that are "embedded . . . in social networks relevant to [their] lives" (p. 146). As with so many aspects of reading motivation, there is still much to understand about the varying impacts of peers on children's and adolescents' motivation to read.

Cost and Risk

Cost is related to the time and effort it will take to do a task, plus the competing values that have to be given up. *Risk* is the anticipation of possible future costs. Very often, the assessment of cost or risk pits one value against another. For example, if you have an old car, you might be motivated to get a new one. But when you consider the time and effort it will take to research and test-drive multiple models, plus the cost of a car payment, you could decide to use that money to save up for a vacation. But if your old car starts to break down a lot, you might change your mind, deciding that the cost of repairing the old car and the risk of getting stranded without transportation outweigh the costs of getting a new one.

Weighing the perceived and possible cost(s) is a vital element in any motivational choice, but it is the element of value that has been the least studied (Wigfield et al., 2009), perhaps because it is a complex factor that varies for each individual and situation. For instance, in the example above, the monetary cost of a new car would mean much less to you if you were rich, and much more if you were having trouble just paying rent. The risk of getting stranded would weigh differently if you needed your car to get to work, than if you lived in a city with decent mass transit. Your own personal likes and dislikes might also impact your perception of cost. If you are a real car buff, shopping for a new car won't feel like effort; it will feel like fun. In addition, for most people, near benefits tend to outweigh distant costs or even distant benefits (Mischel, Ebbesen, & Raskoff Zeiss, 1972). This effect is stronger in people who are younger, more tired, or under more stress. So, the allure of the new car you see on the car lot can sometimes outweigh saving for a vacation next year or maybe even being able to pay your rent next month.

We weigh the same types of complex costs and risks when we make decisions about reading, costs that depend both on the reading context and the individual reader. Consider some of the costs and risks we have already discussed. For a struggling reader, the risk of failure weighs heavily against any benefits of reading, especially if that failure would be public. Risk of public failure is one reason so many people, even those who are now good readers, have painful memories of being forced to read out loud in class; in fact, one study found that adults, even in a laboratory setting, showed increased heart rates and blood pressure when asked to read aloud, compared to reading silently (Ogawa & Shodo, 2001). Even if failure is not immediately public, the effect of failure on a struggling reader's self-concept is often too painful, to the point that trying to read is just not worth the cost (Johnston, 1985). Students whose friends believe reading is "uncool" (Merga, 2014b) are often unwilling to risk their peer relationships by being seen reading. Students in classrooms or schools where external controls and sanctions are strongly emphasized may, overtly or covertly, refuse to do assigned reading to meet their basic human need for autonomy (Deci & Ryan, 1987), to feel like origins rather than pawns.

A major cost factor in reading motivation is the desire to engage in alternative activities—if you are playing sports after school, and then talking and texting on your cell phone to friends after dinner, you probably aren't doing much recreational reading. This conflict between recreational reading and other desirable activities seems to increase as children get older, especially with the growing use of social media and computer gaming by adolescents today (Scholastic, 2015). Ironically, Moje et al. (2008) found that many of these alternate activities actually involved considerable amounts of reading (e.g., reading and writing on Facebook; Internet surfing, reading computer game manuals and walkthroughs). Unfortunately, neither adolescents nor their parents or teachers tended to view these activities as real reading. The jury is still out on whether reading these alternative texts is as beneficial to skill development as reading books is.

Summary of Factors Affecting Value for Reading

Just as with expectancy for success, multiple factors have been demonstrated through research to impact different people's sense of value for reading. Factors affecting value can combine to result in an overall higher or lower value for reading any particular text in a specific context than each would predict singly. Let's consider three students in the same classroom. One student, knowledgeable about race relations in the South, might be intrinsically interested in reading *To Kill a Mockingbird*, a book often assigned in English classes. This student might also like the teacher who assigned the book and identify with some of the characters, so both relational and self-concept-related values may accrue. Because this student has the requisite reading skills, the effort involved in reading the book will not come at too high a cost. This brief description sketches an almost ideal motivational scenario for assigned school reading. Another student, however, who is unaware of and uninterested in the history of race in the South, probably will not find the book interesting or even comprehensible, lacking the prior knowledge to understand the tension that builds throughout the book. If this student must also struggle to read the text and thus anticipates a fairly low grade, much of the utility value in completing the assignment is also lost. The cost to this student, in terms of time, effort, and risk to self-concept, is much higher, and he will be unmotivated to read the book. A third student may prefer science fiction and so might not find the book personally interesting. If this student has the necessary background knowledge and reading ability, and perceives a fairly strong utility value for completing this assignment, the final choice of whether to read the book or not may depend on how attractive the alternative activities are. If it is a rainy weekend, reading the book may seem like a fine idea, but if the student has just bought a new computer game, the cost of postponing playing that new game may be too high, and the book may not get read. These examples of different students from perhaps the same English class demonstrate how the various value-related factors in reading motivation can interact with each other to produce very different types and levels of subjective value for reading even the same book. These factors also help to explain why teachers will probably never find that one perfect book that all of their students are motivated to read, and suggest how different students in the same context may come to have very different goals in reading—the subject of the next section in this chapter.

GOAL ORIENTATIONS IN READING

Expectancy and value factors act together in specific contexts and people to produce different goals for reading. Goal theorists in education have written extensively about four different types of orientations that students tend to adopt in school situations, based on their adoption of *mastery, performance, social,* or *work-avoidant* goals. All of these types of goals have different origins and different effects, and they can all be easily seen in the average classroom of students reading. Consider the five girls in a hypothetical middle school English classroom, based on many we have observed, from the case study that began this chapter. Notice how the various motivational factors we have discussed interact and combine, causing each of the girls to adopt a different orientation to the reading task given to them by Ms. Garvey.

Mastery Goal Orientation

Students adopting mastery goals, also called *learning* or *task-involved* goals (Murphy & Alexander, 2000) are focused mainly on enjoying or learning from what they are reading. They do not tend to compare themselves with others, but rather read most often for reasons related to intrinsic motivation, rather than extrinsic praise or rewards. They tend to have an incremental view of ability and are therefore willing to ask for help if needed and put forward the effort required to develop competence (Dweck, 1986). In the vignette, Shondra exemplifies a reader with a mastery goal orientation. It is easier for Shondra to adopt a mastery goal in this situation than it would be for, say, Delores or Brittany. Shondra has a reasonable expectancy of success because she reads well and therefore has high self-efficacy in reading. She is also confident she will have enough time to read and any support and resources she might need. Finally, because she likes to read and finds the story interesting, the reading has intrinsic interest for her, beyond just doing it well enough to get a good grade on the worksheet. Students like Shondra who take a mastery orientation to reading not only enjoy it more, but also learn more as they read, so they become even better readers (Stanovich, 1986).

Performance Goal Orientations

Students who adopt performance goals, also called *ego-involved* goals (Murphy & Alexander, 2000), often hold an entity view of ability (Dweck, 1986). They are not focused on the reading itself, but are mainly concerned with how they compare to or will be judged by others in the reading situation. They feel that a good or poor performance in reading demonstrates not just what they have learned in reading so far, but reflects on how good or bad a reader they ultimately are, and will always be, thus impacting their self-concept and self-worth as readers.

Linda and Delores both show performance orientations in this situation, but because they have different expectancies of success in the reading task they were assigned, they have adopted different types of performance goals. Linda's actions show a type of *performance approach* goal that is typical of some gifted readers. Her aim is to perform well and thus to look smart in comparison to the other students, earning external recognition, praise, or rewards (i.e., grades). Although she might use more in-depth strategies on a more difficult task, she can accomplish her goal in this situation with only surface-level reading, so that is all she uses, and thus she misses out on any skill improvement or understanding she could gain from the reading. In this way, her concern with performance, though it may result in good grades at the moment, could actually disadvantage her in the future.

Dolores is also concerned with how people will see her as a reader in the classroom, but she has a *performance avoidance* (sometimes called *failure avoidance*) goal. Like many struggling readers, she does not believe she can perform well in reading tasks, so her aim is to avoid situations in which others could judge her reading ability, because the risk of failure seems high. Some students avoid performance judgments by refusing to read or by getting in trouble, so they can leave class, but Dolores has found an alternative strategy that is working for her right now. It is possible that she may adopt a more mastery orientation to this reading assignment when she does it at home, because she will have support and plenty of time there, especially since the story has caught her interest. If she does, her altered goal may help her learn and develop her reading just as Shondra's has. However, many readers who avoid performance situations in class don't have this kind of interest or support at home, so they simply end up avoiding reading, and thus do not develop as readers.

This is probably what has happened to Brittany, who has progressed from avoidance to a performance-related orientation called *learned helplessness* (Dweck, 1975). People experiencing learned helplessness feel they have no control over their situation. There is nothing they can do to either perform better or avoid failure, so they have simply given up. Learned helpless readers have little or no self-efficacy in reading, and they also tend to hold an entity view of ability, believing that no amount of effort will help them improve. Students with a long history of failure in reading often show characteristics of learned helplessness (Chapman & Tunmer, 2003). The learning disability diagnosis Brittany received last year may also have inadvertently contributed to this problem. It made her eligible for extra help, which was good, but it may also have communicated to her and her teacher that there was little use in her trying to learn to read better (Osterholm, Nash, & Kritsonis, 2007).

Julie demonstrates a *social goal orientation* in this classroom situation. Quite simply, the relational value of interacting with her friend is outweighing any value she sees in reading the story. Both she and Linda could also be said to have a *work avoidance orientation* (Nicholls & Miller, 1984). From their point of view, the time and effort necessary to actually read and comprehend the story cost too much, in terms of competing desires, so in part their goal seems to be to put in the very least amount of time and effort necessary to meet the requirements of the assignment.

Each of these students had a different goal that led them to engage or disengage with the same classroom reading assignment, but these goals are not fixed. Once Ms. Garvey understands the various factors impacting their motivations in this situation, there is much she could do to help those who were disengaged move toward more productive reading goals.

WHAT WE CAN DO: CLASSROOM PRACTICES
THAT ENHANCE READING MOTIVATION

Make Sure Students Have Lots of Good Things to Read

Easy access to lots of good things to read is key to nurturing motivated readers (Gambrell, 2011). As discussed in Chapter 1, children who are fortunate enough to grow up with many books and other texts at home are much more likely to become avid readers, and research has repeatedly demonstrated that students with access to larger school libraries become better readers (Achterman, 2009; Krashen, Lee, & McQuillan, 2012; Lance & Russell, 2004). But because school libraries are not always available and may also intimidate struggling readers, classroom libraries are also vital (Chamblis & McKillop, 2000; Pachtman & Wilson, 2006). Both types of libraries need to offer a wide selection of texts, fiction and nonfiction, on a variety of subjects at multiple reading levels, including graphic novels, magazines, and e-texts, so that any reader will be able to find many "interesting texts," that is, texts on his or her reading level that pertain to his or her interests (Guthrie & Wigfield, 2000). Teachers can build classroom libraries at relatively little expense by shopping garage sales, thrifts stores, and public library book sales. Donations can be solicited from friends, parents of older students whose children have outgrown younger books, local businesses, and on websites like Craigslist and Donors Choose. Books and magazines being culled from the school library can also go to classrooms and eventually be given to students. In fact, giving students a chance to own books can be very motivating (Klauda & Wigfield, 2012), and many of these same strategies can be used to obtain books and magazines to give to students as presents or rewards, or to put on "swap" shelves where students can initially pick out a few books for themselves and then swap them for others as they finish them—a strategy found to increase reading among even disadvantaged, failing students (Fader & McNeil, 1968; Knapp, 2013b).

Let Students Choose What They Read

Access to lots of engaging reading material is not much use if students are mostly constrained to reading assigned books and textbooks. Frequently giving students choices about what they read is one form of *autonomy support*—"providing students with opportunities for choice or self-direction while minimizing the use of controlling pressures" (Guthrie et al., 2013, p. 10)—an instructional strategy proven to increase learning goals and engagement in school (Shih, 2008; Ryan & Deci, 2009) because of its impact on multiple motivational factors. Choice increases readers' expectations of success because it lets them control the difficulty and length of what they attempt to read; this personal locus of control may be especially important to struggling or resistant readers (Alexander, 2005; deCharms, 1977). Choice increases value because students can choose to read things that interest them or that offer information they believe will be useful. Increased autonomy also positively impacts self-image. Given these multiple effects, it is not surprising that allowing choice in reading is one of the best proven strategies for enhancing reading motivation (Gambrell, 2011; Krashen, 2006), and one frequently mentioned as highly motivating by children themselves (Knapp & Grattan, 2001; Pachtman & Wilson, 2006). In Scholastic's (2015) survey of over 1,000 K–12 students, 90% or more agreed with the statements, "My favorite books are the ones that I have picked out myself," and, "I am more likely to finish reading a book that I have picked our for myself" (p. 56).

Many students will have no trouble finding books if given a choice, but struggling readers and those unused to choosing their own reading may not necessarily be aware of reading options or their own tastes, so they may need help at first to find books that they can read and enjoy. Such help can come from a school librarian (Chelton, 2003), a teacher who knows them well, or, as discussed below, their friends and classmates, if opportunities for sharing books are built into the classroom reading experience. At other times, when certain topics must be covered or a teacher wants the whole class to share a reading experience, full choice is not an option, but *bounded choices* (Gambrell, 2011) can be a good alternative. If a class is studying volcanoes, for example, a science textbook could be only one of several options offered to students for learning the material; others might include two or three trade books about volcanoes, on different reading levels, plus perhaps a website (e.g., Discovery's *Volcano Explorer* at *http://discoverykids.com/games/volcano-explorer*) and an entry in an online encyclopedia like the Simple English Wikipedia (*http://simple.wikipedia.org/wiki/Main_Page*). A scavenger hunt-type rubric will ensure that each student finds the essential information he or she needs to learn, and class discussion and activities will be enriched as students bring in different information from the different sources they read. In literature, students could be given a choice of several books on the same theme or by the same author, or different versions of the same novel (e.g., graphic, abridged, or full). Even such a modest degree of choice can significantly and positively affect student motivation and engagement in reading (Guthrie & Wigfield, 2000).

Give Students Time to Read

Students have homework. Many participate in after-school activities, and others are responsible for siblings or do other family-related work after school. In many homes, there is no tradition of leisure reading, and television, outdoor play, and electronic gaming are potent sources of distraction. If children are to develop the reading habit, they need time for uninterrupted reading in school (Krashen, 2009). Yet, as pointed out earlier, less than 20 minutes a day is typically allocated in school for reading connected text of any kind, much less personally chosen, engaging texts of the type we have been discussing.

Though no direct instruction is being given when students read independently, such time is far from wasted; researchers have repeatedly found that time allotted for sustained, independent reading is strongly and directly related to gains in both student reading motivation and tested achievement (Allington & Johnston, 2000; Foorman et al., 2006; Garan & DeVoogd, 2008; Hiebert, 2009; Krashen, 2011; Yoon, 2002). Of course, to be most productive, sustained silent reading time needs to be well planned, just like other parts of the school day. The need for a wide and varied selection of reading materials and initial support for some students in making choices has already been discussed. Young students and students unused to reading for long periods of time may at first be unable to sustain attention for a full 20–30 minutes of reading; Gambrell (2011) suggests starting with as little as 10 minutes a day and increasing gradually. As discussed earlier, students who struggle greatly with reading may initially need extra scaffolding from reading partners, audiobooks, or digital devices in order to benefit from sustained reading time.

Finally, though it is tempting to use this time to grade papers or otherwise catch up on work, sustained silent reading is most effective when teachers participate, serving as visible models of the value and pleasure of reading (Methe & Hintze, 2003), and actively share their enjoyment with their students as well.

Make Reading a Social Activity

Indeed, sharing should be part of reading in every classroom. Avid readers almost always like to talk about what they are reading: They belong to book clubs, they share books with their friends, and they often insist on reading "good bits" from their current book to anyone who will listen. This social aspect of reading needs to be more recognized in schools, especially as children get older and peer relationships are increasingly vital. Creating a school or classroom culture of reading involves structuring multiple ways and opportunities for students to share their reading with each other. This can be as informal as just asking students at the end of their reading time what they are reading and what they think of it so far. Students can also give more structured "book commercials," either in person or on video, recommending books they have liked to classmates. Using multimedia tools, they can construct exciting or funny or scary book "trailers" that can be posted on a class website and shared with the school or with the public at large. They can write short reviews of books on school-based websites, or in a protected Goodreads circle, or out in the "real world" on sites dedicated to children's book reviews, such as Spaghetti Book Club (*www.spaghettibookclub.org*) and Teen Ink (*www.teenink.com/reviews/book_reviews*), or even on Amazon. Nanci Atwell (2007) has found that students enjoy using dialogue journals to write back and forth with her and with each other about what they are reading. All of these interactive alternatives encourage comprehension and critical thought about text as well as or better than traditional quizzes and book reports, which tend to decrease students' motivation to read (Pachtman & Wilson, 2006). Finally, literature circles, where students can talk about books during class, have been used effectively in classrooms for decades (Daniels, 1994; Raphael & McMahon, 1994), and their more modern incarnation, student book clubs, have been found especially effective with specially targeted populations, from boys (Scieszka, 2008; Young, 2000) to struggling readers (Stevenson, 2009) to teen mothers (Klor & Nordhausen, 2011).

Support Students' Success in Reading

Students who have experienced failure in reading, sometimes for many years, often regard reading with dislike, at best, or with a sense of learned helplessness, at worst (Alexander, 2005; Chapman & Tunmer, 2003). Simply increasing their actual reading skills, although necessary, is rarely sufficient to help them regain their motivation to read (Morgan et al., 2008; Quirk & Schwanenflugel, 2004). These students need to experience success in reading texts they like before they can begin to expect success or enjoyment in reading. Several of the ideas discussed so far can help struggling readers experience such success. Providing high-interest books with lower reading levels, often known as Hi-Lo books, is a proven strategy for helping struggling readers, useful both as leisure reading and as accessible alternatives for instructional reading (Guthrie & Cox, 2001; Wigfield et al., 2009). One teacher has had great success with lending out Kindles to struggling readers; he believes that the "cool factor" of reading on Kindles, plus the ability to enlarge the text and discretely read books at easier levels, has contributed to the greater-than-average number of books read and the reading gains experienced by his ninth-grade "Kindlers" (Isero, 2014, p. 63).

Providing help in finding interesting texts and introducing comprehension strategies and scaffolds like those discussed in Chapter 8 can increase both students' confidence and their actual success in reading. Low-pressure feedback mechanisms, such as reading logs to track the amount of text read, can also encourage struggling readers to recognize their progress, but Guthrie and Wigfield (2000) warn that making such mechanisms mandatory or allowing them to become competitive between students can be counterproductive. Teacher read-alouds or movies related to books the class is reading can spark students' interest and also give struggling readers a head start on comprehension. Reader's Theater activities can do the same thing, while also giving students a chance to practice and master oral reading of text (Buehl, 2000). The more intensive forms of scaffolding we have already discussed for decoding and vocabulary learning, through partner reading or computer-assisted reading, can help students with even the most disabling reading problems experience initial success and also gain experience in comprehending age-appropriate texts that they would be unable to read on their own (Buehl; Knapp, 2013a; Park, Roberts, Takahashi, & Stodden, 2014).

MEASURING READING MOTIVATION

As this chapter has shown, motivation is a key aspect of the psychology of reading, in that it powerfully impacts the development of reading skill and the amount and quality of reading done from early in school throughout adult life. However, the importance of increasing children's motivation to read is often overlooked in the official definitions and standards adopted by various education panels (e.g., National Institute of Child Health and Human Development, 2000; *www.corestandards.org/ELA-Literacy*), and also in the classroom. Panels that define standards are most interested in measureable goals, and as the testing that accompanies standards is increasingly emphasized, schools and classrooms have tended to focus narrowly on the goals those tests measure (Ravitch, 2011). For a number of reasons, motivation to read is rather difficult to measure.

For one thing, as we have explained, motivation to read is not a unified construct but involves many interrelated factors. Unfortunately, there is not much agreement among scholars about how many and which of these factors should be measured. The Elementary Reading Attitude Survey (ERAS; McKenna & Kear, 1990), one of the earliest and still best known assessments in this area, measures *reading attitude*—students' affective feelings about reading (perhaps closest to what we have described as *intrinsic interest* in reading)—rather than the whole construct of reading motivation. McKenna and Kear divided their assessment into two subscales, one for academic (school-related) reading and one for recreational reading. The Motivation for Reading Questionnaire (MRQ; Wigfield & Guthrie, 1997), another well-known and often-used assessment, by contrast includes 11 different subscales, measuring factors such as *compliance, competition, recognition,* and *curiosity,* as well as more commonly recognized factors such as *reading efficacy* and *social* (relational) aspects. The Motivation to Read Profile (MRP; Gambrell, Palmer, Codling, & Mazzoni, 1996), developed at about the same time as the MRQ, again measures only two factors, this time students' *self-concept as readers* and their *value of reading.* These three popular assessments, all used in numerous research studies since their development, conceptualize and thus measure reading motivation very differently. Just recently, De Naeghel at al. (2012) developed a new measure, the Self-Regulation Questionnaire—Reading Motivation (SRQ-RM), based on Deci and Ryan's (1987) self-determination theory. The SRQ-RM measures four types of motivation (intrinsic, identified, introjected, and external) for both academic and recreational reading, yielding eight factors. Sperling, Sherwood, and Hood (2013) combined and adapted some questions from the MRP and MRQ with newly created questions to come up with the Emergent Readers Motivation and Reading Scale (ERMAS), intended for use with children in PreK and kindergarten. Clearly, just what should be measured when we measure "reading motivation" remains an open question.

The second challenge in measuring reading motivation is that all of these instruments are based on children's self-reports of their own motivation. Certainly, if you want to know about students' reading motivation, it makes sense to ask them, but relying completely on self-report to measure motivation poses several problems. First, self-report measures are notoriously subject to *social desirability* bias; that is, people tend to answer questions in ways that they believe will please the person asking the questions or that will make themselves look better (Crowne & Marlowe, 1960; van de Mortel, 2008). This effect can be conscious or even unconscious, and is especially strong in areas where society has clearly approved or disapproved behaviors. For instance, in self-report studies of nutrition, people consistently overestimate the amount of healthy food and underestimate the amount of junk food they actually eat (Worsley, Baghurst, & Leitch, 1984). An example of the type of question likely to be subject to social desirability is this multiple-choice question from the MRP (Gambrell et al., 1996, p. 522):

16. When I grow up, I will spend

   ☐ none of my time reading

   ☐ very little of my time reading

   ☐ some of my time reading

   ☐ a lot of my time reading

In interviewing children referred to a program for delayed readers, Knapp (1998) in fact found that children as young as second grade responded in socially desirable ways to similar questions. When asked directly whether they liked to read, most would answer that they did, even when teacher report and other evidence (e.g., their inability to name a book or author they had recently enjoyed) suggested that many, in fact, did not enjoy reading on any regular basis. These same students also often maintained that their parents read "a lot" or "all the time," though when they were asked if "grown-ups read very often," they were unsophisticated enough to reply (without noticing the contradiction) that they hardly ever saw grown-ups read. Quirk et al. (2009) similarly noted restricted variability on second-graders' responses, skewed heavily toward positive answers, to the value-related questions on the MRQ. These and other studies indicate that our society's strong and early-conveyed value for reading can bias children's self-reports of their own reading motivation even at relatively young ages, and research on social desirability bias suggests that this problem probably only increases as children get older.

An additional problem with self-report measures in this field is that young children are not very metacognitive; that is, they are not very good at assessing their own ongoing feelings or thoughts (Flavell, Green, Flavell, Harris, & Astington, 1995). Instead, they tend to respond based on the most recent happenings or feelings, lacking the perspective to recall and assess how they have usually felt or performed over time. For example, one question on the ERAS (McKenna & Kear, 1990, p. 634) asks:

20. How do you feel about taking a reading test?

Younger children, especially, are likely to circle the Garfield cartoon that reflects how they felt about their most recent testing experience, rather than how they feel about reading tests in general.

Triangulating teacher or parent observations of actual motivated reading behaviors (e.g., time voluntarily spent reading, enthusiasm for discussing texts) might be useful to both validate and extend the reliability of students' self-assessments of reading motivation, but little research has yet been done along these lines. Several studies (e.g., Jakobsons, 2005; Sperling et al., 2013) have looked at correlations between children's scores on reading motivation self-assessments and parents' or teachers' ratings of children's reading motivation, but have unfortunately found only moderate correlations between what children report and what adults think they are seeing in children. In addition, of course, the rapidly changing nature of reading itself, with the advance of the digital age, poses new issues related to how we conceptualize reading and measure reading motivation. In fact, the developers of both the ERAS and the MRP have recently redesigned or revised their instruments to reflect these changes in how and what students now read (McKenna et al., 2012; Malloy, Marinak, Gambrell, & Mazzoni, 2013). So, while the importance of motivation in reading is clear, the measurement of motivation to read is still a task that is "under development."

CONNECTING TO THE STANDARDS

All of these classroom strategies can help teachers significantly and positively impact their students' motivation to read. While none of the Common Core State Standards specifically require the measurement of students' motivation to read, this omission reflects more on the difficulties of assessing reading motivation than on the importance of motivation to reading. The Anchor Standards for College and Career Readiness in Reading aim to have students "read widely and deeply from among a broad range of high-quality, increasingly challenging literary and informational texts" and "acquire the habits of reading independently and closely, which are essential to their future success" (*www.corestandards.org/ELA-Literacy/CCRA/R*). Neither of these goals will be reached unless students are motivated to read.

QUESTIONS FOR DISCUSSION

1. Does it seem to you that some factors in the expectancy × value model are more important to reading motivation than others? Might these vary with different types or ages of readers?

2. When have you been most motivated or most unmotivated to read? How did various factors from the expectancy × value model influence your motivation? Were there other factors that also influenced you? If you can, compare your story with that of others you know.

3. Choose one of the readers in the case study that opens this chapter. What are several possible strategies Ms. Garvey could use to encourage that student's motivation to read?

4. One reason many schools adopt reading incentive programs such as Accelerated Reader is that many students seem to have very little intrinsic motivation to read. Yet these programs can cost a great deal of money, and, even when done as well as possible, research suggests that extrinsic rewards may not be the best way to motivate readers. Considering the ideas in this chapter, what are some things you think could be done at the school level, rather than just the classroom level, to positively impact students' reading motivation?

FURTHER READINGS

Conradi, K., Jang, B. G., & McKenna, M. C. (2014). Motivation terminology in reading research: A conceptual review. *Educational Psychology Review, 26,* 127–164.

Gambrell, L. (2011). Seven rules of engagement: What's most important to know about motivation to read. *The Reading Teacher, 65*(3), 172–178.

Guthrie, J. T., & Wigfield, A. (2000). Engagement and motivation in reading. In M. L. Kamil, P. B. Mosenthal, P. D. Pearson, & R. Barr (Eds.), *Handbook of reading research* (Vol. 3, pp. 403–422). Mahwah, NJ: Erlbaum.

CHAPTER 10

Linguistic Variation and Reading

CASE STUDY

Mr. Garcia, a fourth-grade teacher, just had Yi-wah, a Chinese immigrant, enroll in his classroom. Yi-wah's parents brought no school records with them when they registered him for school. The school district assigned him to the fourth grade, although he is year older than most of the other children in his grade. His parents say that Yi-wah was a good student in China, and indeed Yi-wah does seem to be well behaved and eager to learn. They indicated that Yi-wah had received English instruction in his provincial school since third grade, 2 years ago—all Chinese students receive this instruction. Unfortunately, he cannot speak English well enough to converse with the other children. Yi-wah has knowledge of the alphabet but does not seem to be able to follow along in reading class. Mr. Garcia is considering how to begin teaching Yi-wah to read in English.

With some minor exceptions, throughout this book we have described reading and learning to read as engaging a fairly universal, linguistically independent, complex set of psychological processes. Our focus has been largely English-centric mostly because the research itself is rather English-centric. This may or may not be a problem, depending on your point of view and the language in which your students are learning to read. By assuming that the characteristics of the languages and writing system do not really matter, we have made an assumption that itself needs to be supported by research—that there are universal elements involved in the skills engaged by reading and learning to read.

LEARNING TO READ IN LANGUAGES THAT ARE NOT ENGLISH

Differences in Writing Systems

Before we begin our discussion of learning to read in a language that is not English, it is important to understand variations among writing systems that may influence reading processes. A *writing system* is a systematic symbolic means for visually recording and communicating spoken language on a (generally) flat surface and, in recent history, (generally) paper, but it also includes signage and, now, a host of digital sources. As languages are written down, their messages become discrete, permanent, visible, and ultimately divorced from the context in which they were written. In these respects writing is not a perfect translation of speech to a visible form (Coulmas, 2003, p. 11).

There are three basic kinds of writing systems: alphabetic, syllabic, and logographic. Essentially the differences among these systems can be described as those systems that encode the distinction between writing what you say and those that encode writing what you mean (Ellis et al., 2004). That is, some writing systems emphasize the transformation of the phonetic qualities of speech onto the page, whereas others transcribe the message of speech more directly and graphically within the writing system.

Alphabetic writing systems represent the phonemes of a language in a fairly economical manner—they do not attempt to represent every possible phonemic variation. As you may recall, the *phoneme* is the smallest unit in the sound system of a language that contrasts one word from another. English is an example of an alphabetic system. The alphabetic system that English uses (the Roman alphabet, which is also used in most Western European countries) does not represent all the phonemes by a single letter, sometimes using multiletter units such as *sh*, *th*, and *ch* to represent particular phonemes.

Further, single letters can represent more than one phoneme (e.g., *g*, *c*). The same letter may relate to a sound that is pronounced a bit differently depending on the linguistic context in which it appears (the /k/ sound in *kangaroo* vs. *keyboard*). These differences can be seen in a spectrograph, but the sounds to which the particular letter relates are close enough because there are no two words that can be contrasted using the distinction.

In English, as we have noted before, there are issues with orthographic regularity and transparency that young readers must overcome while learning to read. This lack of transparency shows up particularly in sight words, but it occurs elsewhere too. By comparison, languages such as Albanian, Spanish, Italian, German, Dutch, and Finnish are examples of alphabetic languages with shallow or transparent orthography. Transparent orthographies are those that map the letters and phonemes very consistently in both directions (i.e., from reading to speech and from speech to spelling). A *consonantal writing system* is a type of an alphabetic writing system wherein only consonant phonemes are represented in the script, with vowels indicated only by a diacritical mark, a mark that appear above or below a consonant, if at all. Arabic and Hebrew are examples of this type of alphabetic system. The commonality in all of these writing systems is that they are based on the incorporation of speech sounds into print.

At the other end of the continuum are *logographic writing systems* in which a single unit of writing stands in for an entire word or morpheme, generally. The Chinese writing system is an example of a logographic system. Not all Chinese characters represent individual morphemes, however, and some morphemes are combinations of characters. The main difference between an alphabetic writing system and a logographic writing system is that the pronunciation of a word in a logographic writing system is not tied directly to the logograph. That is, one cannot determine how to pronounce a character by looking at the components of it. This means that it takes many years to learn to read Chinese. In Chinese, there are 3,500–4,000 commonly used characters, and these are combined to form around 60,000 words (DeFrancis, 1986).

One benefit of logographic writing systems, however, is that it can sometimes communicate across languages and dialects when they share the writing system. For example, persons speaking different dialects of Chinese (and even Japanese, when using the *kanji* system) can understand the general messages conveyed by the written form because the logographs in the message are attached to meaning, not phonology. Some Chinese characters help this process along by depicting meaning in a rather iconic way; for example, the character for *person* looks vaguely like that of a person (人). But, by no means do most characters graphically convey their meaning, and we would venture to assert that most Westerners cannot guess what various characters mean by just looking at them.

Modern Chinese also has phonetic elements. For example, many of the words are written as compounds such that the first character represents the basic meaning and the second provides a hint as to the approximate sound. For example, the word for *stare* is 盯, with the character on the left indicating an eye-related concept and the one on the right the sound (Tong & McBride-Chang, 2010). Sound-indicating units provide pronunciation cuing only at a syllable level, not at the phoneme level. Further, in many cases, the same element can function as either a meaning or pronunciation cue, depending on its position within the character. Between 80 and 90% of the words found in Chinese written corpuses are compounds of this sort (Rayner, Pollatsek, Ashby, & Clifton, 2012, p. 39; Tong & McBride-Chang, 2010). Thus, most written Chinese words have elements of both semantics and phonetic form. It is mainly common words that get written as simple logographic characters without these phonetic cues included. Thus, Chinese, possibly the best understood logographic writing system, is not completely logographic.

There are also *syllabic writing systems* or syllabaries. Like an alphabet, these are phonetic writing systems in which syllables are represented: typically a consonant and a vowel, or just a vowel. Bengali, Kannada, Burmese, Cherokee, Lao, and Thai, among others, use a syllabic writing system. Japanese *hiragana*, which is used when there is no *kanji* equivalent, is also an example of a syllabary. Most syllabaries combine elements of alphabetic and syllabic writing components (e.g., Hindi, Tamil, Kannada) and/or combinations of logographic and syllabic writing components (e.g., Japanese).

As can be seen by our description of various writing systems, the issue of how to represent spoken language in print has been solved differently by each writing system. What are the implications of particular writing systems in relation to learning to read? This question has generated much recent research in the attempt to discern just how much of what we have described in the rest of this book is universal and which is orthography-specific. One active question is whether the characteristics of the writing system likely encourage readers to adapt their processing strategies to the particular demands of the orthography. We address the implications for learning to read in alphabetic, syllabic, and logographic writing systems in the next sections.

Learning to Read in Alphabetic Writing Systems

One question that has occupied researchers studying reading development of the three main alphabetic writing systems is the degree to which orthographic transparency affects learning to read. As noted earlier, orthographic transparency is a main variable distinguishing alphabetic languages. This transparency may influence the strategies that young readers use for translating print to speech. In a truly transparent writing system such as Finnish, all letter names provide the phoneme for the letter, and these sounds are independent of where the letter occurs within a word. Children learning to read Finnish have all the phonemic tools they need after they have mastered 21 letter–sound connections (Aro & Wimmer, 2003). This orthographic transparency has a number of implications for learning to read in alphabetic languages.

First, learning to decode words is relatively easy in orthographically transparent languages because doing so is merely a matter of translating the alphabet into speech sounds in a rather direct way. In fact, it has been shown that children learning to read in orthographically transparent languages learn to read accurately more quickly than those learning to read in orthographically opaque alphabetic languages such as English. For example, Ellis et al. (2004) found that 7-year-old English-speaking children could read only 60% of words sampled accurately, whereas young Albanian readers could read about 80% of words with similar meanings and frequencies. Similarly, Patel, Snowling, and deJong (2004) found that Dutch children in the process of learning to read Dutch named words with greater accuracy and speed than English readers of a similar age and experience.

Another implication of learning to read in transparent writing systems is that word length should have a great effect on word-reading times in orthographically transparent alphabetic languages compared to opaque languages. That is, decoding a word in a transparent language requires the retrieval and assemblage of the pronunciation of each and every letter. This should add up when reading longer words. Ellis and Hooper (2001) showed that word length accounted for greater variance in the reading times of children reading Welch (an orthographically transparent alphabetic language) than it did for children reading English.

According to Ellis et al. (2004), another implication of learning to read in orthographically transparent languages is that transparency encourages young readers to rely on phonology in learning to read words. By contrast, orthographic opacity encourages readers to access the lexicon as an additional step in identifying words (as described by the dual-route model discussed in Chapter 4; see also Coltheart, 2004), because the surface spelling-to-sound translation process cannot be relied upon as readily. This has implications for the kinds of errors that young readers make while reading aloud. For example, German- and Albanian-speaking children, who are leaning to read in orthographically transparent writing systems, are more likely to produce reading errors that are mispronunciations, even to the extent of producing nonwords, rather than merely substituting actual words while reading (Wimmer & Hummer, 1990; Ellis et al., 2004). By contrast, children learning to read English display reading errors that are more likely to be actual words because the young readers might try direct access to the lexicon.

Phonological awareness may be less important to the decoding of orthographically transparent writing systems than for inconsistent ones because transparent systems place a lessened demand on young readers. As any teacher who is teaching children to read in English knows, teaching letter sounds is not nearly enough phonics knowledge for children to be successful. In transparent orthographies, most children, even children who struggle, are able to learn the necessary phonics patterns within a year or so. Children learning to read in an opaque language such as English truly need to have a deep understanding of the phoneme system to be able to map various letter combinations to their respective sounds. They have to be flexible enough to retrieve graphemic units in a variety of sizes ranging from single-letter units to larger-morphemic, multiletter, rime, and even whole-word units (Goswami, 2002; Ziegler & Goswami, 2005). In fact, a number of studies that have compared learning to decode words in transparent and opaque languages have found that phonological awareness is not as important to decoding in transparent languages as it is in opaque languages (Georgiou, Parilla, & Papadopolous, 2008; Georgiou, Torppa, Manolitsis, Lyytinen, & Parilla, 2012; Ziegler et al., 2010). The importance of early phonological awareness is particularly important during the early stages of learning to read words in orthographically opaque languages (Vaessen et al., 2010). Children reading orthographically opaque languages need to have this phonemic knowledge in a deeper, very retrievable, and uniquely identifiable form.

Another implication for learning to read in transparent alphabetic writing systems is that these systems may shift the relative importance of skills necessary for reading comprehension. This shift in strategies would be expected if the writing system likely encourages readers to adapt their processing strategies to the particular demands of the orthography. Indeed, Florit and Cain (2011) identified a shift in the pattern of skills important to learning to read in a meta-analysis comparing predictors of reading comprehension in English to predictors of reading comprehension across a variety of transparent languages.

Consider the simple view of reading discussed in our chapter on theories of reading comprehension. This theory assumes that both decoding skills and linguistic comprehension skills are key contributors to reading comprehension. But what happens when acquiring decoding skills is not particularly difficult and virtually every child acquires them easily? This is what generally happens for children learning orthographically transparent languages. Linguistic comprehension skills might be a greater contributor to reading comprehension in such cases. For readers of opaque languages such as English, basic decoding skills can be a major impediment to comprehension, as we have discussed previously, and their impacts may be more keenly felt for young readers. Linguistic comprehension skills track more closely to reading comprehension skills for young readers of transparent languages, whereas decoding skills track more closely to reading comprehension skills for young readers of English.

Learning to Read in a Syllabary Writing System

The research on children learning to read in syllabary writing systems is comparatively sparse. One prediction that can be made is that children learning to read syllabaries would have poor phonemic awareness skills (Share, 1995). This should occur because the operative unit of analysis of the writing system is the syllable, not the phoneme. Reading in a syllabary might require syllabic awareness, but not phonemic awareness. Mann (1986) found this result for young readers of Japanese *hiragana*. Further, Kobayashi, Haynes, Macaruso, Hook, and Kato (2005) found that syllable deletion skill correlated with reading accuracy among Japanese *hiragana* learners. Pure syllabaries are rare, however. For example, the syllabary system of 71 basic *hiragana* that Japanese children learn to read also has 36 additional symbols that represent phonetic elements (called the *hiragana you-on* system). It is possible that having phonological awareness can assist in the learning of those symbols. Fletcher-Flinn, Thompson, Yamada, and Naka (2011) have reported that

Japanese children learning to read the *hiragana* syllabary with phonological aware-ness are better able to read these 36 symbols than children without good phono-logical awareness. However, phonological awareness did not distinguish children's learning of basic *hiragana*.

As we noted earlier, most syllabaries are, in fact, not pure syllabaries, but rather *alphasyllabaries* or some combination of logographic and syllabic writing. Nag (2007) examined the acquisition of the Kannada alphasyllabary among South Indian 5- to 10-year-old children. This alphasyllabary represents sounds at the level of the syllable in a salient way, but it also has distinctive diacritics that indi-cate subsyllabic information related to vowels. Children learning this alphasyl-labary show strong and early sensitivity to syllable-level phonological awareness, but phoneme-level phonological awareness is fairly late to emerge. Syllable-level phonological awareness is importantly related to reading skills at both younger and older ages. Phonological awareness, which older Kannada-speaking children eventually acquire to the level typically seen in English-speaking counterparts, is mainly related to skill in acquiring the finer details of Kannada print.

Frankly, we need to learn more about how children learn to read in various types of syllabary writing systems. This knowledge will help us understand more than we currently do about how the characteristics of writing systems influence the patterns of underlying skills needed for learning to read.

Learning to Read in Logographic Writing Systems

To be sure, the most researched logographic language to be investigated using psy-cholinguistic methodologies is Chinese. As we have noted earlier, most Chinese words contain characters constructed of a meaning and a phonetic element. In learning to read, children have to learn to identify the general meaning/semantic elements (which may have different interpretations in different contexts), the pro-nunciation of the phonetic elements, and the positioning of these elements within the character to extract the identity of a particular word.

Theoretically, it is unclear how these orthographies map on to the semantic–phonological–orthographic triad reasoning found in word recognition theories for English reading (e.g., Seidenberg & McClelland, 1989). However, we can attempt to draw analogies to components of models originally developed to describe word recognition in English by disassembling these Chinese compounds into their pho-netic, semantic, and orthographic components.

The phonetic component of Chinese compound characters would seem to be most closely related to the phonological representation described by triad models, and the relevant skill that children would need to process them well would prob-ably require phonological awareness. Indeed, phonological awareness is important for learning to read in Chinese, particularly syllabic awareness and tonal awareness (i.e., the knowledge that a particular pronunciation has different meanings when spoken in different tones), which is relevant to the Chinese language and its orthography (Ho & Bryant, 1997; He, Wang, & Anderson, 2005).

The semantic component of the Chinese compound characters would seem to be analogous to the semantic units described by the triad models. If so, morphological awareness should be a relevant underlying skill that allows children to appreciate the meaning subcomponents of these characters. Children who have greater morphological awareness should demonstrate better word reading skills in Chinese (Kuo & Anderson, 2006). For example, McBride-Chang, Shu, Zhou, Wat, and Wagner (2003) examined one element of morphological awareness, the understanding of compounding. They found that children's ability to construct novel compounds based on manipulating constituent morphemes (e.g., "If we see the sun rising in the morning, we call that a sunrise. What should we say when we see the moon rising in the evening?"; p. 746) captured unique variance in kindergarten children's word reading skills. Other ways of measuring morphological awareness have also demonstrated the important contribution that this construct has for the beginning phases of learning to read Chinese words (Tong & McBride-Chang, 2010).

The orthographic component of Chinese characters would seem to be related to children's understanding of the organization of the semantic and phonetic subcomponents within the characters. Indeed, young Chinese readers who have an understanding of this system are better readers (Cheung, Chan, & Chong, 2007). That is, children who know the positioning and functions of the elements within characters display better word reading accuracy and comprehension. Further, Chinese kindergarten children who can identify incorrect elements of Chinese characters altered in a minor way (akin to misspellings) also tend to display stronger word reading (Tong & McBride-Chang, 2010).

Concluding Thoughts about Writing Systems and Learning to Read

At the outset of this chapter, we discussed the issue of whether learning to read engages universal, linguistically independent, complex sets of psychological processes. To a great extent, the research on the influence of writing systems has focused on the process of learning to read words rather than other types of literacy skills discussed in this book (i.e., comprehension, vocabulary). For this reason, our discussion has focused on whether different writing systems engage the same underlying skills for word recognition discussed by the triad (Seidenberg & McClelland, 1989) or dual-route models (Coltheart, 2004) of word recognition.

Research on writing systems has generally taken an individual differences approach to considering the relevance of these factors for learning to read. These methods involve using a variety of correlational methods to distinguish the relationships between component skills and overall word reading skills. Essentially, these skills are considered contributors to reading skills. Differences between these writing systems have been inferred differentially by comparing the strength of correlations from one language to another.

We have noted similarities and differences in the development of the importance of subskills in learning to read. In learning to read transparent alphabetic writing systems, phonological awareness skills are not as strong a differentiator as to who is and is not a good reader. In learning to read in syllabary writing systems, phonological awareness is again important, but only awareness at the syllabic level is needed. In learning to read in logographic writing systems, research on Chinese suggests that, even in this nonalphabetic system, evidence for the importance of phonological, morphological, and orthographic awareness is present. However, direct correspondences between the subskills studied for Chinese and the well-documented subskills studied for learning to read in English were harder to draw directly.

For now, we tentatively conclude that the kinds of underlying skills described by the triad and dual-route models might be all we need to describe learning to read in most writing systems. We need to include the proviso, which is already clear from the research, that the writing system itself will direct the relative importance and characterization of the particular component skills needed for the task. However, it is hard for us to escape the feeling that the theorizing about the development of word reading skills themselves probably would have taken a different turn if we had started from the point of view of Chinese rather than English.

LEARNING TO READ IN A SECOND LANGUAGE

Being able to speak two or more languages is a very common skill both nationally and globally. The 2007 Census Survey estimated the percentage of the population over the age of 5 speaking a language other than English in the United States is around 20% (Shin & Kominski, 2010). Of those speaking a native language other than English, approximately 76% claim to speak English at least well or very well. Bilingual children represent 9.1% of U.S. public school population, and the percentage is growing.

There has been a global escalation of migration in recent years (Connor, Cohn, & Gonzalez-Barrera, 2013), suggesting that the number of bilingual people is increasing around the world as well. It has been estimated that fully one half of the world's population uses two or more languages (or dialects) daily (Grosjean, 2010). Thus, internationally, bilingualism is neither a rarity nor an aberrant skill. Indeed, most bilingual individuals learn and maintain a second language because it serves as a personal and economic resource for them (Ruiz, 1984). Many children around the world learn to read, and read well, in a second language.

Developmental Issues in Learning to Read in a Second Language

As has been emphasized throughout this book, learning to read well rests on a strong foundation of linguistic skills. For bilingual children, developing this strong foundation is complicated.

When children receive native language exposure from birth, they move through reliable sequences of linguistic development. They acquire their first words by the end of their first year, two-word combinations and 50-word vocabulary milestones by 1½ years (Brown, 1973; Nelson, 1973), and complex sentence grammars between preschool and the end of elementary school (Chomsky, 1969). The major acquisitions are thought to be determined by the development of hemispheric specialization for language and frontal lobe maturation in the brain (Diamond, 2002; Kovelman, Baker, & Petitto, 2008). Children receiving bilingual input from birth show the native-like patterns in both their linguistic development and neurological specialization for language (Pearson, Fernandez, & Oller, 1993).

Most immigrant children in the United States, at least, do not receive bilingual input from birth; they receive dominant input from one language only. For many, if not most, bilingual children, the timing and relative exposure to a second language is often delayed until preschool or kindergarten entry. The *sensitive period hypothesis*, as it applies to bilingual individuals (Johnson & Newport, 1989), claims that general proficiency with a second language is strongly linked to the age at which children are exposed to this second language. Adults not having exposure to their second language until later in childhood usually end up with lower proficiency overall in this language as adults (Johnson & Newport, 1989), although perhaps this is not universal (White & Genesee, 1996). The greater fragility of linguistic proficiency in their second language will impact the reading skills of bilingual children learning to read in that language.

Children who acquire their second language upon school entry are acquiring it beyond the period where native-like proficiency is usually found. Indeed, research suggests that, as a general rule, bilingual children from immigrant families perform worse in national assessments of reading than monolingual children (Cheung & Slavin, 2013). On the National Assessment of Educational Progress (2011), only 3% of fourth-grade English language learners (ELLs) scored at or above the proficient level, whereas 46% of non-ELLs scored at the proficient level, a difference that was similar for eighth graders (3% vs. 39%). The effects may be larger for vocabulary skills than actual word reading skills (Mancilla-Martinez & Lesaux, 2011). As a result, the long-term impacts of bilingualism on literacy may be larger on reading comprehension than they are for the relatively constrained skill of word reading (Kieffer, 2010). Unfortunately, bilingual children in the United States also have worse family literacy resources and fewer family learning activities than their monolingual counterparts (Feng, Gai, & Chen, 2014). So, the cause of these lower reading scores may be linguistic, experiential, or both.

Unfortunately, these statistics paint a negative picture of the effects of bilingualism, which is not our goal here. It has been demonstrated that children who have early exposure to two languages do not have these issues with regard to the acquisition of basic literacy skills. Kovelman et al. (2008) compared the literacy performance of early versus late exposure to English for second- and third-grade Spanish–English bilingual children. The bilingual children with early exposure had acquired both languages prior to age 3, whereas those with late exposure acquired English upon preschool or elementary school entry. The performance of these bilingual children was evaluated for phonological awareness and nonword naming (an indicator of decoding knowledge) and compared to demographically similar monolingual English-speaking children. Kovelman et al. found that Spanish–English bilingual second and third graders who learned both languages early were indistinguishable from monolingual English-speaking children on both tasks. Bilingual children with early exposure to English outperformed their late-exposure counterparts on the reading measures. Luckily, for early-exposure children these benefits for learning to read in English did not come at the cost of Spanish proficiency, which is what many parents and teachers worry about. Bilingual children with early exposure performed similarly to their late-exposure counterparts on Spanish phonological awareness, Spanish nonword reading, and a measure of general Spanish linguistic competence. The early-exposure children displayed what Cummins (1994) has called *additive bilingualism* (wherein the first language continues to be developed and maintained as the second language is added) rather than the *subtractive bilingualism* pattern that is often seen (wherein the second language is added at the expense of the first language). This finding suggests that the issue is not bilingualism itself, but rather early exposure to the language in which one is going to learn to read that is important.

A subtractive bilingualism pattern is not a small worry, though, as it is prevalent among bilingual children who are a linguistic minority in a larger linguistically dominant milieu, which is most often the case in the United States (Mancilla-Martinez & Lesaux, 2011). Further, being educated in an environment where the second language dominates linguistically may accelerate these subtractive processes among children who may not yet have a firm command of their first language (Restrepo et al., 2010). Bilingual children in these circumstances nearly always have a larger vocabulary in the language of schooling, and this gap does not close until about fifth grade (Oller & Eilers, 2002). The problem of subtractive bilingualism suggests that strong efforts should be made toward helping children grow linguistically in both languages.

Some research suggests that poverty may be a better explanation of the lower literacy skills found in bilingual children than linguistic background (Lesaux, 2012). ELLs and non-ELLs from similar SES backgrounds appear to be at a similar risk for late-emerging difficulties in literacy (Kieffer, 2010). These findings point to the importance of oral proficiency in the language of literacy regardless of whether children are bilingual or not.

Contributors to Learning to Read in a Second Language

Bialystok (2007) identifies basic precursors to literacy in bilingual individuals that we find useful in considering the attainment of literacy in children learning a second language. These precursors can be seen in Figure 10.1.

Focusing on the left-hand side of this figure, children's oral language skills in their first language (L1) and their second language (L2) are hypothesized to be key underlying skills for L2 literacy. Oral language skills are usually operationalized in studies investigating these skills as knowledge of vocabulary and grammar. Research shows that the relationship between L1 and L2 oral language skills is rather small, surprisingly, although it is statistically significant across studies (Melby-Lervåg & Lervåg, 2011). Children who have good oral language skills in their first language do not always have good oral language skills in their second, although they generally do. Thus, the operative oral language link to acquiring good L2 comprehension is between L2 oral language and L2 literacy. There is, however, a strong relationship between L2 vocabulary knowledge and L2 reading comprehension skills (Jeon & Yamashita, 2014), although this relationship is larger for older children who are reading more complex texts than are younger children. There is also a strong correlation between L2 grammar skills and L2 reading comprehension (Jeon & Yamashita, 2014). Further, it has been shown

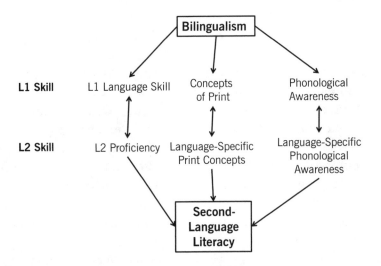

FIGURE 10.1. Relation between bilingualism and first- and second-language literacy acquisition. L1, first language; L2, second language. Adapted from Bialystok (2007). Copyright 2007 by and adapted with permission of John Wiley and Sons.

that listening comprehension skills in L2 have a very strong relationship with L2 reading comprehension (as might be anticipated from the simple view of reading; Jeon & Yamashita, 2014). Thus, L2 language skills have an enormous impact on comprehension of text in children's second language.

Concentrating on the center of this figure, we find hypothesized links between language-specific print concepts and L2 literacy. Print concepts are usually operationalized as orthographic features of the two writing systems and the distance between them. As might be expected, when the languages have similar orthography in L1 and L2, children experience less difficulty in learning to read in their second language. For example, there is a strong correlation between being able to decode in an L1 alphabetic system and in an L2 alphabetic system (Melby-Lervåg & Lervåg, 2011). That is, this finding suggests that children are able to transfer their understanding of alphabetic principles to a new alphabetic system. This transference occurs even when two opaque alphabetic orthographies, such as English and French, are involved (Commissaire, Duncan, & Casalis, 2011; Deacon, Wade-Woolley, & Kirby, 2009). As might be expected, there is almost no transfer in learning to decode words when moving from a nonalphabetic L1 writing system to an alphabetic system (Melby-Lervåg & Lervåg, 2011). In other words, having good decoding skills in Chinese does not confer any particular advantage on learning to decode in English (Bialystok, Luk, & Kwan, 2005). Thus, children's knowledge of print concepts in their first language can often help them to learn to read in a second language, but only if the writing systems share some characteristics.

The right-hand side of Figure 10.1 represents the idea that phonological awareness skills in L1 should help children transfer this knowledge to L2, which will assist their learning to read words in L2. A substantial amount of research has documented that there is a strong relationship between L1 and L2 phonological awareness skills (Melby-Lervåg & Lervåg, 2011). This finding indicates that young readers can transfer their understanding of phonological awareness from their first language to their new one. When they have good phonological awareness in their first language, they can use it to help them learn how to decode in a second language (Bialystok, 2007; Melby-Verlåg & Lervåg, 2011). And, just as for L1 reading, having good decoding skills in L2 helps children understand what they are reading in L2 (Melby-Lervåg & Lervåg, 2011).

At the outset of this section on bilingual reading, we posited that it was important for children to develop strong linguistic skills in their first language to support the decoding and comprehension processes needed for learning to read in a second language. In support of this statement, we have discussed how oral language, decoding, and phonological awareness skills in their first language can be fundamental to children's development of the skills necessary for reading with good comprehension in the second language. Some of these relationships are strong, whereas others are less so.

If we consider the skills that are cited in most theories of reading comprehension, we can see that the research on this topic needs to expand its treatment of the linguistic contributors of L1 on reading comprehension in L2. That is, to a great extent, the research is silent on some major contributors to reading comprehension, such as inferencing skills and prior knowledge, perhaps because it is assumed that these contributors do not change as a child moves from one language to the next, although this should be verified. Thus, these contributions to reading comprehension should be considered to be among the linguistic contributors to comprehension that children may bring with them while learning to read in a second language.

Implications for Instructing Children Who Are Learning to Read in a Second Language and in Different Orthographies

Studies on learning to read in a second language and across writing systems point to the importance of ensuring that children have experience with phonological awareness. Note here that we have called this skill *phonological* awareness rather than *phonemic* awareness, which is a phonological grain size (Ziegler & Goswami, 2005) most associated with learning to read in an alphabetic language. As we noted in our discussion of writing systems, some elements of phonological awareness are more relevant to some orthographies than others. Transfer of phonological awareness may be affected by issues of psycholinguistic grain size relevant to reading in the originating L1 to the target L2 (Branum-Martin, Tao, Garnaat, Bunta, & Francis, 2012). This implies that instructing children in various levels of phonological awareness (phoneme, syllable, and word) may be helpful so that they can pick the level of phonological awareness that is most helpful to learning to read in their second language.

The research further upholds the idea that teachers may wish to capitalize on children's orthographic knowledge if the child's first language is similar to the one in which they are learning to read. For children whose first language is Spanish, it is important to realize that children may bring an expectation about the transparency of print that is not supported in English (Sun-Alperin & Wang, 2011). However, because English is also an alphabetic language, it makes sense to let children know that they can transfer much of their knowledge of consonants, which are similar enough between the two languages to be usefully deployed. Vowel rules will need to be dealt with separately.

Finally, the research supports carrying out instruction to ensure that children have sufficiently developed oral language skills in both languages, but particularly in the language in which they are learning to read. Without it, it is difficult to see how they would succeed in reading comprehension. We need to be mindful of the fact that proficiency in a second language will take years to develop, long after children sound native-like. Teachers should not confuse the apparent achievement of fluent bilingual performance with native-like proficiency. They should provide language-rich environments in which students have access to print as well as opportunities to use language within collaborative experiences with other children and proficient adults (Lesaux, 2012).

The Common Core State Standards stress that "all students should be held to the same high expectations outlined in the . . . Standards. This includes students who are English language learners (ELLs). However, these students may require additional time, appropriate instructional support, and aligned assessments as they acquire both English language proficiency and content area knowledge." Thus, no special standards are designed for ELLs. The standards urge teachers to recognize that "it is possible to achieve the standards for reading and literature, writing and research, language development and speaking and listening without manifesting native-like control of conventions and vocabulary." Teachers should provide the following (*www.corestandards.org/assets/application-for-english-learners.pdf*):

- "Literacy-rich school environments where students are immersed in a variety of language experiences;
- "Instruction that develops foundational skills in English and enables ELLs to participate fully in grade-level coursework;
- "Coursework that prepares ELLs for postsecondary education or the workplace, yet is made comprehensible for students learning content in a second language (through specific pedagogical techniques and additional resources);
- "Opportunities for classroom discourse and interaction that are well-designed to enable ELLs to develop communicative strengths in language arts;
- "Ongoing assessment and feedback to guide learning; and
- "Speakers of English who know the language well enough to provide ELLs with models and support."

DIALECT AND LEARNING TO READ

In the United States, children often find themselves in schools where the dominant language spoken is standard English (sometimes called *mainstream* English), or some close variant of it. This may or may not be the variant of English with which they are most familiar or that they use in everyday life. Instead, they may speak a dialect of English different from their teachers or perhaps different from their classmates. A *dialect* is a variant of a language associated with a particular group of speakers who have a common region and/or social pattern. A dialect of a language is usually distinguishable from its standard variety by its unique features of vocabulary (e.g., do you prefer *faucet* or *spigot*, *pail* or *bucket*?), morphosyntactic uses (do you say *might could* or simply *might*?), and phonology (do you say *north* or *norf*?), including prosody.

Generally, a linguistic system is considered a dialect and not a distinct language when there is mutual intelligibility between the speakers of the standard variant and dialect speakers. However, whether a linguistic system is labeled a standard language or a dialect is usually a matter of power rather than any particular consistent set of linguistic features; or as the sociolinguistic saying goes, "A language is a dialect with an army and navy" (Bright, 1997, p. 469). This saying makes the point that all linguistic systems are, in one way or another, dialects; just some of them serve as the language of schooling. Linguists nearly universally agree that dialects are not impoverished versions of standard dialects. Instead, what gets labeled a *dialect* is the result of a power differential among speakers of the language.

The dialect on which we focus our attention here is an English dialect that goes by several names historically—black English, ebonics, African American vernacular English, or simply, African American English (AAE)—which are all synonyms for the same dialect. In the Southern United States, non-African-American adults speak a dialect that shares many features with AAE because of a shared historical context (Wolfram, 1974). AAE is the dialect around which there is the most information regarding effects of a nonstandard dialect on learning to read.

Key Features of AAE

Before we embark on the implications of AAE for learning to read, it is helpful to understand some of its main identifiers. Common features of AAE used by children are in Table 10.1. AAE is a probabilistic constellation of linguistic features. Speakers of this dialect may use many or few of these features. Note that the speakers themselves may use these features in a contextual way. A given speaker will sometimes omit articles and sometimes not; he or she might sometimes omit the plural -*s* or past tense -*ed* and sometimes not. Further, there is great variability among African American speakers, including children, as to the number and density of features that are used.

Craig et al. (2003) calculated the density of phonological and morphosyntactic features of AAE produced by low-income African American children while reading aloud. They found that a full 94% of the African American children whom they tested produced some AAE features while reading aloud. Older elementary

TABLE 10.1. The Most Frequent Phonological and Morphosyntactic Features of AAE Found in Child Read-Alouds

Feature Description	Example
Common Phonological Features	
Neutralization of diphthong	Our → /ɑɾ/
Substitutions	This → /dɪs/
Deletion of phonemes from consonant clusters	World → /wɣl/
Deletion of consonants following vowels	Mouth → /mau/
Reversal of phonemes within a cluster	Escape → /ɛkskep/
Reduction of an unstressed syllable in a multisyllabic word	Became → /kem/
Substitution of /n/ for /ŋ/ in final word positions	Waiting → /wetn/
Syllable addition to a word	Forests → /foristsiz/
Common Morphosyntactic Features	
Omission of -*ed* on regular past-tense verbs; use of present forms of irregular verbs	"As soon as she open her mouth, she fall straight . . ."
Omission of articles	"This cake is best present of all."
Use of the article "a" regardless of the vowel context	"One day she met a eagle traveling to . . ."
Omission of -*s* to mark number	"Father went to buy some pretty flower."
Omission of prepositions	"She sits and looks birds."
Omission of auxiliaries	"She always comes down when it time to eat."

Note. Based on Craig, Thompson, Washington, and Potter (2003).

school children tended to produce fewer AAE features than younger children. This finding has been replicated by others using groups of African American children from a variety of locations in the United States (Charity, Scarborough, & Griffin, 2004). Phonological features were produced more often than morphosyntactic features. Most of the AAE features produced during oral reading were the same ones that previous studies had shown are produced spontaneously by African American children during free play (e.g., Washington & Craig, 1994). However, there are differing production rates in oral narratives, oral readings, and written narratives (Thompson, Craig, & Washington, 2004), suggesting that some literacy contexts lend themselves to greater use of AAE than others. Still the presence of AAE in literacy tasks suggests that children bring their linguistic knowledge of AAE with them to school activities, just as do speakers of standard English.

Implications of AAE for Learning to Read

A great deal of research has investigated the link between AAE and learning to read. Some of the thinking about dialect and its influence on learning to read has been framed as concerns about *dialect interference* (Goodman, 1965). That is, the concern is that using a minority dialect will cause children to show lower reading achievement than they might if they spoke standard English. At this point, we must restate that the similarities between AAE and standard English are overwhelming. Thus, understanding English should allow African American children to transfer the vast bulk of their linguistic knowledge to the process of learning to read. This transfer is positive and helpful.

Analysis of the NAEP, however, shows a persistent gap between African American and European American children in their performance on national assessments of reading. Half of African American children failed to achieve basic reading levels on the 2013 fourth-grade NAEP compared to 21% of their European American peers (Nations Report Card, 2013). This racial gap in reading skills has been intractable for over 20 years, possibly for as long as people have been tracking reading achievement. This has occurred despite increased pressure on states to address this gap instructionally by imposing accountability measures (Nichols, Glass, & Berliner, 2012). Unfortunately, whatever benefits, if any, these accountability measures may have had on student achievement have probably been eroded by the simultaneous resegregation and isolation of the schools that African American children increasingly attend (Condron, Tope, Steidl, & Freeman, 2013).

One view is that African American children's relative lack of familiarity with standard English may be one source of the disparity in reading skills in African American and European American children (beyond poverty). To test this hypothesis, Charity et al. (2004) asked African American children to repeat verbatim sentences designed to tap some of the AAE features. If children had difficulty doing this task without introducing AAE, it probably meant that they had less familiarity with standard English. Indeed, children who were able to do this task displayed better reading achievement than those who could not, even after SES variables were controlled for. This finding suggests that children who have a basic understanding of standard English might attain higher reading achievement scores than those who do not.

Sociolinguists Ogbu and Simons (1998) argue that the difficulties experienced by disadvantaged children speaking AAE are not caused by dialect issues per se, because these are minor. Instead, they are caused by identity issues and nonlanguage issues such as understanding when and where to use AAE. Children are expected to use AAE when addressing members of their own community; it is considered rude not to do so. Refusing to use AAE with other members of the community is viewed as an attempt to distance oneself from the community. Children are expected to use standard English when they are at school, generally, and switch back to AAE when they return home. Older children understand this expectation.

Like children of immigrants, the first language of most African American children is AAE, not standard English. Children usually acquire standard English dialect upon school entry. For African American children just entering school, the mismatch between the language of schooling and language of the home may influence their transition into school (LeMoine, 2001), as well as their beginning efforts in learning to read. So one might expect that it would take a number of years before children understand the intricacies of this new dialect.

African American children learn to code-switch between dialects, much as bilingual children shift between languages. When carried out between dialects, this is called *dialect shifting*. Some African American children as young as preschool have been observed attempting dialect shifting when narrating wordless storybooks, suggesting that they have already come to understand the sociolinguistic imperative to use standard English in carrying out school tasks (Connor & Craig, 2006). Indeed, the inability to shift dialects (as the Charity et al., 2004, findings are interpreted as indicating) might be a persistent source of problems for acquiring literacy (Ogbu & Simons, 1998). On the positive side, dialect shifting can be viewed as an indicator of strong linguistic flexibility and linguistic skill.

In support of this idea, Craig, Zhang, Hensel, and Quinn (2009) examined the written versus spoken productions of elementary school children with the view that children's writings had previously been shown to reveal fewer features of AAE. It was their hypothesis that a comparison of written and oral productions might provide an indicator of children's ability to shift dialects. They found that the presence and density of AAE features in oral narratives were unrelated to children's reading assessment scores, although presence of AAE features within written narratives was. Thus, there is support for the hypothesis that states that the ability to shift dialects among African American children is related to their developing skill in reading.

Whether dialect is causal to producing the lower reading assessment scores of young African Americans learning to read or whether its effects are mediated by some other factor is unclear. The view that dialect has some causal role in the reduced level of reading skills among African American students is not universally accepted. Terry (2012), for example, points out that children's use of AAE dialect is relatively unimportant once their emergent literacy skills are taken into account. Others claim that the ability to shift dialects in literacy contexts (i.e., when the context demands it) is a linguistic achievement in itself that is predictive of better literacy achievement (Craig, Kolenic, & Hensel, 2014). Certainly, we feel that dialect interference is probably a relatively minor player in reading achievement in contrast to larger sociological impacts.

We believe that there is enough evidence at this point to suggest that merely being a speaker of AAE is not an enormous issue for literacy outcomes by itself. Instead, the ability to shift dialects when the context demands it matters most. This metalinguistic skill represents a positive benefit for speakers of AAE. Learning flexibility in language use can be a goal of instruction. Teachers can promote the use of AAE in everyday speech among members of the community if they simultaneously encourage children to engage their linguistic flexibility by shifting into standard English when the context demands it.

CONNECTING TO THE STANDARDS

The Common Core State Standards do not explicitly address issues of dialect until fifth grade. Specifically, in fifth grade, there is a standard that requires teachers to instruct children on how to "adapt speech to a variety of contexts and tasks, using formal English when appropriate to task and situation" (CSS.ELA-Literacy. SL.5.6). Children are expected to be able to "compare and contrast the varieties of English (e.g., *dialects, registers*) used in stories, dramas, or poems" (CCSS.ELA-Literacy.l.5.3.B). Throughout the standards is an emphasis that children should demonstrate acquisition and proficiency with standard varieties of English.

Some researchers, such as Paris (2012), object to having similar standards and similar policies for both dialect speakers and bilingual children because the standards have an explicit goal of creating a monocultural, monolingual society. Instead he urges that we develop "pedagogy that seeks to perpetuate and foster—to sustain—linguistic, literate, and cultural pluralism as part of the democratic project of schooling" (p. 93). Others think that dialect instruction should occur much earlier than the Common Core State Standards deal with it, be carried out in a positive atmosphere, and be more linguistically systematic (Terry, 2008).

Where you stand on the importance of AAE depends, we suspect, on whether you believe that maintaining linguistic differences among speakers of English has a societal value. Well beyond the psychology of reading, we point to research that indicates the use of AAE is a key aspect of familial, community, and ethnic identity. The development of a positive identity, including ethnic identity, has been shown to have positive impact on school achievement in general (Altschul, Oyserman, & Bybee, 2006).

According to Siegel (1999), there are basically three instructional approaches to considering AAE dialect in the classroom. Instrumental programs teach children to read and write in AAE first, and then move children gradually toward using standard dialect. Accommodation programs do not use dialect in literacy instruction, but allow children to use it in the classroom in their own personal interactions if they wish. Awareness programs explicitly train children to recognize and appreciate the differences between standard English and AAE and to recognize linguistic variation as the natural and interesting aspect of language that it is. Often in these awareness programs, texts containing dialect are used and overt discussions regarding dialect are held within the classroom, particularly focusing on the utility of code switching. Usually instruction involving some overt, positive attention to dialect is somewhat more successful than programs that do not provide it, but the reasons for it are unclear (Terry, 2008). Certainly, the positive motivation and the cultural affirmation that children gain from such experiences are important by themselves.

CONCLUSION

Throughout this chapter we have tried to emphasize several points. How well individuals ultimately read will depend a great deal on the languages they speak and the requirements of the written form in the target language in which they are reading. The writing system and its characteristics, the proficiency that we have for the language we are reading in, and the specifics of the linguistic foundation that we bring to the task of learning to read are all determining factors.

QUESTIONS FOR DISCUSSION

1. Considering what you now know about the characteristics of various alphabets, what might a perfect alphabet for learning to read look like, if you could start from scratch? What implications does your alphabet have for cognitive processing?

2. What strategies might families use to maximize the likelihood that their child would end up both bilingual and biliterate?

3. What might be the optimal approach for addressing dialect issues within the classroom?

4. Returning to the case study of Yi-wah presented in this chapter, what have you learned that might affect the advice you give to Mr. Garcia regarding how to instruct Yi-wah to read in English?

FURTHER READINGS

Bialystok, E. (2007). Acquisition of literacy in bilingual children: A framework for research. *Language learning, 57*(1), 45–77.

Rayner, K., Pollatsek, A., Ashby, J., & Clifton, C. (2012). *The psychology of reading,* New York: Psychology Press.

Thompson, C. A., Craig, H. K., & Washington, J. A. (2004). Variable production of African American English across oral and literacy contexts. *Language, Speech, and Hearing Services in Schools, 35*(3), 269–282.

CHAPTER 11

Why Reading?

THE PSYCHOSOCIAL BENEFITS OF READING

CASE STUDY

Beverly, now age 70, grew up as the daughter of a short-order cook and a cafeteria worker in a small, Midwestern city. Beverly's parents, who both had dropped out of high school to help support their families, were determined that their daughter would go on to graduate. Even before Beverly attended school, her mother took her to the public library every week, even though getting there required a change of buses. They would spend many spare moments reading books, so reading came fairly easy to Beverly in elementary school; indeed, she became an avid reader. Even as an adolescent, she was known as a bit of a bookworm. Although her teachers didn't expect much of her, Beverly always did well enough in school and tested well. So, the local college offered her the scholarship she needed to attend college, which allowed her to become a teacher. Reading was a constant avocation throughout her life. As a teacher, she passed on her love of words and children's literature to her young charges. Beverly was a leader among teachers in her school, known for staying informed about the latest trends in education. She had an uncanny ability to relate well to the parents, children, administrators, and political leaders who came through her high-poverty school. Despite her modest beginnings, Beverly did well for herself. Now, in retirement, she looks forward to leading her book club meetings, being politically and socially active, and perhaps even helping a child or two to learn to read along the way.

The purpose of this chapter is to outline the benefits of becoming literate. It is probably obvious to you by now that the psychosocial benefits that can be accrued through reading are probably myriad. We have already described how literacy changes the number and kinds of words we know, the depth with which we know them, and our general knowledge about the world. In Chapter 9, we outlined the research that shows that developing a motivation to read and actually reading avidly enable us to become better readers per se. What we want to illustrate in this chapter is how psychosocial benefits of reading extend well beyond those provided by the simple enjoyment of reading.

In recent years, the United States has seen a marked decline in the number of adults who engage in a pattern of reading for pleasure (National Endowment for the Arts, 2007). The Pew Research Center noted recently that nearly a quarter of adults have reported not reading a single book within the past year, not in electronic, paper, or even audio forms (Weissmann, 2014). This number has been growing over the past decades, up from 8% in 1978 identifying themselves as nonpleasure readers. It is obvious that American families are spending less on books than ever before (National Endowment for the Arts, 2007).

Particularly problematic is the percentage of teens who report hardly ever or never reading for pleasure. This number has increased from only 9% in the mid-1980s to approximately 27% now (National Center for Educational Statistics, 2013). The biggest source of decline in reading patterns for teens and young adults is in the area of reading fiction (National Endowment for the Arts, 2007). The comparisons to the reading patterns of adults in their lives are striking.

E-readers and tablets now offer appealing alternatives to traditional books for this age group, but currently most teenagers who do read spend more time reading regular books than reading books on these other electronic types of devices (Common Sense Media, 2014). So, change in format seems to have done little to entice young teens to read. Still, among college students, various forms of electronic reading comprise a substantial part of their daily reading habits (Acheson, Wells, & MacDonald, 2008).

This decline in voluntary reading is a problem because the issue is being felt in the workplace. Employers rank reading and writing skills as among the top deficiencies noted for new hires coming out of high school (National Endowment for the Arts, 2007). The percentage of employers who rate U.S. workers as deficient in basic reading comprehension skills is 38%, and this percentage rises to 72% for writing skills (Casner-Lotto & Barrington, 2006). Indeed, internationally, U.S. workers rank among the bottom third of developed countries in terms of the literacy skills desired by employers, as determined by the Organization for Economic Cooperation and Development (OECD Statistics Canada, 2011). The difficulty of English orthography, vocabulary, or other peculiarities of English cannot be blamed here, because other English-speaking populations, such as Canadians and Australians, perform better internationally.

The purpose of this chapter is to provide an answer to some basic questions, "Why reading?" Just why should reading be so important to us? Does it really matter if adults stop reading for pleasure? Does it really matter if children never achieve solid reading skills, or if they never adopt a love for reading? In this chapter, you will learn about some of the many ways in which reading and reading skills change lives.

COGNITIVE BENEFITS OF READING

It is probably not surprising that there are numerous cognitive benefits for people who read a lot. One of these benefits, which we hope to have made evident from research cited throughout this book, is the continued growth of basic reading skills. Basic reading skills account for things such as the ability to decode and to read simple texts fluently. Psychologists have been interested in capturing benefits besides these basic benefits in reading skills by estimating readers' exposure to print. Exposure to print can be thought of as being different from basic reading skill. *Exposure to print* refers to the amount of voluntary reading, generally, that adults do. As adults engage in print literacy in a variety of ways through books, newspapers, and magazines, they also increase their print exposure. Print exposure is thought to be responsible for the well-known "Matthew effects" on reading (Stanovich, 1986; Cunningham & Stanovich, 1998) whereby persons who read a lot become more proficient over time. However, reading is also responsible for a variety of other cognitive benefits.

Stanovich and his colleagues have been interested the potential role that exposure to print can play in accounting for the cognitive growth seen among some adults but not others. How much one reads can be difficult to assess because people tend to overestimate the amount of time that they actually read. So a more objective measure of print exposure is needed. To assess print exposure, Stanovich and his colleagues have developed objective measures of print exposure that asks adults, college students, or children to complete a checklist regarding how they spend their time (reading is one of them); a questionnaire regarding their reading habits (i.e., whether they read for pleasure, how many books they read in the past year, how much they liked to read); an author recognition test; and a magazine recognition test; they then formed a composite of exposure to print with these measures. In Table 11.1 we provide some examples of the items that Stanovich and Cunningham (1992) and Cunningham and Stanovich (1992) have used to assess print exposure in adults and children. What is noticeable about this print exposure assessment is that it is not filled with tricky or obscure authors or books but, rather, ones with which most teachers might be reasonably familiar.

As a culture, we tend to think that people who read a lot (who would have done well on the print assessment, presumably) probably have acquired a lot of "book smarts," knowledge that is valued in the academic world. But will they have attained knowledge that is really practical for the real world? Using measures of print exposure, research has shown that among the benefits that people accrue

TABLE 11.1. Examples of Items on Measures of Print Exposure

Author Recognition (for adults)	Title recognition (for children)
• Stephen J. Gould	• *A Light in the Attic*
• Andrew Greeley	• *How to Eat Fried Worms*
• Frank Herbert	• *Call of the Wild*
• Erica Jong	• *The Indian in the Cupboard*
• Judith Krantz	• *The Polar Express*
• Stephen King	• *Heidi*
• Robert Ludlum	• *James and the Giant Peach*
• James Michener	• *Dr. Doolittle*
• Studs Terkel	• *Ramona the Pest*
• Alvin Toffler	• *Harriet the Spy*
• J. R. R. Tolkien	• *The Lion, the Witch, and the Wardrobe*
• Alice Walker	• *Freedom Train*
• Tom Wolfe	• *Island of the Blue Dolphins*

Note. There are also foils included in the assessments, which are not presented here. Developed by Stanovich and Cunningham (1992).

from reading a lot is higher levels of practical knowledge. *Practical knowledge* refers to knowledge that is directly relevant to living in a complex technological society. It can include information such as what a carburetor is, what substances may be carcinogenic, what the relation is between the prime lending rate and the rate that the average consumer pays when borrowing money, and which fruits have the most vitamin C. This is the kind of knowledge that one can acquire through experience, exposure to the media, and direct social exchange of information, but we can attain this information much more quickly from reading. Stanovich and Cunningham (1993) have shown that adults who read a lot tend to have a greater amount of this sort of practical knowledge.

Practical knowledge is one aspect of a general set of cognitive skills called *crystallized intelligence.* Crystallized intellectual abilities are those cognitive abilities related to one's experiential history and generally include skills such as vocabulary, general knowledge base, and related skills acquired through experience (Salthouse, 1988). Crystallized intelligence also includes various elements of cultural literacy (Hirsch, 1987)—that is, general cultural knowledge of science, history, geography, economics, literature, art, philosophy, and even psychology, among other things. These types of knowledge are either maintained at a relatively constant level or they increase developmentally throughout most of the adult years. For example, Stanovich, West, and Harrison (1995) gave college students and older adults several tests of cultural literacy and vocabulary and found that older adults generally had stronger crystallized intelligence than did college students.

Stanovich et al. (1995) found that exposure to print was a significant predictor of crystallized intelligence even after fluid intelligence (i.e., the ability to solve problems independent of previous specific practice or instruction; Cattell, 1941), years of education, and age were controlled. In fact, exposure to print accounted for between 12.5 and 15.4% of the variance in individual differences in intelligence in adulthood. Other investigators have also found that the results of a simple rating scale, on which adults compare themselves to their cohort in terms of reading habits, correlate with tests of verbal intelligence as well (Acheson et al., 2008). These researchers have concluded that, to a great extent, reading is one way in which literacy can make you smarter.

Stanovich and his colleagues have shown that the same basic principle applies to children. Echols, West, Stanovich, and Zehr (1996) asked fourth- through sixth-grade children to complete a book title recognition test, on which children had to select real titles of books they had read and avoid fake titles (which they could not have read). This assessment of print exposure was correlated with both standardized assessments of vocabulary and general knowledge base. The researchers found that the exposure-to-print measure in fourth grade predicted individual differences in the growth of both of these forms of crystallized intelligence over the next 2 years (not to mention growth in reading skills 2 years later). Cunningham and Stanovich (1998) later showed that exposure to print was a predictor of growth in vocabulary (as a crystallized intelligence measure) as much as 10 years later, above and beyond the reading and vocabulary skills children already displayed in early elementary school.

On the low end of the print-exposure spectrum are individuals with dyslexia who have difficulty in learning to read, and who, we can assume generally often avoid reading when possible. Correspondingly, research has shown that children with dyslexia tend to show a pattern of decreasing IQ as they get older (Shaywitz et al., 1995), although not all children with dyslexia show this decrease. For children with dyslexia who manage to learn to read reasonably well (we can assume through dint of effort and practice), there is a pattern of IQ growth in childhood, as compared to children with dyslexia who remain persistently poor readers throughout childhood (Ferrer, Shaywitz, Holahan, Marchione, & Shaywitz, 2009).

Print exposure has neurological impacts as well. Goldman and Manis (2013) examined the cortical thickness of areas related to reading in adults reporting varying degrees of exposure to print. Gray matter thickening might be expected to occur over in the developing brain as readers form new connections between neurons and the axons that lie within the brain areas used during reading myelinate: the occipital–temporal junction, which includes the visual word form area on the fisiform gyrus; the inferior frontal gyrus/Broca's area; the superior temporal gyrus/Wernicke's area; the angular gyrus; and the supramarginal gyrus. Presumably exposure to print provides a cumulative impact on cortical thickness. The researchers found that print exposure was the most consistent correlate of cortical thickness in these reading areas of the brain. Print exposure was even more sensitive to accounting for cortical thickness than standardized assessments such as reading comprehension or sight word reading.

Simply learning to read has impacts on our brains, too, as we have noted throughout this book. Evidence of this impact can be found in neurological changes that occur in the brains of formerly illiterate adults who learn to read late. Dehaene et al. (2010) compared currently illiterate adults with formerly illiterate adults who had learned to read as adults. They found that the establishment of literacy in adulthood increased the visual word form area response to orthographic patterns, which is probably not surprising. Learning to read caused a reorganization of visual cortical networks to develop subareas that now showed enhanced responsiveness to print. Further, formerly illiterate adults engaged a broader network within the brain as they read. Learning to read in adulthood permitted the entire spoken language network in the left hemisphere to become engaged by the process of reading print.

Reading a lot may produce a kind of cognitive reserve that is protective for the brain. Such a cognitive reserve may help to forestall the onset of cognitive decline with age. Limited literacy has been associated with increased risk of dementia among older adults (>70 years). In fact, low literacy has been found to be more predictive of earlier Alzheimer's disease onset than is education level (Kaup et al., 2013).

You might be curious as to whether exposure to print on the Internet has cognitive benefits similar to the ones we have described here. It probably does. Jackson et al. (2006) provided home Internet access and computers to children who did not previously have them. Children demonstrated an improvement in achievement within 16 months of going online. The Internet is text heavy, so it is likely that print exposure had a lot to do with this improvement. Leu et al. (2007) point out that online reading may enhance skills that we associate with high intelligence, such as reading critically, as well as locating and synthesizing information across documents. Children read to answer the questions that they have and to promote their curiosity.

The combined message of all of this research is that reading has a positive impact on intelligence and general cognitive functioning. This impact is true for children, as well as both young and older adults. Those who read a lot of text continue to grow in intelligence, whereas those who do not either stagnate or decline.

SOCIAL–EMOTIONAL BENEFITS OF LITERACY

There are numerous social–emotional benefits of literacy. Most of us appear to know this intuitively. For example, many of us use reading as a way of distracting ourselves or relaxing after a hard and stressful day. We may read for a few minutes before trying to go to sleep. Surprisingly, there is little research regarding the effectiveness of reading for producing a sense of relaxation and general stress reduction. A relatively small study by Jin (1992), however, suggests that there is some efficacy to this practice. After inducing stress in participants experimentally, Jin examined the effects of tai chi, brisk walking, meditation, or reading for an hour to recover from the effects of stress. After these treatments, including reading, salivary corti-sol levels had dropped significantly in these adults. Cortisol is a hormone produced by the adrenal cortex; psychological stress results in elevated levels. Lowered cor-tisol levels can be interpreted as an objective sign that participants have relaxed. Further, participants reported that their mood had also improved. Thus, the four treatments, including reading, were effective in reducing mood disturbance caused by mental and/or emotional stressors. We can tentatively say that there is some evidence for the view that reading has the personal benefit of improving our gen-eral state of mind at the end of a long hard day.

Among the social–emotional benefits of reading is the growth in social–cognitive skills that the individual derives from reading. Empathy is one of these skills that has been most studied with regard to reading. *Empathy* occurs when we experience the understanding of another person's condition from his or her, rather than our own, perspective. Empathy is a key cognitive skill that helps us to navi-gate the complexities of social relationships so that we can better maintain them (Saxe, Carey, & Kanwisher, 2004). Empathy allows us to attend to and perhaps deal more sensitively with the emotional states of others.

Reading fiction, in particular, has been linked with increased empathy. Because we often experience emotions in response to the circumstances of fic-tional characters, it has been hypothesized that reading fiction allows us to men-tally simulate, manipulate, and perhaps improve our social understanding of the emotional states of others in a way that translates into our own lives. In a related series of studies, Mar, Oatley, Hirsh, dela Paz, and Peterson (2006) have shown that adults who read a lot of fiction perform better on objective tests of empathy than nonreaders. In fact, this finding of increased empathy could not be attributed to simply reading a lot, because adults who are frequent readers of informational text do not display the same benefits. High informational text readers may actu-ally perform worse relative to nonreaders (although this effect varies from study to study; Mar, Oatley, & Peterson, 2009)!

To determine the potential benefits of reading fiction, Mar and his colleagues asked adults to complete a print-exposure assessment modeled after the one devel-oped by West, Stanovich, and Mitchell (1993), described previously, but they distin-guished the reading of fictional from informational reading. Adults also completed a test of empathy wherein they selected the mental state verb that best represented the emotions being depicted by actors acting out various emotions (Baron-Cohen, Wheelwright, Hill, Raste, & Plumb, 2001). This type of test has been shown to dis-tinguish the empathy skills of typical adults from adults known to have difficulties in empathy, such as adults with autism and those with Alzheimer's. Mar et al. (2009) found that adults who had read a lot fiction showed significantly higher empathy scores, even after various personality and intelligence traits were factored out.

Literary fiction may be more important to producing this effect than popular fiction, that is, action/thrillers, romance novels, and the like. Literary fiction is different because it has an increased capacity to challenge readers' thinking and expectations. It is more likely to provoke readers to search for meaning and understanding, thereby promoting cognitive and emotional growth. Kidd and Castano (2013) carried out a series of experiments in which adults were given different types of texts to read: literary fiction, popular fiction, or nonfiction. Then they were examined on tests of empathy to determine the immediate effects that this reading had on their understanding of empathy. Readers of literary fiction showed enhanced performance on several objective measures of empathy than readers of popular fiction or nonfiction did.

What is interesting about this series of studies is that the improvements in empathy caused by the experience of reading literary fiction were induced experimentally. That is, the improvements on measures of empathy could not be attributed to a priori differences among individuals in their preferences for one particular genre over another. It appears that if one wishes to enhance empathy among particular groups of individuals, employing literary fiction in interventions might be a strategy that we can take. Indeed, Shapiro, Morrison, and Boker (2004) successfully used the reading of drama, fiction, and poetry related to illness to improve empathy in first-year medical students, at least in the short term.

Similarly, improvements have been found in children's empathy following an intervention designed to increase empathy and social understanding through literature. Lysaker, Tonge, Gauson, and Miller (2011) used what they called *relationally oriented reading instruction* to promote second- and third-grade children's ability to infer and imagine the thoughts and feelings of others. The children, who were chosen because they were experiencing difficulties with social relationships, were provided with books depicting adults or children who were working through social–emotional problems. Teachers engaged the children in discussions related to the thoughts, feelings, intentions, and emotions of the book characters. The teacher expressed empathy for the characters and modeled her thinking about how she inferred the characters' feelings. The children were asked to do the same, and they wrote a reader response to the books. After 8 weeks of intervention, children displayed a significant improvement on objective measures of empathy.

Although both the Shapiro et al. (2004) and the Lysaker et al. (2011) studies found improvements in empathy after a literature intervention, the effects were examined only in a short-term way. It seems likely that prolonged exposure to literary fiction may eventually produce a more permanent effect on levels of empathy. However, the effects of reading fiction on the development of a permanent increase in empathy over the long haul has to be demonstrated. Studies by Mar and colleagues are promising in this respect.

Another social–emotional benefit of literacy is the improvements in *self-esteem* and *self-efficacy* that adults accrue from merely learning to read. This type

TABLE 11.2. Examples of Self-Concept and Self-Efficacy Rating Items to Evaluate Changes as a Function of Participation in an Adult Basic Literacy Education Program

Self-concept (0—not at all; 1—somewhat; 2—very much)	Self-efficacy (0—never; 1—sometimes; 2—all the time)
How good are you as a housewife?	Have you ever shopped in a supermarket by yourself?
How smart do you find yourself?	Have you ever taken a bus by yourself?
How skillful do you find yourself?	Have you ever done a transaction in a bank by yourself?
How successful do you find yourself?	Have you ever paid bills by yourself?
How pleased are you with yourself?	Have you ever crossed the bridge (to the other side of the city) by yourself?

Note. Based on Kagitcibasi, Goksen, and Gülgöz (2005).

of benefit has been studied by researchers engaged in providing basic adult literacy education internationally to adults who were not able to attend school or who did not learn to read well enough to become functionally literate during the short period that they did attend school (Burchfield, Hua, Baral, & Rocha, 2002; Kagitcibasi, Goksen, & Gulgoz, 2005). For example, Kagitcibasi et al. (2005) found that women attending such programs showed stronger self-concept and self-efficacy after completing one of these programs lasting four months. Table 11.2 presents examples of questions measuring self-concept and self-efficacy used in the study. Note that none of these relate to literacy specifically, so changes in the way that participants rate self-concept and self-efficacy could be viewed as general changes in benefits that adults receive after participation in these programs.

SOCIETAL BENEFITS OF LITERACY

Literacy is now so ubiquitous that we no longer really consider its effects on thought, our understandings of the world, our societal organization, and our activities as citizens. There have been major *historical changes* that have been attributed to literacy. Historians have theorized about the effects that literacy has had on the progress of human societies as literacy became more commonplace and texts more widely available. They have generally concluded that literacy's effects on human societies have been nothing less than revolutionary. Marshall McLuhan (1963), for example, suggested that the advent of widespread literacy was responsible for ushering in *modernity* as we currently know it.

According to Olson (1986), as more people became literate, they began to use written documents in their reasoning about a host of topics in preference to relying on oral communication. Essentially, literacy prioritized the written word over oral transmission of information. Texts began to be seen as given and objective, whereas interpretations began to be seen as subjective and personal. Without text and literacy, the distinction between the message and its interpretation was not obvious.

According to historians such as Innis (1951; cf. Olson, 1986), this distinction underlying written and oral communication was responsible for instigating historical changes in the practice of science, which now relied on written evidence. It produced written codification of law for resolving legal matters. It produced religious changes such as the Reformation. It essentially established a common ground of information on which to base attitudes and values. With literacy, debates could now be had about what was written in texts and what those texts really meant. It allowed scientists, for example, to distinguish facts from hypotheses; it enabled our legal system to distinguish the written law from our interpretations of it. Olson (1986) points out that the distinction between what a text says and what it means is an important developmental milestone. It is one that children come to understand as they acquire literacy. Historically, we have gone through the same change.

Not all societies have benefited from literacy to the same extent. UNESCO reports that 15.7% of the world's adults were illiterate in 2014, with the greatest concentration of illiterate adults being in South and West Asia, and Sub-Saharan Africa. Nearly two-thirds of illiterate people are women. In West Africa, illiteracy may actually be increasing (UNESCO, 2014a). Social and societal changes have been documented by various studies investigating changes that occur in adults when they learn to read through basic literacy education programming. These changes exist at many levels, including political, health-related, and economic.

Participation in adult basic literacy education programs has been connected with a host of benefits in the political sphere (Stromquist, 2008). For example, women participating in these programs have shown increased participation in elections, growth in political knowledge, and engagement in community activities (Boggs, Buss, & Yarnell, 1979; Burchfield et al., 2002; Kagitcibasi et al., 2005). They are more likely to vote, to know the names of their local their representatives, and to consider themselves eligible for political participation. They are more aware of their rights as citizens and show greater participation in local community organizations. These findings are rather consistent regardless of the global political context in which the studies have taken place (e.g., Turkey, Nepal, Bolivia, United States). Thus, becoming literate is a very powerful force for encouraging women to access their rights as citizens.

When mothers attain basic literacy through adult basic literacy programs, their children benefit. Specifically, attaining basic literacy increases participation in their children's schooling. Even though both literate and nonliterate mothers appreciate the value of schooling, literate mothers seem to feel empowered by their newly acquired literacy to support their children in the educational arena. They are more likely to be involved in their children's schooling in supportive ways, such as meeting their children's teachers and discussing school progress with children (Burchfield et al., 2002). Carr-Hill et al. (2001) reported that literacy class participants were nearly twice as likely to discuss schoolwork and check homework compared to mothers who had not participated in a literacy class.

Research suggests that learning to read may have a significant impact on *health behavior*. In particular, participation in adult basic literacy education directed at women has resulted in women's changed health behavior, even when health behavior is not a direct target of the literacy program. For example, Burchfield et al. (2002) found that women who attended basic literacy education programs were more likely to seek medical attention and seek immunization for themselves and their families, and know more about family planning than those who had not attended such programs. It should be pointed out here that women who go to basic literacy classes are probably getting a host of advantages beyond literacy that might account for the vast personal benefits that they enjoy.

Literacy is intricately linked to *economic growth*. Obtaining very basic skills such as those offered by most adult basic literacy education programs may not be enough to produce noticeable changes in economic status, although it probably helps. There may be cultural reasons limiting the impact of such programs on family income, particularly for women whose husbands may not permit them to participate in the workplace (Kagitcibasi et al., 2005). However, it has been observed that literacy matters for farmers in Mozambique who are considerately more likely to grow cash crops when they are literate than when they are not (UNESCO, 2014).

Across societies there is no simple and direct relationship between literacy and economic growth. For example, Coulombe, Tremblay, and Marchand (2004), using data from the International Adult Literacy Survey (IALS), found that differences on average of literacy skill levels among OECD countries explained 55% of the differences in economic growth between 1960 and 1994. However, Sachs and Warner (2001) found an S-shaped relationship between economic growth and literacy skills, with maximum effect of increased literacy occurring when literacy rates were neither very high nor very low. Thus, regions with very high or very low literacy rates do not benefit from small increases in literacy skills, but economically developing countries do.

CONCLUSION

By no means should the reader of this chapter assume that we have outlined all the potential benefits of reading and learning to read. However, we have described some of the research demonstrating that learning to read has a host of fundamental benefits for both the individuals and the societies in which they live.

As individuals, readers simply accrue more knowledge. They simply know more. Over time, they expand their intellect and improve their brains. This improvement lasts well into old age. Adults who read experience reductions in stress and increased empathy, self-esteem, and self-efficacy, which most likely have an impact on their social relationships and general happiness.

Societies who develop literacy also change. As a whole, their cultures come to understand the distinction between facts and interpretations and organize their institutions around this idea. Adults who learn to read show increased civic participation and more informed health behavior, which benefits their communities and countries. Countries whose leaders focus on literacy as a goal are rewarded with enhanced economic growth.

As we can see, the psychological and social benefits of literacy and learning to read are many. The importance of fostering a love of reading simply cannot be overstated.

QUESTIONS FOR DISCUSSION

1. Is the decline in time spent reading books for pleasure important now that people read on the Internet? What impact might the switch to primarily reading from the Internet have on the cognitive benefits that individuals derive from reading over a lifetime?

2. Research shows that increased empathy is one benefit that individuals derive from reading fiction. What other benefits might we look for?

3. Research suggests that individuals who read informational text primarily might not be as empathetic as those who read fiction. What social or cognitive benefits might we look for among those who read informational text primarily?

4. Consider the case study of Beverly presented at the beginning of this chapter. What have we learned in this chapter that might help to account for the outcome of Beverly's long association with being an avid reader?

FURTHER READINGS

Burchfield, S., Hua, H., Iturry, T., & Rocha, V. (2002). A longitudinal study of the effect of integrated literacy and basic education programs on the participation of women in social and economic development in Bolivia. USAID, Office of Women in Development. *http://datatopics.worldbank.org/hnp/files/edstats/BOLdprep02.pdf.*

Stanovich, K. E., West, R. F., & Harrison, M. R. (1995). Knowledge growth and maintenance across the life span: The role of print exposure. *Developmental Psychology, 31*(5), 811.

References

Acheson, D. J., Wells, J. B., & MacDonald, M. C. (2008). New and updated tests of print exposure and reading abilities in college students. *Behavior Research Methods, 40*(1), 278–289.

Achterman, D. (2009). A new California study: School libraries give students a better chance at success. *CSLA Journal, 33*(1), 26–27.

Adams, M. J. (1990). *Beginning to read: Thinking and learning about print.* Cambridge, MA: MIT Press.

Adams, M. J. (2010–2011, Winter). Advancing our students' language and literacy: The challenge of complex texts. *American Educator,* 3–11.

Adams, M. J., & Collins, A. (1977). *A schema–theoretic view of reading* (Technical Report No. 32). Champaign University of Illinois at Urbana–Champaign, Center for the Study of Reading.

Adams, M. J., Foorman, B. R., Lundberg, I., & Beeler, T. (1998). *Phonemic awareness in young children: A classroom curriculum.* Baltimore, MD: Brookes.

Adolf, S. M., Catts, H. W., & Little, T. D. (2006). Should the simple view of reading include a fluency component? *Reading and Writing, 19,* 933–958.

Adorni, R., Manfredi, M., & Proverbio, A. M. (2013). Since when or how often?: Dissociating the roles of age of acquisition (AoA) and lexical frequency in early visual word processing. *Brain and Language, 124,* 132–141.

Adrián, J. E., Clemente, R. A., & Villanueva, L. (2007). Mothers' use of cognitive state verbs in picture-book reading and the development of children's understanding of mind: A longitudinal study. *Child Development, 78*(4), 1052–1067.

Afflerbach, P., Cho, B. Y., Kim, J. Y., Crassas, M. E., & Doyle, B. (2013). Reading: What else matters besides strategies and skills? *The Reading Teacher, 66*(6), 440–448.

Afflerbach, P., Pearson, P. D., & Paris, S. G. (2008). Clarifying differences between reading skills and reading strategies. *The Reading Teacher, 61*(5), 364–373.

Akhondi, M., Malayeri, F. A., & Samad, A. A. (2011). How to teach expository text structure to facilitate reading comprehension. *The Reading Teacher, 64*(5), 368–372.

Alexander, P. A. (2005). The path to competence: A lifespan developmental perspective on reading. *Journal of Literacy Research, 37*(4), 413.

Allbritton, D. (2004). Strategic production of predictive inferences during comprehension. *Discourse Processes, 38*(3), 309–322.

Allington, R. L. (1977). If they don't read much, how they ever gonna get good? *Journal of Reading, 21,* 57–61.

Allington, R. L. (2014). How reading volume affects both reading fluency and reading achievement. *International Electronic Journal of Elementary Education, 7*(1), 13–26.

Allington, R. L., & Cunningham, P. M. (2006). *Schools that work: Where all children read and write.* Boston: Allyn & Bacon.

Allington, R. L., & Johnston, P. H. (2000). *What do*

we know about effective fourth-grade teachers and their classrooms? Report Series 13010. Albany, NY: National Research Center on English Learning and Achievement.

Al Otaiba, S., & Petscher, Y., Pappamihiel, N. E., Williams, R. S., Dyrlund, A. K., & Connor, C. (2009). Modeling oral reading fluency and development in Latino students: A longitudinal study across second and third grade. *Journal of Educational Psychology, 101*(2), 315–329.

Altschul, A., Oyserman, D., & Bybee, D. (2006). Racial–ethnic identity in mid-adolescence: Content and change as predictors of academic achievement. *Child Development, 77*(5), 1155–1169.

Alvermann, D. E., Smith, L. C., & Readence, J. E. (1985). Prior knowledge activation and the comprehension of compatible and incompatible text. *Reading Research Quarterly, 20*(4), 420–436.

Amenta, S., & Crepaldi, D. (2012). Morphological processing as we know it: An analytical review of morphological effects in visual word identification. *Frontiers in Psychology, 3*, 1–12.

Ames, W. S. (1966). The development of a classification scheme of contextual aids. *Reading Research Quarterly, 2*, 57–82.

Anderson, J. R. (1983). A spreading activation theory of memory. *Journal of Verbal Learning and Verbal Behavior, 22*, 261–295.

Anderson, R. C. (1994). Role of the reader's schema in comprehension, learning, and memory. In R. B. Ruddell & H. Singer (Eds.), *Theoretical models and processes of reading* (pp. 469–482). Newark, DE: International Reading Association.

Anderson, R. C., & Freebody, P. (1981). Vocabulary knowledge. In J. T. Guthrie (Ed.), *Comprehension and teaching: Research reviews* (pp. 77–117). Newark, DE: International Reading Association.

Anderson, R. C., Hiebert, E. H., Scott, J. A., & Wilkinson, I. (1985). *Becoming a nation of readers*. Washington, DC: National Institute of Education.

Anderson, R. C., & Pearson, P. D. (1984). A schema–theoretic view of basic processes in reading comprehension. In P. D. Pearson, R. Barr, M. L. Kamil, & P. Mosenthal (Eds.), *Handbook of reading research* (pp. 255–291). New York: Longman.

Anderson, R. C., & Pichert, J. W. (1978). Recall of previously unrecallable information following a shift in perspective. *Journal of Verbal Learning and Verbal Behavior, 17*, 1–12.

Anderson, R. C., Reynolds, R. E., Schallert, D. L., & Goetz, E. T. (1977). Frameworks for comprehending discourse. *American Educational Research Journal, 14*(4), 367–381.

Anderson, R. C., Wilson, P. T., & Fielding, L. G. (1988). Growth in reading and how children spend their time outside of school. *Reading Research Quarterly, 23*, 285–303.

Andrus, M. R., & Roth, M. T. (2002). Health literacy: A review. *Pharmacotherapy: The Journal of Human Pharmacology and Drug Therapy, 22*(3), 282–302.

Anglin, J. M. (1993). Vocabulary development: A morphological analysis. *Monographs of the Society for Research in Child Development, 58*(10).

Anmarkrud, Ø., & Bråten, I. (2009). Motivation for reading comprehension. *Learning and Individual Differences, 19*(2), 252–256.

Anthony, J. L., & Lonigan, C. J. (2004). The nature of phonological awareness: Converging evidence from four studies of preschool and early grade school children. *Journal of Educational Psychology, 96*, 43–55.

Apel, K., & Diehm, M. S. (2014). Morphological awareness intervention with kindergarteners, first, and second grade students from low SES homes: A small efficacy study. *Journal of Learning Disabilities, 47*(1), 65–75.

Applebee, A. N., & Langer, J. A. (1983). Instructional scaffolding: Reading and writing as natural language activities. *Language Arts, 60*(2), 168–175.

Applegate, A. J., & Applegate, M. D. (2004). The Peter effect: Reading habits and attitudes of preservice teachers. *The Reading Teacher, 57*(6), 554–563.

Armbruster, B. B., Anderson, T. H., & Meyer, J. L. (1991). Improving content-area reading using instructional graphics. *Reading Research Quarterly, 26*(4), 393–416.

Armbruster, B. B., Osborn, J. H., & Davidson, A. L. (1985). Readability formulas may be dangerous to your textbooks. *Educational Leadership, 42*, 18–20.

Arnold, J. E. (1998). Reference form and discourse patterns. Doctoral dissertation, Stanford University, Stanford, CA.

Arnold, J. E., Brown-Schmidt, S., & Trueswell, J. (2007). Children's use of gender and order-of-mention during pronoun comprehension. *Language and Cognitive Processes, 22*(4), 527–565.

Arnold, J. E., Eisenband, J. G., Brown-Schmidt, S., & Trueswell, J. C. (2000). The rapid use of gender information: Evidence of the time course of pronoun resolution from eye tracking. *Cognition, 76*, B13–B26.

Aro, M., & Wimmer, H. (2003). Learning to read: English in comparison to six more regular orthographies. *Applied Psycholinguistics, 24*(4), 621–635.

Asselin, M. (2004). Supporting sustained engagements with texts. *Teacher Librarian, 31*(3), 51–52.

Astington, J. W., & Olson, D. R. (1990). Metacognitive and metalinguistic language: Learning to talk about thought. *Applied Psychology: An International Review, 39*, 71–87.

Atkinson, J. W. (1964). *An introduction to motivation.* Princeton, NJ: Van Nostrand.

Atkinson, R. C., & Shiffrin, R. M. (1968). Human memory: A proposed system and its control processes. In K. W. Spence & J. T. Spence (Eds.), *The psychology of learning and motivation* (Vol. 2, pp. 89–195). London: Academic Press.

Atwell, N. (2007). *The reading zone: How to help kids become skilled, passionate, habitual, critical readers.* New York: Scholastic.

Au, K. H. P. (1980). Participation structures in a reading lesson with Hawaiian children: Analysis of a culturally appropriate instructional event. *Anthropology and Education Quarterly, 11*(2), 91–115.

Ausabel, D. P. (1978). In defense of advance organizers: A reply to the critics. *Review of Educational Research, 48*, 251–257.

Baddeley, A. D., Thomson, N., & Buchanan, M. (1975). Word length and the structure of short-term memory. *Journal of Verbal Learning and Verbal Behavior, 14*(6), 575–589.

Baird, G. L., Scott, W. D., Dearing, E., & Hamill, S. K. (2009). Cognitive self-regulation in youth with and without learning disabilities: Academic self-efficacy, theories of intelligence, learning vs. performance goal preferences, and effort attributions. *Journal of Social and Clinical Psychology, 28*(7), 881–908.

Baker, L. (1984). Spontaneous versus instructed use of multiple standards for evaluating comprehension: Effects of age, reading proficiency and type of standard. *Journal of Experimental Child Psychology, 38*, 289–311.

Baker, L., Scher, D., & Mackler, K. (1997). Home and family influences on motivations for reading. *Educational Psychologist, 32*(2), 69–82.

Baker, L., & Wigfield, A. (1999). Dimensions of children's motivation for reading and their relations to reading activity and reading achievement. *Reading Research Quarterly, 34*(4), 452–477.

Balota, D. A., Yap, M. J., & Cortese, M. J. (2006). Visual word recognition: The journey from features to meaning (a travel update). In M. Traxler & M. A. Gernsbacher (Eds.), *Handbook of psycholinguistics* (2nd ed., pp. 285–375). London: Academic Press.

Bandura, A. (1994). Self-efficacy. In V. S. Ramachaudran (Ed.), *Encyclopedia of human behavior* (Vol. 4, pp. 71–81). New York: Academic Press.

Bar-Ilan, L., & Berman, R. A. (2007). Developing register differentiation: The Latinate–Germanic divide in English. *Linguistics, 45*(1), 1–35.

Barnes, M. A., Dennis, M., & Haefele-Kalvaitis, J. (1996). The effects of knowledge availability and knowledge accessibility on coherence and elaborative inferencing in children from six to fifteen years of age. *Journal of Experimental Child Psychology, 61*, 216–241.

Baron-Cohen, S., Wheelwright, S., Hill, J., Raste, J., & Plumb, I. (2001). The "Reading the Mind in the Eyes" test revised version: A study with normal adults, and adults with Asperger syndrome or high-functioning autism. *Journal of Child Psychology and Psychiatry, 42*, 241–251.

Baumann, J. F., Edwards, E. C., Boland, E. M., Olejnik, S., & Kame'enui, E. J. (2003). Vocabulary tricks: Effects of instruction in morphology and context on fifth-grade students' ability to derive and infer word meanings. *American Educational Research Journal, 40*(2), 447–494.

Beals, D., & Tabors, P. O. (1995). Arboretum, bureaucratic, and carbohydrates: Preschoolers' exposure to rare vocabulary at home. *First Language, 15*, 57–76.

Beaver, W. (1996). Is it time to replace the SAT? *Academe, 82*(3), 37–39.

Beck, I. L., & McKeown, M. G. (1981). Developing questions that promote comprehension: The story map. *Language Arts, 58*, 913–918.

Beck, I. L., & McKeown, M. (1990). Conditions of vocabulary acquisition. In R. Barr, M. L. Kamil, P. B. Mosenthal, & P. D. Pearson, (Eds.), *Handbook of reading research* (Vol. 2, pp.789–814). New York: Longman.

Beck, I. L., & McKeown, M. G. (2001). Inviting students into the pursuit of meaning. *Educational Psychology Review, 13*(3), 225–241.

Beck, I. L., McKeown, M. G., & McCaslin, E. S. (1983). Vocabulary development: All contexts are not created equal. *The Elementary School Journal, 83*(3), 177–181.

Beck, I. L., McKeown, M. G., Sandora, C., Kucan, L., & Worthy, J. (1996). Questioning the author: A yearlong classroom implementation to engage students with text. *Elementary School Journal, 96*(4), 385–414.

Beck, I. L., McKeown, M. G., Sinatra, G. M., & Loxterman, J. A. (1991). Revising social studies text from a text-processing perspective: Evidence of improved comprehensibility. *Reading Research Quarterly, 26*(3), 251–276.

Becker, M., McElvany, N., & Kortenbruck, M. (2010). Intrinsic and extrinsic reading motivation as predictors of reading literacy: A longitudinal study. *Journal of Educational Psychology, 102*(4), 773.

Bedard J., & Chi, M. T. H. (1992). Expertise. *Current Directions in Psychological Science, 1*, 135–139.

Ben-Ishai, L., Matthews, H., & Levin-Epstein, J. (2014). *Scrambling for stability: The challenges of job schedule volatility and child care.* Washington, DC: Center for Law and Social Policy.

Benjamin, R. G., & Schwanenflugel, P. J. (2010). Text complexity and oral reading prosody in young readers. *Reading Research Quarterly, 45*(4), 388–404.

Benjamin, R. G., Schwanenflugel, P. J., Meisinger, E. B., Groff, C., Kuhn, M. R., & Steiner, L. (2013). A spectrographically grounded scale for evaluating reading expressiveness. *Reading Research Quarterly, 48*(2), 105–133.

Bergen, L., Grimes, T., & Potter, D. (2005). How attention partitions itself during simultaneous message presentations. *Human Communication Research, 31*, 311–336.

Berkeley, S., Mastropieri, M. A., & Scruggs, T. E. (2011). Reading comprehension strategy instruction and attribution retraining for secondary students with learning and other mild disabilities. *Journal of Learning Disabilities, 44*(1), 18–32.

Berl, M. M., Duke, E. S., Mayo, J., Rosenberger, L. R., Moore, E. N., VanMeter, J., et al. (2010). Functional anatomy of listening and reading comprehension during development. *Brain and Language, 114*(2), 115–125.

Berlin, B., Breedlove, D. E., & Raven, P. H. (1973). General principles of classification and nomenclature in folk biology. *American Anthropologist, 75*(1), 214–242.

Berliner, D. C. (1992). Telling the stories of educational psychology. *Educational Psychologist, 27*(2), 13–161.

Berndt, R. S., Reggia, J. A., & Mitchum, C. C. (1987). Empirically derived probabilities for grapheme-to-phoneme correspondences in English. *Behavior Research Methods, Instrumentation, and Computers, 19*, 1–9.

Berninger, V., Nagy, W., Carlisle, J., Thomson, J., Hoffer, D., Abbott, S., et al. (2003). Effective treatment for dyslexics in grades 4 to 6. In B. Foorman (Ed.), *Preventing and remediating reading difficulties: Bringing science to scale* (pp. 382–417). Timonium, MD: York Press.

Berns, G. S., Blaine, K., Prietula, M. J., & Pye, B. E. (2013). Short-and long-term effects of a novel on connectivity in the brain. *Brain Connectivity, 3*(6), 590–600.

Berridge, G., & Goebel, V. (2013). Examining the effectiveness of the accelerated reader program in college students enrolled in a teacher education program. *International Research in Education, 1*(1), 116–128.

Besner, D. (1990). Does the reading system need a lexicon? In D. A. Balota, G. B. Flores d'Arcaise, & K. Rayner (Eds.), *Comprehension processes in reading* (pp. 73–99). Hillsdale, NJ: Erlbaum.

Best, R., Floyd, R. G., & McNamara, D. S. (2004, April). *Understanding the fourth-grade slump: Comprehension difficulties as a function of reader aptitudes and text genre.* Paper presented at 85th annual meeting of the American Educational Research Association, Newport Beach, CA.

Bialystok, E. (2007). Acquisition of literacy in bilingual children: A framework for research. *Language Learning, 57*, 45–77.

Bialystok, E., Luk, G., & Kwan, E. (2005). Bilingualism, biliteracy, and learning to read: Interactions among languages and writing systems. *Scientific Studies of Reading, 9*, 43–61.

Biemiller, A. (2003). Vocabulary: Needed if more children are to read well. *Reading Psychology, 24*, 323–335.

Biemiller, A., & Slonim, N. (2001). Estimating root word vocabulary growth in normative and advantaged populations: Evidence for a common sequence of vocabulary acquisition. *Journal of Educational Psychology, 93*(3), 498–520.

Binder, K. S., Tighe, E., Jiang, Y., Kaftanski, K., Qi, C., & Ardoin, S. P. (2013). Reading expressively and understanding thoroughly: An examination of prosody in adults with low literacy skills. *Reading and Writing, 26*(5), 665–680.

Blair, R., & Savage, R. (2006). Name writing but not environmental print recognition is related to letter–sound knowledge and phonological awareness in pre-readers. *Reading and Writing, 19*(9), 991–1016.

Bleasdale, F. A. (1987). Concreteness dependent associative priming: Separate lexical organization for concrete and abstract words. *Journal of Experimental Psychology: Learning, Memory, and Cognition, 13*, 582–594.

Blunsdon, B., Reed, K., & McNeil, N. (2003). Experiential learning in social science theory: An investigation of the relationship between student enjoyment and learning. *Journal of Further and Higher Education, 27*(1), 3–14.

Boggs, D., Buss, F., & Yarnell, S. (1979). Adult basic education in Ohio: Program impact evaluation. *Adult Education, 29*(2), 123–140.

Bookheimer, S. (2002). Functional MRI of language: New approaches to understanding the cortical organization of semantic processing. *Annual Review of Neuroscience, 25*(1), 151–188.

Bovair, S., & Kieras, D. (1985). A guide to propositional analysis for research on technical prose. In B. K. Britton & J. B. Black (Eds.), *Understanding expository text* (pp. 315–362). Hillsdale, NJ: Erlbaum.

Bowers, P. N., Kirby, J. R., & Deacon, S. H. (2010). The effects of morphological instruction on literacy skills: A systematic review of the literature. *Review of Educational Research, 80*(2), 144–179.

Bracken, S. S. (2005). Oral language and reading: Reply to Bracken. *Developmental Psychology, 41*(6), 1000–1002.

Bradley, B. A., & Jones, J. (2007). Sharing alphabet books in early childhood classrooms. *The Reading Teacher, 60*(5), 452–463.

Bradley, L., & Bryant, P. E. (1983). Categorizing sounds and learning to read: A causal connection. *Nature, 301,* 419–521.

Bradley, R. H. (1994). The HOME inventory: Review and reflections. In H. W. Ree (Ed.), *Advances in child development and behavior* (Vol. 25, pp. 241–288). San Diego, CA: Academic Press.

Bradley, R. H., Caldwell, B. M., Rock, S. L., & Harris, P. T. (1986). Early home environment and the development of competence: Findings from the Little Rock longitudinal study. *Children's Environments Quarterly, 3*(1), 10–22.

Brainerd, C. J., & Reyna, V. F. (1990). Gist is the grist: Fuzzy trace theory and the new intuitionism. *Developmental Review, 10*(1), 3–47.

Bransford, J. D., & Johnson, M. K. (1972). Contextual prerequisites for understanding: Some investigations of comprehension and recall. *Journal of Verbal Learning and Verbal Behavior, 11*(6), 717–726.

Branum-Martin, L., Tao, S., Garnaat, S., Bunta, F., & Francis, D. J. (2012). Meta-analysis of bilingual phonological awareness: Language, age, and psycholinguistic grain size. *Journal of Educational Psychology, 104*(4), 932.

Brasseur-Hock, I. F., Hock, M. F., Kieffer, M. J., Biancarosa, G., & Deshler, D. D. (2011). Adolescent struggling readers in urban schools: Results of a latent class analysis. *Learning and Individual Differences, 21,* 438–452.

Braunger, J., & Lewis, J. P. (1998). *Building a knowledge base in reading.* Newark, DE: International Reading Association.

Bredekamp, S., & Copple, C. (1997). *Developmentally appropriate practice in early childhood programs* (rev. ed.). Washington, DC: National Association for the Education of Young Children.

Brem, S., Bach, S., Kucian, K., Guttorm, T. K., Martin, E., Lyytinen, H., et al. (2010). Brain sensitivity to print emerges when children learn letter–speech sound correspondences. *Proceedings of the National Academy of Sciences, 107* (17), 7939–7944.

Brenner, D., Hiebert, E. H., & Tompkins, R. (2009). How much and what are third graders reading? In E. H. Hiebert (Ed.), *Reading more, reading better* (pp. 118–140). New York: Guilford Press.

Bridwell, N. (1988). *Clifford's birthday party.* New York: Scholastic.

Bright, W. (1997). A language is a dialect with an Army and a Navy. *Language in Society, 26*(3), 469.

Britton, B. K., & Gülgöz, S. (1991). Using Kintsch's computational model to improve instructional text: Effects of repairing inference calls on recall and cognitive structures. *Journal of Educational Psychology, 83*(3), 329.

Brooks, R., & Meltzoff, A. N. (2008). Infant gaze following and pointing predict accelerated vocabulary growth through two years of age: A longitudinal, growth curve modeling study. *Journal of Child Language, 35*(1), 207–220.

Brooks, W., & McNair, J. C. (2009). "But this story of mine is not unique": A review of research on African American children's literature. *Review of Educational Research, 79*(1), 125–162.

Brooks-Gunn, J., & Duncan, G. J. (1997). The effects of poverty on children. *The Future of Children, 7*(2), 55–71.

Brown, A. L., Campione, J. C., & Barclay, C. R. (1979). Training self-checking routines for estimating test readiness: Generalization from list learning to prose recall. *Child Development, 30,* 501–512.

Brown, A. L., Day, J. D., & Jones, R. S. (1983). The development of plans for summarizing texts. *Child Development, 54*(4), 968–979.

Brown, B. A., Ryoo, K., & Rodriguez, J. (2010). Pathway towards fluency: Using "disaggregate instruction" to promote science literacy. *International Journal of Science Education, 32*(11), 1465–1493.

Brown, C., Snodgrass, T., Kemper, S. J., Herman, R., & Covington, M. A. (2008). Automatic measurement of propositional idea density from part-of-speech tagging. *Behavior Research Methods, 40*(2), 540–545.

Brown, R. (1957). Linguistic determinism and the part of speech. *Journal of Abnormal and Social Psychology, 55,* 1–5.

Brown, R. (1973). *A first language: The early stages.* Cambridge, MA: Harvard University Press.

Brown, R. (2008). The road not yet taken: A transactional strategies approach to comprehension instruction. *The Reading Teacher, 61*(7), 538–547.

Bryan, G., Fawson, P. C., & Reutzel, D. R. (2003). Sustained silent reading: Exploring the value of literature discussion with three non-engaged readers. *Reading Research and Instruction, 43*(1), 47–73.

Brysbaert, M., Buchmeier, M., Conrad, M., Jacobs, A. M., Bölte, J., & Böhl, A. (2011). The word frequency effect: A review of recent developments and implications for the choice of frequency estimates in German. *Experimental Psychology, 58*(5), 412–424.

Brysbaert, M., & New, B. (2009). Moving beyond Kucera and Francis: A critical evaluation of current word frequency norms and the introduction of a new and improved word frequency measure for American English. *Behavior Research Methods, Instruments, and Computers, 30*, 272–277.

Buchweitz, A., Mason, R. A., Tomitch, L. M. B., & Just, M. A. (2009). Brain activation for reading and listening comprehension: An fMRI study of modality effects and individual differences in language comprehension. *Psychology and Neuroscience, 2*(2), 111–123.

Buck, G., Tatsuoka, K., & Kostin, I. (1997). The subskills of reading: Rule-space analysis of a multiple-choice test of second language reading comprehension. *Language Learning, 47*(3), 423–466.

Buehl, D. (2000). *Classroom strategies for interactive learning.* Newark, DE: International Reading Association.

Burani, C., Marcolini, S., De Luca, M., & Zoccolotti, P. (2008). Morpheme-based reading aloud: Evidence from dyslexic and skilled Italian readers. *Cognition, 108*(1), 243–262.

Burchfield, S. H., Hua, H., Baral, D., & Rocha, V. (2002). A longitudinal study of the effect of integrated literacy and basic education programs on women's participation in social and economic development in Nepal. Washington, DC: Office for Women in Development, Agency for International Development. Retrieved from *http:// datatopics.worldbank.org/hnp/files/edstats/BOLd-prep02.pdf.*

Burchfield, S. H., Hua, H., Iturry, T., & Rocha, V. (2002). A longitudinal study of the effect of integrated literacy and basic education programs on the participation of women in social and economic development in Bolivia. USAID, Office of Women in Development. Retrieved from *http:// datatopics.worldbank.org/hnp/files/edstats/BOLd-prep02.pdf.*

Burgess, S. R., Hecht, S. A., & Lonigan, C. J. (2002). Relations of the home literacy environment (HLE) to the development of reading related abilities: A one-year longitudinal study. *Reading Research Quarterly, 37*(4), 408–426.

Burgess, T. W. (1920). *Mrs. Peter Rabbit.* Boston: Little, Brown & Co.

Burgess, C., & Simpson, G. B. (1988). Neuropsychology of lexical ambiguity resolution: The contribution of divided visual field studies.. In G. Adriaens, S. L. Small, G. W. Cottrell, & M. K. Tanenhaus (Eds.), *Lexical ambiguity resolution: Perspectives from psycholinguistics, neuropsychology, and artificial intelligence* (pp. 411–430). San Mateo, CA: Morgan Kaufmann Publishers.

Bus, A. G., & van IJzendoorn, M. H. (1995). Mothers reading to their 3-year-olds: The role of mother–child attachment security in becoming literate. *Reading Research Quarterly, 30*(4), 998–1015.

Bus, A. G., van IJzendoorn, M. H., & Pellegrini, A. D. (1995). Joint book reading makes for success in learning to read: A meta-analysis on intergenerational transmission of literacy. *Review of Educational Research, 65*(1), 1–21.

Byrne, B., & Fielding-Barnsley, R. (1991). Evaluation of a program to teach phonemic awareness to young children. *Journal of Educational Psychology, 83*, 451–455.

Caccamise, D., & Snyder, L. (2005). Theory and pedagogical practices of text comprehension. *Topics in Language Disorders, 25*(1), 5–20.

Cain, K., & Oakhill, J. V. (1999). Inference making ability and its relation to comprehension failure in young children. *Reading and writing, 11*(5–6), 489–503.

Cain, K., & Oakhill, J. (2006). Assessment matters: Issues in the measurement of reading comprehension. *British Journal of Educational Psychology, 76*, 697–708.

Cain, K., Oakhill, J. V., Barnes, M. A., & Bryant, P. E. (2001). Comprehension skill, inference-making ability, and their relation to knowledge. *Memory and Cognition, 29*(6), 850–859.

Caldwell, B. M., & Bradley, R. H. (1984). *Home observation for measurement of the environment.* Little Rock: Center for Applied Studies in Education, University of Arkansas at Little Rock.

Caldwell, B. M., & Bradley, R. H. (2003). *Home inventory administration manual.* Tempe: Family & Human Dynamics Research Institute, University of Arizona.

Caldwell, B. M., Heider, J., & Kaplan, B. (1966, September). *The inventory of home stimulation.* Paper presented at the annual meeting of the American Psychological Association, New York.

Camilli, G., Wolfe, P. M., & Smith M. L. (2006). Meta-analysis and reading policy: Perspectives on teaching children to read. *Elementary School Journal, 107*, 27–36.

Campbell, J. M., Bell, S. K., & Keith, L. K. (2001). Concurrent validity of the Peabody Picture Vocabulary Test—Third Edition as an intelligence and achievement screener for low SES African American children. *Assessment, 8*(1), 85–94.

Campuzano, L., Dynarski, M., Agodini, R., & Rall, K. (2009). *Effectiveness of reading and mathematics software products: Findings from two student cohorts.* Washington, DC: Institute of Education Sciences.

Cappella, E., & Weinstein, R. S. (2001). Turning around reading achievement: Predictors of high school students' academic resilience. *Journal of Educational Psychology, 93*(4), 758.

Cardoso-Martins, C., Rodrigues, L. A., & Ehri, L. C. (2003). Place of environmental print in reading development: Evidence from nonliterate adults. *Scientific Studies of Reading, 7*(4), 335–355.

Carducci-Bolchazy, M. (1978). A survey of the use of reading readiness tests. *Reading Horizons, 18*(3), 209–212.

Carlisle, J. F., & Stone, C. A. (2005). Exploring the role of morphemes in word reading. *Reading Research Quarterly, 40*, 428–449.

Carlson, E., Jenkins, F., Li, T., & Brownell, M. (2013). The interactions of vocabulary, phonemic awareness, decoding, and reading comprehension. *Journal of Educational Research, 106*, 120–131.

Carlson, K., Dickey, M. W., Frazier, L., & Clifton, C. (2009). Information structure expectations in sentence comprehension. *Quarterly Journal of Experimental Psychology, 62*, 114–139.

Carreiras, M., Armstrong, B. C., Perea, M., & Frost, R. (2014). The what, when, where, and how of visual word recognition. *Trends in Cognitive Sciences, 18*(2), 90–98.

Carr-Hill, R., Okech, A., Katahoire, A., Kakooza, T., Ndidde, A., & Oxenham, J. (2001). *Adult literacy programs in Uganda.* Washington, DC: Human Development Africa Region, The World Bank.

Carroll, J. B., & White, M. N. (1973). Word frequency and age of acquisition as determiners of picture naming latency. *Quarterly Journal of Experimental Psychology, 12*, 85–95.

Carson, K. L., Gillon, G. T., & Boustead, T. M. (2013). Classroom phonological awareness instruction and literacy outcomes in the first year of school. *Language, Speech, and Hearing Services in the Schools, 44*, 147–160.

Carver, R. P. (2000). *The causes of high and low reading achievement.* Mahwah, NJ: Erlbaum.

Casenhiser, D. M. (2005). Children's resistance to homonymy: An experimental study of pseudohomonyms. *Journal of Child Language, 32*(2), 319–343.

Casner-Lotto, J., & Barrington, L. (2006). *Are they really ready to work?* Washington, DC: The Conference Board, Corporate Voices for Working Families, Partnership for 21st Century Skills and Society for 32 Human Resource Management.

Cassar, M., & Treiman, R. (1997). The beginnings of orthographic knowledge: Children's knowledge of double letters in words. *Journal of Educational Psychology, 89*, 631–644.

Casteel, C. P., Isom, B. A., & Jordan, K. F. (2000). Creating confident and competent readers: Transactional strategies instruction. *Intervention in School and Clinic, 36*(2), 67–74.

Castles, A., & Coltheart, M. (1996). Cognitive correlates of developmental surface dyslexia: A single case study. *Cognitive Neuropsychology, 13*, 25–50.

Castles, A., & Nation, K. (2006). How does orthographic learning happen? In S. Andrews (Ed.), *From inkmarks to ideas: Challenges and controversies about word recognition and reading* (pp. 151–179). London: Psychology Press.

Cattell, R. B. (1941). Some theoretical issues in adult intelligence testng. *Psychological Bulletin, 38*, 592.

Catts, H. W., Adlof, S. M., & Weismer, S. E. (2006). Language deficits in poor comprehenders: A case for the simple view of reading. *Journal of Speech, Language, and Hearing Research, 49*, 278–293.

Cervetti, G. N., Bravo, M. A., Hiebert, E. H., Pearson, P. D., & Jaynes, C. A. (2009). Text genre and science content: Ease of reading, comprehension, and reader preference. *Reading Psychology, 30*, 487–511.

Chafe, W. (1982). Integration and involvement in speaking, writing, and oral literature. In D. Tannen (Ed.), *Spoken and written language: Exploring orality and literacy* (Vol. 9, pp. 35–53). Norwood, NJ: Ablex.

Chafe, W., & Danielewicz, J. (1986). Properties of spoken and written language. In R. Horowitz & S. J. Samuels (Eds.), *Comprehending oral and written language* (pp. 81–113). New York: Academic Press.

Chafe, W., & Tannen, D. (1987). The relation between written and spoken language. *Annual Review of Anthropology, 16*, 383–407.

Chall, J. S. (1996). *Stages of reading development* (2nd ed.). Fort Worth, TX: Harcourt-Brace.

Chall, J. S., & Jacobs, V. A. (2003). The classic study on poor children's fourth grade slump. *American Educator, 27*(1), 14–15.

Chambliss, M. J., & McKillop, A. M. (2000). Creating a print- and technology-rich classroom library to entice children to read. In L. Baker, M. J. Dreher, & J. T. Guthrie (Eds.), *Engaging young readers* (pp. 94–118). New York: Guilford Press.

Chandler, K. (1999). Reading relationships: Parents, adolescents, and popular fiction by Stephen King. *Journal of Adolescent and Adult Literacy, 43*, 228–239.

Chapman, J. W., & Tunmer, W. E. (2003). Reading difficulties, reading-related self-perceptions, and strategies for overcoming negative self-beliefs. *Reading and Writing Quarterly, 19*(1), 5–24.

Chapman, J. W., Tunmer, W. E., & Prochnow, J. E. (2000). Early reading-related skills and performance, reading self-concept, and the development of academic self-concept: A longitudinal study. *Journal of Educational Psychology, 92*(4), 703.

Chard, D. J. (2011). 6 minutes of "eyes-on-text" can make a difference: Whole-class choral reading as an adolescent fluency strategy. *Reading Horizons, 51*(1), 1–20.

Chard, D. J., & Osborn, J. (1999). Phonics and word-recognition instruction in early reading programs: Guidelines for accessibility. *Learning Disabilities Research and Practice, 14*(2), 107–117.

Charity, A. H., Scarborough, H. S., & Griffin, D. M. (2004). Familiarity with school English in African American children and its relation to early reading achievement. *Child Development, 75*(5), 1340–1356.

Chase, C. H., & Tallal, P. (1990). A developmental, interactive activation model of the word superiority effect. *Journal of Experimental Child Psychology, 49*, 448–487.

Cheatham, J. P., & Allor, J. H. (2012). The influence of decodabilty in early reading text on reading achievement: A review of the evidence. *Reading and Writing, 25*, 2223–2246.

Chelton, M. K. (2003). Readers' advisory services 101. *Library Journal, 128*, 18.

Cheng, K. (2005). *Designing type.* New Haven, CT: Yale University Press.

Cherland, M. R. (1994). *Private practices: Girls reading fiction and constructing identity.* London: Taylor & Francis.

Cheung, A. C. K., & Slavin, R. E. (2012). How features of educational technology applications affect student reading outcomes: A meta-analysis. *Educational Research Review, 7*, 198–215.

Cheung, A. C. K., & Slavin, R. E. (2013). Effects of educational technology applications on reading outcomes for struggling readers: A best-evidence synthesis. *Reading Research Quarterly, 48*(3), 277–299.

Cheung, H., Chan, M., & Chong, K. (2007). Use of orthographic knowledge in reading by Chinese–English bi-scriptal children. *Language Learning, 57*(3), 469–505.

Chi, M. T. H., & Bassock, M. (1989). Learning from examples via self-explanations. In L. B. Resnick (Ed.), *Knowing, learning, and instruction: Essays in honor of Robert Glaser* (pp. 251–282). Hillsdale, NJ: Erlbaum.

Chiarello, C. (2003). Parallel systems for processing language: Hemispheric complementarity in the normal brain. In M. T. Banich & M. Mack (Eds.), *Mind, brain, and language: Multidisciplinary perspectives* (pp. 229–247). Hillsdale, NJ: Erlbaum.

Chiesi, H. L., Spilich, G. J., & Voss, J. F. (1979). Acquisition of domain-related information in relation to high and low domain knowledge. *Journal of Verbal Learning and Verbal Behavior, 18*, 257–273.

Chomsky, C. (1969). *The acquisition of syntax in children from 5 to 10.* Cambridge, MA: MIT Press.

Chomsky, N. (1959). A review of B. F. Skinner's *Verbal Behavior. Language, 35*(1), 26–58.

Choo, T. O. L., Eng, T. K., & Ahmad, N. (2011). Effects of reciprocal teaching strategies on reading comprehension. *Reading Matrix: An International Online Journal, 11*(2).

Cipielewski, J., & Stanovich, K. E. (1992). Predicting growth in reading ability from children's exposure to print. *Journal of Experimental Child Psychology, 54*(1), 74–89.

Clark, C., & De Zoysa, S. (2011). *Mapping the interrelationships of reading enjoyment, attitudes, behaviour and attainment: An exploratory investigation.* London: National Literacy Trust.

Clark, C., Osborne, S., & Akerman, R. (2008). *Young people's self-perception as readers.* London: National Literacy Trust.

Clark, E. V. (2007). Young children's uptake of new words in conversation. *Language in Society, 36*, 157–182.

Clark, E. V. (2010). Adult offer, word-class, and child uptake in early lexical acquisition. *First Language, 30*(3–4), 250–269.

Clark, J. M., & Paivio, A. (2004). Extensions of the Paivio, Yuille, and Madigan (1968) norms. *Behavior Research Methods, Instruments, and Computers, 36*(3), 371–383.

Clarke, A. T., & Kurtz-Costes, B. (1997). Television viewing, educational quality of the home environment, and school readiness. *Journal of Educational Research, 90*(5), 279–285.

Clay, M. M. (1975). *What did I write?* Aucklund, New Zealand: Heinemann.

Clay, M. M. (1979). *Early detection of reading difficulties.* Portsmouth, NH: Heinemann.

Clinton, V., & van den Broek, P. (2012). Interest, inferences, and learning from texts. *Learning and Individual Differences, 22*(6), 650–663.

Clymer, T. L. (1963). The utility of phonic generalizations in the primary grades. *The Reading Teacher, 16*, 252–258.

Clymer, T. L., & Barrett, T. (1966). *Clymer–Barrett Prereading Battery.* Princeton, NJ: Personnel Press.

Coch, D., Mitra, P., & George, E. (2012). Behavioral and ERP evidence of word and pseudoword superiority effects in 7- and 11-year-olds. *Brain Research, 1486,* 68–81.

Coerr, E. (1977). *Sadako and the thousand paper cranes.* London: Puffin Books.

Cole, R. W. (2008). *Educating everybody's children: Diverse teaching strategies for diverse learners.* Alexandria, VA: Association for Supervision and Curriculum Development.

Coleman, J. S., Campbell, E. Q., Hobson, C. J., McPartland, J., Mood, A. M., Weinfeld, F. D., et al. (1966). *Equality of educational opportunity.* Washington, DC: U.S. Government Printing Office.

Coleman-Jensen, A., Gregory, C., & Singh, A. (2014). Household food security in the United States in 2013. Retrieved November 10, 2014, from *www.ers.usda.gov/media/1565410/err173_summary.pdf.*

Collins, A., Brown, J. S., & Newman, S. E. (1989). Cognitive apprenticeship: Teaching the craft of reading, writing and mathematics. In L. B. Resnick (Ed.), *Knowing, learning, and instruction: Essays in honor of Robert Glaser* (pp. 453–494). Hillsdale, NJ: Erlbaum.

Collins, A. M., & Loftus, E. F. (1975). A spreading-activation theory of semantic processing. *Psychological Review, 82,* 407–428.

Coltheart, M. (2004). Are there lexicons? *Quarterly Journal of Experimental Psychology Section A, 57*(7), 1153–1171.

Coltheart, M., Rastle, K., Perry, C., Langdon, R., & Ziegler, J. (2001). DRC: A dual route cascaded model of visual word recognition and reading aloud. *Psychological Review, 108,* 204–256.

Coltheart, V., & Leahy, J. (1992). Children's and adults' reading of nonwords: Effects of regularity and consistency. *Journal of Experimental Psychology: Learning, Memory, and Cognition, 18,* 718–729.

Commissaire, E., Duncan, L. G., & Casalis, S. (2011). Cross-language transfer of orthographic processing skills: A study of French children who learn English at school. *Journal of Research in Reading, 34*(1), 59–76.

Common Sense Media. (2014). *Children, teens, and reading: A Common Sense Media brief.* Washington, DC: Author.

Compton, D. L., Fuchs, D., Fuchs, L. S., Elleman, A. M., & Gilbert, J. K. (2008). Tracking children who fly below the radar: Latent transition modeling of students with late-emerging reading disability. *Learning and Individual Differences, 18*(3), 329–337.

Condron, D. J., Tope, D., Steidl, C. R., & Freeman, K. J. (2013). Racial segregation and the black/white achievement gap, 1992 to 2009. *Sociological Quarterly, 54*(1), 130–157.

Conger, R. D., & Elder, G. H., Jr. (1994). *Families in troubled times: Adapting to change in rural America.* Hillsdale, NJ: Aldine.

Conger, R. D., Wallace, L. E., Sun, Y., Simons, R. L., McLoyd, V. C., & Brody, G. H. (2002). Economic pressure in African American families: A replication and extension of the family stress model. *Developmental Psychology, 38*(2), 179.

Connor, C. M., & Craig, H. K. (2006). African American preschoolers' language, emergent literacy skills, and use of African American English: A complex relation. *Journal of Speech, Language, and Hearing Research, 49*(4), 771–792.

Connor, P., Cohn, D., & Gonzalez-Barrerra, A. (2013). Changing patterns of global migration and remittances. Retrieved from *www.pewresearch.org.*

Connors, F. A. (2009). Attentional control and the simple view of reading. *Reading and Writing, 22,* 591–613.

Conradi, K., Jang, B. G., & McKenna, M. C. (2014). Motivation terminology in reading research: A conceptual review. *Educational Psychology Review, 26,* 127–164.

Cook, A. E., Limber, J. E., & O'Brien, E. J. (2001). Situation-based context and the availability of predictive inferences. *Journal of Memory and Language, 44,* 220–234.

Cooperative Children's Book Center. (2014). *Children's books by and about people of color published in the United States.* Retrieved January 19, 2015, from *http://ccbc.education.wisc.edu/books/pcstats.asp.*

Corpus, J. H., McClintic-Gilbert, M. S., & Hayenga, A. O. (2009). Within-year changes in children's intrinsic and extrinsic motivational orientations: Contextual predictors and academic outcomes. *Contemporary Educational Psychology, 34*(2), 154–166.

Cortese, M. J., & Schock, J. (2013). Imageability and age of acquisition effects in disyllabic word recognition. *Quarterly Journal of Experimental Psychology, 66*(5), 946–972.

Cortese, M. J., Simpson, G. B., & Woolsey, S. (1997). Effects of association and imageability on phonological mapping. *Psychonomic Bulletin and Review, 4*(2), 226–231.

Coulmas, F. (2003). *Writing systems: An introduction to their linguistic analysis.* Boston: Cambridge University Press.

Coulombe, S., Tremblay, J. F., & Marchand, S. (2004). *International Adult Literacy Survey.* Literacy Scores Human Capital and Growth Across 14 OECD Countries. Report No. 89552. Ottawa, Ontario, Canada: Statistics Canada.

Covington, M. V. (1992). *Making the grade: A self-worth perspective on motivation and school reform.* New York: Cambridge University Press.

Cozijn, R., Commandeur, E., Vonk, W., & Noordman, L. G. (2011). The time course of the use of implicit causality information in the processing of pronouns: A visual world paradigm study. *Journal of Memory and Language, 64*(4), 381–403.

Craig, H. K., Kolenic, G. E., & Hensel, S. L. (2014). African American English-speaking students: A longitudinal examination of style shifting from kindergarten through second grade. *Journal of Speech, Language, and Hearing Research, 57*(1), 143–157.

Craig, H. K., Thompson, C. A., Washington, J. A., & Potter, S. L. (2003). Phonological features of child African American English. *Journal of Speech, Language, and Hearing Research, 46*(3), 623–635.

Craig, H. K., Zhang, L., Hensel, S. L., & Quinn, E. J. (2009). African American English-speaking students: An examination of the relationship between dialect shifting and reading outcomes. *Journal of Speech, Language, and Hearing Research, 52*, 839–855.

Cramer, E. H., & Castle, M. (1994). *Fostering the love of reading.* Newark, DE: International Reading Association.

Cromley, J. G., & Azevedo, R. (2007). Testing and refining the direct and inferential mediation model of reading comprehension. *Journal of Educational Psychology, 99*(2), 311–325.

Cromley, J. G., Snyder-Hogan, L. E., & Luciw-Dubas, U. A. (2010). Reading comprehension of scientific text: A domain-specific test of the direct and inferential mediation model of reading comprehension. *Journal of Educational Psychology, 102*(3), 687–700.

Cronin, V., Farrell, D., & Delaney, M. (1999). Environmental print and word reading. *Journal of Research in Reading, 22*(3), 271–282.

Crosson, A. C., & Lesaux, N. K. (2010). Revisiting assumptions about the relationship of fluent reading to comprehension: Spanish-speakers' text-reading fluency in English. *Reading and Writing, 23*, 475–494.

Crowne, D. P., & Marlowe, D. (1960). A new scale of social desirability independent of psychopathology. *Journal of Consulting Psychology, 24*(4), 349–354.

Csikszentmihalyi, M. (1990). *Flow: The psychology of optimal experience.* New York: Harper Perennial.

Cummins, J. (1994). The acquisition of English as a second language. In K. Spangenberg-Urbschat & R. Pritchard (Eds.), *Kids come in all languages: Reading instruction for ESL students* (pp. 36–62). Newark, DE: International Reading Association.

Cunningham, A. E., & Stanovich, K. E. (1992). Tracking the unique effects of print exposure: Associations with vocabulary, general knowledge, and spelling. *Journal of Educational Psychology, 83*(2), 264–274.

Cunningham, A. E., & Stanovich, K. E. (1998). The impact of print exposure on word recognition. In J. Metsala & L. Ehri (Eds.), *Word recognition in beginning literacy* (pp. 235–262). Mahwah, NJ: Erlbaum.

Curenton, S. M., & Justice, L. M. (2008). Children's preliteracy skills: Influence of mothers' education and beliefs about shared-reading interactions. *Early Education and Development, 19*(2), 261–283.

Daane, M. C., Campbell, J. R., Grigg, W. S., Goodman, M. J., & Oranje, A. (2005). *Fourth-grade students reading aloud: NAEP 2002 special study of oral reading.* The nation's report card (NCES 2006469). Washington, DC: U.S. Department of Education, Institute of Education Sciences.

Dale, E., & O'Rourke, J. (1981). *The living word vocabulary.* Chicago: World Book/Childcraft International.

Dalton, B., & Grisham, D. L. (2011). eVoc strategies: 10 ways to use technology to build vocabulary. *The Reading Teacher, 64*(5), 306–317.

D'Andrade, R. G. (1995). *The development of cognitive anthropology.* Cambridge, UK: Cambridge University Press.

Dandurand, F., & Shultz, T. R. (2011). A fresh look at vocabulary spurts. Available at *http://mindmodeling.org/cogsci2011/papers/0268/paper0268.pdf.*

Dang, T.-D., Chen, G.-D., Dang, G., Li, L.-Y., & Nurkhamid (2013). RoLo: A dictionary interface that minimizes extraneous cognitive load of lookup and supports incidental and incremental learning of vocabulary. *Computers and Education, 61*, 251–260.

Daniel, S. S., Walsh, A. K., Goldston, D. B., Arnold, E. M., Reboussin, B. A., & Wood, F. B. (2006). Suicidality, school dropout, and reading problems among adolescents. *Journal of Learning Disabilities, 39*(6), 507–514.

Daniels, H. (1994). *Literature circles: Voice and choice in the student-centered classroom.* York, ME: Stenhouse.

Davidson, D., & Tell, D. (2005). Monolingual and bilingual children's use of mutual exclusivity in the naming of whole objects. *Journal of Experimental Child Psychology, 92*(1), 25–45.

Davis, Z. T., & McPherson, M. D. (1989). Story map instruction: A road map for reading comprehension. *The Reading Teacher, 43*(3), 232–240.

Deacon, S. H., Wade-Woolley, L., & Kirby, J. R.

(2009). Flexibility in young second-language learners: Examining the language specificity of orthographic processing. *Journal of Research in Reading, 32*(2), 215–229.

DeBaryshe, B. D. (1995). Maternal belief systems: Linchpin in the home reading process. *Journal of Applied Developmental Psychology, 16*(1), 1–20.

DeBaryshe, B. D., Binder, J. C., & Buell, M. J. (2000). Mothers' implicit theories of early literacy instruction: Implications for children's reading and writing. *Early Child Development and Care, 160*(1), 119–131.

deCharms, R. (1977). Pawn or origin?: Enhancing motivation in disaffected youth. *Educational Leadership, 34*(6), 444–448.

Deci, E. L., Koestner, R., & Ryan, R. M. (1999). A meta-analytic review of experiments examining the effects of extrinsic rewards on intrinsic motivation. *Psychological Bulletin, 125*(6), 627.

Deci, E. L., & Ryan, R. M. (1987). The support of autonomy and the control of behavior. *Journal of Personality and Social Psychology, 53*(6), 1024.

Deci, E. L., Vallerand, R. J., Pelletier, L. G., & Ryan, R. M. (1991). Motivation and education: The self-determination perspective. *Educational Psychologist, 26*(3–4), 325–346.

DeFelice, C. L. (2010). Mapping the chapter: One way to tackle the CTE textbook. *Techniques: Connecting Education and Careers, 85*(4), 40–45.

DeFrancis, J. (1986). *The Chinese language: Fact and fantasy.* Honolulu: University of Hawaii Press.

Dehaene, S., Cohen, L., Sigman, M., & Vinckier, F. (2005). The neural code for written words: A proposal. *Trends in Cognitive Sciences, 9*(7), 335–341.

Dehaene, S., Pegado, F., Braga, L. W., Ventura, P., Filho, G. N., Jobert, A., et al. (2010). How learning to read changes the cortical networks for vision and language. *Science, 330,* 1359–1364.

de Jong, P. F., & Leseman, P. P. (2001). Lasting effects of home literacy on reading achievement in school. *Journal of School Psychology, 39*(5), 389–414.

De Marie, D., Aloise-Young, P., Prideaux, C., Muransky-Doran, J., & Gerda, J. H. (2004). College students' memory for vocabulary in their majors: Evidence for a nonlinear relation between knowledge and memory. *Canadian Journal of Experimental Psychology, 58,* 181–195.

De Naeghel, J., Van Keer, H., Vansteenkiste, M., & Rosseel, Y. (2012). The relation between elementary students' recreational and academic reading motivation, reading frequency, engagement, and comprehension: A self-determination theory perspective. *Journal of Educational Psychology, 104*(4), 1006.

DeNavas-Walt, C., Proctor, B. D., & Smith, J. C. (2013). *Income, poverty, and health insurance coverage in the United States: 2012.* Washington, DC: U.S. Census Bureau.

Denes, P. B. (1963). On the statistics of spoken English. *Journal of the Acoustic Society of America, 35*(6), 892–904.

Deno, S. L. (1985). Curriculum-based measurement: The emerging alternative. *Exceptional Children, 52,* 219–232.

Deno, S. L., Fuchs, L. S., Martson, D. B., & Shin, J. (2001). Using curriculum-based measurement to establish growth standards for students with learning disabilities. *School Psychology Review, 30,* 507–524.

Denton, C. A., Barth, A. E., Fletcher, A. E., Wexler, J., Vaughn, S., Cirino, P. T., et al. (2011). The relations among oral and silent reading fluency and comprehension in middle school: Implications for identification and instruction of students with reading difficulties. *Scientific Studies of Reading, 15*(2), 109–135.

Denton, K., & West, J. (2002). *Children's reading and mathematics achievement in kindergarten and first grade* (NCES 2002-125). Washington, DC: U.S. Government Printing Office.

De Temple, J. M., & Tabors, P. O. (1996, August). *Children's story re-telling as a predictor of early reading achievement.* Paper presented at the biennial meeting of the International Society for the Study of Behavioral Development, Quebec City, Quebec, Canada.

Dewey, J. (1938). *Experience and education.* New York: McMillan.

Diamond, A. (2002). Normal development of prefrontal cortex from birth to young adulthood: Cognitive functions, anatomy, and biochemistry. In D. Stuss & R. Knight (Eds.), *Principles of frontal lobe function* (pp. 466–503). New York: Oxford University Press.

Dickinson, D. K., & Snow, C. E. (1987). Interrelationships among prereading and oral language skills in kindergarteners from two social classes. *Early Childhood Research Quarterly, 2,* 1–25.

Dimino, J. A., Taylor, R. M., & Gersten, R. M. (1995). Synthesis of the research on story grammar as a means to increase comprehension. *Reading and Writing Quarterly: Overcoming Learning Difficulties, 11*(1), 53–72.

Di Stasio, M. R., Savage, R., & Abrami, P. C. (2012). A follow-through study of the ABRACADABRA web-based literacy intervention in grade 1. *Journal of Research in Reading, 35*(1), 69–86.

Di Vesta, F. J., & Walls, R. T. (1970). Factor analysis of the semantic attributes of 487 words and some relationships to the conceptual behavior of fifth-grade children. *Journal of Educational Psychology, 61*(62), 1–15.

Dochy, F., Segers, M., & Buehl, M. M. (1999). The relation between assessment practices and outcomes of studies: The case of research on prior knowledge. *Review of Educational Research, 69*(2), 145–186.

Dolch, E. W. (1936). A basic sight vocabulary. *Elementary School Journal, 36*, 456–460.

Dole, J. A., Duffy, G. G., Roehler, L. R., & Pearson, P. D. (1991). Moving from the old to the new: Research on reading comprehension instruction. *Review of Educational Research, 61*, 239–264.

Dole, J. A., Valencia, S. W., Greer, E. A., & Wardrop, J. L. (1991). Effects of two types of prereading instruction on the comprehension of narrative and expository text. *Reading Research Quarterly, 26*, 142–159.

Donahue, P. L., Finnegan, R. J., Lutkus, A. D., Allen, N. L., & Campbell, J. R. (2001). *The nation's report card: Fourth grade reading, 2000* (NCES 2001-499). Washington, DC: U.S. Department of Education, Institute of Education Sciences.

Donovan, C. A., Smolkin, L. B., & Lomax, R. G. (2000). Beyond the independent-level text: Considering the reader–text match in first graders' self-selections during recreational reading. *Reading Psychology, 21*, 309–333.

Dooling, D. J., & Christiaansen, R. E. (1977). Episodic and semantic aspects of memory for prose. *Journal of Experimental Psychology: Human Learning and Memory, 3*(4), 428–436.

Dougherty, J. W. D. (1978). Salience and relativity in classification. *American Ethnologist, 5*, 66–80.

Downey, D. B. (1995). When bigger is not better: Family size, parental resources, and children's educational performance. *American Sociological Review, 60*(5), 746–761.

Downey, D. B. (2001). Number of siblings and intellectual development: The resource dilution explanation. *American Psychologist, 56*(6–7), 497.

Drouin, M., Horner, S. L., & Sondergeld, T. A. (2012). Alphabet knowledge in preschool: A Rasch model analysis. *Early Childhood Research Quarterly, 27*(3), 543–554.

Dudley-Marling, C., & Lucas, K. (2009). Pathologizing the language and culture of poor children. *Language Arts, 86*(5), 362–370.

Duff, F. J., Fieldsend, E., Bowyer-Crane, C., Hulme, C., Smith, G., Gibbs, S., et al. (2008). Reading with vocabulary intervention: Evaluation of an instruction for children with poor response to reading intervention. *Journal of Research in Reading, 31*(3), 319–336.

Duff, F. J., & Hulme, C. (2012). The role of children's phonological and semantic knowledge in learning to read words. *Scientific Studies of Reading, 16*(6), 504–525.

Duffy, G. G. (1993). Rethinking strategy instruction: Four teachers' development and their low achievers' understandings. *Elementary School Journal, 93*(3) 231–247.

Duke, N. K., & Pearson, P. D. (2002). Effective practices for developing reading comprehension. In A. E. Farstrup & S. J. Samuels (Eds.), *What research has to say about reading instruction* (Vol. 3, pp. 205–242). Newark, DE: International Reading Association.

Dumont, R., & Willis, J. O. (2007). Peabody Picture Vocabulary Test—Third Edition. In C. R. Reynolds & E. Fletcher-Janzen (Eds.), *Encyclopedia of special education* (p. 1522). New York: Wiley.

Dunabeitia, J. A., Dimitropoulou, M., Grainger, J., Hernandez, J. A., & Carreiras, M. (2012). Differential sensitivity of letters, numbers, and symbols to character transpositions. *Journal of Cognitive Neuroscience, 24*(7), 1610–1624.

Duncan, G. J., & Murnane, R. J. (2014). *Restoring opportunity: The crisis of inequality and the challenge for American education.* Cambridge, MA: Harvard Education Press.

Dunifon, R., & Kowaleski-Jones, L. (2007). The influence of grandparents in single-mother families. *Journal of Marriage and Family, 69*(2), 465–481.

Dunn, L., Beach, S. A., & Kontos, S. (1994). Quality of the literacy environment in day care and children's development. *Journal of Research in Childhood Education, 9*(1), 24–34.

Dunn, L. M., & Dunn, L. M. (1981). *Manual for the Peabody Picture Vocabulary Test—Revised.* Circle Pines, MN: American Guidance Service.

Durham, R. E., Farkas, G., Hammer, C. S., Tomblin, J. B., & Catts, H. W. (2007). Kindergarten oral language skill: A key variable in the intergenerational transmission of socioeconomic status. *Research in Social Stratification and Mobility, 25*(4), 294–305.

Durik, A. M., Vida, M., & Eccles, J. S. (2006). Task values and ability beliefs as predictors of high school literacy choices: A developmental analysis. *Journal of Educational Psychology, 98*(2), 382.

Durkin, D. (1978). What classroom observations reveal about reading comprehension instruction. *Reading Research Quarterly, 14*(4), 481–533.

Durkin, D. (1993). *Teaching them to read.* Boston: Allyn & Bacon.

Dweck, C. S. (1975). The role of expectations and attributions in the alleviation of learned helplessness. *Journal of Personality and Social Psychology, 31*(4), 674.

Dweck, C. S. (1986). Motivational processes affecting learning. *American Psychologist, 41*(10), 1040.

Dweck, C. S., & Leggett, E. L. (1988). A social–cognitive approach to motivation and personality. *Psychological Review, 95*(2), 256.

Dweck, C. S., & Master, A. (2009). Self-theories and motivation: Students' beliefs about intelligence. In K. R. Wentzel & A. Wigfield (Eds.), *Handbook of motivation in school* (pp. 123–140). New York: Taylor & Francis.

Dyer, J. R., Shatz, M., & Wellman, H. M. (2000). Young children's storybooks as a source of mental state information. *Cognitive Development, 15*(1), 17–37.

Eccles, J. S. (2005). Subjective task value and the Eccles et al. model of achievement-related choices. In A. J. Elliot & C. S. Dweck (Eds.), *Handbook of competence and motivation* (pp. 105–121). New York: Guilford Press.

Echols, L. D., West, R. F., Stanovich, K. E., & Zehr, K. S. (1996). Using children's literacy activities to predict growth in verbal cognitive skills: A longitudinal investigation. *Journal of Educational Psychology, 88*(2), 296–304.

Edmunds, K. M., & Bauserman, K. L. (2006). What teachers can learn about reading motivation through conversations with children. *The Reading Teacher, 59*(5), 414–424.

Edwards, J., Beckman, M. E., & Munson, B. (2004). The interaction between vocabulary size and phonotactic probability effects on children's production accuracy and fluency in nonword repetition. *Journal of Speech, Language, and Hearing Research, 47*, 421–436.

Edwards, P. A. (1992). Involving parents in building reading instruction for African-American children. *Theory into Practice, 31*(4), 350–359.

Edwards, P. A. (1995). Empowering low-income mothers and fathers to share books with young children. *The Reading Teacher, 48*(7), 558–564.

Ehri, L. C. (1976). Do words really interfere in naming pictures? *Child Development, 47*, 502–505.

Ehri, L. C. (1991). Phases in learning to read words by sight. *Journal of Research in Reading, 18*(2), 116–125.

Ehri, L. C. (2005). Learning to read words: Theory, findings, and issues. *Scientific Studies of Reading, 9*(2), 167–188.

Ehri, L. C., & McCormick, S. (1998). Phases of word learning: Implications for instruction with delayed and disabled readers. *Reading and Writing Quarterly: Overcoming Learning Difficulties, 14*(2), 135–163.

Ehri, L. C., Nunes, S. R., Willows, D. M., Schuster, B. V., Yaghoub-Zadeh, Z., & Shanahan, T. (2001). Phonemic awareness instruction helps children learn to read: Evidence from the National Reading Panel's meta-analysis. *Reading Research Quarterly, 36*, 250–287.

Ehri, L. C., & Wilce, L. S. (1979). Does word training increase or decrease interference in a Stroop task? *Journal of Experimental Child Psychology, 27*, 352–364.

Ehri, L. C., & Wilce, L. S. (1985). Movement into reading: Is the first stage of printed word learning visual or phonetic? *Reading Research Quarterly, 20*(2), 163–179.

Ehri, L. C., & Wilce, L. S. (1987). Does learning to spell help beginners learn to read words? *Reading Research Quarterly, 22*, 47–65.

Ehrlich, M. F., Remond, M., & Tardieu, H. (1999). Processing of anaphoric devices in young skilled and less skilled comprehenders: Differences in metacognitive monitoring. *Reading and Writing, 11*, 29–63.

Elleman, A. M., Lindo, E., Morphy, P., & Compton, D. L. (2009). The impact of vocabulary instruction on passage-level comprehension of school-age children: A meta-analysis. *Journal of Research on Educational Effectiveness, 2*, 1–44.

Ellis, A. W., & Lambon Ralph, M. A. (2000). Age of acquisition effects in adult lexical processing reflect loss of plasticity in maturing systems: Insights from connectionist networks. *Journal of Experimental Psychology: Learning, Memory, and Cognition, 26*, 1103–1123.

Ellis, N. C., & Hooper, A. (2001). Why learning to read is easier in Welsh than in English: Orthographic transparency effects evinced with frequency-matched tests. *Applied Psycholinguistics, 22*(4), 571–599.

Ellis, N. C., Natsume, M., Stavropoulou, K., Hoxhallari, L., van Daal, V. H., Polyzoe, N., et al. (2004). The effects of orthographic depth on learning to read alphabetic, syllabic, and logographic scripts. *Reading Research Quarterly, 39*(4), 438–468.

Englemann, S., & Bruner, E. (1969). *Distar reading program*. Chicago: SRA.

Evans, G. A. L., Ralph, M. A. L., & Woollams, A. M. (2012). What's in a word?: A parametric study of semantic influences on visual word recognition. *Psychonomic Bulletin and Review, 19*, 325–331.

Evans, M. A., Reynolds, K., Shaw, D., & Pursoo, T. (2011). Parental explanations of vocabulary during shared book reading: A missed opportunity. *First Language, 31*, 195–213.

Evans, M. A., & Saint-Aubin, J. (2013). Addressing the effects of reciprocal teaching on the receptive and expressive vocabulary of 1st-grade students. *Journal of Educational Psychology, 105*(3), 596–608.

Evans, M. D. R., Kelly, J., & Sikora, J. (2014). Scholarly culture and academic performance in 42 nations. *Social Forces, 92*(4), 1573–1605.

Eysenck, M. W. (1974). Age differences in incidental learning. *Developmental Psychology, 10*(6), 936–941.

Fader, D. N., & McNeil, E. B. (1968). *Hooked on books: Program and proof.* New York: Berkley Books.

Fang, Z., Schleppegrell, M. J., & Cox, B. E. (2006). Understanding the language demands of schooling: Nouns in academic registers. *Journal of Literacy Research, 38*(3), 247–273.

Farrant, B. M., & Zubrick, S. R. (2012). Early vocabulary development: The importance of joint attention and parent–child book reading. *First Language, 32*(3), 343–364.

Farver, J. A. M., Xu, Y., Lonigan, C. J., & Eppe, S. (2013). The home literacy environment and Latino Head Start children's emergent literacy skills. *Developmental Psychology, 49*(4), 775.

Feather, N. T. (1959). Subjective probability and decision under uncertainty. *Psychological Review, 66,* 150–164.

Feng, L., Gai, Y., & Chen, X. (2014). Family learning environment and early literacy: A comparison of bilingual and monolingual children. *Economics of Education Review, 39,* 110–130.

Fenson, L., Marchman, V. A., Thal, D., Dale, P., Reznick, S., & Bates, E. (2007). *MacArthur–Bates Communicative Development Inventories: User's guide and technical manual* (2nd ed.). Baltimore, MD: Brookes.

Fernandez-Fein, S., & Baker, L. (1997). Rhyme and alliteration sensitivity and relevant experiences among preschoolers from diverse backgrounds. *Journal of Literacy Research, 29*(3), 433–459.

Ferrer, E., Shaywitz, B. A., Holahan, J. M., Marchione, K., & Shaywitz, S. E. (2009). Uncoupling of reading and IQ over time: Empirical evidence for a definition of dyslexia. *Psychological Science, 21*(1), 93–101.

Ferstl, E. C., Neumann, J., Bogler, C., & von Cramon, D. Y. (2008). The extended language network: A meta-analysis of neuroimaging studies on text comprehension. *Human Brain Mapping, 29*(5), 581–593.

Fiebach, C. J., Friederici, A. D., Muller, K., von Cramon, D. Y., & Hernandez, A. E. (2003). Distinct brain representations for early and late learned words. *NeuroImage, 19,* 1627–1637.

First Book. (n.d.). The impact of First Book. Retrieved November 30, 2014, from *http://aborc. firstbook.org/images/stories/orc_doc/impact_of_ first_book.pdf*.

Fischler, I. (1977). Semantic facilitation without association in a lexical decision task. *Memory and Cognition, 5*(3), 335–339.

Fischler, I., & Bloom, P. A. (1979). Automatic and attentional processes in the effects of sentence contexts on word recognition. *Journal of Verbal Learning and Verbal Behavior, 18,* 1–20.

Fiset, D., Blais, C., Ethier-Majcher, C., Arguin, M., Bub, D., & Gosselin, F. (2008). Features for identification of uppercase and lowercase letters. *Psychological Science, 19*(11), 1161–1168.

Flavell, J. H., Green, F. L., Flavell, E. R., Harris, P. L., & Astington, J. W. (1995). Young children's knowledge about thinking. *Monographs of the Society for Research in Child Development, 60*(1), i–113.

Fletcher, C. R., & Bloom, C. P. (1988). Causal reasoning in the comprehension of simple narrative texts. *Journal of Memory and Language, 27,* 235–244.

Fletcher, K. L., & Speirs Neumeister, K. L. (2012). Research on perfectionism and achievement motivation: Implications for gifted students. *Psychology in the Schools, 49*(7), 668–677.

Fletcher-Flinn, C. M., Thompson, G. B., Yamada, M., & Naka, M. (2011). The acquisition of phoneme awareness in children learning the Hiragana syllabary. *Reading and Writing, 24*(6), 623–633.

Florit, E., & Cain, K. (2011). The simple view of reading: Is it valid for different types of alphabetic orthographies? *Educational Psychology Review, 23*(4), 553–576.

Foertsch, M. A. (1992). *Reading in and out of school.* Darby, PA: Diane Publishing.

Foorman, B. R., Schatschneider, C., Eakin, M. N., Fletcher, J. M., Moats, L. C., & Francis, D. J. (2006). The impact of instructional practices in grades 1 and 2 on reading and spelling achievement in high poverty schools. *Contemporary Educational Psychology, 31*(1), 1–29.

Foraker, S., & McElree, B. (2007). The role of prominence in pronoun resolution: Availability versus accessibility. *Journal of Memory and Language, 56,* 357–383.

Fordham, S., & Ogbu, J. U. (1986). Black students' school success: Coping with the "burden of 'acting white.'" *Urban Review, 18*(3), 176–206.

Franzke, M., Kintsch, E., Caccamise, D., Johnson, N., & Dooley, S. (2005). Summary Street®: Computer support for comprehension and writing. *Journal of Educational Computing Research, 33*(1), 53–80.

Frazier, L., Carlson, K., & Clifton, C. (2006). Prosodic phrasing is central to language comprehension. *Trends in Cognitive Sciences, 10*(6), 244–249.

Frishkoff, G. A., Collins-Thompson, K., Perfetti, C.

A., & Callan, J. (2008). Measuring incremental changes in word knowledge: Experimental validation and implications for learning and assessment. *Behavior Research Methods, 40*(4), 907–925.

Frishkoff, G. A., Perfetti, C. A., Collins-Thompson, K. (2011). Predicting robust vocabulary growth from measures of incremental learning. *Scientific Studies of Reading, 15*(1), 71–91.

Fry, E. (2000). *1,000 instant words*. Westminster, CA: Teacher Created Resources.

Fry, E. (2004). Phonics: A large phoneme–grapheme frequency count revisited. *Journal of Literacy Research, 36*(1), 85–98.

Fuchs, D., Fuchs, L. S., Mathes, P. G., Lipsey, M. W., & Roberts, P. H. (2001). Is "learning disabilities" just a fancy term for low achievement?: A meta-analysis of reading differences between low achievers with and without the label. Retrieved February 1, 2015, from *www.ldaofky.org/LD/Is%20LD%20just%20another%20term%20for%20low%20achievement.pdf*.

Fujimaki, N., Hayakawa, T., Ihara, A., Wei, Q., Montezuma, S., Terazono, Y., et al. (2009). Early neuronal activation for lexico-semantic access in the left anterior temporal area analyzed by an fMRI-assisted MEG multidipole method. *NeuroImage, 44*, 1093–1102.

Fukkink, R. G., & deGlopper, K. (1998). Effects of instruction on deriving word meaning from context: A meta-analysis. *Review of Educational Research, 68*(4), 450–469.

Fullilove, M. T., & Wallace, R. (2011). Serial forced displacement in American cities, 1916–2010. *Journal of Urban Health, 88*(3), 381–389.

Gaitens, J. M., Dixon, S. L., Jacobs, D. E., Nagaraja, J., Strauss, W., Wilson, J. W., et al. (2009). Exposure of U.S. children to residential dust lead, 1999–2004: I. Housing and demographic factors. *Environmental Health Perspectives, 117*(3), 461–467.

Gajria, M., Jitendra, A. K., Sood, S., & Sacks, G. (2007). Improving comprehension of expository text in students with LD: A research synthesis. *Journal of Learning Disabilities, 40*(3), 210–225.

Gallimore, R., & Goldenberg, C. (1993). Activity settings of early literacy: Home and school factors in children's emergent literacy. In E. Forman, N. Minick, & A. Stone (Eds.), *Education and mind: The integration of institutional, social, and developmental processes* (pp. 315–335). New York: Oxford University Press.

Gambrell, L. B. (1984). How much time do children spend reading during teacher-directed reading instruction. In J. Niles & L. Harris (Eds.), *Changing perspectives on research in reading/language processing and instruction. Thirty-third yearbook of the National Reading Conference* (pp. 193–198). New York: National Reading Conference.

Gambrell, L. B. (1996). Creating classroom cultures that foster reading motivation. *The Reading Teacher, 50*, 14–25.

Gambrell, L. B. (2011). Seven rules of engagement: What's most important to know about motivation to read. *The Reading Teacher, 65*(3), 172–178.

Gambrell, L. B., & Bales, R. J. (1986). Mental imagery and the comprehension-monitoring performance of fourth- and fifth-grade poor readers. *Reading Research Quarterly, 21*, 454–464.

Gambrell, L. B., & Jaywitz, P. B. (1993). Mental imagery, text illustrations and children's story comprehension and recall. *Reading Research Quarterly, 28*, 265–273.

Gambrell, L. B., & Koskinen, P. S. (2002). Imagery: A strategy for enhancing comprehension. In C. C. Block & M. Pressley (Eds.), *Comprehension instruction: Research-based best practices* (pp. 305–318). New York: Guilford Press.

Gambrell, L. B., Palmer, B. M., Codling, R. M., & Mazzoni, S. A. (1996). Assessing motivation to read. *The Reading Teacher, 49*(7), 518–533

Ganger, J., & Brent, M. (2004). Reexamining the vocabulary spurt. *Developmental Psychology, 40*, 621–632.

Garan, E. M., & DeVoogd, G. (2008). The benefits of sustained silent reading: Scientific research and common sense converge. *The Reading Teacher, 62*(4), 336–344.

Gardner, D. (2007). Children's immediate understanding of vocabulary: Contexts and dictionary definition. *Reading Psychology, 28*, 331–373.

Garner, R. (1980). Monitoring of understanding: An investigation of good and poor readers' awareness of induced miscomprehension of text. *Journal of Reading Behavior, 12*, 55–63.

Garrod, S. C., & Sanford, A. J. (1994). Resolving sentences in a discourse context: How discourse representation affects language understanding. In M. A. Gernsbacher (Ed.), *Handbook of psycholinguistics* (pp. 675–698). San Diego, CA: Academic Press.

Garvin, A., & Walter, E. (1991). *The relationships among children's storybook reading behavior and knowledge about print concepts in kindergarten and their reading ability in first grade*. Available from ERIC (ED380795).

Gaskins, I. (2005). *Success with struggling readers: The benchmark school approach*. New York: Guilford Press.

Gates, A. I., & MacGinitie, W. H. (1968). *Gates–MacGinitie Reading Tests: Readiness skills*. New York: Teachers College Press.

Gathercole, S. E., & Baddeley, A. D. (1993). Phonological working memory: A critical building block for reading development and vocabulary acquisition? *European Journal of Psychology of Education, 8,* 259–272.

Gee, J. P. (1992). *The social mind: Language, ideology, and social practice.* New York: Bergin & Garvey.

Gee, J. P. (2003). A sociocultural perspective on early literacy development. In S. B. Neumann & D. K. Dickinson (Eds.), *Handbook of early literacy research* (Vol. 1, pp. 30–42). New York: Guilford Press.

Gentner, D. (1982). *Why nouns are learned before verbs: Linguistic relativity versus natural partitioning.* Center for the Study of Reading Technical Report; No. 257.

Georgiou, G. K., Parrila, R., & Papadopoulos, T. C. (2008). Predictors of word decoding and reading fluency across languages varying in orthographic consistency. *Journal of Educational Psychology, 100*(3), 566–580.

Georgiou, G. K., Torppa, M., Manolitsis, G., Lyytinen, H., & Parrila, R. (2012). Longitudinal predictors of reading and spelling across languages varying in orthographic consistency. *Reading and Writing, 25*(2), 321–346.

Gergen, K. J. (1985). The social constructionist movement in modern psychology. *American Psychologist, 40*(3), 266–275.

Gerhand, S., & Barry, C. (1998). Word frequency effects in oral reading are not merely age-of-acquisition effects in disguise. *Journal of Experimental Psychology: Learning, Memory, and Cognition, 24,* 267–283.

Gernsbacher, M. A. (1984). Resolving 20 years of inconsistent interactions between lexial familiarity and orthography, concreteness, and polysemy. *Journal of Experimental Psychology: General, 113,* 256–281.

Gernsbacher, M. A., Goldsmith, H. H., & Robertson, R. R. (1992). Do readers mentally represent characters' emotional states? *Cognition and Emotion, 6*(2), 89–111.

Gerrig, R. J. (1986). Process models and pragmatics. *Advances in Cognitive Science, 1,* 23–42.

Gerrig, R. J., Horton, W. S., & Stent, A. (2011). Production and comprehension of unheralded pronouns: A corpus analysis. *Discourse Processes, 48*(3), 161–182.

Gersten, R., Fuchs, L. S., Williams, J. P., & Baker, S. (2001). Teaching reading comprehension strategies to students with learning disabilities: A review of research. *Review of Educational Research, 71,* 279–230.

Gesell, A. L. (1925). *The mental growth of the preschool child.* New York: Macmillan.

Gibbs, R. W. (1994). Figurative thought and figurative language. In M. A. Gernsbacher (Ed.), *Handbook of psycholinguistics* (pp. 411–446). San Diego, CA: Academic Press.

Gibson, J. J., & Gibson, E. (1955). Perceptual learning: Differentiation or enrichment? *Psychological Review, 62,* 32–41.

Gilhooly, K. J., & Gilhooly, M. L. M. (1979). Age-of-acquisition effects in lexical decision and episodic memory tasks. *Memory and Cognition, 7,* 214–223.

Gilhooly, K. J., & Gilhooly, M. L. M. (1980). The validity of age-of-acquisition ratings. *British Journal of Psychology, 71,* 105–110.

Gillon, G. T. (2004). *Phonological awareness: From research to practice.* New York: Guilford Press.

Gilmore, G. C., Hersh, H., Caramazza, A., & Griffin, J. (1979). Multidimensional letter similarity derived from recognition errors. *Perception and Psychophysics, 25*(5), 425–431.

Giora, R. (2007). Is metaphor special? *Brain and Language, 100*(2), 111–114.

Goldman, J. G., & Manis, F. R. (2013). Relationships among cortical thickness, reading skill, and print exposure in adult readers. *Scientific Studies of Reading, 17*(3), 163–176.

Golinkoff, R. M., Hirsh-Pasek, K., Mervis, C. B., Frawley, W. B., & Parillo, M. (1995). Lexical principles can be extended to the acquisition of verbs. In M. Tomasello & W. E. Merriman (Eds.), *Beyond names for things: Young children's acquisition of verbs* (pp. 185–221). Hillsdale, NJ: Erlbaum.

Golova, N., Alario, A. J., Vivier, P. M., Rodriguez, M., & High, P. C. (1999). Literacy promotion for Hispanic families in a primary care setting: A randomized, controlled trial. *Pediatrics, 103*(5), 993–997.

Gonzalez, N., Moll, L. C., & Amanti, C. (2005). *Funds of knowledge: Theorizing practices in households, communities, and classrooms.* Mahwah, NJ: Erlbaum.

Good, R. H., III, & Kaminski, R. A. (2010). *Dynamic Indicators of Basic Early Literacy Skills* (6th ed.). Eugene, OR: Dynamic Measurement Group.

Goodman, K. S. (1965). Dialect barriers to reading comprehension. *Elementary English, 42*(8), 6–12.

Goodman, K. S., & Goodman, Y. M. (1979). Learning to read is natural. In L. B. Resnick & P. A. Waver (Eds.), *Theory and practice of early reading* (Vol. 1, pp. 137–154). Hillsdale, NJ: Erlbaum.

Goodman, Y. M. (1986). Children coming to know literacy. In W. H. Teale & E. Sulzby (Ed.), *Emergent literacy: Writing and reading* (pp. 1–14). Norward, NJ: Ablex.

Goodman, Y. M., Goodman, K. S., & Martens, P. (2002). Text matters: Readers who learn with decodable texts. In D. L. Schalbert, C. M. Fairbanks, J. Orthy, B. Maloch, & J. V. Hoffman

(Eds.), *51st yearbook of the National Reading Conference* (pp. 186–203). Oak Creek, WI: National Reading Conference.

Goodwin, A. P., & Ahn, S. (2010). A meta-analysis of morphological interventions: Effects on literacy achievement of children with literacy difficulties. *Annals of Dyslexia, 60,* 183–208.

Goodwin, A. P., & Ahn, S. (2013). A meta-analysis of morphological interventions in English: Effects on literacy outcomes for school-age children. *Scientific Studies of Reading, 17*(4), 257–285.

Goodwin, A. P., Gilbert, J. K., & Cho, S.-J. (2013). Morphological contributions to adolescent word reading: An item response approach. *Reading Research Quarterly, 48*(1), 39–60.

Goodwin, K., & Highfield, K. (2012, March). *iTouch and iLearn: An examination of "educational" apps.* Paper presented at the Early Education and Technology for Children conference, Salt Lake City, UT.

Gordon, P. C., Grosz, B. J., & Gilliom, L. A. (1993). Pronouns, names, and the centering of attention in discourse. *Cognitive Science, 17,* 311–347.

Goswami, U. (2002). Phonology, reading development, and dyslexia: A cross-linguistic perspective. *Annals of Dyslexia, 52,* 141–163.

Goswami, U., & Bryant, P. (1989). The interpretation of studies using the reading level design. *Journal of Reading Behavior, 21,* 413–424.

Goswami, U., & Bryant, P. (1990). *Phonological skills and learning to read.* Hove, UK: Erlbaum.

Gottfried, A. E., Fleming, J. S., & Gottfried, A. W. (2001). Continuity of academic intrinsic motivation from childhood through late adolescence: A longitudinal study. *Journal of Educational Psychology, 93*(1), 3.

Graesser, A. C., & McNamara, D. S. (2011). Computational analyses of multilevel discourse comprehension. *Topics in Cognitive Science, 3,* 371–398.

Graesser, A. C., McNamara, D. S., & Kulikowich, J. M. (2011). Coh-Metrix: Providing multi-level analyses of text characteristics. *Educational Researcher, 40,* 223–234.

Graesser, A. C., Millis, K. K., & Zwaan, R. A. (1997). Discourse comprehension. *Annual Review of Psychology, 48,* 163–189.

Graesser, A. C., Singer, M., & Trabasso, T. (1994). Constructing inferences during narrative text comprehension. *Psychological Review, 101*(3), 371–395.

Graham, S., & Hebert, M. (2010). *Writing to read: Evidence for how writing can improve reading.* New York: Carnegie Corporation.

Grainger, J., Rey, A., & Dufau, S. (2008). Letter perception: From pixels to pandemonium. *Trends in Cognitive Sciences, 12*(10), 381–387.

Graves, M. F., & Watts-Taffe, S. (2008). For the love of words: Fostering word consciousness in young readers. *The Reading Teacher, 62*(3), 185–193.

Greenberg, M. S., Westcott, D. R., & Bailey, S. E. (1998). When believing is seeing: The effect of scripts on eyewitness memory. *Law and Human Behavior, 22*(6), 685–694.

Greene, B. B. (2001). Testing reading comprehension of theoretical discourse with cloze. *Journal of Research in Reading, 24*(1), 82–98.

Greene, S. B., Gerrig, R. J., McKoon, G., & Ratcliff, R. (1994). Unheralded pronouns and management by common ground. *Journal of Memory and Language, 33*(4), 511–526.

Greenfield, J. (2014). E-book growth slows to single digits in U.S. in 2013. Retrieved December 10, 2014, from *www.digitalbookworld.com/2014/ebook-growth-slows-to-single-digits-in-u-s-in-2013.*

Greenleaf, C. L., & Hinchman, K. (2009). Reimagining our inexperienced adolescent readers: From struggling, striving, marginalized, and reluctant to thriving. *Journal of Adolescent and Adult Literacy, 53*(1), 4–13.

Gregory, E. (2001). Sisters and brothers as language and literacy teachers: Synergy between siblings playing and working together. *Journal of Early Childhood Literacy, 1*(3), 301–322.

Grolnick, W. S., & Ryan, R. M. (1987). Autonomy in children's learning: An experimental and individual difference investigation. *Journal of Personality and Social Psychology, 52*(5), 890.

Grosjean, F. (2010). Bilingualism's best kept secret. Available at *www.psychologytoday.com/blog/life-bilingual/201011/bilingualisms-best-kept-secret.*

Grosz, B. J., Weinstein, S., & Joshi, A. K. (1995). Centering: A framework for modeling the local coherence of discourse. *Computational Linguistics, 21*(2), 203–225.

Gruenbaum, E. A. (2012). Common literacy struggles with college students: Using the reciprocal teaching technique. *Journal of College Reading and Learning, 42*(2), 109–116.

Gurlitt, J., & Renkl, A. (2010). Prior knowledge activation: How different concept mapping tasks lead to substantial differences in cognitive processes, learning outcomes, and perceived self-efficacy. *Instructional Science, 38*(4), 417–433.

Guthrie, J. T., & Cox, K. E. (2001). Classroom conditions for motivation and engagement in reading. *Educational Psychology Review, 13*(3), 283–302.

Guthrie, J. T., Hoa, A. L. W., Wigfield, A., Tonks, S. M., Humenick, N. M., & Littles, E. (2007). Reading motivation and reading comprehension growth in the later elementary years. *Contemporary Educational Psychology, 32*(3), 282–313.

Guthrie, J. T., Klauda, S. L., & Ho, A. N. (2013).

Modeling the relationships among reading instruction, motivation, engagement, and achievement for adolescents. *Reading Research Quarterly, 48*(1), 9–26.

Guthrie, J. T., Van Meter, P., Hancock, G. R., Alao, S., Anderson, E., & McCann, A. (1998). Does concept-oriented reading instruction increase strategy use and conceptual learning from text? *Journal of Educational Psychology, 90*(2), 261.

Guthrie, J. T., & Wigfield, A. (2000). Engagement and motivation in reading. In M. L. Kamil, P. B. Mosenthal, P. D. Pearson, & R. Barr (Eds.), *Handbook of reading research* (Vol. 3, pp. 403–422). Mahwah, NJ: Erlbaum.

Guthrie, J. T., Wigfield, A., Barbosa, P., Perencevich, K. C., Taboada, A., Davis, M. H., et al. (2004). Increasing reading comprehension and engagement through concept-oriented reading instruction. *Journal of Educational Psychology, 96*(3), 403.

Guthrie, J. T., Wigfield, A., Humenick, N. M., Perencevich, K. C., Taboada, A., & Barbosa, P. (2006). Influences of stimulating tasks on reading motivation and comprehension. *Journal of Educational Research, 99*(4), 232–246.

Guthrie, J. T., Wigfield, A., Metsala, J., & Cox, K. (2004). Motivational and cognitive predictors of text comprehension and reading amount. In R. B. Ruddell & N. Unrau (Eds.), *Theoretical models and processes of reading* (Vol. 5, pp. 929–953). Newark, DE: International Reading Association.

Gutierrez-Palma, N., & Palma-Reyes, A. (2007). Stress sensitivity and reading performance in Spanish: A study with children. *Journal of Research in Reading, 30*(2), 157–168.

Guttentag, R. E., & Haith, M. M. (1978). Automatic processing as a function of age and reading ability. *Child Development, 49*, 707–716.

Hagood, B. F. (1997). Reading and writing with help from story grammar. *Teaching Exceptional Children, 29*(4), 10–14.

Hairrell, A., Rupley, W., & Simmons, D. (2011). The state of vocabulary research. *Literacy Research and Instruction, 50*, 253–271.

Hall, L. A. (2010). The negative consequences of becoming a good reader: Identity theory as a lens for understanding struggling readers, teachers, and reading instruction. *Teachers College Record, 112*(7), 1792–1829.

Hamilton, C. E., & Schwanenflugel, P. J. (2011). *PAVEd for Success: Building vocabulary and language development in young learners.* Baltimore, MD: Brookes.

Hamilton, C. E., & Shinn, M. R. (2003). Characteristics of word callers: An investigation of the accuracy of teachers' judgments of reading comprehension and oral reading skills. *School Psychology Review, 32*(2), 228–240.

Hamilton, S. T., Freed, E. M., & Long, D. L. (2013). Modeling reader and text interactions during narrative comprehension: A test of the lexical quality hypothesis. *Discourse Processes, 50*, 139–163.

Hamston, J., & Love, K. (2003). "Reading relationships": Parents, boys, and reading as cultural practice. *Australian Journal of Language and Literacy, 26*, 44–57.

Hanna, P. R., Hanna, J. S., Hodges, R. E., & Rudorf, E. H. (1966). *Phoneme–grapheme correspondences as cues to spelling improvement.* Washington, DC: U.S. Department of Health, Education, and Welfare.

Hansen, J., & Pearson, P. D. (1983). An instructional study: Improving the inferential comprehension of good and poor fourth-grade readers. *Journal of Educational Psychology, 75*, 821–829.

Hardyck, C. D., & Petrinovich, L. F. (1970). Subvocal speech and comprehension level as a function of the difficulty level of reading material. *Journal of Verbal Learning and Verbal Behavior, 9*, 647–652.

Hargreaves, I. S., Pexman, P. M., Pittman, D. J., & Goodyear, B. G. (2011). Tolerating ambiguity: Ambiguous words recruit the left inferior frontal gyrus in the absence of a behavioral effect. *Experimental Psychology, 58*(1), 19–30.

Harlaar, N., Dale, P. S., & Plomin, R. (2007). From learning to read to reading to learn: Substantial and stable genetic influence. *Child Development, 78*(1), 116–131.

Harn, B. A., Stoolmiller, M., & Chard, D. J. (2008). Measuring dimensions of the alphabetic principle on the reading development of first graders. *Journal of Learning Disabilities, 41*(2), 143–157.

Harpaz, Y., & Lavidor, M. (2012). Context modulates hemispheric asymmetries in the resolution of lexical ambiguity. *Journal of Cognitive Psychology, 24*(4), 428–440.

Harrison, C. (2010). Why do policy-makers find the "simple view of reading" so attractive, and why do I find it so morally repugnant? In K. Hall, U. Goswami, C. Harrison, S. Ellis, & J. Soler (Eds.), *Interdisciplinary perspectives on learning to read: Culture, cognition, and pedagogy* (pp. 207–218). New York: Routledge.

Harrison, M. L., & Stroud, J. B. (1950). *The Harrison–Stroud Reading Readiness Profiles.* Boston: Houghton Mifflin.

Hart, B., & Risley, T. R. (1995). *Meaningful differences in the everyday experience of young American children.* Baltimore, MD: Brookes.

Hart, B., & Risley, T. R. (2003). The early catastrophe: The 30-million word gap by age 3. *American Educator, 27*, 4–9.

Hart, J. T. (1967). Memory and the memory-monitoring process. *Journal of Verbal Learning and Verbal Behavior, 6*, 685–691.

Hart, M. S. (2004). Gutenberg mission statement. Available at *www.gutenberg.org*.

Harter, S. (2008). The developing self. In W. Damon, R. M. Lerner, D. Kuhn, R. S. Siegler, & N. Eisenberg (Eds.), *Child and adolescent development: An advanced course* (pp. 216–261). Hoboken, NJ: Wiley.

Harter, S., Whitesell, N. R., & Junkin, L. J. (1998). Similarities and differences in domain-specific and global self-evaluations of learning-disabled, behaviorally disordered, and normally achieving adolescents. *American Educational Research Journal, 35*(4), 653–680.

Hasbrouck, J., & Tindal, G. A. (2006). Oral reading fluency norms: A valuable assessment tool for reading teachers. *The Reading Teacher, 59*, 636–644.

Hayes, D. P., Wolfer, L. T., & Wolfe, M. F. (1996). Schoolbook simplification and its relation to the decline in SAT—Verbal Scores. *American Educational Research Journal, 33*(2), 489–508.

He, Y., Wang, Q., & Anderson, R. C. (2005). Chinese children's use of subcharacter information about pronunciation. *Journal of Educational Psychology, 97*(4), 572.

Heath, S. B. (1982a). Questioning at home and at school: A comparative study. In G. Spindler (Ed.), *Doing the ethnography of schooling* (pp. 102–131). New York: Holt, Rinehart & Winston.

Heath, S. B. (1982b). What no bedtime story means: Narrative skills at home and school. *Language in Society, 11*(2), 49–76.

Heath, S. B. (1983). *Ways with words: Language, life, and work in communities and classrooms.* Cambridge, UK: Cambridge University Press.

Heath, S. B. (1989). Oral and literate traditions among black Americans living in poverty. *American Psychologist, 44*(2), 367.

Hecht, S. A., Burgess, S. R., Torgesen, J. K., Wagner, R. K., & Rashotte, C. A. (2000). Explaining social class differences in growth of reading skills from beginning kindergarten through fourth-grade: The role of phonological awareness, rate of access, and print knowledge. *Reading and Writing: An Interdisciplinary Journal, 12*, 99–127.

Herman, P. A. (1985). The effect of repeated readings on reading rate, speech pauses, and word recognition accuracy. *Reading Research Quarterly, 20*(5), 553–565.

Hernandez, A. E., & Fiebach, C. J. (2006). The brain bases of reading late learned words: Evidence from functional MRI. *Visual Cognition, 13*, 1027–1043.

Hiebert, E. H. (2002). *Quick reads.* Upper Saddle River, NJ: Modern Curriculum Press.

Hiebert, E. H. (2005). The effects of text difficulty on second graders' fluency development. *Reading Psychology, 26*, 183–209.

Hiebert, E. H. (2009). *Reading more, reading better.* New York: Guilford Press.

Hiebert, E. H., & Fisher, C. W. (2007). Critical word factor in texts for beginning readers. *Journal of Educational Research, 101*, 3–11.

Hiebert, E. H., & Reutzel, R. (2010). Revisiting silent reading in 2020 and beyond. In E. H. Hiebert & D. R. Reutzel (Eds.), *Revisiting silent reading: New directions for teachers and researchers* (pp. 290–299). Newark, DE: International Reading Association.

Higgins, E. L., & Raskind, M. H. (2005). The compensatory effectiveness of the Quicktionary Reading Pen II on the reading comprehension of students with learning disabilities. *Journal of Special Education Technology, 20*(1), 31.

Hildebrandt, N. (1994). The Reicher–Wheeler effect and models of deep and phonological dyslexia. *Journal of Neurolinguistics, 8*(1), 1–18.

Hilden, K. R., & Pressley, M. (2007). Self-regulation through transactional strategies instruction. *Reading and Writing Quarterly, 23*(1), 51–75.

Hildreth, G., Griffiths, N., & McGauvran, M. (1965). *Metropolitan Readiness Tests.* New York: Harcourt, Brace & World.

Hill, M. (1991). Writing summaries promotes thinking and learning across the curriculum: But why are they so difficult to write? *Journal of Reading, 34*(7), 536–539.

Hill, N. E. (2001). Parenting and academic socialization as they relate to school readiness: The roles of ethnicity and family income. *Journal of Educational Psychology, 93*(4), 686–697.

Hirsch, E. D. (1987). *Cultural literacy: What every American needs to know.* Boston: Houghton Mifflin.

Hirshman, E., & Durante, R. (1992). Prime identification and semantic priming. *Journal of Experimental Psychology: Learning, Memory, and Cognition, 18*(2), 255–265.

Ho, C. S. H., & Bryant, P. (1997). Phonological skills are important in learning to read Chinese. *Developmental Psychology, 33*(6), 946.

Hobbs, J. R. (1979). Coherence and coreference. *Cognitive Science, 3*, 67–90.

Hodgson, C., & Ellis, A. W. (1998). Last in, first to go: Age of acquisition and naming in the elderly. *Brain and Language, 64*(1), 146–163.

Hoffman, J. V. (2009). In search of the "simple view" of reading comprehension. In S. E. Israel & G.

G. Duffy (Eds.), *Handbook of research on reading comprehension* (pp. 54–66). New York: Routledge.

Hoien, T., Lundberg, I., Stanovich, K. E., & Bjaalid, I.-K. (1995). Components of phonological awareness. *Reading and Writing, 7,* 171–188.

Holmes, B. C., & Allison, R. W. (1985). The effect of four modes of reading on children's reading comprehension. *Reading Research and Instruction, 25,* 9–20.

Hoover, W., & Gough, P. (1990). The simple view of reading. *Reading and Writing: An Interdisciplinary Journal, 2,* 127–160.

Horner, S. L. (2005). Categories of environmental print: All logos are not created equal. *Early Childhood Education Journal, 33*(2), 113–119.

Houck, B. D., & Ross, K. (2012). Dismantling the myth of learning to read and reading to learn. *ASCD Express, 7*(11). Retrieved from *www.ascd. org/ascd-express/vol7/711-houck.aspx.*

Houston, D., Wu, J., Ong, P., & Winer, A. (2004). Structural disparities of urban traffic in Southern California: Implications for vehicle-related air pollution exposure in minority and high-poverty neighborhoods. *Journal of Urban Affairs, 26,* 565–592.

Houston-Price, C., Caloghiris, Z., & Raviglione, E. (2010). Language experience shapes the development of the mutual exclusivity bias. *Infancy, 15*(2), 125–150.

Howard, V. (2011). The importance of pleasure reading in the lives of young teens: Self-identification, self-construction and self-awareness. *Journal of Librarianship and Information Science, 43*(1), 46–55.

Huang, Y. T., & Gordon, P. C. (2011). Distinguishing the time course of lexical and discourse processes through context, coherence, and quantified expressions. *Journal of Experimental Psychology: Learning, Memory, and Cognition, 37*(4), 966–978.

Hudson, R. F., Isakson, C., Richman, T., Lane, H. B., & Arriaza-Allen, S. (2011). An examination of a small-group decoding intervention for struggling readers: Comparing accuracy and automaticity criteria. *Learning Disabilities Research and Practice, 26*(1), 15–27.

Hudson, R. F., Lane, H. B., & Pullen, P. C. (2008). Introduction: Understanding theory and practice in reading fluency instruction. *Reading and Writing Quarterly, 25*(1), 1–3.

Hudson, R. F., Pullen, P. C., Lane, H. B., & Torgesen, J. K. (2009). The complex nature of reading fluency: A multidimensional view. *Reading and Writing Quarterly, 25,* 4–32.

Huey, E. B. (1908). *The history and pedagogy of reading: With a review of the history of reading and writing and of methods, texts and hygiene in reading.* New York: Macmillan.

Hughes-Hassell, S., & Rodge, P. (2007). The leisure reading habits of urban adolescents. *Journal of Adolescent and Adult Literacy, 51*(1), 22–33.

Hunt, J. M. (1961). *Intelligence and experience.* New York: Wiley.

Hutchison, K. A. (2003). Is semantic priming due to association strength or feature overlap? A microanalytic review. *Psychonomic Bulletin and Review, 10*(4), 785–813.

Hutzler, F., Ziegler, J. C., Perry, C., Wimmer, H., & Zorzi, M. (2004). Do current connectionist learning models account for reading development in different languages? *Cognition, 91,* 273–296.

Hymes, J. L. (1958). *Before the child reads.* New York: Harper & Row.

Idol, L. (1987). Group story mapping: A comprehension strategy for both skilled and unskilled readers. *Journal of Learning Disabilities, 20,* 196–205.

Inhoff, A. W., & Rayner, K. (1986). Parafoveal word processing during eye fixations in reading: Effects of word frequency. *Perception and Psychophysics, 40*(6), 431–439.

Innis, H. (1951). *The bias of communication.* Toronto, Ontario, Canada: University of Toronto Press.

Isero, M. (2014). Rekindle the love of reading: Giving students Kindles reinvigorates young readers and improves their reading achievement. *Phi Delta Kappan, 95*(7), 61.

Ivey, G., & Broaddus, K. (2001). "Just plain reading": A survey of what makes students want to read in middle school classrooms. *Reading Research Quarterly, 36,* 350–377.

Ivey, G., & Johnston, P. H. (2013). Engagement with young adult literature: Outcomes and processes. *Reading Research Quarterly, 48*(3), 255–275.

Jackendoff, R. (2002). *Foundations of language: Brain, meaning, grammar, evolution.* New York: Oxford University Press.

Jackson, L. A., Von Eye, A., Biocca, F. A., Barbatsis, G., Zhao, Y., & Fitzgerald, H. E. (2006). Does home Internet use influence the academic performance of low-income children? *Developmental Psychology, 42*(3), 429.

Jacobs, D. E., Kelly, T., & Sobolewski, J. (2007). Linking public health, housing, and indoor environmental policy: Successes and challenges at local and federal agencies in the United States. *Environmental Health Perspectives, 115*(6), 976–982.

Jakobsons, L. J. (2005). Child, teacher, and parent reports of motivation and their predictive relations to reading achievement and reading quantity. Unpublished thesis. Available at *http://diginole.lib.fsu.edu/etd/3665.*

James, K. H. (2010). Sensori-motor experience leads to changes in visual processing in the developing brain. *Developmental Science, 13*(2), 279–288.

James, K. H., James, T. W., Jobard, G., Wong, A. C., & Gauthier, I. (2005). Letter processing in the visual system: Different activation patterns for single letters and strings. *Cognitive, Affective, and Behavioral Neuroscience, 5*(4), 452–466.

James, W. (1890). *Principles of psychology* (Vols. 1–2). New York: Holt.

Jarmulowicz, L., Taran, V. L., & Seek, J. (2012). Metalinguistics, stress accuracy, and word reading: Does dialect matter? *Language, Speech, and Hearing Services in Schools, 43*(4), 410–423.

Jenkins, J. R., Peyton, J. A., Sanders, E. A., & Vadasy, P. F. (2004). Effects of reading decodable texts in supplemental first-grade tutoring. *Scientific Studies of Reading, 8*, 53–85.

Jeon, E. H., & Yamashita, J. (2014). L2 reading comprehension and its correlates: A meta-analysis. *Language Learning, 64*(1), 160–212.

Jin, P. (1992). Efficacy of Tai Chi, brisk walking, meditation, and reading in reducing mental and emotional stress. *Journal of Psychosomatic Research, 36*(4), 361–370.

Jobard, G., Vigneau, M., Mazoyer, B., & Tzourio-Mazoyer, N. (2007). Impact of modality and linguistic complexity during reading and listening tasks. *NeuroImage, 34*, 784–800.

Johnson, C. J., & Anglin, J. M. (1995). Qualitative developments in the content and form of children's definitions. *Journal of Speech and Hearing Research, 38*(3), 612–629.

Johnson, J. S., & Newport, E. L. (1989). Critical period effects in second language learning: The influence of maturational state on the acquisition of English as a second language. *Cognitive Psychology, 21*(1), 60–99.

Johnson, R. E. (1969). The validity of the Clymer–Barrett Prereading Battery. *The Reading Teacher, 22*(7), 609–614.

Johnston, F., Invernizzi, M., & Bear, D. R. (2004). *Words their way: Word sorts for letter name-alphabetic spellers*. Upper Saddle River, NJ: Pearson.

Johnston, P. H. (1984). Prior knowledge and reading comprehension test bias. *Reading Research Quarterly, 19*(2), 219–239.

Johnston, P. H. (1985). Understanding reading disability: A case study approach. *Harvard Educational Review, 55*(2), 153–178.

Johnston, R. A., & Barry, C. (2006). Age of acquisition and lexical processing. *Visual Cognition, 13*, 789–845.

Johnston, R. S., McGeown, S., & Watson, J. E. (2012). Long-term effects of synthetic versus analytic phonics teaching on the reading and spelling ability of 10-year-old boys and girls. *Reading and Writing, 25*, 1365–1384.

Johnston, T. C., & Kirby, J. R. (2006). The contribution of naming speed to the simple view of reading. *Reading and Writing, 19*, 339–361.

Jones, C. D., Clark, S. K., & Reutzel, D. R. (2013). Enhancing alphabet knowledge instruction: Research implications and practical strategies for early childhood educators. *Early Childhood Education Journal, 41*, 81–89.

Jones, C. D., & Reutzel, D. R. (2012). Enhanced alphabet knowledge instruction: Exploring a change of frequency, focus, and distributed cycles of review. *Reading Psychology, 33*, 448–464.

Jones, L. L. (2012). Prospective and retrospective processing in associative mediated priming. *Journal of Memory and Language, 66*, 52–67.

Jones, M. N., & Mewhort, D. J. K. (2004). Case-sensitive letter and bigram frequency counts from large-scale English corpora. *Behavior Research Methods, Instruments, and Computers, 36*, 388–396.

Jones, T., & Brown, C. (2011). Reading engagement: A comparison between e-books and traditional print books in an elementary classroom. *Online Submission, 4*(2), 5–22.

Joseph, H. S. S. L., Nation, K., & Liversedge, S. P. (2013). Using eye movements to investigate word frequency effects in children's sentence reading. *School Psychology Review, 42*(2), 207–222.

Joshi, R. M., & Aaron, P. G. (2000). The component model of reading: Simple view of reading made a little more complex. *Reading Psychology, 21*(2), 85–97.

Juel, C., & Roper/Schneider, D. (1985). The influence of basal readers on first grade reading. *Reading Research Quarterly, 20*, 134–152.

Juhasz, B. J., & Rayner, K. (2006). The role of age of acquisition and word frequency in reading: Evidence from eye fixation durations. *Visual Cognition, 13*(7/8), 846–863.

Juola, J. F., Schadler, M., Chabot, R. J., & McCaughey, M. W. (1978). The development of visual information processing skills related to reading. *Journal of Experimental Child Psychology, 25*, 459–476.

Juslin, P. N., & Laukka, P. (2003). Communication of emotions in vocal expression and music performance: Different channels, same code? *Psychological Bulletin, 129*(5), 770–814.

Justice, L. M., Pence, K., Bowles, R. P., & Wiggins, A. (2006). An investigation of four hypotheses concerning the order by which 4-year-old children learn the alphabet letters. *Early Childhood Research Quarterly, 21*, 374–389.

Kaakinen, J. K., Hyönä, J., & Keenan, J. M. (2003). How prior knowledge, WMC, and relevance of information affect eye fixations in expository text. *Journal of Experimental Psychology: Learning, Memory, and Cognition, 29*(3), 447.

Kagitcibasi, C., Goksen, F., & Gülgöz, S. (2005). Functional adult literacy and empowerment of women: Impact of a functional literacy program in Turkey. *Journal of Adolescent and Adult Literacy, 48*(6), 472–489.

Kamide, Y. (2008). Anticipatory processes in sentence processing. *Language and Linguistic Compass, 2*(4), 647–670.

Kaup, A., Simonsick, E., Harris, T., Satterfield, S., Metti, A., Ayonayon, H., et al. (2013). Limited literacy predicts dementia incidence among older adults. *Alzheimer's and Dementia, 9*(4), 628.

Kay, J., & Katz, C. (2012). Pollution, poverty, and people of color. Retrieved November 25, 2014, from *www.environmentalhealthnews.org/ehs/news/2012/pollution-poverty-and-people-of-color-richmond-day-1/pollution-poverty-people-of-color-series-summary*.

Keenan, J. M., & Betjemann, R. S. (2006). Comprehending the Gray Oral Reading Test without reading it: Why comprehension tests should not include passage-independent items. *Scientific Studies of Reading, 10*(4), 363–380.

Keenan, J. M., Betjemann, R. S., & Olson, R. K. (2008). Reading comprehension tests vary in the skills they assess: Differential dependence on decoding and oral comprehension. *Scientific Studies of Reading, 12*, 281–300.

Keene, E., & Zimmerman, S. (1997). *Mosaic of thought*. Portsmouth, NH: Heinemann.

Kellas, G., Paul, S. T., Martin, M., & Simpson, G. B. (1991). Contexual feature activation and meaning activation. In G. B. Simpson (Ed.), *Understanding word and sentence* (pp. 47–71). New York: North-Holland.

Kendeou, P., Bohn-Gettler, C., White, M. J., & Van Den Broek, P. (2008). Children's inference generation across different media. *Journal of Research in Reading, 31*(3), 259–272.

Kendeou, P., & van den Broek, P. (2007). The effects of prior knowledge and text structure on comprehension processes during reading of scientific texts. *Memory and Cognition, 35*(7), 1567–1577.

Kenner, C., Ruby, M., Jessel, J., Gregory, E., & Arju, T. (2007). Intergenerational learning between children and grandparents in East London. *Journal of Early Childhood Research, 5*(3), 219–243.

Kessler, B., & Treiman, R. (2003). Is English spelling chaotic?: Misconceptions concerning its irregularity. *Reading Psychology, 24*, 267–289.

Kidd, D. C., & Castano, E. (2013). Reading literary fiction improves theory of mind. *Science, 342*, 377–380.

Kids Count. (n.d.). Data retrieved November 11, 2014, from *http://datacenter.kidscount.org/data/tables/43-children-in-poverty#detailed/1/any/false/36,868,867,133,38/any/321,322*.

Kieffer, M. J. (2010). Socioeconomic status, English proficiency, and late emerging reading difficulties. *Educational Researcher, 39*, 484–486.

Kim, Y.-S., Petscher, Y., Schatschneider, C., & Foorman, B. (2010). Does growth rate in oral reading fluency matter in predicting reading comprehension achievement? *Journal of Educational Psychology, 102*(3), 652–667.

Kim, Y.-S., Wagner, R. K., & Lopez, D. (2011). Developmental relations between reading fluency and reading comprehension: A longitudinal study from grade 1 to grade 2. *Journal of Experimental Child Psychology, 113*, 93–111.

Kintsch, E. (1990). Macroprocesses and microprocesses in the development of summarization skill. *Cognition and Instruction, 7*(3), 161–195.

Kintsch, W. (1988). The use of knowledge in discourse processing. *Psychological Review, 95*, 163–218.

Kintsch, W. (1998). *Comprehension: A paradigm for comprehension*. Cambridge, UK: Cambridge University Press.

Kintsch, W. (2004). The construction–integration model of text comprehension and its implications for instruction. In N. Onrau & R. B. Ruddell (Eds.), *Theoretical models and processes of reading* (Vol. 5, pp. 1270–1328). Newark, DE: International Reading Association.

Kintsch, W. (2010). Comprehension: Standards for grades 4 and 5. Available at *www.reading.org/Libraries/book-supplements/bk767Supp-Kintsch.pdf*.

Kintsch, W., & Keenan, J. (1973). Reading rate and retention as a function of the number of propositions in the base structure of sentences. *Cognitive Psychology, 5*, 257–274.

Kintsch, W., & van Dijk, T. A. (1978). Toward a model of text comprehension and production. *Psychological review, 85*(5), 363–394.

Kirby, J. R., & Savage, R. S. (2008). Can the simple view deal with the complexities of reading? *Literacy, 42*(2), 75–82.

Klauda, S. L. (2009). The role of parents in adolescents' reading motivation and activity. *Educational Psychology Review, 21*(4), 325–363.

Klauda, S. L., & Guthrie, J. T. (2008). Relationships of three components of reading fluency to reading comprehension. *Journal of Educational Psychology, 100*(2), 310–321.

Klauda, S. L., & Wigfield, A. (2012). Relations of perceived parent and friend support for recreational reading with children's reading motivations. *Journal of Literacy Research, 44*(1), 3–44.

Klingner, J. K., & Vaughn, S. (1996). Reciprocal teaching of reading comprehension strategies for students with learning disabilities who use English as a second language. *Elementary School Journal, 96*(3), 275–293.

Klor, E., & Nordhausen, S. (2011). *Serving teen parents: From literacy to life skills.* Santa Barbara, CA: ABC-CLIO.

Knapp, N. F. (1998, April). *The child's conception of reading interview: A concretized, qualitative instrument for investigating children's concepts of reading.* Paper presented at the annual meeting of the American Educational Research Association, San Diego, CA.

Knapp, N. F. (1999, December). *"Reading the words" vs. "reading for meaning": An old debate from a younger perspective.* Paper presented at the annual meeting of the National Reading Conference, Orlando, FL.

Knapp, N. F. (2013a, May). *Teacher-centered professional development: Five years of progress.* Paper presented at the annual conference of the American Educational Research Association, San Francisco, CA.

Knapp, N. F. (2013b, December). *The reading apprenticeship: A pattern of success with struggling readers.* Paper presented at the annual conference of the Literacy Research Association, Dallas, TX.

Knapp, N. F. (2015, December). *Expectancy × value in reading motivation: A framework for research and practice.* Paper for presentation at the Annual Meeting of the Literacy Research Association, Carlsbad, CA.

Knapp, N. F., & Grattan, K. W. (2001). Learning from students about learning to read. *Language and Literacy Spectrum, 11,* 40–51.

Knapp, N. F., & Winsor, A. P. (1998). A reading apprenticeship for delayed primary readers. *Reading Research and Instruction, 38*(1), 13–29.

Kobayashi, M. S., Haynes, C. W., Macaruso, P., Hook, P. E., & Kato, J. (2005). Effects of mora deletion, nonword repetition, rapid naming, and visual search performance on beginning reading in Japanese. *Annals of Dyslexia, 55*(1), 105–128.

Kohl, H. (1992). I won't learn from you!: Thoughts on the role of assent in learning. *Rethinking Schools, 7*(1), 16–17, 19.

Kohn, A. (1993). Why incentive plans cannot work. *Harvard Business Review, 71*(5), 2–7.

Kohn, A. (2014). The trouble with calls for universal high-quality pre-K. Retrieved November 30, 2014, from *www.washingtonpost.com/blogs/answer-sheet/wp/2014/02/01/the-trouble-with-calls-for-universal-high-quality-pre-k.*

Kontos, S., & Wilcox-Herzog, A. (1997). Teachers' interactions with children: Why are they so important? Research in review. *Young Children, 52*(2), 4–12.

Korat, O. (2005). Contextual and non-contextual knowledge in emergent literacy development: A comparison between children from low SES and middle SES communities. *Early Childhood Research Quarterly, 20,* 220–238.

Koriat, A., Greenberg, S. N., & Kreiner, H. (2002). The extraction of structure during reading: Evidence from reading prosody. *Memory and Cognition, 30*(2), 270–280.

Kovelman, I., Baker, S. A., & Petitto, L. A. (2008). Age of first bilingual language exposure as a new window into bilingual reading development. *Bilingualism: Language and Cognition, 11*(2), 203–223.

Kozol, J. (1991). *Savage inequalities: Children in America's schools.* New York: Crown.

Kozol, J. (1996). *Amazing grace: The lives of children and the conscience of a nation.* New York: Harper Perennial.

Kozol, J. (2000). *Ordinary resurrections: Children in the years of hope.* New York: Crown.

Kragler, S. (1995). The transition from oral to silent reading. *Reading Psychology, 16,* 395–408.

Krashen, S. D. (2005). Is in-school free reading good for children?: Why the National Reading Panel Report is (still) wrong. *Phi Delta Kappan, 86*(6), 444–447.

Krashen, S. D. (2006). Free reading. *School Library Journal, 52*(9), 42–45.

Krashen, S. D. (2009). Anything but reading. *Knowledge Quest, 37*(5), 18–25.

Krashen, S. D. (2011). *Free voluntary reading.* Englewood, CO: Libraries Unlimited.

Krashen, S. D., Lee, S., & McQuillan, J. (2010). An analysis of the PIRLS (2006) data: Can the school library reduce the effect of poverty on reading achievement? *CSLA (California School Library Association) Journal, 34*(1), 26–28.

Krashen, S. D., Lee, S., & McQuillan, J. (2012). Is the library important?: Multivariate studies at the national and international level. *Journal of Language and Literacy Education, 8*(1), 26–36.

Kucan, L., & Beck, I. L. (1997). Thinking aloud and reading comprehension research: Inquiry, instruction, and social interaction. *Review of Educational Research, 67*(3), 271–299.

Kucera, H., & Francis, W. (1967). *Computational*

analysis of present day American English. Providence, RI: Brown University Press.

Kuhl, P. K. (2004). Early language acquisition: Cracking the speech code. *Nature Reviews Neuroscience, 5,* 831–843.

Kuhn, M. R. (2005). A comparative study of small group fluency instruction. *Reading Psychology, 26,* 127–146.

Kuhn, M. R., Schwanenflugel, P. J., & Meisinger, E. B. (2010). Aligning theory and assessment of reading fluency: Automaticity, prosody, and definitions of fluency. *Reading Research Quarterly, 45*(2), 232–253.

Kuhn, M. R., Schwanenflugel, P. J., Morris, R. D., Morrow, L. M., Bradley, B. A., Meisinger, E., et al. (2006). Teaching children to become fluent and automatic readers. *Journal of Literacy Research, 38,* 357–387.

Kuhn, M. R., & Stahl, S. A. (2003). Fluency: A review of developmental and remedial practices. *Journal of Educational Psychology. 95*(1), 3–21.

Kuo, L. J., & Anderson, R. C. (2006). Morphological awareness and learning to read: A cross-language perspective. *Educational Psychologist, 41*(3), 161–180.

Kutas, M., Lindamood, T. E., & Hilliard, S. A. (1984). Word expectancy and event-related potentials during sentence processing. In S. Kornblum & J. Requin (Eds.), *Preparatory states and processes* (pp. 217–234). Hillsdale, NJ: Erlbaum.

Kutner, M., Greenberg, E., Jin, Y., Boyle, B., Hsu, Y., & Dunleavy, E. (2007). *Literacy in Everyday Life: Results From the 2003 National Assessment of Adult Literacy* (NCES 2007-08). Washington, DC: National Center for Education Statistics.

Lai, S. A. (2014). *Validating the use of D.* Unpublished dissertation, University of Georgia, Athens, GA.

Lai, S. A., Benjamin, R. G., Schwanenflugel, P. J., & Kuhn, M. R. (2014). The longitudinal relationship between reading fluency and reading comprehension skills in second grade children. *Reading and Writing Quarterly, 30*(2), 116–138.

Laing, E., & Hulme, C. (1999). Phonological and semantic processes influence beginning readers' ability to learn to read words. *Journal of Experimental Child Psychology, 73,* 183–207.

Lambon Ralph, M. A., Graham, K. S., Ellis, A. W., & Hodges, J. R. (1998). Naming in semantic dementia—what matters? *Neuropsychologia, 36,* 775–784.

Lance, K. C., & Russell, B. (2004). Scientifically based research on school libraries and academic achievement: What is it? How much of it do we have? How can we do it better? *Knowledge Quest, 32*(5), 13–17.

Lass, B. (1982). Portrait of my son as an early reader. *The Reading Teacher, 36,* 20–28.

Lassonde, K. A., & O'Brien, E. J. (2009). Contextual specificity in the activation of predictive inferences. *Discourse Processes, 46*(5), 426–438.

Layzer, J. I., Goodson, B. D., & Moss, M. (1993). *Observational study of early childhood programs, final report, volume I: Life in preschool.* Cambridge, MA: Abt Associates.

Leavell, A. S., Tamis-LeMonda, C. S., Ruble, D. N., Zosuls, K. M., & Cabrera, N. J. (2012). African American, white and Latino fathers' activities with their sons and daughters in early childhood. *Sex Roles, 66*(1–2), 53–65.

Lee, J. M., Clark, W. W., & Lee, D. M. (1934). Measuring reading readiness. *Elementary School Journal, 34*(9), 656–666.

LeMoine, N. R. (2001). Language variation and literacy acquisition in African American students. In J. L. Harris, A. G. Kamhi, & K. E. Pollock (Eds.), *Literacy in African American communities* (pp. 169–94). Mahwah, NJ: Erlbaum.

León, J. A., & Carretero, M. (1995). Intervention in comprehension and memory strategies: Knowledge and use of text structure. *Learning and Instruction, 5*(3), 203–220.

Lesaux, N. K. (2012). Reading and reading instruction for children from low-income and non-English-speaking households. *The Future of Children, 22*(2), 73–88.

Lesaux, N. K., Kieffer, M. J., Faller, S. E., & Kelley, J. G. (2010). The effectiveness and ease of implementation of an academic vocabulary intervention for linguistically diverse students in urban middle schools. *Reading Research Quarterly, 45*(2), 196–228.

Leu, D. J., Zawilinski, L., Castek, J., Banerjee, M., Housand, B., Liu, Y., et al. (2007). What is new about the new literacies of online reading comprehension? In L. S. Rush, J. Eakle, & A. Berger (Eds.), *Secondary school literacy: What research reveals for classroom practices* (pp. 37–68). Urbana, IL: National Council of Teachers of English.

Lever, R., & Sénéchal, M. (2011). Discussing stories: On how a dialogic reading intervention improves kindergartners' oral narrative construction. *Journal of Experimental Child Psychology, 108*(1), 1–24.

Levin, I., & Bus, A. G. (2003). How is emergent writing based on drawing?: An analyses of children's products and their sorting by children and mothers. *Developmental Psychology, 39,* 891–905.

Levin, J. R., Shriberg, L. K., & Berry, J. K. (1983). A concrete strategy for remembering abstract prose. *American Educational Research Journal, 20,* 277–290.

Levinson, S. (2001). Covariation between spatial language and cognition, and its implications for language learning. In M. Bowerman & S. Levinson (Eds.), *Language acquisition and conceptual development* (pp. 566–588). New York: Cambridge University Press.

Lewin, K. (1938). *The conceptual representation and the measurement of psychological forces.* Durham, NC: Duke University Press.

Lewis, M., & Samuels, S. J. (2005). Read more, read better?: A meta-analysis of the literature on the relationship between exposure to reading and reading achievement. Retrieved December 10, 2014, from *www.tc.umn.edu/samue001/final%20 version.pdf.*

Lexia Learning Systems. (2003). *Early reading.* Concord, MA: Author.

Lieff, J. (2012). Neuronal connections and the mind: The Connectome. Retrieved February 8, 2015, from *http://jonlieffmd.com/blog/neuronal-connections-and-the-mind-the-connectome.*

Linan-Thompson, S., Cirino, P. T., & Vaughn, S. (2007). Determining English language learners' response to intervention: Questions and some answers. *Learning Disability Quarterly, 30,* 185–195.

Linderholm, T. (2002). Predictive inference generation as a function of working memory capacity and causal text constraints. *Discourse Processes, 34*(3), 259–280.

Lipson, M. Y. (1982). Learning new information from text: The role of prior knowledge and reading ability. *Journal of Literacy Research, 14*(3), 243–261.

Lloyd, S. L. (2004). Using comprehension strategies as a springboard for student talk. *Journal of Adolescent and Adult Literacy, 48*(2), 114–124.

Lockhead, G., & Crist, W. B. (1980). Making letters distinctive. *Journal of Educational Psychology, 72*(4), 483–493.

Logan, G. D. (1997). Automaticity and reading: Perspectives from the instance theory of automatization. *Reading and Writing Quarterly, 13*(2), 123–146.

Logan, S., Medford, E., & Hughes, N. (2011). The importance of intrinsic motivation for high and low ability readers' reading comprehension performance. *Learning and Individual Differences, 21*(1), 124–128.

Long, D. L., & De Ley, L. (2000). Implicit causality and discourse focus: The interaction of text and reader characteristics in pronoun resolution. *Journal of Memory and Language, 42*(4), 545–570.

Long, D. L., & Golding, J. M. (1993). Superordinate goal inferences: Are they automatically generated during comprehension? *Discourse Processes, 16*(1–2), 55–73.

Lonigan, C. J., Burgess, S. R., & Anthony, J. L. (2000). Development of emergent literacy and early reading skills in preschool children: Evidence from a latent-variable longitudinal study. *Developmental Psychology, 36,* 596–613.

Lonigan, C. J., & Whitehurst, G. J. (1998). Relative efficacy of parent and teacher involvement in a shared-reading intervention for preschool children from low-income backgrounds. *Early Childhood Research Quarterly, 13,* 263–290.

Lott, J. R. (1990). The effect of conviction on the legitimate income of criminals. *Economics Letters, 34*(4), 381–385.

Lovett, M. W., Lacerenza, L., Borden, S. L., Frijters, J. C., Steinback, K. A., & De Palma, M. (2000). Components of effective remediation for developmental reading disabilities: Combining phonological and strategy-based instruction to improve outcomes. *Journal of Educational Psychology, 92,* 263–283.

Lucas, M. (1999). Context effects in lexical access: A meta-analysis. *Memory and Cognition, 27*(3), 385–398.

Lundberg, I., Frost, J., & Peterson, O. (1988). Effects of an extensive program for stimulating phonological awareness in preschool children. *Reading Research Quarterly, 23,* 263–284.

Lynch, J. S., van den Broek, P., Kremer, K. E., Kendeou, P., White, M., & Lorch, E. P. (2008). The development of narrative comprehension in its relation to other early reading skills. *Reading Psychology, 29,* 327–365.

Lysaker, J. T., Tonge, C., Gauson, D., & Miller, A. (2011). Reading and social imagination: What relationally oriented reading instruction can do for children. *Reading Psychology, 32,* 520–566.

Mabie, G. E. (2002, March). A life with young learners: An interview with Bettye M. Caldwell. *Educational Forum, 66*(1), 40–49.

Macaruso, P., & Rodman, A. (2011). Efficacy of computer-assisted instruction for the development of early literacy skills in young children. *Reading Psychology, 32,* 172–196.

MacGinitie, W. H. (1969). Evaluating readiness for learning to read: A critical review and evaluation of research. *Reading Research Quarterly, 4*(3), 396–410.

Magliano, J. P., Baggett, W. B., Johnson, B. K., & Graesser, A. C. (1993). The time course of generating causal antecedent and causal consequence inferences. *Discourse Processes, 16*(1–2), 35–53.

Magliano, J. P., & Millis, K. K. (2003). Assessing reading skill with a think-aloud procedure and latent semantic analysis. *Cognition and Instruction, 21*(3), 251–283.

Maguire, E. A., Frith, C. D., & Morris, R. G. M.

(1999). The functional neuroanatomy of comprehension and memory: The importance of prior knowledge. *Brain, 122*(10), 1839–1850.

Males, M. (2009). The role of poverty in California teenagers' fatal traffic crash risk. *Californian Journal of Health Promotion, 7*(1), 1–13.

Malloy, J. A., Marinak, B. A., Gambrell, L. B., & Mazzoni, S. A. (2013). Assessing motivation to read. *The Reading Teacher, 67*(4), 273–282.

Malvern, D. D., & Richards, B. J. (2002). Investigating accommodation in language proficiency interviews using a new measure of lexical diversity. *Language Testing, 19*(1), 85–104.

Malvern, D. D., Richards, B. J., Chipere, N., & Durán, P. (2004). *Lexical diversity and language development: Quantification and assessment.* Basingstoke, UK: Palgrave.

Mancilla-Martinez, J., & Lesaux, N. K. (2011). The gap between Spanish speakers' word reading and word knowledge: A longitudinal study. *Child Development, 82*(5), 1544–1560.

Mandler, J. M., & Johnson, N. S. (1977). Remembrance of things parsed: Story structure and recall. *Cognitive Psychology, 9*, 111–151.

Mann, V. (1986). Phonological awareness: The role of reading experience. *Cognition, 24*, 65–92.

Mar, R. A., Oatley, K., Hirsh, J., dela Paz, J., & Peterson, J. B. (2006). Bookworms versus nerds: Exposure to fiction versus non-fiction, divergent associations with social ability, and the simulation of fictional social worlds. *Journal of Research in Personality, 40*, 694–712.

Mar, R. A., Oatley, K., & Peterson, J. B. (2009). Exploring the link between reading fiction and empathy: Ruling out individual differences and examining outcomes. *Communications, 34*, 407–429.

Marchman, V. A., & Fernald, A. (2008). Speed of word recognition and vocabulary knowledge in infancy predict cognitive and language outcomes in later childhood. *Developmental Science, 11*(3), F9–F16.

Marée, T. J., van Bruggen, J. M., & Jochems, W. M. (2013). Effective self-regulated science learning through multimedia-enriched skeleton concept maps. *Research in Science and Technological Education, 31*(1), 16–30.

Marinak, B. A., & Gambrell, L. B. (2008). Intrinsic motivation and rewards: What sustains young children's engagement with text? *Literacy Research and Instruction, 47*(1), 9–26.

Markman, E. M., Wasow, J. L., & Hansen, M. B. (2003). Use of the mutual exclusivity assumption by young word learners. *Cognitive Psychology, 47*(3), 241–275.

Marks, G. N. (2006). Family size, family type, and student achievement: Cross-national differences and the role of socioeconomic and school factors. *Journal of Comparative Family Studies, 37*(1), 1–24.

Marr, D. (1982). *Vision: A computational investigation into the human representation and processing of visual information.* San Francisco: Freeman.

Marsh, G., Desberg, P., & Cooper, J. (1977). Developmental strategies in reading. *Journal of Reading Behavior, 9*, 391–394.

Masonheimer, P. E., Drum, P. A., & Ehri, L. C. (1984). Does environmental print identification lead children into word reading? *Journal of Literacy Research, 16*(4), 257–271.

Matsumoto, A., Iidaka, T., Haneda, K., Okada, T., & Sadato, N. (2005). Linking semantic priming effect in functional MRI and event-related potentials. *Neuroimage, 24*(3), 624–634.

Mayor, J., & Plunkett, K. (2011). A statistical estimate of infant and toddler vocabulary size from CDI analysis. *Developmental Science, 14*(4), 769–785.

McBride-Chang, C. (1999). The ABCs of the ABCs: The development of letter-name and letter-sound knowledge. *Merrill–Palmer Quarterly, 45*, 285–308.

McBride-Chang, C., Shu, H., Zhou, A., Wat, C. P., & Wagner, R. K. (2003). Morphological awareness uniquely predicts young children's Chinese character recognition. *Journal of Educational Psychology, 95*(4), 743.

McCabe, A. (1997). Cultural background and storytelling: A review and implications for schooling. *Elementary School Journal, 97*(5), 453–473.

McCabe, J., Fairchild, E., Grauerholz, L., Pescosolido, B. A., & Tope, D. (2011). Gender in twentieth-century children's books: Patterns of disparity in titles and central characters. *Gender and Society, 25*(2), 197–226.

McCarthey, S. (1999). Identifying teacher practices that connect home and school. *Education and Urban Society, 32*, 83–107.

McClelland, J. L., & O'Regan, J. K. (1981). Expectations increase the benefit derived from parafoveal information in reading words aloud. *Journal of Experimental Psychology: Human Perception and Performance, 7*, 634–644.

McClelland, J. L., & Rumelhart, D. E. (1981). An interactive activation model of context effects in letter perception: Part 1. An account of basic findings. *Psychological Review, 88*, 375–407.

McDaniel, C. (2004). Critical literacy: A questioning stance and the possibility for change. *The Reading Teacher, 570*(5), 472–481.

McDonald, S. A., & Shillock, R. C. (2003). Low-level predictive inference in reading: The influence of transitional probabilities on eye movements. *Vision Research, 43,* 1735–1751.

McFalls, E. M., Schwanenflugel, P. J., & Stahl, S. (1996). Influence of word meaning on the acquisition of a reading vocabulary in second-grade children. *Reading and Writing: An Interdisciplinary Journal, 8,* 235–250.

McKenna, M. C., Conradi, K., Lawrence, C., Jang, B. G., & Meyer, J. P. (2012). Reading attitudes of middle school students: Results of a U.S. survey. *Reading Research Quarterly, 47*(3), 283–306.

McKenna, M. C., & Kear, D. J. (1990). Measuring attitude toward reading: A new tool for teachers. *The Reading Teacher, 43*(9), 626–639.

McKenna, M. C., Kear, D. J., & Ellsworth, R. A. (1995). Children's attitudes toward reading: A national survey. *Reading Research Quarterly, 30*(4), 934–956.

McKeown, M. G. (1985). The acquisition of word meaning from context by children of high and low ability. *Reading Research Quarterly, 20,* 482–496.

McKeown, M. G. (1993). Creating effective definitions for young word learners. *Reading Research Quarterly, 28*(1), 16–31.

McKeown, M. G., & Beck, I. L. (1990). The assessment and characterization of young learners' knowledge of a topic in history. *American Educational Research Journal, 27*(4), 688–726.

McKeown, M. G., & Beck, I. L. (2004). Transforming knowledge into professional development resources: Six teachers implement a model of teaching for understanding text. *Elementary School Journal, 104*(5), 391–408.

McKeown, M. G., Beck, I. L., & Worthy, M. J. (1993). Grappling with text ideas: Questioning the author. *The Reading Teacher, 46*(7), 560–566.

McKool, S. S., & Gespass, S. (2009). Does Johnny's reading teacher love to read?: How teachers' personal reading habits affect instructional practices. *Literacy Research and Instruction, 48*(3), 264–276.

McKoon, G., & Ratcliff, R. (1986). Inferences about predictable events. *Journal of Experimental Psychology: Learning, Memory, and Cognition, 12*(1), 82–91.

McLuhan, M. (1963). *The Gutenberg galaxy.* Toronto, Ontario, Canada: University of Toronto.

McNamara, D. S., Graesser, A. C., McCarthy, P. M., & Cai, Z. (2014). *Automated evaluation of text and discourse with Coh-Metrix.* New York: Cambridge University Press.

McNamara, D. S., & Kendeou, P. (2011). Translating advances in reading comprehension research to educational practice. *International Electronic Journal of Elementary Education, 4*(1), 33–46.

McNamara, D. S., Kintsch, E., Songer, N. B., & Kintsch, W. (1996). Are good texts always better?: Interactions of text coherence, background knowledge, and levels of understanding in learning from text. *Cognition and Instruction, 14*(1), 1–43.

McNamara, T. P. (1992). Theories of priming: I. Associative distance and lag. *Journal of Experimental Psychology: Learning, Memory, and Cognition, 18*(6), 1173–1190.

McNamara, T. P. (2005). *Semantic priming: Perspectives from memory and word recognition.* New York: Psychology Press.

McNicol, S. J., & Dalton, P. (2002). "The best way is always through the children": The impact of family reading. *Journal of Adolescent and Adult Literacy, 46*(3), 248–253.

McRae, K., de Sa, V. R., & Seidenberg, M. S. (1997). On the nature and scope of featural representations of word meaning. *Journal of Experimental Psychology: General, 126,* 99–130.

Meara, P. M. (1981). Vocabulary acquisition: A neglected aspect of language learning. *Language Teaching and Linguistics Abstracts, 14,* 221–246.

Meara, P. M., & Olmos Alcoy, J. C. (2010). Words as species: An alternative approach to estimating productive vocabulary size. *Reading in a Foreign Language, 22*(1), 222–236.

Meisinger, E. B., Bradley, B. A., Schwanenflugel, P. J., & Kuhn, M. R. (2009). Myth and reality of the word caller: The relationship between teacher nominations and prevalence among elementary school children. *School Psychology Quarterly, 24,* 147–159.

Meisinger, E. B., Bradley, B. A., Schwanenflugel, P. J., & Kuhn, M. R. (2010). Teachers' perception of word callers and related literacy concepts. *School Psychology Review, 39*(1), 54–68.

Melby-Lervåg, M., & Lervåg, A. (2011). Cross-linguistic transfer of oral language, decoding, phonological awareness, and reading comprehension: A meta-analysis of the correlational evidence. *Journal of Research in Reading, 34*(1), 114–135.

Melby-Lervåg, M., Lyser, S.-A., & Hulme, C. (2012). Phonological skills and their role in learning to read: A meta-analytic review. *Psychological Review, 138*(2), 322–352.

Merga, M. K. (2014a). Exploring the role of parents in supporting recreational book reading beyond primary school. *English in Education, 48*(2), 149–163.

Merga, M. K. (2014b). Peer group and friend influences on the social acceptability of adolescent book reading. *Journal of Adolescent and Adult Literacy, 57*(6), 472–482.

Mervis, C. B., & Bertrand, J. (1994). Acquisition of the novel name–nameless category (N3C) principle. *Child Development, 65*(6), 1646–1662.

Mervis, C. B., & Bertrand, J. (1995). Early lexical acquisition and the vocabulary spurt: A response to Goldfield and Reznick. *Journal of Child Language, 22*, 461–468.

Methe, S. A., & Hintze, J. M. (2003). Evaluating teacher modeling as a strategy to increase student reading behavior. *School Psychology Review, 32*(4), 617–622.

Metsala, J. L. (1997). An examination of word frequency and neighborhood density in the development of spoken-word recognition. *Memory and Cognition, 25*(1), 47–56.

Metsala, J. L. (1999). The development of phonemic awareness in reading-disabled children. *Applied Psycholinguistics, 20*(1), 149–158.

Meyer, B. J. F. (1985). Prose analysis: Purposes, procedures, and problems. In B. K. Britten & J. B. Black (Eds.), *Understanding expository text: A theoretical and practical handbook for analyzing explanatory text* (pp. 11–64). Hillsdale, NJ: Erlbaum.

Meyer, B. J. F., Brandt, D. M., & Bluth, G. J. (1980). Use of top-level structure in text: Key for reading comprehension of ninth-grade students. *Reading Research Quarterly, 16*, 72–103.

Meyer, B. J. F., & Ray, M. N. (2011). Structure strategy interventions: Increasing reading comprehension of expository text. *International Electronic Journal of Elementary Education, 4*(1), 127–152.

Meyer, B. J. F., & Wijekumar, K. (2007). A web-based tutoring system for the structure strategy: Theoretical background, design, and findings. In D. S. McNamara (Ed.), *Reading comprehension strategies: Theories, interventions, and technologies* (pp. 347–375). Mahwah, NJ: Erlbaum.

Meyer, D. E., & Schvaneveldt, R. W. (1971). Facilitation in recognizing pairs of words: Evidence of a dependence between retrieval operations. *Journal of Experimental Psychology, 90*, 227–234.

Michaels, S. (1981). "Sharing time": Children's narrative styles and differential access to literacy. *Language in Society, 10*(3), 423–442.

Michaels, S., & Collins, J. (1984). Oral discourse styles: Classroom interaction and the acquisition of literacy. In D. Tannen (Ed.), *Coherence in spoken and written discourse* (pp. 219–244). Norwood, NJ: Ablex.

Miller, G. A., & Gildea, P. M. (1987). How children learn words. *Scientific American, 257*(3), 94–99.

Miller, J., & Schwanenflugel, P. J. (2006). Prosody of syntactically complex sentences in the oral reading of young children. *Journal of Educational Psychology, 98*(4), 839–853.

Miller, J., & Schwanenflugel, P. J. (2008). A longitudinal study of the development of reading prosody as a dimension of oral reading fluency in early elementary school children. *Reading Research Quarterly, 43*, 336–354.

Miller, S. D., & Smith, D. E. (1985). Differences in literal and inferential comprehension after reading orally and silently. *Journal of Educational Psychology, 77*, 341–348.

Mischel, W., Ebbesen, E. B., & Raskoff Zeiss, A. (1972). Cognitive and attentional mechanisms in delay of gratification. *Journal of Personality and Social Psychology, 21*(2), 204.

Miyake, N., & Norman, D. A. (1979). To ask a question, one must know enough to know what is not known. *Journal of Verbal Learning and Verbal Behavior, 18*, 357–364.

Moje, E. B., Overby, M., Tysvaer, N., & Morris, K. (2008). The complex world of adolescent literacy: Myths, motivations, and mysteries. *Harvard Educational Review, 78*(1), 107–154.

Mokhtari, K., & Thompson, H. B. (2006). How problems of reading fluency and comprehension are related to difficulties in syntactic awareness skills in fifth graders. *Reading Research and Instruction, 46*(1), 73–94.

Mol, S. E., & Bus, A. G. (2011). To read or not to read: A meta-analysis of print exposure from infancy to early adulthood. *Psychological Bulletin, 137*(2), 267–296.

Mol, S. E., Bus, A. G., & de Jong, M. T. (2009). Interactive book reading in early education: A tool to stimulate print knowledge as well as oral language. *Review of Educational Research, 79*(2), 979–1007.

Mol, S. E., Bus, A. G., de Jong, M. T., & Smeets, D. J. (2008). Added value of dialogic parent–child book readings: A meta-analysis. *Early Education and Development, 19*(1), 7–26.

Moll, L. C. (Ed.). (1992). *Vygotsky and education: Instructional implications and applications of sociohistorical psychology.* New York: Cambridge University Press.

Moll, L. C., Amanti, C., Neff, D., & Gonzalez, N. (1992). Funds of knowledge for teaching: Using a qualitative approach to connect homes and classrooms. *Theory into Practice, 31*(2), 132–141.

Moore, C., & Furrow, D. (1991). The development of language of belief: The expression of relative certainty. In D. Frye & C. Moore (Eds.), *Children's theories of mind: Mental states and social understanding* (pp. 173–193). Hillsdale, NJ: Erlbaum.

Morgan, H. (2013). Multimodal children's e-books help young learners in reading. *Early Childhood Education Journal, 41*(6), 477–483.

Morgan, P. L., & Fuchs, D. (2007). Is there a bidirectional relationship between children's reading skills and reading motivation? *Exceptional Children, 73*(2), 165–183.

Morgan, P. L., Fuchs, D., Compton, D. L., Cordray, D. S., & Fuchs, L. S. (2008). Does early reading failure decrease children's reading motivation? *Journal of Learning Disabilities, 41*(5), 387–404.

Morrison, C. M., Chappell, T. D., & Ellis, A. W. (1997). Age of acquisition norms for a large set of object names and their relation to adult estimates and other variables. *Quarterly Journal of Experimental Psychology, 50A*, 528–559.

Morrison, C. M., & Ellis, A. W. (1995). The role of word frequency and age of acquisition in word naming and lexical decision. *Journal of Experimental Psychology: Learning, Memory, and Cognition, 21*, 116–133.

Mulder, G., & Sanders, T. J. M. (2012). Causal coherence relations and levels of discourse representation. *Discourse Processes, 49*(6), 501–522.

Murphy, P. K., & Alexander, P. A. (2000). A motivated exploration of motivation terminology. *Contemporary Educational Psychology, 25*(1), 3–53.

Muter, V., Hulme, C., Snowling, M. J., & Stevenson, J. (2004). Phonemes, rimes, vocabulary, and grammatical skills as foundations of early reading development: Evidence from a longitudinal study. *Developmental Psychology, 40*, 665–681.

Nag, S. (2007). Early reading in Kannada: The pace of acquisition of orthographic knowledge and phonemic awareness. *Journal of Research in Reading, 30*(1), 7–22.

Nagengast, B., Marsh, H. W., Scalas, L. F., Xu, M. K., Hau, K. T., & Trautwein, U. (2011). Who took the "x" out of expectancy–value theory?: A psychological mystery, a substantive–methodological synergy, and a cross-national generalization. *Psychological Science, 22*(8), 1058–1066.

Nagy, W. E., & Anderson, R. C. (1984). How many words are there in printed school English? *Reading Research Quarterly, 19*(3), 304–330.

Nagy, W. E., & Herman, P. (1987). Depth and breadth of vocabulary knowledge: Implications for acquisition and instruction. In M. G. McKeown & M. E. Curtis (Eds.), *The nature of vocabulary acquisition* (pp. 19–35). Hillsdale, NJ: Erlbaum.

Nagy, W. E., & Townsend, D. (2012). Words as tools: Learning academic vocabulary as language acquisition. *Reading Research Quarterly, 47*(1), 91–108.

Nathanson, S., Pruslow, J., & Levitt, R. (2008). The reading habits and literacy attitudes of inservice and prospective teachers: Results of a questionnaire survey. *Journal of Teacher Education, 59*(4), 313–321.

Nation, I. S. P. (2001). *Learning vocabulary in another language.* New York: Cambridge University Press.

Nation, K., Angell, P., & Castles, A. (2007). Orthographic learning via self-teaching in children learning to read English: Effects of exposure, durability, and context. *Journal of Experimental Child Psychology, 96*, 71–84.

Nation, K., & Snowling, M. (1997). Assessing reading difficulties: The validity and utility of current measures of reading skill. *British Journal of Educational Psychology, 67*(3), 359–370.

Nation, K., & Snowling, M. J. (2004). Beyond phonological skills: Broader language skills contribute to the development of reading. *Journal of Research in Reading, 27*, 342–356.

National Assessment of Educational Progress. (2011). The nation's report card. Retrieved from *http://nationsreportcard.gov/reading_/nat_g4.asp?tab_idtab2&subtab_id=Tab_7#chart.*

National Association for the Education of Young Children. (2002). *Early learning standards: Creating the conditions for success.* Washington, DC: Author.

National Association for the Education of Young Children. (2014). *NAEYC early childhood program standards and accreditation criteria and guidance for assessment.* Washington, DC: Author. Retrieved November 30, 2014, from *www.naeyc.org/academy/files/academy/file/AllCriteriaDocument.pdf.*

National Center for Early Development and Learning. (2005). Prekindergarten in eleven states: NCEDL's multi-state study of prekindergarten and study of state-wide early education programs (SWEEP). Preliminary descriptive report. Available at *www.fpg.unc.edu/ncedl/pdfs/SWEEP_MS_summary_final.pdf.*

National Center for Education Statistics. (2013). *The nation's report card: Trends in academic progress 2012* (NCES 2013-456). Washington, DC: Author. Available at *http://nces.ed.gov/nationsreportcard.*

National Early Literacy Panel. (2008). *Developing early literacy.* Washington, DC: National Institute for Literacy.

National Endowment for the Arts. (2007). *To read or not to read: A question of national consequence* (Research Report #47). Washington, DC: Author.

National Endowment for the Arts. (2015). How a nation engages with art: Highlights from the survey of public participation in the arts (rev.). Retrieved January 16, 2015, from *http://arts.gov/sites/default/files/highlights-from-2012-sppa-revised-jan2015.pdf*.

National Governors Association Center for Best Practices & Council of Chief State School Officers. (2010). *Common Core State Standards for English language arts and literacy in history/social studies, science, and technical subjects*. Washington, DC: Author.

National Institute of Child Health and Human Development. (2000). *Report of the National Reading Panel. Teaching children to read: An evidence-based assessment of the scientific research literature on reading and its implications for reading instruction: Reports of the subgroups* (NIH Publication No. 00-4754). Washington, DC: U.S. Government Printing Office.

National Institute of Child Health and Human Development Early Child Care Research Network. (2005). Pathways to reading: The role of oral language in the transition to reading. *Developmental Psychology, 41*(2), 428–444.

Nation's Report Card. (2013). What poportions of student groups are reaching proficient? Retrieved from *www.nationsreportcard.gov/reading_math_2013/#/student-groups*.

Neely, J. H. (1991). Semantic priming effects in visual word recognition: A selective review of current findings and theories. In D. Besner & G. W. Humphreys (Eds.), *Basic processes in reading: Visual word recognition* (pp. 264–336). Hillsdale, NJ: Erlbaum.

Neisser, U. (1967). *Cognitive psychology*. New York: Appleton, Century, Crofts.

Nelson, K. (1973). Structure and strategy in learning to talk. *Monographs of the Society for Research in Child Development, 38*, 1–135.

Nelson, R. O., & Wein, K. S. (1974). Training letter discrimination by presentation of high-confusion versus low-confusion alternative. *Journal of Educational Psychology, 66*(6), 926–931.

Nesbit, J. C., & Adesope, O. O. (2006). Learning with concept and knowledge maps: A meta-analysis. *Review of Educational Research, 76*(3), 413–448.

Neuman, S. B. (1988). The displacement effect: Assessing the relation between television viewing and reading performance. *Reading Research Quarterly, 23*(4), 414–440.

Neuman, S. B. (1991). *Literacy in the television age*. Norwood, NJ: Ablex.

Neuman, S. B., & Celano, D. (2001). Access to print in low-income and middle-income communities: An ecological study of four neighborhoods. *Reading Research Quarterly, 36*(1), 8–26.

Neuman, S. B., & Celano, D. (2012). *Giving our children a fighting chance: Affluence, literacy, and the development of information capital*. New York: Teachers College Press.

Neumann, M. M., Hood, M., & Ford, R. M. (2013a). Using environmental print to enhance emergent literacy and print motivation. *Reading and Writing, 26*(5), 771–793.

Neumann, M. M., Hood, M., Ford, R. M., & Neumann, D. L. (2011). The role of environmental print in emergent literacy. *Journal of Early Childhood Literacy, 12*(3), 231–258.

Neumann, M. M., Hood, M., Ford, R. M., & Neumann, D. L. (2013b). Letter and numeral identification: Their relationship with early literacy and numeracy skills. *European Early Childhood Education Research Journal, 21*(4), 489–501.

Newcombe, P. I., Campbell, C., Siakaluk, P. D., & Pexman, P. M. (2012). Effects of emotional and sensorimotor knowledge in semantic processing of concrete and abstract nouns. *Frontiers in Human Neuroscience, 6*, article #275.

Nicholls, J. G., & Miller, A. (1984). Conceptions of ability and achievement motivation. In R. Ames & C. Ames (Eds.), *Research on motivation in education: Student motivation* (Vol. 1, pp. 39–73). New York: Academic Press.

Nichols, S. L., Glass, G. V., & Berliner, D. C. (2012). High-stakes testing and student achievement: Updated analyses with NAEP data. *Education Policy Analysis Archives, 20*(20).

Nilsen, E., & Bourassa, D. (2008). Word-learning performance in beginning readers. *Canadian Journal of Experimental Psychology, 62*(2), 110–116.

Nilsson, N. L. (2005). How does Hispanic portrayal in children's books measure up after 40 years?: The answer is "It depends." *The Reading Teacher, 58*(6), 534–548.

Nippold, M. A., & Sun, L. (2008). Knowledge of morphologically complex words: A developmental study of older children and young adolescents. *Language, Speech, and Hearing Services in the Schools, 39*, 365–373.

Nist, S. L., & Olejnik, S. (1995). The role of context and dictionary definition on varying levels of word knowledge. *Reading Research Quarterly, 30*(2), 172–193.

Noordman, L., Dassen, I., Swerts, M., & Terken, J. (1999). Prosodic markers of text structure. In K. van Hoek, A. Kibrik, & L. Noordman (Eds.), *Discourse studies in cognitive linguistics: Selected papers from the 5th international cognitive linguistics conference* (pp. 133–148). Amsterdam, The Netherlands: Benjamins.

Norton, M. I., & Ariely, D. (2011). Building a better

America: One wealth quintile at a time. *Perspectives on Psychological Science, 6*(1), 9–12.

Norwalk, K. E., DiPerna, J. C., Lei, P.-W., & Wu, Q. (2012). Examining early literacy skill differences among children in Head Start via latent profile analysis. *School Psychology Quarterly, 27,* 170–183.

Nunes, T., Bryant, P., & Barros, R. (2012). The development of word recognition and its significance for comprehension and fluency. *Journal of Educational Psychology, 104*(4), 959–973.

Oakhill, J. (1984). Inferential and memory skills in children's comprehension of stories. *British Journal of Educational Psychology, 54,* 31–39.

Oakhill, J., Hartt, J., & Samols, D. (2005). Levels of comprehension monitoring and working memory in good and poor comprehenders. *Reading and Writing, 18*(7–9), 657–686.

Oakhill, J., & Patel, S. (1991). Can imagery training help children who have comprehension problems? *Journal of Research in Reading, 12,* 106–115.

OECD Statistics Canada. (2011). *Literacy for life: Further results from the Adult Literacy and Life Skills Survey.* Ottawa: OECD Publishing.

O'Flahavan, J., Gambrell, L. B., Guthrie, J., Stahl, S., Baumann, J. F., & Alvermann, D. E. (1992). Poll results guide activities of research center. *Reading Today, 10*(1), 12.

Ogawa, E., & Shodo, H. (2001). Effects of aloud/silent reading, reading speed, Type A behavior pattern, and preference of material on the cardiovascular reactivity during reading tasks. *Japanese Journal of Physiological Psychology and Psychophysiology, 19*(1), 25–32.

Ogbu, J. U. (2003). *Black students in an affluent suburb: A study of academic disengagement.* Mahwah, NJ: Erlbaum.

Ogbu, J. U. (2004). Collective identity and the burden of "acting White" in Black history, community, and education. *Urban Review, 36*(1), 1–35.

Ogbu, J. U., & Simons, H. D. (1998). Voluntary and involuntary minorities: A cultural-ecological theory of school performance with some implications for education. *Anthropology and Education Quarterly, 29*(2), 155–188.

Ogle, D. (2009). Creating contexts for inquiry: From KWL to PRC2. *Knowledge Quest, 38*(1), 56–61.

Oldfather, P., & Dahl, K. (1994). Toward a social constructivist reconceptualization of intrinsic motivation for literacy learning. *Journal of Literacy Research, 26*(2), 139–158.

Oliver, K. (2009). An investigation of concept mapping to improve the reading comprehension of science texts. *Journal of Science Education and Technology, 18*(5), 402–414.

Oller, D. K., & Eilers, R. E. (Eds.). (2002). *Language and literacy in bilingual children* (Vol. 2). Clevedon, UK: Multilingual Matters.

Olson, D. R. (1986). The cognitive consequences of literacy. *Canadian Psychology, 27*(2), 109–121.

Olson, R. K., Gillis, J. J., Rack, J. P., DeFries, J. C., & Fulker, D. W. (1991). Confirmatory factor analysis of word recognition and process measures in the Colorado Reading Project. *Reading and Writing, 3,* 235–248.

O'Mara, J., & Laidlaw, L. (2011). Living in the iWorld: Two literacy researchers reflect on the changing texts and literacy practices of childhood. *English Teaching: Practice and Critique, 10*(4), 149–159.

Ordóñez, C. L., Carlo, M. S., Snow, C., & McLaughlin, B. (2002). Depth and breadth of vocabulary in two languages: Which vocabulary skills transfer? *Journal of Educational Psychology, 94*(4), 719–728.

Ornaghi, V., Brockmeier, J., & Gavazzi, I. G. (2011). The role of language games in children's understanding of mental states: A training study. *Journal of Cognition and Development, 12*(2), 239–259.

Osterholm, K., Nash, W. R., & Kritsonis, W. A. (2007). Effects of labeling students "learning disabled": Emergent themes in the research literature 1970 through 2000. *Focus on Colleges, Universities, and Schools, 1*(1), 1–11.

Ouellette, G. P. (2006). What's meaning got to do with it?: The role of vocabulary in word reading and reading comprehension. *Journal of Educational Psychology, 98*(3), 554–566.

Ouellette, G. P., & Beers, A. (2010). A not-so-simple view of reading: How oral vocabulary and visual-word recognition complicate the story. *Reading and Writing, 23*(2), 189–208.

Pachtman, A. B., & Wilson, K. A. (2006). What do the kids think? *The Reading Teacher, 59*(7), 680–684.

Pacton, S., Perruchet, P., Fayol, M., & Cleeremans, A. (2001). Implicit learning in real world context: The case of orthographic regularities. *Journal of Experimental Psychology: General, 130,* 401–426.

Pae, H. K., Greenburg, D., & Morris, R. D. (2012). Construct validity and measurement invariance of the Peabody Picture Vocabulary Test–III Form A. *Language Assessment Quarterly, 9*(2), 152–171.

Paige, D. D., Rasinski, T. B., & Magpuri-Lavell, T. (2012). Is fluent, expressive reading important for high school readers? *Journal of Adolescent and Adult Literacy, 56*(1), 67–76.

Paivio, A. (1968). A factor-analytic study of word attributes and verbal learning. *Journal of Verbal Learning and Verbal Behavior, 7,* 41–49.

Palincsar, A. S., & Brown, A. L. (1984). Reciprocal teaching of comprehension-fostering and comprehension-monitoring activities. *Cognition and Instruction, 1,* 117–175.

Paratore, J. R. (2002). Home and school together: Helping beginning readers succeed. In S. J. Samuels & A. Farstrup (Eds.), *What research has to say about reading instruction* (pp. 48–68). Newark, DE: International Reading Association.

Paratore, J. R., & Dougherty, S. (2011). Home differences and reading difficulty. In A. McGill-Franzen& Allington, R. L. (Eds.), *Handbook of reading disability research* (pp. 93–109). New York: Routledge.

Parault, S. J., & Williams, H. M. (2010). Reading motivation, reading amount, and text comprehension in deaf and hearing adults. *Journal of Deaf Studies and Deaf Education, 15*(2), 120–135.

Parault Dowds, S. J., Haverback, H. R., & Parkinson, M. M. (2014). Classifying the context clues in children's text. *Journal of Experimental Education.*

Paris, D. (2012). Culturally sustaining pedagogy: A needed change in stance, terminology, and practice. *Educational Researcher, 41*(3), 93–97.

Paris, S. G. (2005). Reinterpreting the development of reading skills. *Reading Research Quarterly, 40*(2), 184–202.

Paris, S. G., Lindauer, B. K., & Cox, G. L. (1977). The development of inferential comprehension. *Child Development, 48*(4), 1728–1733.

Paris, S. G., Lipson, M. Y., & Wixson, K. K. (1983). Becoming a strategic reader. *Contemporary Educational Psychology, 8*(3), 293–316.

Paris, S. G., & McNaughton, S. (2010). Social and cultural influences on children's motivation for reading. In D. Wise, R. Andrews, & J. Hoffman (Eds.), *The Routledge international handbook of English language and literacy teaching* (pp. 11–21). New York: Routledge.

Parish-Morris, J., Mahajan, N., Hirsh-Pasek, K., Golinkoff, R. M., & Collins, M. F. (2013). Once upon a time: Parent–child dialogue and storybook reading in the electronic era. *Mind, Brain, and Education, 7*(3), 200–211.

Park, H. J., Roberts, K. D., Takahashi, K., & Stodden, R. (2014). Using Kurzweil 3000 as a reading intervention for high school struggling readers: Results of a research study. Retrieved January 20, 2015, from *http://scholarworks.calstate.edu/bitstream/handle/10211.3/121970/JTPD201406-p105-113.pdf?sequence=1.*

Park, Y. (2011). How motivational constructs interact to predict elementary students' reading performance: Examples from attitudes and self-concept in reading. *Learning and Individual Differences, 21*(4), 347–358.

Partin, K., & Hendricks, C. G. (2002). The relationship between positive adolescent attitudes toward reading and home literary environment. *Reading Horizons, 43*(1), 8.

Patel, A. D., Peretz, I., Tramo, M., & Labreque, R. (1998). Processing prosody and musical patterns: A neuropsychological investigation. *Brain and Language, 61,* 123–144.

Patel, T. K., Snowling, M. J., & deJong, P. F. (2004). A cross-linguistic comparison of children learning to read in English and Dutch. *Journal of Educational Psychology, 96*(4), 785–797.

Paulson, E. J. (2006). Self-selected reading for enjoyment as a college developmental reading approach. *Journal of College Reading and Learning, 36*(2), 51–58.

Pavonetti, L. M., Brimmer, K. M., & Cipielewski, J. F. (2002). Accelerated Reader: What are the lasting effects on the reading habits of middle school students exposed to Accelerated Reader in elementary grades? *Journal of Adolescent and Adult Literacy, 46*(4), 300–311.

Pearson, B. Z., Fernandez, S. C., & Oller, D. K. (1993). Lexical development in bilingual infants and toddlers: Comparison to monolingual norms. *Language Learning, 43*(1), 93–120.

Pearson, P. D., & Gallagher, M. C. (1983). The instruction of reading comprehension. *Contemporary Educational Psychology, 8,* 317–344.

Pelli, D. G., Burns, C. W., Farell, B., Moore-Page, D. C. (2006). Feature detection and letter identification. *Vision Research, 46,* 4646–4674.

Pepi, A., Alesi, M., & Geraci, M. (2004). Theories of intelligence in children with reading disabilities: A training proposal. *Psychological Reports, 95*(3), 949–952.

Perfetti, C. A. (2007). Reading ability: Lexical quality to comprehension. *Scientific Studies of Reading, 11*(4), 357–383.

Perfetti, C. A., Beck, I., Bell, L. C., & Hughes, C. (1987). Phonemic knowledge and learning to read are reciprocal: A longitudinal study of first grade children. *Merrill–Palmer Quarterly, 33,* 283–319.

Perlman, C. L., Borger, J., Collins, C. B., Elenbogan, J. C., & Wood, J. (1996, April). *The effect of time limits on learning disabled students' scores on standardized tests.* Paper presented at the annual meeting of the National Council on Measurement in Education, New York.

Peters, E. E., & Levin, J. R. (1986). Effects of a mnemonic imagery strategy on good and poor readers' prose recall. *Reading Research Quarterly, 21*(2), 179–192.

Pew Charitable Trusts. (2011). The state of children's dental health. Retrieved November 21, 2014, from *www.pewtrusts.org/en/research-and-analysis/reports/0001/01/01/the-state-of-childrens-dental-health*.

Philips, S. U. (1972). Participant structures and communicative competence: Warm Springs children in community and classroom. In C. B. Cazden, V. P. John, & D. Hymes (Eds.), *Functions of language in the classroom* (pp. 370–394). New York: Teachers College Press.

Phillips, B. M., Clancy-Menchetti, J., & Lonigan, C. J. (2008). Successful phonological awareness instruction with preschool children: Lessons from the classroom. *Topics in Early Childhood Special Education, 28*(1), 3–17.

Phillips, B. M., & Lonigan, C. J. (2009). Variations in the home literacy environment of preschool children: A cluster analytic approach. *Scientific Studies of Reading, 13*(2), 146–174.

Phillips, B. M., Piasta, S. B., Anthony, J. L., Lonigan, C. J., & Francis, D. J. (2012). IRTs of the ABCs: Children's letter name acquisition. *Journal of School Psychology, 50*, 461–481.

Piaget, J. (1970). Piaget's theory. In P. H. Mussen (Ed.), *Carmichael's handbook of child psychology* (Vol. 1, pp. 703–733). New York: Wiley.

Piaget, J., & Inhelder, B. (1969). *The psychology of the child*. New York: Basic Books.

Piasta, S. B. (2006). Acquisition of alphabetic knowledge: Examining letter- and child-level factors in a single comprehensive model. *Electronic Theses, Treatises and Dissertations,* paper 931, Florida State University.

Piasta, S. B., Petscher, Y., & Justice, L. M. (2012). How many letters should preschoolers in public programs know?: The diagnostic efficiency of various preschool letter-naming benchmarks for predicting first-grade literacy achievement. *Journal of Educational Psychology, 104*(4), 945–958.

Piasta, S. B., & Wagner, R. K. (2010a). Developing early literacy skills: A meta-analysis of alphabet learning and instruction. *Reading Research Quarterly, 45*(1), 8–38.

Piasta, S. B., & Wagner, R. K. (2010b). Learning letter names and sounds: Effects of instruction, letter type, and phonological processing skill. *Journal of Experimental Child Psychology, 105*, 324–344.

Pichert, J. A., & Anderson, R. C. (1977). Taking different perspectives on a story. *Journal of Educational Psychology, 69*, 309–315.

Pike, M. M., Barnes, M. A., & Barron, R. W. (2010). The role of illustrations in children's inferential comprehension. *Journal of Experimental Child Psychology, 105*(3), 243–255.

Pikulski, J. J. (1988). Questions and answers. *The Reading Teacher, 42*(1), 76.

Pinheiro, A. P., Vasconcelos, M., Dias, M., Arrais, N., & Gonclaves, O. F. (2015). The music of language: An ERP investigation of the effects of musical training on emotional prosody processing. *Brain and Language, 140*, 24–34.

Pinker, S., & Ullman, M. T. (2002). The past and future of the past tense. *Trends in Cognitive Science, 6*, 456–463.

Plaut, D. C., & Booth, J. R. (2000). Individual and developmental differences in semantic priming: Empirical and computational support for a single-mechanism account of lexical processing. *Psychological Review, 107*(4), 786–823.

Pressley, G. M. (1976). Mental imagery helps eight-year-olds remember what they read. *Journal of Educational Psychology, 68*, 355–359.

Pressley, M., Duke, N. K., Gaskins, I. W., Fingeret, L., Halladay, J., Hilden, K., et al. (2009). Working with struggling readers: Why we must get beyond the simple view of reading and visions of how it might be done. In T. Gutkin & C. R. Reynolds (Eds.), *The handbook of school psychology* (4th ed., pp. 522–546). New York: Wiley.

Pressley, M., El-Dinary, P. B., Gaskins, I., Schuder, T., Bergman, J. L., Almasi, J., et al. (1992). Beyond direct explanation: Transactional instruction of reading comprehension strategies. *Elementary School Journal, 92*, 513–555.

Pressley, M., Johnson, C. J., Symons, S., McGoldrick, J. A., & Kurita, J. A. (1989). Strategies that improve children's memory and comprehension of text. *Elementary School Journal, 90*(1), 3–32.

Priebe, S. J., Keenan, J. M., & Miller, A. C. (2012). How prior knowledge affects word identification and comprehension. *Reading and Writing, 25*, 131–149.

Prior, S. M., Fenwick, K. D., Saunders, K. S., Ouellette, R., O'Quinn, C., & Harvey, S. (2011). Comprehension after oral and silent reading: Does grade level matter? *Literacy Research and Instruction, 50*, 183–194.

Prior, S. M., & Welling, K. A. (2001). "Read in your head": A Vygotskian analysis of the transition from oral to silent reading. *Reading Psychology, 22*, 1–15.

Protopapas, A., Simos, P. G., Sideridis, G. D., & Mouzaki, A. (2012). The components of the simple view of reading: A confirmatory factor analysis. *Reading Psychology, 33*(3), 217–240.

Puranik, C. S., & Lonigan, C. J. (2012). Name-writing proficiency, not length of name, is associated with preschool children's emergent literacy skills. *Early Childhood Research Quarterly, 27*, 284–294.

Puranik, C. S., Lonigan, C. J., & Kim, Y.-S. (2011).

Contributions of emergent literacy skills to name writing, letter writing, and spelling in preschool children. *Early Childhood Research Quarterly, 26,* 465–474.

Purcell-Gates, V. (1988). Lexical and syntactic knowledge of written narrative held by well-read-to kindergartners and second graders. *Research in the Teaching of English, 22*(2), 128–160.

Purcell-Gates, V. (1996). Stories, coupons, and the *TV Guide*: Relationships between home literacy experiences and emergent literacy knowledge. *Reading Research Quarterly, 31*(4), 406–428.

Purcell-Gates, V., & Dahl, K. (1991). Low-SES children's success and failure at early literacy learning in skills-based classrooms. *Journal of Reading Behavior, 23,* 1–34.

Quemart, P., Casalis, S., & Cole, P. (2011). The role of form and meaning in the processing of written morphology: A priming study in French developing readers. *Journal of Experimental Child Psychology, 109,* 478–496.

Quian, D. (1999). Assessing the roles of depth and breadth of vocabulary knowledge in reading comprehension. *Canadian Modern Language Review, 56*(2), 282–307.

Quirk, M. P., & Beem, S. (2012). Examining the relations between reading fluency and reading comprehension for English Language learners. *Psychology in the Schools, 49*(6), 539–553.

Quirk, M. P., & Schwanenflugel, P. J. (2004). Do supplemental remedial reading programs address the motivational issues of struggling readers?: An analysis of five popular programs. *Literacy Research and Instruction, 43*(3), 1–19

Quirk, M. P., Schwanenflugel, P. J., & Webb, M. Y. (2009). A short-term longitudinal study of the relationship between motivation to read and reading fluency skill in second grade. *Journal of Literacy Research, 41*(2), 196–227.

Radvansky, G. A., Gerard, L. D., Zacks, R. T., & Hasher, L. (1990). Younger and older adults' use of mental models as representations for text materials. *Psychology and Aging, 5,* 209–214.

Radvansky, G. A., Zwaan, R. A., Curiel, J. M., & Copeland, D. E. (2001). Situation models and aging. *Psychology and Aging, 16,* 145–160.

Raikes, H., Alexander Pan, B., Luze, G., Tamis-LeMonda, C. S., Brooks-Gunn, J., Constantine, J., et al. (2006). Mother–child bookreading in low-income families: Correlates and outcomes during the first three years of life. *Child Development, 77*(4), 924–953.

Ramus, F., Hauser, M. D., Miller, C., Morris, D., & Mehler, J. (2000). Language discrimination by human newborns and by cotton-top tamarin monkeys. *Science, 288,* 349–351.

Raphael, T. E., & Au, K. H. (2005). QAR: Enhancing comprehension and test taking across grades and content areas. *The Reading Teacher, 59*(3), 206–221.

Raphael, T. E., & McMahon, S. I. (1994). Book club: An alternative framework for reading instruction. *The Reading Teacher, 48*(2), 102–116.

Raphael, T. E., & Pearson, P. D. (1985). Increasing students' awareness of sources of information for answering questions. *American Educational Research Journal, 22,* 217–236.

Rasinski, T. V., Rikli, A., & Johnston, S. (2009). Reading fluency: More than automaticity?: More than a concern for the primary grades? *Reading Research and Instruction, 48*(4), 350–361.

Rastle, K., & Davis, M. H. (2008). Morphological decomposition based on the analysis of orthography. *Language and Cognitive Processes, 23*(7–8), 942–971.

Rattan, A., Good, C., & Dweck, C. S. (2012). "It's OK—not everyone can be good at math": Instructors with an entity theory comfort (and demotivate) students. *Journal of Experimental Social Psychology, 48*(3), 731–737.

Ravitch, D. (2011). *The death and life of the great American school system: How testing and choice are undermining education.* New York: Basic Books.

Rawson, K. A., & Kintsch, W. (2004). Exploring encoding and retrieval effects of background information on text memory. *Discourse Processes, 38,* 323–344.

Rayner, K., Ashby, J., Pollatsek, A., & Reichle, E. D. (2004). The effects of frequency and predictability on eye fixations in reading: Implications for the E-Z Reader model. *Journal of Experimental Psychology: Human Perception and Performance, 30,* 720–732.

Rayner, K., & Duffy, S. A. (1986). Lexical complexity and fixation times in reading: Effects of word frequency, verb complexity, and lexical ambiguity. *Memory and Cognition, 14,* 191–201.

Rayner, K., Pollatsek, A., Ashby, J., & Clifton, C. (2012). *Psychology of reading.* New York: Psychology Press.

Rayner, K., & Well, A. D. (1996). Effects of contextual constraint on eye movements in reading: A further examination. *Psychonomic Bulletin and Review, 3,* 504–509.

Razfar, A., & Gutierrez, K. (2003). Reconceptualizing early childhood literacy: The sociocultural influence. In N. Hall, J. Larson, & J. Marsh (Eds.), *Handbook of early childhood literacy* (pp. 34–47). New York: Sage.

Reardon, S. F., & Bischoff, K. (2011). Income inequality and income segregation. *American Journal of Sociology, 116*(4), 1092–1153.

Recht, D. R., & Leslie, L. (1988). Effect of prior knowledge on good and poor readers' memory of text. *Journal of Educational Psychology, 80*, 16–20.

Reichenberg, M., & Kent, L. Ä. (2014). An intervention study in grade 3 based upon reciprocal teaching. *Journal of Education and Learning (EduLearn), 8*(2), 122–131.

Reicher, G. M. (1969). Perceptual recognition as a function of meaningfulness of stimulus material. *Journal of Experimental Psychology, 81*(2), 275–280.

Reisner, M. (2010). *Dora's birthday surprise.* New York: Random House (Golden Books).

Reitsma, P. (1983). Printed word learning in beginning readers. *Journal of Experimental Child Psychology, 75*, 321–339.

Reschly, A. L., Busch, T. W., Betts, J., Deno, S. L., & Long, J. D. (2009). Curriculum-based measurement of oral reading as an indicator of reading achievement: A meta-analysis of the correlational evidence. *Journal of School Psychology, 47*, 427–469.

Restrepo, M. A., Castilla, A. P., Schwanenflugel, P. J., Neuharth-Pritchett, S., Hamilton, C. E., & Arboleda, A. (2010). Effects of an add-on Spanish program on sentence length, complexity, and grammaticality growth in Spanish-speaking children attending English-only preschools. *Language, Speech, and Hearing Services in Schools, 41*, 3–13.

Restrepo, M. A., Schwanenflugel, P. J., Blake, J., Neuharth-Pritchett, S., Cramer, S., & Ruston, H. (2006). Performance on the PPVT-III and the EVT: Applicability of the measures with African-American and European-American preschool children. *Language, Hearing, and Speech Services in the Schools, 37*, 17–27.

Retelsdorf, J., Köller, O., & Möller, J. (2011). On the effects of motivation on reading performance growth in secondary school. *Learning and Instruction, 21*(4), 550–559.

Reutzel, D. R. (1992). Breaking the letter-a-week tradition. *Childhood Education, 69*(1), 20–23.

Reutzel, D. R. (2003). Reading environmental print: What is the role of concepts about print in discriminating young readers' responses? *Reading Psychology, 24*(2), 123–162.

Reutzel, D. R., Spichtig, A. N., & Petscher, Y. (2012). Exploring the value added of a guided, silent reading intervention: Effects on struggling third-grade readers' achievement. *Journal of Educational Research, 105*, 404–415.

Reyhner, J., & Jacobs, D. T. (2002). Preparing teachers of American Indian and Alaska native students. *Action in Teacher Education, 24*(2), 85–93.

Reynolds, R., Taylor, M., Steffenson, M. S., Shirey, L. L., & Anderson, R. C. (1982) Cultural schemata and reading comprehension. *Reading Research Quarterly, 17*(3), 353–366.

Rinsland, H. D. (1945). *A basic vocabulary of elementary school children.* New York: Macmillan.

Rissman, J., Eliassen, J. C., & Blumstein, S. E. (2003). An event-related fMRI investigation of implicit semantic priming. *Cognitive Neuroscience, 15*(8), 1160–1175.

Ritchey, K. A. (2011). How generalization inferences are constructed in expository text comprehension. *Contemporary Educational Psychology, 36*, 280–288.

Roberts, B., Povich, D., & Mather, M. (2013). Low-income working families. Retrieved November 29, 2014, from *www.workingpoorfamilies.org/wp-content/uploads/2013/01/Winter-2012_2013-WPFP-Data-Brief.pdf.*

Roberts, J., Jurgens, J., & Burchinal, M. (2005). The role of home literacy practices in preschool children's language and emergent literacy skills. *Journal of Speech, Language, and Hearing Research, 48*, 345–359.

Roberts, S. M., & Lovett, S. B. (1994). Examining the "F" in gifted: Academically gifted adolescents' physiological and affective responses to scholastic failure. *Journal for the Education of the Gifted, 17*(3), 241–259.

Robertson, D. A., Gernsbacher, M. A., Guidotti, S. J., Robertson, R. R., Irwin, W., Mock, B. J., et al. (2000). Functional neuroanatomy of the cognitive process of mapping during discourse comprehension. *Psychological Science, 11*(3), 255–260.

Robinson, B., & Mervis, C. (1999). Comparing productive vocabulary measures from the CDI and a systematic diary study. *Journal of Child Language, 26*(1), 177–185.

Robinson, F. P. (1961). Study skills for superior students in secondary school. *The Reading Teacher, 15*(1), 29–37.

Rochford, G., & Williams, M. (1962). Studies in the development and breakdown of the use of names: Part I. The relation between norminal dysphasia and the acquisition of vocabulary in childhood. *Journal of Neurology, Neurosurgery, and Psychiatry, 25*, 222–233.

Rodriguez, M. (2000, April). *Home literacy in the everyday life of three Dominican families.* Presentation at the annual conference of the American Educational Research Association, New Orleans, LA.

Rogers, C. (1959). A theory of therapy: Personality relationships as developed in the client-centered framework. In S. Koch (Ed.), *Psychology: A study of a science: Vol. 3. Formulations of the person and the social context* (pp. 184–256). New York: McGraw Hill.

Rogoff, B., & Chavajay, P. (1995). What's become of research on the cultural basis of cognitive development? *American Psychologist, 50*(10), 859–877.

Rogoff, B., & Lave, J. E. (1984). *Everyday cognition: Its development in social context.* Cambridge, MA: Harvard University Press.

Rosenshine, B., & Meister, C. (1994). Reciprocal teaching: A review of the research. *Review of Educational Research, 64*(4), 479–530.

Rosin, H. (2013). The touch-screen generation. *The Atlantic, 311*(3), 356–365.

Roth, F. P., Speece, D. L., & Cooper, D. H. (2002). A longitudinal analysis of the connection between oral language and early reading. *Journal of Educational Research, 95*(5), 259–272.

Rothkopf, E. Z., & Billington, M. J. (1979). Goal-guided learning from text: Inferring a descriptive processing model from inspection times and eye movements. *Journal of Educational Psychology, 71*(3), 310–327.

Rubin, D. C. (1980). 51 properties of 125 words: A unit analysis of verbal behavior. *Journal of Verbal Learning and Verbal Behavior, 19*(6), 736–755.

Rude, R. T. (1973). Readiness tests: Implications for early childhood education. *The Reading Teacher, 26*, 572–580.

Ruiz, R. (1984). Orientations in language planning. *NABE Journal of Research and Practice, 8*(2), 15–34.

Rumelhart, D. E. (1980). Schemata: The building blocks of cognition. In R. J. Spiro, B. C. Bruce, & W. F. Brewer (Eds.), *Theoretical issues in reading comprehension* (pp. 35–58). Mahwah, NJ: Erlbaum.

Rupp, A. A., Ferne, T., & Choi, H. (2006). How assessing reading comprehension with multiple-choice questions shapes the construct: A cognitive processing perspective. *Language Testing, 23*(4), 441–474.

Ruston, H. P., & Schwanenflugel, P. J. (2010). Effects of a conversation intervention on the expressive vocabulary development of prekindergarten children. *Language, Speech, and Hearing Services in Schools, 41*(3), 303–313.

Ryan, R. M., & Deci, E. L. (2000). Intrinsic and extrinsic motivations: Classic definitions and new directions. *Contemporary Educational Psychology, 25*(1), 54–67.

Ryan, R. M., & Deci, E. L. (2009). Promoting self-determined school engagement: Motivation, learning, and well-being. In K. R. Wenzel & A. Wigfield (Eds.), *Handbook of motivation at school* (pp. 171–195). New York: Routledge.

Ryan, R. M., & Grolnick, W. S. (1986). Origins and pawns in the classroom: Self-report and projective assessments of individual differences in children's perceptions. *Journal of Personality and Social Psychology, 50*(3), 550.

Sabis-Burns, D. (2011). Taking a critical look at Native Americans in children's literature. In L. A. Smolen & R. A. Oswald (Eds.), *Multicultural literature and response: Affirming diverse voices* (pp. 131–152). Santa Barbara, CA: Libraries Unlimited.

Sachs, J. D., & Warner, A. M. (2001). The curse of natural resources. *European Economic Review, 45*(4), 827–838.

Säily, T., Nevalainen, T., & Siirtola, H. (2011). Variation in noun and pronoun frequencies in a sociohistorical corpus of English. *Literary and Linguistic Computing.*

Salthouse, T. A. (1988). Resource-reduction interpretations of cognitive aging. *Developmental Review, 8*(3), 238–272.

Sameroff, A. J., & Haith, M. M. (1996). *The five to seven year shift: The age of reason and responsibility.* Chicago: University of Chicago Press.

Samuels, S. J. (2006). Reading fluency: Its past, present, and future. In T. Rasinski, C. Blachowicz, & K. Lems (Eds.), *Fluency instruction: Research-based best practices* (pp. 7–20). New York: Guilford Press.

Sanacore, J. (2000). Promoting the lifetime reading habit in middle school students. *The Clearing House, 73*(3), 157–161.

Sandelands, L. E., Brockner, J., & Glynn, M. A. (1988). If at first you don't succeed, try, try again: Effects of persistence-performance contingencies, ego involvement, and self-esteem on task persistence. *Journal of Applied Psychology, 73*(2), 208–216.

Sanford, A. J., Filik, R., Emmott, C., & Morrow, L. (2008). They're digging up the road again: The processing cost of institutional they. *Quarterly Journal of Experimental Psychology, 61*(3), 372–380.

Sanocki, T., & Dyson, M. C. (2012). Letter processing and font information during reading: Beyond distinctiveness, where vision meets design. *Attention, Perception, and Psychophysics, 74*(1), 132–145.

Sattler, J. M. (1988). *Assessment of children* (3rd ed.). San Diego, CA: Author.

Saxe, R., Carey, S., & Kanwisher, N. (2004). Understanding other minds: Linking developmental psychology and functional neuroimaging. *Annual Review of Psychology, 55,* 87–124.

Scarborough, H. S., & Dobrich, W. (1994). On the efficacy of reading to preschoolers. *Developmental Review, 14*(3), 245–302.

Schadler, M., & Thissen, D. M. (1981). The development of automatic word recognition and reading skill. *Memory and Cognition, 9,* 132–141.

Schank, R. C., & Abelson, R. P. (1975, September). Scripts, plans, and knowledge. In *Proceedings of the 4th International Joint Conference on Artificial Intelligence* (Vol. 1, pp. 151–157). San Francisco: Morgan Kaufmann.

Schmidt, N. (1998). Quantifying word association responses: What is native-like? *System, 26,* 389–401.

Schneider, E. F. (2014). A survey of graphic novel collection and use in American public libraries. *Evidence Based Library and Information Practice, 9*(3), 68–79.

Scholastic. (2015). Kids and families reading report (5th ed.). Retrieved January 10, 2015, from *www.scholastic.com/readingreport*.

Schreuder, R., & Baayen, H. (1995). Modeling morphological processing. In L. B. Feldman (Ed.), *Morphological aspects of language processing* (pp. 131–154). Hillsdale, NJ: Erlbaum.

Schunk, D. H., & Zimmerman, B. J. (1997). Developing self-efficacious readers and writers: The role of social and self-regulatory processes. *Reading Engagement: Motivating Readers through Integrated Instruction, 34,* 50.

Schwanenflugel, P. J. (1986). Completion norms for final words of sentences using a multiple production measure. *Behavior Research Methods, Instrumentation, and Computers, 18,* 363–371.

Schwanenflugel, P. J. (1991). Why are abstract concepts hard to understand? In P. J. Schwanenflugel (Ed.), *The psychology of word meanings* (pp. 223–250). Hillsdale, NJ: Erlbaum.

Schwanenflugel, P. J., & Akin, C. E. (1994). Developmental trends in lexical decisions for abstract and concrete words. *Reading Research Quarterly, 29,* 251–263.

Schwanenflugel, P. J., Hamilton, A. M., Kuhn, M. R., Wisenbaker, J., & Stahl, S. A. (2004). Becoming a fluent reader: Reading skill and prosodic features in the oral reading of young readers. *Journal of Educational Psychology, 96,* 119–129.

Schwanenflugel, P. J., Hamilton, C. E., Neuharth-Pritchett, S., Restrepo, M. A., Bradley, B. A., & Webb, M.-Y. (2010). PAVEd for Success: An evaluation of a comprehensive literacy program for 4-year-old children. *Journal of Literacy Research, 42,* 227–275.

Schwanenflugel, P. J., Harnishfeger, K. K., & Stowe, R. W. (1988). Context availability and lexical decisions for abstract and concrete words. *Journal of Memory and Language, 27,* 499–520.

Schwanenflugel, P. J., Henderson, R., & Fabricius, W. V. (1998). Developing theory of mind in older childhood: Evidence from verb extensions. *Developmental Psychology, 34,* 512–524.

Schwanenflugel, P. J., Kuhn, M. R., Morris, R. D., Morrow, L. M., Meisinger, E. B., & Woo, D. G. (2009). Insights into fluency instruction: Short- and long-term effects of two reading programs. *Literacy Research and Instruction, 48,* 318–336.

Schwanenflugel, P. J., & LaCount, K. (1988). Semantic relatedness and the scope of facilitation for upcoming words in sentences. *Journal of Experimental Psychology: Learning, Memory, and Cognition, 14,* 344–354.

Schwanenflugel, P. J., Meisinger, E., Wisenbaker, J. M., Kuhn, M. R., Strauss, G. P., & Morris, R. D. (2006). Becoming a fluent and automatic reader in the early elementary school years. *Reading Research Quarterly, 41,* 496–522.

Schwanenflugel, P. J., Morris, R. K., Kuhn, M. R., Strauss, G. P., & Sieczko, J. M. (2008). The influence of word unit size on the development of Stroop interference in early word decoding. *Reading and Writing: An Interdisciplinary Journal, 21,* 177–203.

Schwanenflugel, P. J., & Noyes, C. R. (1996). Context availability and the development of word reading skill. *Journal of Literacy Research, 28,* 35–54.

Schwanenflugel, P. J., & Ruston, H. P. (2007). The process of becoming a fluent reader: From theory to practice. In M. R. Kuhn & P. J. Schwanenflugel (Eds.), *Fluency in the classroom* (pp. 1–16). New York: Guilford Press.

Schwanenflugel, P. J., & Shoben, E. J. (1983). Differential context effects in the comprehension of abstract and concrete verbal materials. *Journal of Experimental Psychology: Learning, Memory, and Cognition, 9,* 82–102.

Schwanenflugel, P. J., Stahl, S. A., & McFalls, E. L. (1997). Partial word knowledge and vocabulary growth during reading comprehension. *Journal of Literacy Research, 29,* 531–553.

Schwanenflugel, P. J., & Stowe, R. W. (1989). Context availability and the processing of abstract and concrete words in sentences. *Reading Research Quarterly, 24,* 114–126.

Schwanenflugel, P. J., Westmoreland, M. R., & Benjamin, R. G. (2015). Reading fluency skill and the prosodic marking of linguistic focus. *Reading and Writing, 29,* 9–30.

Schwanenflugel, P. J., & White, C. R. (1991). The influence of paragraph information on the processing of upcoming words. *Reading Research Quarterly, 26,* 160–177.

Scieszka, J. (2008). *Guys write for guys read.* New York: Viking.

Sciurba, K. (2014). Texts as mirrors, texts as windows. *Journal of Adolescent and Adult Literacy, 58*(4), 308–316.

Scott, J. A., & Nagy, W. E.(2004). Developing word consciousness. In J. F. Bauman & E. J. Kame'enui (Eds.), *Vocabulary instruction: Research to practice* (pp. 201–217). New York: Guilford Press.

Segal-Drori, O., Korat, O., Shamir, A., & Klein, P. S. (2010). Reading electronic and printed books with and without adult instruction: Effects on emergent reading. *Reading and Writing, 23*(8), 913–930.

Seidenberg, M. S., & McClelland, J. L. (1989). A distributed developmental model of word recognition and naming. *Psychological Review, 96,* 523–568.

Seidenberg, M. S., Tanenhaus, M. K., Leiman, J. M., & Bienkowski, M. (1982). Automatic access of the meanings of ambiguous words in context: Some limitations of knowledge-based processing. *Cognitive Psychology, 14*(4), 489–537.

Seidenberg, M. S., Waters, G. S., Barnes, M. A., & Tanenhaus, M. K. (1984). When does irregular spelling or pronunciation influence word recognition? *Journal of Verbal Learning and Verbal Behavior, 23,* 383–404.

Sénéchal, M. (1997). The differential effect of storybook reading on preschoolers' acquisition of expressive and receptive vocabulary. *Journal of Child Language, 24*(1), 123–138.

Sénéchal, M., & LeFevre, J. A. (2002). Parental involvement in the development of children's reading skill: A five-year longitudinal study. *Child development, 73*(2), 445–460.

Sénéchal, M., LeFevre, J. A., Thomas, E. M., & Daley, K. E. (1998). Differential effects of home literacy experiences on the development of oral and written language. *Reading Research Quarterly, 33*(1), 96–116.

Sénéchal, M., Ouellette, G., Pagan, S., & Lever, R. (2012). The role of invented spelling on learning to read in low-phoneme awareness kindergarteners: A randomized-control-trial study. *Reading and Writing, 25,* 917–934.

Sereno, S. C., O'Donnell, P. J., & Rayner, K. (2006). Eye movements and lexical ambiguity resolution: Investigating the subordinate-bias effect. *Journal of Experimental Psychology: Human Perception and Performance, 32*(2), 335–350.

Shallice, T., & Warrington, E. K. (1980). Single and multiple component central dyslexic syndromes. In M. Coltheart, K. Patterson, & J. C. Marshall (Eds.), *Deep dyslexia* (pp. 119–145). London: Routledge & Kegan Paul.

Shallice, T., Warrington, E. K., & McCarthy, R. (1983). Reading without semantics. *Quarterly Journal of Experimental Psychology, 35A,* 111–138.

Shanahan, T., Kamil, M. L., & Tobin, A. W. (1982). Cloze as a measure of intersentential comprehension. *Reading Research Quarterly, 17*(2), 229–255.

Shanahan, T., Mulhern, M., & Rodriguez-Brown, F. (1995). Project FLAME: Lessons learned from a family literacy program for linguistic minority families. *The Reading Teacher, 48*(7), 586–593.

Shany, M. T., & Biemiller, A. (1995). Assisted reading practice: Effects on performance for poor readers in grades 3 and 4. *Reading Research Quarterly, 30*(3), 382–395.

Shapiro, A. M. (2004). How including prior knowledge as a subject variable may change outcomes of learning research. *American Educational Research Journal, 41*(1), 159–189.

Shapiro, J., Morrison, E., & Boker, J. (2004). Teaching empathy to first year medical students: Evaluation of an elective literature and medicine course. *Education Health, 17,* 73–84.

Share, D. L. (1995). Phonological recoding and self-teaching: Sine qua non of reading acquisition. *Cognition, 55,* 151–218.

Share, D. L. (2004). Knowing letter names and learning letter sounds: A causal connection. *Journal of Experimental Child Psychology, 88,* 213–233.

Share, D. L., & Leikin, M. (2003). Language impairment at school entry and later reading disability: Connections at lexical and supra-lexical levels of reading. *Scientific Studies of Reading, 8,* 87–110.

Sharps, M. J., & Wertheimer, M. (2000). Gestalt perspectives on cognitive science and on experimental psychology. *Review of General Psychology, 4*(4), 315.

Shatz, M., Wellman, H. M., & Silber, S. (1983). The acquisition of mental verbs: A systematic investigation of the first reference to mental state. *Cognition, 14,* 301–321.

Shaywitz, B. A., Holford, T. R., Holahan, J. M., Fletcher, J. M., Stuebing, K. K., Francis, D. J., et al. (1995). A Matthew effect for IQ but not for reading: Results from a longitudinal study. *Reading Research Quarterly, 30*(4), 894–906.

Shell, D. F., Colvin, C., & Bruning, R. H. (1995). Self-efficacy, attribution, and outcome expectancy mechanisms in reading and writing achievement: Grade-level and achievement-level differences. *Journal of Educational Psychology, 87*(3), 386.

Shelley-Tremblay, J. F. (2010). Theories of semantics. In J. Guendouzi, F. Loncke, & M. Williams (Eds.), *The handbook of psycholinguistic and cognitive processes: Perspectives in communication disorders* (pp. 209–225). New York: Taylor & Francis.

Shih, S. (2008). The relation of self-determination and achievement goals to Taiwanese eighth graders' behavioral and emotional engagement in schoolwork. *Elementary School Journal, 108*(4), 313–334.

Shin, F. (2001). Motivating students with *Goosebumps* and other popular books. *CSLA Journal (California School Library Association), 25*(1), 15–19.

Shin, H. B., & Kominski, R. A. (2010). *Language use in the United States: 2007* (American Community Survey Reports [ACS-12]). Washington, DC: U.S. Census Bureau.

Shinn, M. R., & Shinn, M. M. (2002). *AIMSweb training workbook: Administration and scoring of reading maze for use in general outcome measurement.* Eden Prairie, MN: Edformation.

Shore, W. J., & Durso, F. T. (1990). Partial knowledge in vocabulary acquisition: General constraints and specific detail. *Journal of Educational Psychology, 82*(2), 315–318.

Shuler, C. (2009). *iLearn; A content analysis of the iTunes app store's education section,* New York: Joan Ganz Cooney Center at Sesame Workshop.

Siegel, J. (1999). Stigmatized and standardized varieties in the classroom: Interference or separation? *TESOL Quarterly, 33*, 701–728.

Silberglitt, B., Burns, M. K., Madyun, N. H., & Lail, K. E. (2006). Relationship of reading fluency assessment data with state accountability test scores: A longitudinal comparison of grade levels. *Psychology in the Schools, 43*, 527–535.

Silveri, M. C., Cappa, A., Mariotti, P., & Puopolo, M. (2002). Naming in patients with Alzheimer's disease: Influence of age of acquisition and categorical effects. *Journal of Clinical and Experimental Neuropsychology, 24*, 755–764.

Silverman, S. W., & Ratner, N. B. (1997). Syntactic complexity, fluency, and accuracy of sentence imitation in adolescents. *Journal of Speech, Language, and Hearing Research, 40*(1), 95–106.

Singer, H., & Donlan, D. (1982). Active comprehension: Problem-solving schema with question generation for comprehension of complex short stories. *Reading Research Quarterly, 17*(2), 166–186.

Slater, W. H., Graves, M. F., & Piché, G. L. (1985). Effects of structural organizers on ninth-grade students' comprehension and recall of four patterns of expository text. *Reading Research Quarterly, 20*(2), 189–202.

Slater, W. H., & Horstman, F. R. (2002). Teaching reading and writing to struggling middle school and high school students: The case for reciprocal teaching. *Preventing School Failure: Alternative Education for Children and Youth, 46*(4), 163–166.

Smeets, D. J. H., & Bus, A. G. (2012). Interactive electronic storybooks for kindergartners to promote vocabulary growth. *Journal of Experimental Child Psychology, 112*, 36–55.

Smith, C. L. (2004). Topic transitions and durational prosody in reading aloud: Production and modeling. *Speech Communication, 42*(3–4), 247–270.

Smith, E. E., Shoben, E. J., & Rips, L. J. (1974). Structure and process in semantic memory: A featural model for semantic decisions. *Psychological Review, 81*(3), 214–241.

Smith, F. (1988). *Joining the literacy club: Further essays into education.* Portsmouth, NH: Heinemann.

Smith, M., & Wilhelm, J. (2002). *"Reading don't fix no Chevys": Literacy in the lives of young men.* Portsmouth, NH: Heinemann.

Smith, N. J., & Levy, R. (2013). The effect of word predictability on reading time is logarithmic. *Cognition, 128*, 302–319.

Smith, S. F. (2014). Testing a multicomponent model of reading comprehension for seventh- and eighth-grade students. *Dissertation Abstracts International Section A: Humanities and Social Sciences, 74*(11-A)(E).

Smith, S. S., & Dixon, R. G. (1995). Literacy concepts of low- and middle-class four-year-olds entering preschool. *Journal of Educational Research, 88*, 243–253.

Smythe, P. C., Stennett, R. G., Hardy, M., & Wilson, H. R. (1970). Developmental patterns in elemental skills: Knowledge of upper-case and lower-case letter names. *Journal of Literacy Research, 3*, 24–33.

Snow, C. E. (1983). Literacy and language: Relationships during the preschool years. *Harvard Educational Review, 53*(2), 165–189.

Snow, C. E. (1990). The development of definitional skill. *Journal of Child Language, 17*(3), 697–710.

Snow, C. E., & Blum-Kulka, S. (2002). From home to school: School-age children talking with adults. In S. Blum-Kulba & C. E. Snow (Eds.), *Talking to adults: The contribution of multiparty discourse to language acquisition* (pp. 327–341). Mahwah, NJ: Erlbaum.

Sokal, L., & Piotrowski, C. (2011). My brother's teacher?: Siblings and literacy development in the home. *Education Research International.* DOI: 10.1155/2011/253896.

Solomyak, O., & Marantz, A. (2010). Evidence for early morphological decomposition in visual word recognition. *Journal of Cognitive Neuroscience, 22*(9), 2042–2057.

Sonnenschein, S., Stapleton, L. M., & Benson, A. (2010). The relation between the type and amount of instruction and growth in children's reading competencies. *American Educational Research Journal, 47*(2), 358–389.

Speer, N. K., Zacks, J. M., & Reynolds, J. R. (2007). Human brain activity time-locked to narrative event boundaries. *Psychological Science, 18*(5), 449–455.

Sperling, R. A., Sherwood, T. P., & Hood, A. M. (2013). Relating motivation to read and emergent reading skills: A measurement validation study. *Reading Psychology, 34*(5), 461–485.

Spooner, A. L. R., Baddeley, A. D., & Gathercole, S. E. (2004). Can reading accuracy and comprehension be separated in the Neale Analysis of Reading Ability? *British Journal of Educational Psychology, 74*, 187–204.

Spörer, N., Brunstein, J. C., & Kieschke, U. L. F. (2009). Improving students' reading comprehension skills: Effects of strategy instruction and reciprocal teaching. *Learning and Instruction, 19*(3), 272–286.

Stadler, M. A., Watson, M., & Skahan, S. (2007). Rhyming and vocabulary: Effects of lexical restructuring. *Communication Disorders Quarterly, 28*(4), 197–205.

Stahl, K. A. D. (2007). Creating opportunities for comprehension instruction within fluency-oriented reading. In M. Kuhn & P. J. Schwanenflugel (Eds.), *Fluency in the classroom* (pp. 55–74). New York: Guilford Press.

Stahl, S. A. (1999). *Vocabulary development.* Cambridge, MA: Brookline Books.

Stahl, S. A. (2004). What do we know about fluency?: Findings of the National Reading Panel. In P. McCardle & V. Chhabra (Eds.), *The voice of evidence in reading research* (pp. 187–211). Baltimore, MD: Brookes.

Stahl, S. A., Duffy-Hester, A. M., & Stahl, K. A. D. (1998). Everything you wanted to know about phonics (but were afraid to ask). *Reading Research Quarterly, 33*(3), 338–355.

Stahl, S. A., & Fairbanks, M. M. (1986). The effects of vocabulary instruction: A model-based meta-analysis. *Review of Educational Research, 56*(1), 72–110.

Stahl, S. A., & Heubach, K. (2005). Fluency-oriented reading instruction. *Journal of Literacy Research, 37*, 25–60.

Stanovich, K. E. (1986). Matthew effects in reading: Some consequences of individual differences in the acquisition of literacy. *Reading Research Quarterly, 21*(4), 360–407.

Stanovich, K. E. (1994). Romance and reality. *The Reading Teacher, 47*, 280–291.

Stanovich, K. E., & Cunningham, A. E. (1992). Studying the consequences of literacy within a literate society: The cognitive correlates of print exposure. *Memory and Cognition, 20*(1), 51–68.

Stanovich, K. E., & Cunningham, A. E. (1993). Where does knowledge come from?: Specific associations between print exposure and information acquisition. *Journal of Educational Psychology, 85*(2), 211.

Stanovich, K. E., West, R. F., & Feeman, D. J. (1981). A longitudinal study of sentence context effects in second grade children: Tests of the interactive-compensatory model. *Journal of Experimental Child Psychology, 32*, 185–199.

Stanovich, K. E., West, R. F., & Harrison, M. R. (1995). Knowledge growth and maintenance across the life span: The role of print exposure. *Developmental Psychology, 31*(5), 811.

Stein, N. L., & Glenn, C. G. (1979). An analysis of story comprehension in elementary school children. In R. Freedle (Ed.), *Discourse processing: Multidisciplinary perspectives* (pp. 137–181). Norwood, NJ: Ablex.

Sternberg, R. J. (1987). Most vocabulary is learned from context. In M. G. McKeown & M. E. Curtis (Eds.), *The nature of vocabulary acquisition* (pp. 89–105). Hillsdale, NJ: Erlbaum.

Stetter, M. E., & Hughes, M. T. (2010a). Computer-assisted instruction to enhance the reading comprehension of struggling readers: A review of the literature. *Journal of Special Education Technology, 25*(4), 1–16.

Stetter, M. E., & Hughes, M. T. (2010b). Using story grammar to assist students with learning disabilities and reading difficulties improves their comprehension. *Education and Treatment of Children, 33*(1), 115–151.

Steubing, K. K., Barth, A. E., Cirino, P. T., Francis, D. J., & Fletcher, J. M. (2008). A response to recent reanalyses of the National Reading Panel Report: Effects of systematic phonics instruction are practically significant. *Journal of Educational Psychology, 100*(1), 123–134.

Stevenson, S. (2009). My Bluford High boys: How a book club for reluctant readers proved the naysayers wrong. *School Library Journal, 55*(5), 34–36.

Stipek, D. J. (1981). Children's perceptions of their own and their classmates' ability. *Journal of Educational Psychology, 73*, 404–410.

Stipek, D. J. (1993). *Motivation to learn: From theory to practice.* Boston: Allyn & Bacon.

Stipek, D. J. (2006). Accountability comes to preschool: Can we make it work for young children? *Phi Delta Kappan, 87*(10), 741.

Stipek, D. J., & Daniels, D. H. (1988). Declining perceptions of competence: A consequence of changes in the child or in the educational environment? *Journal of Educational Psychology, 80*(3), 352.

Stites, M. C., Federmeier, K. D., & Stine-Morrow, E. A. L. (2013). Cross-age comparisons reveal multiple strategies for lexical ambiguity resolution during natural reading. *Journal of Experimental Psychology: Learning, Memory, and Cognition, 39*(6), 1823–1841.

Storch, S. A., & Whitehurst, G. J. (2002). Oral language and code-related precursors to reading: Evidence from a longitudinal structural model. *Developmental Psychology, 38*, 934–947.

Strain, E., Patterson, K., & Seidenberg, M. S. (1995). Semantic effects in single-word naming. *Journal of Experimental Psychology: Learning, Memory, and Cognition, 21*, 1140–1154.

Strommen, L. T., & Mates, B. F. (2004). Learning to love reading: Interviews with older children and teens. *Journal of Adolescent and Adult Literacy, 48*(3), 188–200.

Stromquist, N. P. (2008). The political benefits of adult literacy: Presumed and real effects. *International Multilingual Research Journal, 2*(1–2), 88–101.

Stroop, J. R. (1935). Studies of interference in serial verbal reactions. *Journal of Experimental Psychology, 18*(6), 643–662.

Stuart, M., Stainthorp, R., & Snowling, M. (2008). Literacy as a complex activity: Deconstructing the simple view of reading. *Literacy, 42*(2), 59–66.

Suggate, S. P. (2010). Why what we teach depends on when: Grade and reading intervention modality moderate effect size. *Developmental Psychology, 46*(6), 1556–1579.

Sulzby, E. (1985). Children's emergent reading of favorite storybooks: A developmental study. *Reading Research Quarterly, 20*(4), 458–481.

Sulzby, E., & Teale, W. H. (1991). Emergent literacy. In R. Barr, M. L. Kamil, P. B. Mosenthal, & P. D. Pearson (Eds.), *Handbook of reading research* (Vol. 2, pp. 727–757). New York: Longman.

Sulzby, E., & Teale, W. H. (2003). The development of the young child and the emergence of literacy. In S. B. Neuman & D. K. Dickinson (Eds.), *Handbook of early literacy research* (pp. 727–757). New York: Longman.

Sun-Alperin, M. K., & Wang, M. (2011). Cross-language transfer of phonological and orthographic processing skills from Spanish L1 to English L2. *Reading and Writing, 24*(5), 591–614.

Svetina, D., Gorin, J. S., & Tatsuoka, K. K. (2011). Defining and comparing the reading comprehension construct: A cognitive–psychometric modeling approach. *International Journal of Testing, 11*, 1–23.

Swanborn, M. S. L., & deGlopper, K. (1999). Incidental word learning while reading: A meta-analysis. *Review of Educational Research, 69*, 261–285.

Swets, B., Desmet, T., Hambrick, D. Z., & Ferreira, F. (2007). The role of working memory in syntactic ambiguity resolution: A psychometric approach. *Journal of Experimental Psychology: General, 136*(1), 64–81.

Taft, M. (2004). Morphological decomposition and the reverse base frequency effect. *Quarterly Journal of Experimental Psychology Section A, 57*(4), 745–765.

Taft, M., & Ardasinski, S. (2006). Obligatory decomposition in reading prefixed words. *The Mental Lexicon, 1*(2), 183–199.

Tanenhaus, M. K., Leiman, J. M., & Seidenberg, M. S. (1979). Evidence for multiple stages in the processing of ambiguous words in syntactic contexts. *Journal of Verbal Learning and Verbal Behavior, 18*, 427–440.

Taraban, R., Rynearson, K., & Kerr, M. (2000). College students' academic performance and self-reports of comprehension strategy use. *Reading Psychology, 21*(4), 283–308.

Tarchi, C. (2010). Reading comprehension of informative texts in secondary school: A focus on direct and indirect effects of reader's prior knowledge. *Learning and Individual Differences, 20*, 415–420.

Taylor, B. M., & Beach, R. W. (1984). The effects of text structure instruction on middle grade students' comprehension and production of expository text. *Reading Research Quarterly, 19*, 134–146.

Taylor, C. D., Meisinger, E. B., & Floyd, R. G. (2013). Variations in directions and overt timing on oral reading accuracy, fluency, and prosody. *School Psychology Review, 42*(4), 437–447.

Taylor, D. L. (2004). "Not just boring stories": Reconsidering the gender gap for boys. *Journal of Adolescent and Adult Literacy, 48*(4), 290–298.

Taylor, D. L., & Dorsey-Gaines, C. (1988). *Growing up literate*. Portsmouth, NH: Heinemann.

Taylor, J. (1986). *Dudley and the strawberry shake*. New York: Putnam Juveniles.

Tayor, W. L. (1957). "Cloze" readability scores as indices of individual differences in comprehension and aptitude. *Journal of Applied Psychology, 41*, 19–26.

Teale, W. H. (1986). Home background and young children's literacy development. In W. H. Teale

& E. Sulzby (Eds.), *Emergent literacy: Writing and reading* (pp. 173–206). Norwood, NJ: Ablex

Terry, N. P. (2008). Addressing African American English in early literacy assessment and instruction. *Perspectives on Communication Disorders and Sciences in Culturally and Linguistically Diverse Populations, 15*(2), 54–61.

Terry, N. P. (2012). Examining relationships among dialect variation and emergent literacy skills. *Communication Disorders Quarterly, 33*(2), 67–77.

Thom, E. E., & Sandhofer, C. M. (2009). More is more: The relationship between vocabulary size and word extension. *Journal of Experimental Child Psychology, 104,* 466–473.

Thompson, C. A., Craig, H. K., & Washington, J. A. (2004). Variable production of African American English across oral and literacy contexts. *Language, Speech, and Hearing Services in Schools, 35*(3), 269–282.

Thompson, G., Madhuri, M., & Taylor, D. (2008). How the Accelerated Reader program can become counterproductive for high school students. *Journal of Adolescent and Adult Literacy, 51*(7), 550–560.

Thorndike, E. L. (1917). Reading as reasoning: A study of mistakes in paragraph reading. *Journal of Educational Psychology, 8,* 323–332.

Thorndike, R. L. (1973). Reading as reasoning. *Reading Research Quarterly, 9*(2), 135–147.

Till, R. E., Mross, E., & Kintsch, W. (1988). Time course of priming for associate and inference words in a discourse context. *Memory and Cognition, 16,* 283–298.

Tilstra, J., McMaster, K., van den Broek, P., Kendeou, P., & Rapp, D. (2009). Simple but complex: Components of the simple view of reading across grade levels. *Journal of Reseaerch in Reading, 32,* 383–401.

Tomasello, M. (1995). Joint attention as social cognition. In C. Moore & P. Dunham (Eds.), *Joint attention: Its origins and role in development* (pp. 103–130). Hillsdale, NJ: Erlbaum.

Tong, X., & McBride-Chang, C. (2010). Developmental models of learning to read Chinese words. *Developmental Psychology, 46*(6), 1662.

Torgesen, J. K., Wagner, R., & Rashotte, C. (1999). *TOWRE–2: Test of Word Reading Efficiency.* Austin, TX: PRO-ED.

Torgerson, C. J., Brooks, G., & Hall, J. (2006). *A systematic review of the research literature on the use of phonics in the teaching of reading and spelling.* London: Department for Education and Skills (DfES).

Totsika, V., & Sylva, K. (2004). The home observation for measurement of the environment revisited. *Child and Adolescent Mental Health, 9*(1), 25–35.

Treiman, R., & Broderick, V. (1998). What's in a name: Children's knowledge about the letters in their own names. *Journal of Experimental Child Psychology, 70*(2), 97–116.

Treiman, R., & Kessler, B. (2004). The case of case: Children's knowledge and use of upper- and lowercase letters. *Applied Psycholinguistics, 25,* 413–428.

Treiman, R., Pennington, B. F., Shriberg, L. D., & Boada, R. (2008). Which children benefit from letter names in learning letter sounds? *Cognition, 106*(3), 1322–1338.

Treiman, R., Tincoff, R., Rodriguez, K., Mouzaki, A., & Francis, D. J. (1998). The foundations of literacy: Learning the sounds of letters. *Child Development, 69,* 1524–1540.

Treiman, R., Weatherston, S., & Berch, D. (1994). The role of letter names in children's learning of phoneme–grapheme relations. *Applied Psycholinguistics, 15,* 97–122.

Treisman, A. (1996). The binding problem. *Current Opinion in Neurobiology, 6*(2), 171–178.

Trelease, J. (2013). *The read-aloud handbook* (7th ed.). East Rutherford, NJ: Penguin.

Turnbull, K. L. P., Bowles, R. P., Skibbe, L. E., Justice, L. M., & Wiggins, A. K. (2010). Theoretical explanations for preschoolers' lower case alphabet knowledge. *Journal of Speech, Language, and Hearing Research, 53,* 1757–1768.

Turner, J. C. (1995). The influence of classroom contexts on young children's motivation for literacy. *Reading Research Quarterly, 30*(3), 410–441.

Turner, J. C., & Paris, S. G. (1995). How literacy tasks influence children's motivation for literacy. *The Reading Teacher, 48*(8), 662–673.

Urbach, J. (2010). Beyond story grammar: Looking at stories through cultural lenses. *Education and Urban Society, 44*(4), 392–411.

UNESCO. (2014). Education for All Global Monitoring Report: Teaching and learning—achieving quality for all. Available at *http://unesdoc.unesco.org/images/0022/002256/225660e.pdf.*

U.S. Department of Health and Human Services, Administration for Children and Families. (2005). *Head Start impact study: First year findings.* Washington, DC: Author.

U.S. Department of Housing and Urban Development. (n.d.). Understanding neighborhood effects of concentrated poverty. Retrieved November 30, 2014, from *www.huduser.org/portal/periodicals/em/winter11/highlight2.html.*

Vacca, R. T. (1996). The reading wars: Who will be the winners, who will be the losers? *Reading Today, 14*(2), 3.

Vaessen, A., Bertrand, D., Tóth, D., Csépe, V., Faísca, L., Reis, A., et al. (2010). Cognitive development of fluent word reading does not qualitatively differ between transparent and opaque orthographies. *Journal of Educational Psychology, 102*(4), 827–842.

Van de Mortel, T. F. (2008). Faking it: Social desirability response bias in self-report research. Downloaded from *http://epubs.scu.edu.au/cgi/viewcontent.cgi?article=1001&context=hahs_pubs*.

van den Broek, P., Bohn-Gettler, C., Kendeou, P., Carlson, S., & White, M. J. (2011). When a reader meets a text: The role of standards of coherence in reading comprehension. In T. M. McCrudden, J. Magliano, & G. Schraw (Eds.), *Text relevance and learning from text* (pp. 123–140). Greenwich, CT: Information Age Publishing.

van den Broek, P., & Gustafson, M. (1999). Comprehension and memory for texts: Three generations of reading research. In S. R. Goldman, A. C. Graesser, & P. van den Broek (Eds.), *Narrative comprehension, causality, and coherence* (pp. 15–34). Mahwah, NJ: Erlbaum.

van den Broek, P., Lorch, R. F., Linderholm, T., & Gustafson, M. (2001). The effects of readers' goals on inference generation and memory for texts. *Memory and Cognition, 29*(8), 1081–1087.

Van der Schoot, M., Vasbinder, A. L., Horsley, T. M., Reijntjes, A., & van Lieshout, E. C. D. M. (2009). Lexical ambiguity resolution in good and poor comprehenders: An eye fixation and self-paced reading study in primary school children. *Journal of Educational Psychology, 101*(1), 21–36.

van Kleeck, A. (2006). Fostering inferential language during book sharing with preschoolers: A foundation for later text comprehension strategies. In A. van Kleeck (Ed.), *Sharing books and stories to promote language and literacy* (pp. 269–318). San Diego, CA: Plural Publishing.

van Kleeck, A., & Schuele, C. M. (2010). Historical perspectives on literacy in early childhood. *American Journal of Speech–Language Pathology, 19*(4), 341–355.

Vellutino, F. R., Scanlon, D. M., & Tanzman, M. S. (1994). Components in reading ability: Issues and problems in operationalizing word identification, phonological coding, and orthographic coding. In G. R. Lyon (Ed.), *Frames of reference for the assessment of learning disabilities: New views on measurement issues* (pp. 279–329). Baltimore, MD: Brookes.

Verhaeghen, P. (2003). Aging and vocabulary scores: A meta-analysis. *Psychology and Aging, 18*(2), 332–339.

Villaume, S., & Wilson, L. (1989). Preschool children's explorations of letters in their own names. *Applied Psycholinguistics, 10*, 283–300.

Virtue, S., Haberman, J., Clancy, Z., Parrish, T., & Jung Beeman, M. (2006). Neural activity of inferences during story comprehension. *Brain Research, 1084*(1), 104–114.

von Glasersfeld, E. (1989). Cognition, construction of knowledge and teaching. *Synthese, 80*, 121–141.

Vousden, J. I. (2008). Units of English spelling-to-sound mapping: A rational approach to reading instruction. *Applied Cognitive Psychology, 22*, 247–272.

Vousden, J. I., Ellefson, M. R., Solity, J., & Chater, N. (2011). Simplifying reading: Applying the simplicity principle to reading. *Cognitive Science, 35*, 34–78.

Vygotsky, L. S. (1978). *Mind in society: The development of higher psychological processes.* Cambridge, MA: Harvard University Press.

Vygotsky, L. S. (1986). *Thought and language* (A. Kozulin, Ed.). Cambridge, MA: MIT Press. (Original work published 1934)

Wadsworth, M. E., & Rienks, S. L. (2012). Stress as a mechanism of poverty's ill-effects on children. Retrieved November 29, 2014, from *www.apa.org/pi/families/resources/newsletter/2012/07/stress-mechanism.aspx*.

Wagner, R. K., Torgesen, J. K., & Rashotte, C. A. (1994). The development of reading-related phonological processing abilities: New evidence of bidirectional causality from a latent variable longitudinal study. *Developmental Psychology, 30*, 73–87.

Walberg, H., & Marjoribanks, K. (1973). Differential mental abilities and home environment: A canonical analysis. *Developmental Psychology, 9*, 363–368.

Wang, H.-C., Pomplun, M., Chen, M., Ko, H., & Rayner, K. (2010). Estimating the effect of word predictability on eye movements in Chinese reading using latent semantic analysis and transitional probability. *Quarterly Journal of Experimental Psychology, 63*(7), 1374–1386.

Washington, J. A., & Craig, H. K. (1994). Dialectal forms during discourse of poor, urban, African American preschoolers. *Journal of Speech, Language, and Hearing Research, 37*(4), 816–823.

Wasik, B. A. (2001). Teaching the alphabet to young children. *Young Children, 56*, 34–40.

Wasik, B. A., Bond, M. A., & Hindman, A. (2006). The effects of a language and literacy intervention on Head Start children and teachers. *Journal of Educational Psychology, 98*(1), 63–74.

Wasik, B. A., & Hindman, A. H. (2014). Understanding the active ingredients in effective preschool vocabulary intervention: An exploratory study of teacher and child talk during book reading. *Early Education and Development, 25*(7), 1035–1056.

Waters, G. S., Seidenberg, M. S., & Bruck, M. (1984). Children's and adults' use of spelling–sound information in three reading tasks. *Memory and Cognition, 12*(3), 293–305.

Watson, A., Kehler, M., & Martino, W. (2010). The problem of boys' literacy underachievement: Raising some questions. *Journal of Adolescent and Adult Literacy, 53*(5), 356–361.

Webb, M.-Y., Schwanenflugel, P. J., & Kim, S. (2004). A construct validation study of phonological awareness for children entering prekindergarten. *Journal of Psychoeducational Assessment, 22*, 304–319.

Wechsler, D. (1939). *The measurement of adult intelligence.* Baltimore, MD: Williams & Witkins.

Weiner, B. (1985). An attributional theory of achievement motivation and emotion. *Psychological Review, 92*(4), 548.

Weinstein, R. S., Gregory, A., & Strambler, M. J. (2004). Intractable self-fulfilling prophecies fifty years after *Brown v. Board of Education. American Psychologist, 59*(6), 511.

Weisleder, A., & Fernald, A. (2013). Talking to children matters: Early language experience strengthens processing and builds vocabulary. *Psychological Science, 24*(11), 2143–2152.

Weissmann, J. (2014, January). The decline of the American book lover. Available at *www.theatlantic.com/business/archive/2014/01/the-decline-of-the-american-book-lover/283222.*

Wennerstrom, A. (2001). *The music of everyday speech: Prosody and discourse analysis.* London: Oxford University Press.

West, R. F., Stanovich, K. E., & Mitchell, H. R. (1993). Reading in the real world and its correlates. *Reading Research Quarterly, 28*, 34–50.

Western, B. (2007). Mass imprisonment and economic inequality. *Social Research, 74*(2), 509–532.

What Works Clearinghouse. (2007). *WWC intervention report: Waterford early reading program.* Washington, DC: U.S. Department of Education, Institute of Education Sciences.

White House, Office of the Press Secretary, The. (2014). Invest in US: The White House summit on early childhood education. Retrieved December 1, 2014, from *www.whitehouse.gov/the-press-office/2014/12/10/fact-sheet-invest-us-white-house-summit-early-childhood-education.*

White, K. (1982). The relation between socioeconomic status and academic achievement. *Psychological Bulletin, 9*, 461–481.

White, L., & Genesee, F. (1996). How native is near-native?: The issue of ultimate attainment in adult second language acquisition. *Second Language Research, 12*, 238–265.

White, T. G., Graves, M. F., & Slater, W. H. (1990). Growth of reading vocabulary in diverse elementary schools: Decoding and word meaning. *Journal of Educational Psychology, 82*, 281–290.

White, T. G., Sowell, J., & Yanagihara, A. (1989). Teaching elementary students to use word-part clues. *The Reading Teacher, 42*(4), 302–308.

Whitehurst, G. J., Arnold, D. S., Epstein, J. N., Angell, A. L., Smith, M., & Fischel, J. E. (1994). A picture book reading intervention in day care and home for children from low-income families. *Developmental Psychology, 30*, 679–689.

Whitehurst, G. J., & DeBaryshe, B. D. (1989). Observational learning and language acquisition: Principles of learning, systems, and tasks. In G. E. Speidel & K. E. Nelson (Eds.), *The many faces of imitation in language learning* (pp. 251–276). New York: Springer.

Whitehurst, G. J., & Lonigan, C. J. (1998). Child development and emergent literacy. *Child Development, 69*, 848–872.

Whitehurst, G. J., & Lonigan, C. J. (2001). Emergent literacy: Development from prereaders to readers. In S. B. Neuman & D. K. Dickinson (Eds.), *Handbook of early literacy research* (pp. 11–29). New York: Guilford Press.

Wible, C. G., Han, S. D., Spencer, M. H., Kubicki, M., Niznikiewicz, M. H., Jolesz, F. A., et al. (2006). Connectivity among semantic associates: An fMRI study of semantic priming. *Brain and Language, 97*(3), 294–305.

Wigfield, A., & Cambria, J. (2010). Students' achievement values, goal orientations, and interest: Definitions, development, and relations to achievement outcomes. *Developmental Review, 30*(1), 1–35.

Wigfield, A., & Eccles, J. S. (2000). Expectancy–value theory of achievement motivation. *Contemporary Educational Psychology, 25*(1), 68–81.

Wigfield, A., & Eccles, J. S. (2002). The development of competence beliefs, expectancies for success, and achievement values from childhood through adolescence. In A. Wigfield & J. S. Eccles (Eds.) *Development of achievement motivation* (pp. 91–120). New York: Academic Press.

Wigfield, A., Eccles, J. S., & Pintrich, P. R. (1996). Development between the ages of 11 and 25. In D. C. Berliner & R. C. Calfee (Eds.), *Handbook of educational psychology* (pp. 148–185). Mahwah, NJ: Erlbaum.

Wigfield, A., Eccles, J. S., Yoon, K. S., Harold, R. D., Arbreton, A. J., Freedman-Doan, C., et al. (1997). Change in children's competence beliefs and subjective task values across the elementary school years: A 3-year study. *Journal of Educational Psychology, 89*(3), 451.

Wigfield, A., & Guthrie, J. T. (1995). *Dimensions of children's motivations for reading: An initial study.* Reading Research Report No. 34.

Wigfield, A., & Guthrie, J. T. (1997). Relations of children's motivation for reading to the amount and breadth of their reading. *Journal of Educational Psychology, 89*, 420–432.

Wigfield, A., Guthrie, J. T., Tonks, S., & Perencevich, K. C. (2004). Children's motivation for reading: Domain specificity and instructional influences. *Journal of Educational Research, 97*(6), 299–310.

Wigfield, A., Tonks, S., & Klauda, S. L. (2009). Expectancy–value theory. In K. R. Wentzel & A. Wigfield (Eds.), *Handbook of motivation at school* (pp. 55–75). New York: Routledge.

Wijekumar, K., Meyer, B. J. F., Lei, P., Lin, Y., Johnson, L. A., Spielvogel, J. A., et al. (2014). Multisite randomized controlled trial examining intelligent tutoring of structure strategy for fifth-grade readers. *Journal of Research on Educational Effectiveness, 7*(4), 331–357.

Wilkinson, K. S., & Houston-Price, C. (2013). Once upon a time, there was a pulchritudinous princess . . . : The role of word definitions and multiple story contexts in children's learning of difficult vocabulary. *Applied Psycholinguistics, 34*, 591–613.

Wilks, C., & Meara, P. (2002). Understanding word webs: Graph theory and the notion of density in second language word association networks. *Second Language Research, 18*, 303–324.

Williams, J. P. (2007). Literacy in the curriculum: Integrating text structure and content area instruction. In D. S. McNamara (Ed.), *Reading comprehension strategies: Theories, interventions, and technologies* (pp. 199–219). New York: Taylor & Francis.

Williams, J. P., & Ackerman, M. D. (1971). Simultaneous and successive discrimination of similar letters. *Journal of Educational Psychology, 62*(2), 132–137.

Williams, J. P., Hall, K. M., Lauer, K. D., Stafford, K. B., DeSisto, L. A., & deCani, J. S. (2005). Expository text comprehension in the primary grade classroom. *Journal of Educational Psychology, 97*(4), 538.

Williams, J. P., Pollini, S., Nubla-Kung, A. M., Snyder, A. E., Garcia, A., Ordynans, J. G., et al. (2014). An intervention to improve comprehension of cause/effect through expository text structure instruction. *Journal of Educational Psychology, 106*(1), 1–17.

Williams, K. T. (2007). *Expressive Vocabulary Test, Second Edition.* Circle Pines, MN: AGS.

Williams, L. M. (2008). Book selections of economically disadvantaged black elementary students. *Journal of Educational Research, 102*(1), 51–64.

Willingham, D. T. (2003). Students remember what they think about. *American Educator, 27*(2), 37–41.

Willingham, D. T. (2006). How knowledge helps. *American Educator, 30*(1), 30–37.

Wimmer, H., & Hummer, P. (1990). How German-speaking first graders read and spell: Doubts on the importance of the logographic stage. *Applied Psycholinguistics, 11*(4), 349–368.

Wing, C. S., & Scholnick, E. K. (1986). Understanding the language of reasoning: Cognitive, linguistic, and developmental influences. *Journal of Psycholinguistic Research, 15*, 383–401.

Winograd, P. N. (1984). Strategic difficulties in summarizing texts. *Reading Research Quarterly, 19*(4), 404–425.

Wolf, M., & Katzir-Cohen, T. (2001). Reading fluency and its intervention. *Scientific Studies of Reading, 5*(3), 211–239.

Wolfe, A. (2002). Confessions of a just-in-time reader: Reflections on the development of strategic competence in reading. *Language Learning Journal, 26*(1), 4–10.

Wolfram, W. (1974). The relationship of white southern speech to vernacular black English. *Language, 50*, 498–527.

Wolter, B. (2006). Lexical network structures and L2 vocabulary acquisition: The role of L1 lexical/conceptual knowledge. *Applied Linguistics, 27*(4), 741–747.

Wood, D., Bruner, J. S., & Ross, G. (1976). The role of tutoring in problem solving. *Journal of Child Psychology and Psychiatry, 17*(2), 89–100.

Worden, P. E., & Boettcher, W. (1990). Young children's acquisition of alphabet knowledge. *Journal of Reading Behavior, 22*(3), 277–295.

Worsley, A., Baghurst, K. I., & Leitch, D. R. (1984). Social desirability response bias and dietary inventory responses. *Human Nutrition. Applied Nutrition, 38*(1), 29–35.

Worthy, J., & Invernizzi, M. A. (1995). Linking reading with meaning: A case study of a hyperlexic reader. *Journal of Literacy Research, 27*(4), 585–603.

Wright, J. C., Huston, A. C., Murphy, K. C., St. Peters, M., Pinon, M., Scantlin, R., et al. (2001). The relations of early television viewing to school readiness and vocabulary of children from low-income families: The early window project. *Child Development, 72*(5), 1347–1366.

Wuori, D. (1999). Beyond letter of the week: Authentic literacy comes to kindergarten. *Young Children, 54*, 24–25.

Xin, Y. P., Wiles, B., & Lin, Y. Y. (2008). Teaching conceptual model-based word problem story grammar to enhance mathematics problem solving. *Journal of Special Education, 42*(3), 163–178.

Yamagata, K. (2007). Differential emergence of representational systems: Drawings, letters, and numerals. *Cognitive Development, 22*(2), 244–257.

Yang, Y. F. (2006). Reading strategies or comprehension monitoring strategies? *Reading Psychology, 27*(4), 313–343.

Yap, M. J., Balota, D. A., Sibley, D. E., & Ratcliff, R. (2012). Individual differences in visual word recognition: Insights from the English Lexicon Project. *Journal of Experimental Psychology: Human Perception and Performance, 38*(1), 53–79.

Yarkoni, T., Speer, N. K., & Zacks, J. M. (2008). Neural substrates of narrative comprehension and memory. *NeuroImage, 41*(4), 1408–1425.

Yarosz, D. J., & Barnett, W. S. (2001). Who reads to young children?: Identifying predictors of family reading activities. *Reading Psychology, 22*(1), 67–81.

Yoon, J. C. (2002). Three decades of sustained silent reading: A meta-analytic review of the effects of SSR on attitude toward reading. *Reading Improvement, 39*(4), 186–195.

Young, G. (2013). Assistive technology for students with learning disabilities: Perceptions of students and their parents. *Technology-Mediated Learning*, 77–83.

Young, J. (2000). Boy talk: Critical literacy and masculinities. *Reading Research Quarterly, 35*(3), 312.

Yurovsky, D., Fricker, D. C., Yu, C., & Smith, L. B. (2014). The role of partial knowledge in statistical word learning. *Psychonomic Bulletin and Review, 21*, 1–22.

Zareva, A. (2012). Partial word knowledge: Frontier words in the L2 lexicon. *International Review of Applied Linguistics in Language Teaching, 50*, 277–301.

Zareva, A., Schwanenflugel, P., & Nikolova, Y. (2005). Relationship between lexical competence and language proficiency: Variable sensitivity. *Studies in Second Language Acquisition, 27*(4), 567–595.

Zdrazilova, L., & Pexman, P. M. (2013). Grasping the invisible: Semantic processing of abstract words. *Psychonomic Bulletin and Review, 20*, 1312–1318.

Zeece, P. D., & Wallace, B. M. (2009). Books and good stuff: A strategy for building school to home literacy connections. *Early Childhood Education Journal, 37*(1), 35–42.

Zevenbergen, A. A., Whitehurst, G. J., & Zevenbergen, J. A. (2003). Effects of a shared-reading intervention on the inclusion of evaluative devices in narratives of children from low-income families. *Journal of Applied Developmental Psychology, 24*(1), 1–15.

Zevin, J. D., & Seidenberg, M. S. (2002). Age of acquisition effects in word reading and other tasks. *Journal of Memory and Language, 47*, 1–29.

Zevin, J. D., & Seidenberg, M. S. (2004). Age-of-acquisition effects in reading aloud: Tests of cumulative frequency and frequency trajectory. *Memory and Cognition, 32*, 31–38.

Zhang, H. (2005). Activation of themes during narrative reading. *Discourse Processes, 40*(1), 57–82.

Ziegler, J. C., Bertrand, D., Tóth, D., Csépe, V., Reis, A., Faísca, L., et al. (2010). Orthographic depth and its impact on universal predictors of reading a cross-language investigation. *Psychological Science, 21*(4), 551–559.

Ziegler, J. C., & Goswami, U. (2005). Reading acquisition, developmental dyslexia, and skilled reading across languages: A psycholinguistic grain size theory. *Psychological Bulletin, 131*, 3–29.

Zuckerman, B. (2009). Promoting early literacy in pediatric practice: Twenty years of Reach Out and Read. *Pediatrics, 124*, 1660–1665.

Zwaan, R. A., Radvansky, G. A., Hilliard, A. E., & Curiel, J. M. (1998). Constructing multidimensional situation models during reading. *Scientific Studies of Reading, 2*(3), 199–220.

Author Index

Subject Index

Note. *f* or *t* following a page number indicates a figure or a table.

351